A Widow's Tale And Other Stories

by

Mrs. Oliphant

Double 9
BOOKS

A Widow's Tale And Other Stories
by Mrs. Oliphant

ISBN: 978-93-60462-03-1

Published by

DOUBLE 9 BOOKS

2/13-B, Ansari Road
Daryaganj, New Delhi – 110002
info@double9books.com
www.double9books.com
Tel. 011-40042856

ABOUT THE AUTHOR

Margaret Oliphant Wilson Oliphant was a Scottish author and historical writer who usually wrote under the name Mrs. Oliphant. She was born Margaret Oliphant Wilson on April 4, 1828, and died on June 20, 1897. She writes "domestic realism, the historical novel, and tales of the supernatural" as her short stories. Margaret Oliphant was born in Wallyford, near Musselburgh, East Lothian. She was the only daughter and youngest child still living of Margaret Oliphant (1789–17 September 1854) and Francis W. Wilson, a clerk. We lived in Lasswade, Glasgow, and Liverpool when she was a child. In Wallyford, a street called Oliphant Gardens is named after her. As a girl, she was always trying new things with writing. Passages in the Life of Mrs. Margaret Maitland, her first book, came out in 1849. This was about the mostly successful Scottish Free Church movement, which was something her folks agreed with. Next came Caleb Field in 1851, the same year she met publisher William Blackwood in Edinburgh and was asked to write for Blackwood's Magazine. She did so for the rest of her life and wrote over 100 articles, including one that criticized Arthur Dimmesdale in Nathaniel Hawthorne's "The Scarlet Letter."

CONTENTS

INTRODUCTORY NOTE

I remember well my first meeting with Mrs Oliphant a dozen years ago, how she "ordered" me to Windsor where she was then living (I like to think that it was an order, and obeyed as such by her very loyal subject), and that I was as proud to go, and as nervous, as those must be who make the same journey by command of another lady resident in the same place. I have an odd recollection too of buying my first umbrella for this occasion—for no reason apparently except that I wanted to impress her.

They say she was not tall, but she seemed tremendous to me that day. I find an old letter in which I dwelt on the height of her and her grand manner, so that evidently the umbrella was of little avail. In her presence, I think, those whose manner is of to-day must always have felt suddenly boorish. She belonged to a politer age: you never knew it more surely than when she was putting you at your ease with a graciousness that had something of a command in it. Mrs Oliphant was herself the fine Scots gentlewoman she drew so incomparably in her books, most sympathetic when she unbent and a ramrod if she chose—the *grande dame* at one moment, almost a girl, it might be, the next (her sense of fun often made her a girl again), she gave you the impression of one who loved to finger beautiful things, and always wore rare caps and fine lace as if they were part of her. She could be almost fearsomely correct, and in the middle of it become audacious (for there was a dash of the Bohemian about her); her likes and dislikes were intense; in talk she was extremely witty without trying to be so (she was often, I think, amused and surprised to hear what she had just said); her eyes were so expressive, and such a humorous gleam leapt into them when you attempted to impress her (with anything more pretentious than an umbrella), that to catch sight of them must often to the grandiloquent have been to come to an abrupt stop; and, more noticeable perhaps than anything else, she was of an intellect so alert that one wondered she ever fell asleep. That was but a first impression, a photograph of externals, little to be read in it of the beautiful soul and most heroic woman who was the real Mrs Oliphant. The last time I saw her, which was shortly before her death, I knew her better. The wit had all gone out of her eyes, though not quite from her talk; her face had grown very sweet and soft, and what had started to be the old laugh often ended pitifully. The two sons who had been so much to her were gone, and for the rest of her days she never forgot it, I think, for the length of a smile. She was less the novelist now than a pathetic figure in a novel. She was as brave as ever, but she had less self-control; and so, I suppose it was, that the more exquisite part of her, which the Scotswoman's reserve had kept hidden, came to the surface and dwelt for that last year in her face, as if to let all those who looked on Mrs Oliphant know what she was before she bade them good-bye.

I wonder if there is among the younger Scottish novelists of to-day any one so foolish as to believe that he has a right to a stool near this woman, any one who has not experienced a sense of shame (and some rage at his heart) if he found that for the moment his little efforts were being taken more seriously than hers: I should like to lead the simple man by the ear down the long procession of her books. It is too long a procession, though there are so many fine figures in it—men and women and boys (the boy in 'Sir Tom' is surely among the best in fiction) in the earlier stories, nearly all women in the latest; but whether they would have been greater books had she revised one instead of beginning another is probably to be doubted. Not certainly because the best of them could not have been made better. That is obvious to almost any reader: there nearly always comes a point in Mrs Oliphant's novels where almost any writer of the younger school, without a sixth part of her capacity, could have stepped in with advantage. Often it is at the end of a fine scene, and what he would have had to tell her was that it was the end, for she seldom seemed to know. Even 'Kirsteen,' which I take to be the best, far the best, story of its kind that has come out of Scotland for the last score of years, could have been improved by the comparative duffer. Condensation, a more careful choice of words, we all learn these arts in the schools nowadays—they are natural to the spirit of the age; but Mrs Oliphant never learned them, they were contrary to her genius (as to that of some other novelists greater than she), and they would probably have trammelled her so much that the books would have lost more than they gained. We must take her as she was, believing that she knew the medium which best suited her talents, though it was not the best medium.

Her short stories, of which this book is a sample, contain some of her finest work,—indeed nearly all of her deepest imaginings have appeared, as it happens, in this form. There is nothing in this volume that deserves to rank with, say, 'Old Lady Mary,' nor has it the rippling humour of the delicious 'Chronicles of Carlingford': its tale of the Fellow of his college who becomes a raving lunatic because society has discovered that his mother sells butter would be quite unworthy of inclusion were it not for the noble figure of the mother; yet the book has numberless flashes of insight, several of those women "no longer in the first flush of youth" of whom Mrs Oliphant wrote always with abundant sympathy, and latterly as if she loved them the best, and at least one sweet love story in "Mademoiselle" (Mademoiselle writes such a charming love letter, saying No, that if she had dropped it on the way to the post-office the first man who picked it up and read it would have rushed her to the registrar); and as if all this were not enough, she gives us in "Queen Eleanor and Fair Rosamond" as terrible and grim a picture of a man tired of fifty years of respectability as was ever written. One would have liked to be able to pitchfork the son out of the story, because he will talk, and, after the supreme situation, to drop the curtain on the analysis of Queen Eleanor's state of mind. But it is a story to set you thinking. Mrs Oliphant wrote so many short stories that she forgot their names and what they were about, but readers, I think, will not soon forget this one; and if not this, when shall their hearts grow cold and their admiration wane for the wonderful woman of whom it is but the thousandth part?

J. M. BARRIE.

CHAPTER I

The Bamptons were expecting a visitor that very afternoon: which made it all the more indiscreet that young Fitzroy should stay so long practising those duets with May. It was a summer afternoon, warm and bright, and the drawing-room was one of those pretty rooms which are as English as the landscape surrounding them—carefully carpeted, curtained, and cushioned against all the eccentricities of an English winter, yet with all the windows open, all the curtains put back, the soft air streaming in, the sunshine not too carefully shut out, the green lawn outside forming a sort of velvety extension of the mossy soft carpet in which the foot sank within. This combination is not common in other countries, where the sun is so hot that it has to be shut out in summer, and coolness is procured by the partial dismantling of the house. From the large open windows the trees on the lawn appeared like members of the party, only a little withdrawn from those more mobile figures which were presently coming to seat themselves round the pretty table shining with silver and china which was arranged under the acacia. Miss Bampton, who had been watching its arrangement, cast now and then an impatient glance at the piano where May sat, with Mr Fitzroy standing over her. He was not one of the county neighbours, but a young man from town, a visitor, who had somehow fallen into habits of intimacy it could scarcely be told why. And though he was visiting the Spencer-Jacksons, who were well known and sufficiently creditable people, nobody knew much about Mr Fitzroy. It is a good name: but then it is too good a name to belong to a person of whom it can be said that nobody knows who he is. A Fitzroy ought to be so very easily identified: it ought to be known at once to which of the families of that name he belongs—very distantly perhaps—as distantly as you please; but yet he must somehow belong to one of them.

This opinion Miss Bampton, who was a great genealogist, had stated over and over again, but without producing any conviction in her hearers. Her father asked hastily what they had to do with Fitzroy that they should insist on knowing to whom he belonged. And May turned round upon her little, much too high, heel and laughed. What did she care who he was? He had a delightful baritone, which "went" beautifully with her own soprano. He was very nice-looking. He had been a great deal abroad, and his manners were beautiful, with none of the stiffness of English manners. He did not stand and stare like Bertie Harcourt, or push between a girl and anything she wanted like the new curate. He knew exactly how to steer between these two extremes, to be always serviceable without being officious, and to insinuate a delightful compliment without saying it right out. This was May's opinion of the matter: and then he had such a delightful voice! So that this stranger had come into the very front of affairs at Bampton-Leigh, to the disturbance of the general balance of society, and of many matters much more important than an agreeable visitor, which were going on there. For example, Bertie Harcourt had almost been banished from the house: and he was a young squire of the neighbourhood with a good estate and very serious intentions; while the Spencer-Jacksons, with whom Mr Fitzroy was staying, were not above half pleased to have their novelty, their new man, absorbed in this way. Mrs Spencer-Jackson was a lively young woman who liked to have a cavalier on hand, whom she could lend, so to speak, to a favourite girl as a partner, whether at carpet dance or picnic, and dispose of according to her pleasure—an arrangement which Mr Fitzroy had much interfered with by devoting himself to Bampton-Leigh.

These things were being turned over in her mind by Miss Bampton, while she sat looking out upon the lawn where everything looked so fresh and cool under the trees. She was busy with her usual knitting, but this did not in any way interfere with the acuteness of her senses, or the course of her thoughts. Though May and she were spoken of as if on the same level, as the Miss Bamptons, this lady was twenty years older than her sister, and had discharged for half of that time the functions of mother to that heedless little girl. May had made Julia old, indeed, when she had no right to be considered old. When the mother died she had been a handsome quiet young woman, thirty indeed, which is considered, though quite falsely, an unromantic age yet quite capable of being taken for twenty-eight, or even twenty-five, and with admirers and prospects of her own. After her mourning was over she had become Miss Bampton, the feminine head of the house, managing everything, receiving the few guests her father cared to see, who were almost all contemporaries of his own, as if she were as old as any of them—and had moved up to a totally different level of life. Such a transformation is not unusual in a widower's house. Miss Bampton took the position of her father's wife rather than of his daughter, and no one thought it strange. If she sacrificed any feelings of her own in doing so, no one found it out. She was a mother to May; she had found her position, it seemed, taken possession of her place in the world, at the head of a house which was her own house, though it was not her husband's but her father's. It was generally supposed that the position suited her admirably, and that she had never wished for any other: which indeed I agree was very probably the case, though in such matters no one can ever be confident. It was thus that she happened to be so absorbed in May, so watchful of this (she thought) undesirable interposition of Mr Fitzroy, of the partial withdrawal of Bertie Harcourt, and of many things of equal, or rather equally little, moment to the general world.

And this was the afternoon when Nelly Brunton, the little widowed cousin from India, was coming on her first visit since her return. It was true that a year had elapsed or more since the death of Nelly's husband: but Miss Bampton felt that to receive the poor little widow in the very midst of the laughter, the songs, the foolish conversation and excitement of a love affair, or at the least a strong flirtation, was the most inappropriate thing that could be conceived. Poor Nelly with her life ended, so soon—come back with all gaieties and gladness for ever shut out, the music silenced, the very sight of a man (Miss Bampton felt) made painful to her—to a life much more subdued and quiet than old-maidenhood, she who had always been such a bright little thing, full of fun and nonsense! Good Julia figured her cousin to herself in a widow's cap (which, however, whatever people may say, is a most becoming head-dress to a young woman), pale, smiling quietly when her sympathy was called upon, shrinking aside a little from a laugh, thinking of nothing but her two little children, in whom she would, no doubt, poor thing, begin to live a subdued life by proxy—and whom she had called, in that very touching letter, the sole consolations of her life. Poor little Nelly! who would no doubt break down altogether when she came in to this old place, which she had known in the brightness of her youth—and who ought, at least, to be received by her relations alone, not in a stranger's presence. Miss Bampton grew very restless and unhappy as the time went on. She heard the pony carriage drive out, which May ought to have driven down to the station to meet her cousin. May had found time to run out to tell Johnson that he must go himself, that she could not be ready, and the sound of the wheels upon the gravel felt like a reproach to Julia, who was not in the least to blame. How dreadful to send only a servant to meet her—considering how much had come and gone since she last stopped at that station! When the carriage had gone, Miss Bampton, who felt it her duty, though she was not in the least wanted, to remain in the drawing-room while all this practising was going on, could not keep still. She went and came into the inner drawing-room, she took out books from the shelves and put them back again, she laid down her knitting and took it up, she looked at the clock first in one room, then in another, and compared them with her watch. Finally, she came up to the performers just as they came to the end of a song.

"That was very nice," Miss Bampton said. "I think you have it perfect. May, poor Nelly may be here at any moment; don't you think you should shut the piano before she comes in?"

"Why?" said May, swinging round upon her stool to look her sister in the face.

"Oh! well, dear, I don't know that I can explain. Nelly, that used to be so fond of all these things herself, coming home a widow, deprived of everything—I think that explains itself, dear."

"Is this lady, then, a statue of woe, covered with crape and white caps and streamers?" said Fitzroy.

"I think I see Nelly like that," cried May, with her fingers running up and down the keys. "We can manage this trio when Nelly comes. You know, Julia, she was always the merriest little thing, ready for any fun. What nonsense to try to make us frightened of Nelly!"

"In the first place, she is much older than you are," said Miss Bampton, with something as nearly like anger as she ever showed to her sister, "so how you can speak so confidently—I can't tell, I am sure, whether she may wear a widow's cap. They don't, I believe, in India; but I am very certain, May, that you should have gone down to the station to meet her, and that it will be a painful thing for her, poor dear, though I hope the feeling may not last—to come back to this house after her trouble, she that has been so happy here."

"Why does she come, then?" said May, with a pout. "If I had thought we were to give up everything to Nelly, and go sighing through all the house——"

"Weep upon her shoulder," suggested the young man, in a low tone.

"I must say," cried Miss Bampton, fluttering her feathers like a dove enraged, "that though this sort of talk may be funny and fashionable and all that, I find it in very bad taste. There is the carriage coming back, and if you have no real sympathy for your cousin, I hope you'll at least shut down the piano and meet her without a song on your lips and a grin on your face!"

This tremendous Parthian shaft Miss Bampton discharged as she hurried out, with an almost pleased consciousness, soon to be changed into remorse, of the force of the dart. A grin on May's face! To think that her laugh, which Mr Fitzroy compared to silver bells and all manner of pretty things, should be spoken of as a grin! May closed the piano with a noise like a blow.

"We shall have to stop, I suppose," she said, impatiently, "though I did want so much to try over that last again."

"And I suppose I ought to fly," said Fitzroy. "Must I? I should like to have one peep at this wonderful widow before I leave you, dissolved in tears— —"

"Oh, don't talk nonsense!" said May, with the faintest little frown upon her forehead. It is one thing to laugh or jeer in your own person at your family arrangements, and quite another thing to have your laugh echoed by a stranger. "I suppose I must go and meet her," she added, quickly, and hurried out, leaving him alone by the piano.

If Mr Fitzroy had been a young man of delicate feelings, it is probable that he would have disappeared by the window, and delivered his friends from his unnecessary presence at such a moment. But his feelings were quite robust so far as other people were concerned, and his curiosity was piqued. He stood calmly, therefore, and waited till the party returned. He listened to Miss Bampton's little cries and exclamations, subdued by the distance but yet distinguishable. "Dear Nelly! dear Nelly! So glad, so glad to see you! Welcome back to us all! Welcome! oh, my dear, my dear!" Then a little sound of crying, then "Oh, Nelly, dear!" from May; and kisses, and a note or two of a new voice, "Dear old Ju! dear Maysey," different, not like the tones of the sisters, which resembled, much unlike as their personalities were. Then there sounded old Mr Bampton's tremulous bass. "Well, Nelly, my dear; glad to see you back again." To all this commotion Percy Fitzroy listened, amused at the self-revelation in the different tones. It was highly impertinent on his part to stay, and without reason; but his mind was not much disturbed by that.

Then the little procession streamed in, May first, pushing open the door, Miss Bampton after, with the new-comer's arm affectionately and tightly drawn through hers, Mr Bampton lumbering behind, with his heavy tread. The new-comer—ah! she was certainly worth a second look. She was covered with crape, with a long veil falling almost to her feet; but it was apparent to Fitzroy's very sharp and experienced eyes that the crape was rusty and brown, and probably *d'occasion*, put on for her first appearance and to impress her relations. I don't know what it was in Mrs Brunton's face which gave the young man of the world this impression. There are people who understand each other without a word, at a glance. Mrs Brunton's face was a very pretty one, much prettier than May's, who had not much more than the *beauté de diable*, the first freshness and bloom of a country girl, to recommend her. The young widow had better features; she had a lurking something in the corners of her mouth, which looked like "a spice of wickedness" to the audacious stranger. She lifted her eyes with a little sentiment to survey "the dear old room," prepared to sigh; but caught, with a lightning glance, the unknown young man in it, with the faintest elevation of her eyebrows, postponing for a moment that "suspiration of forced breath," which, however, followed all the same, with only an infinitesimal delay. "The dear old room," said Nelly; "nothing changed except— —" and then came the round, full, long-drawn sigh. Mr Fitzroy felt that he had done well to wait; there was fun to be anticipated here. He caught May's eyes slightly dubious, and elevated his own brows with a look that called back the smile to her face. Then he crossed the room to the door, under shadow of Mr Bampton's back, and giving a little pressure to her hand in parting, whispered "To-morrow?" as if it were for that question he had stayed. May gave him a smile and a nod, and he hastened away. What could be more discreet? Even Miss Bampton, full of wrath against him for his lingering, opened her mouth in surprise when she found he had disappeared so unobtrusively, and had nothing to say.

CHAPTER II

When Mrs Brunton's bonnet with the long veil was taken off, and her long cloak, which was half covered with crape, she presented a very agreeable figure in a well-fitting dress, which indeed was black, but in no special way gloomy, and pleasantly "threw up" her light brown hair and pretty complexion. The crape, which was rather shabby, was indeed more or less worn—if not for effect as Percy Fitzroy supposed—at least by way of response to a natural prejudice in favour of "deep" mourning, which Nelly knew to exist among the English kindred, apt as they were to forget that a long time had elapsed since that crape was a necessity and quite congenial to her feelings. The tears which had come to her eyes when she first saw her cousins, the sigh with which she had greeted the dear old room (though kept back for half a second by the unexpected sight of a stranger), were quite authentic and genuine. Much indeed had passed over her head since she had been last there, much since she had met the "dear old Ju" and little Maysey of her youthful recollections. The over-experienced young man who had fixed his cynical eyes upon Mrs Brunton set it all down as fictitious, with a wisdom which is still more ignorant and silly than foolishness. He took the smile of a buoyant nature which lay *perdu* about the corners of her mouth for an equally cynical amusement at the *rôle* she had to play. And he was entirely wrong, as such penetrating observers usually are. She was ready to smile whenever an occasion should arise, but at that moment she was very ready to cry. When they took her out upon the well-known lawn, and established her in the very same old chair which she remembered, before the same tea-things, the old silver teapot, the china which she would have recognised anywhere, Nelly burst out crying in spite of herself. "I don't believe there is a cup cracked of the whole set," she said; "and to think how many things have happened to me!" May, quite touched, threw herself down on her knees by Nelly's side and clasped her arms round her cousin's waist ("And I dared to think the child was unfeeling!" Miss Bampton, remorseful, said to herself), while Julia bent over her and kissed her, and even old Mr Bampton stroked her shoulder with his heavy hand, saying, "You must keep up your heart, Nelly—you must try to keep up your heart." And then presently they all dried their eyes, and sat down in comfortable chairs and took their tea.

It was all as natural as the sunshine and the rain. Mrs Brunton had not perhaps great cause to be an inconsolable widow; and she was not so. Her husband, had he been the bereaved person, would probably by this time have married again, and she had no thought of doing that. But she had felt his loss keenly, and the change in her life and all the unexpected differences in her lot which separated her from so many of her contemporaries to whom nothing had happened. Fortunately the unfortunates in this world often come to feel a certain superiority in their experience to those who have had no trouble, to whom nothing has happened, which modifies the great inequalities of the balance; and this had some share in Nelly's feelings. The cousins had been happy and at peace all the time during which she had "gone through" so much; but she felt herself on such a height of experience and development over their heads as no words could say. They had never known what trouble was—they were here with their old china, their old silver teapot, polished! as if that was the great business in life; not a cup was cracked, not a chair displaced, old Sinnett the butler stepping softly across the noiseless grass, with the cake basket, just as he had always done. After Nelly had cried with a full heart, she laughed, looking round, as she took her tea. "Does nothing ever happen over here?" she said; "are you all exactly as you used to be before I went away?"

"Ju has never gone off, you see; she can't bring any man to the point," said the old heavy father with a laugh.

"Oh, papa!" said the gentle Julia—"but Nelly knows your naughty ways."

"Yes, I know my uncle's naughty ways—and that he gives thanks on his knees night and morning that Julia has never brought any man to the point: for what would Bampton-Leigh do without her?" Nelly cried.

"Oh, there's me!" said May.

"That little thing!" said Mr Bampton; "she is in the other line, quite the other line. I can't go out for my walk in the morning but some young fellow or other comes trying to make up to me—I'm May's father, Nelly, nowadays: that's what I am to those young men."

"I saw one in the drawing-room," said Mrs Brunton; "I suppose it was one of them. It gave me quite a start to see a stranger there."

"And very bad taste of him," said Miss Bampton, reddening; "the very worst taste! I suppose he stopped to see whether you were nice-looking enough to please him, Nelly."

"Nothing of the sort!" cried May; "he stopped to finish a song we were practising. Julia is always saying disagreeable things of Mr Fitzroy."

Nelly had not the air of finding it very disagreeable that the young man had waited to see whether she was nice-looking. She smoothed back her hair, which curled a little on her forehead, and said with a smile: "That was why you couldn't come to meet me at the station, May."

"It is for a concert in the village," said May, with a great flush of colour.

"Oh!" said Julia hastily, "you must not think, Nelly, it was the child's fault. I gave all the hints I could, but we could not get him to go away. He is one of those society men, as people call them, who do exactly what they please and never mind what you say."

"Julia is so dreadfully prejudiced—she is nothing but a bundle of prejudices!"

"And is there nothing new but Mr Fitzroy?—if that is his name," Nelly said.

Then they began to tell her of all the vicissitudes of the country life, the people who had been married, the children who had been born, a point on which Nelly, being a mother herself, was very curious—and the sons who had gone away to seek their fortune. Mr Bampton by this time had taken his tea and gone in again, so that the ladies were alone with their gossip; and Mrs Brunton sat and listened with a smile, in the relief of having got the first meeting over, and the first shock of the old recollections. She felt at her ease now, not disturbed by any fear of criticism, or of meeting in Julia's eye a reminder that she ought to have had her hair covered by a cap. If truth must be told, it had wounded Julia's feelings much to see her cousin take off her bonnet so simply, without putting up her hand to her head and saying "But I have no cap!" as ladies who wear that article generally do. Miss Bampton, however, had still a hope that when Nelly dressed for the evening it might appear, covering her with the appropriate crown of sorrow. All was not lost as yet, though already indeed Julia had begun to feel a regret that the pretty hair should so covered up, and was in a state of mind to forgive Nelly if that outward and visible sign was not in her wardrobe at all.

When Nelly came down to dinner it was a shock, but not so great a shock as Miss Bampton, had she foreseen it, would have expected. She had no cap—but then her dress was in such very good taste! It was of very thin black stuff, almost transparent, faintly showing her shoulders and arms through, but made quite up to the throat and of a material which was very black and "deep," with no lustre or reflections in it, not even jet or any of the deadly-lively ornaments with which mourning is "lighted up." It made her look very slim, very young, very much like a girl—but poor Nelly could not help that. And nothing, Miss Bampton said to herself, could be nicer than Nelly was. She asked May about her concert that was coming off, and begged that she might be told what songs she was going to sing. "I might help you a little," she said; "I could play your accompaniments at least." And so she did, helping her, for Nelly was a good musician, and giving her a great many hints—as good as a lesson, May acknowledged. And later in the evening when Mr Bampton came in and asked if she could not sing for him that old-fashioned song she used to sing, Nelly, sighing a little, and smiling, and with a tear in her eyes, sang "My mother bids me bind my hair" with a pathos in her voice for Lubin who was away, that made the good Julia cry. She dashed off after that into another lighter song that meant nothing, to take away the taste of the first, she said, which was a little too much for her. Oh no, she had not given up her singing—but nobody had asked her for that old song for years.

"Shows what fools they are nowadays—in music as well as everything else," Mr Bampton said.

The next day Nelly offered most good-naturedly to help May and Mr Fitzroy with their accompaniments—and the next they tried the trio, which was accomplished with great success. She was a better musician and had a much finer voice than May—and before her visit was half over it was she who sang with Fitzroy, taking the leading part in all the concerted music. There were two or three small parties, and it was decided by everybody that it was with Nelly's soprano, not May's, that the baritone went so well. "Dear May's is a delicious little voice," said Mrs Spencer-Jackson, "so pure and so sweet; but Mrs Brunton has a great deal of execution, and she has been so well trained. It is what I call artificial singing, not sweet and child-like, like dear May's. But then so is Percy Fitzroy's—these are the two that go together." Perhaps there was a secret inclination on the part of Mrs Spencer-Jackson to give a little prick to the Bamptons, who had stolen her young man from her. But he was now more away from her than ever. He had always something that called him to Bampton-Leigh, and, if she had disliked to have him carried off by May, there was a still stronger reason for objecting to his entire absorption in Mrs Brunton. However, among most of the audience which listened to their music—whether in the continual rehearsal of which all but the singers were tired—or at the village concert where Nelly, "for such a good motive," was persuaded to lay aside her scruples and take a part—the same idea was prevalent. These were the two that went together. It had always been a delusion in respect to May Bampton. Her little chirp of a voice never could hold its place along with Mr Fitzroy's baritone: which shows how people deceive themselves when their own vanity is concerned. Thus the whole neighbourhood concurred in the verdict. And poor little May, much surprised, was left out of it without any preparation or softening to her of the event. Percy Fitzroy had never been her lover, so that there was nothing at all to blame him for. If the girl had taken foolish notions into her head, there was nobody to blame but herself.

May, for her part, was so much surprised when Fitzroy transferred his attentions to her cousin that she could not believe her eyes. He came as often as ever, and he was ready enough to throw her a crumb of kindness, a scrap of compliment, a morsel of conversation in something of the old tones. She was not jealous of Nelly, or what she and Julia called her strong voice; but when the little girl, new to all perfidies, perceived that the man who had hung about her and charmed her was turning all the artillery of whispers and glances in another direction, and that Nelly, in her black dress—Nelly, who was a widow, who ought to be entirely above the region of flirtation—was the object of these seductions, a cruel astonishment was the first feeling in her breast. She had been flattered and pleased and amused by the little *éclat* of Fitzroy's subjugation. She now stood by in amazement, and watched the change without understanding it. At first everybody had been so sorry for Nelly; and it was easy to imagine that Fitzroy, too, shared that admirable sentiment. A widow, so young! though, now that it came to this, May began secretly to count up Nelly's years, and to decide that at thirty Nelly was not so very young; that she had quite reached the shady side of life, when troubles were to be calculated upon. At twenty, thirty is a great age: it means more than maturity—it is the beginning of decadence. After all, why was Nelly so much to be pitied? And there was such a thing as carrying pity too far. May did not know how to account at first for the change in her own feelings towards her cousin, any more than for the change in her own position, so strangely brought about—the change from being the first, always considered, to being in a manner nobody at all.

CHAPTER III

Miss Bampton's sentiments during this sudden change of circumstances were more remarkable than those of May, for she was as much dismayed and startled as her sister, and much more angry, understanding the whole process better; while at the same time she was, in the midst of her indignation, more or less satisfied to see that Fitzroy's attentions, which had made her so uneasy, were coming to an end. This is a state of mind which it is very difficult to describe in so many words. The excellent Julia would have believed herself ready, before Nelly came, to welcome anything which should break the charm of the stranger's fascinations, and restore May to her previous much more trustworthy suitor; but when this deliverance came in the shape of Mrs Brunton, her anger and resentment and sense of downfall were quite unreasonable. That any one—any man in his senses—should turn from May to Nelly! that the fresh and delightful bloom of the girl should be left neglected for the attractions of the maturer woman; that May, in her *own house*, the young princess of everything, should be thrust into the second place, and Nelly—*Nelly*, whose day was over—made the principal attraction! This was almost more than Miss Bampton could bear. And to see May sitting by with her needlework, or pretending to read, while Nelly and Fitzroy sang, and turned over the music and talked to each other, as musical people do, "Do you remember that phrase?" "Oh, don't you recollect this?" with a few bars played on the piano, and how "the melody comes in here," and how "that cadenza was repeated there," and so forth and so forth, interspersed with exclamations of ecstatic admiration—produced in Julia's mind an exasperation which it was almost impossible to subdue. Even Mr Bampton, who took so little notice, had said once or twice, "Why isn't May singing?" when he came in for his cup of tea. And May, taking it all like the darling she was, not sulky at all, saying a word when there was any room for her to come in, making her first experience in life, but so sweetly, so patiently, through all her surprise.

This changed altogether, however, the character of the scene in the drawing-room at Bampton-Leigh, where now the two sisters, who were the mistresses of the place, pursued their occupations almost as if they had been alone, while the little vaudeville, operetta, genteel comedy, or whatever you please to call it, went on at the piano. Miss Bampton felt that she had no call whatever to provide the scenery, as it were—the good piano, the pretty room, the tea-table, with all its *agréments*—for this drama. When May was the heroine it was all befitting and natural—but for Nelly! Miss Bampton's fingers trembled over her knitting, as she sat bursting with indignation. The only thing to console her was that she had never in her life so admired her little sister. How beautifully May behaved! When Julia, in an access of that fury which sometimes moves the mildest, said fiercely, under her breath, to her sister working at the window, "I can't bear this much longer!" May lifted up pathetic eyes and cried, "Why? You used to like it well enough," said the young martyr, steadily, yet with a pale cheek, ignoring any change. Oh, what a darling she was! and set aside in her own house by that little Nelly, a widow, who ought to be thinking of very different things.

I do not know how to justify Nelly's conduct in these circumstances, and yet I do not think she was so much to blame as appears at a first glance. Mrs Brunton's spirit, much subdued and cast down for a time, had risen before she came to visit her relations in the country, by the natural movement of life and youth, and the sense that after all her existence was not over, though she had tried hard to persuade herself that it was. It was not at all over; it was very warm and lively in her veins, despite of everything she had gone through. Poor Jack was gone. She had been very faithful to Jack, suffering no one to say a word against him either living or dead. She had not blamed him for giving very little thought to the comfort of his wife and children after he was gone. But now that he was gone, and his grave green, and her crape rusty and worn out, it was not natural that she should continue to pose, like a statue of woe leaning upon an urn. That was not at all the *rôle* which she had felt herself to be capable of playing. And she had never felt herself the venerable matron which she appeared to May. She was young; her blood was still running fast in her veins; her little children made no claim yet upon her for anything but kisses and smiles, and the cares which an excellent nurse made light. And Nelly, for a long time sequestered from every amusement, amused herself with relish as soon as it came within her reach. She was scarcely aware at first that she was taking May's admirer from her. Little Maysey! Why, she was only a child, not old enough for that sort of diversion. She had plunged into the music, into the fun, into that little excitement of flirtation which comes on so easily, without intention, without at all perceiving any other effect. And, indeed, she only awoke to what she had done quite suddenly one evening when there was a dinner-party at Bampton-Leigh, and when, after the gentlemen came back to the drawing-room, she had been called upon to sing with Mr Fitzroy for the delight of the party, and without waiting for any special entreaty had complied. When they sang one song they were asked for another, in the most natural way in the world.

"That is one of May's songs," said some one who was near the piano.

"Oh, is it?" cried Nelly. "I have sung it several times with Mr Fitzroy."

"But it is one of May's songs all the same," insisted this injudicious person. "I have heard her sing it very often, also with Mr Fitzroy."

"Yes," said young Harcourt, who was present, and who was still more angry than Julia to see May seated at the other end of the room talking to an old lady. "It is certainly one of May's songs: and nobody could sing it so sweetly," the young man added, with fire in his eyes.

"By the way," said the indiscreet person, "how is it, with so much music going on, that we have not had a song from May?"

"Oh, May—has not been singing much for some time," said Miss Bampton, with a little quiver in her voice.

And Mrs Brunton, startled, gave a sudden look round the room. She saw Fitzroy placing the music upon the piano in a deliberate, conscious way, which made it apparent to her suddenly awakened faculties that he was aware of the meaning in these words; and she caught young Harcourt's look fixed somewhat fiercely upon herself: and Julia, who had turned her head away and would not look at her at all: and May, in the background, smiling and talking to the old lady, talking very fast, smiling a little more than she meant, looking pale and "out of it"—that curious condition which is not to be described, but which betrays itself to a looker-on. All this Nelly saw with a sudden awakening to the real state of affairs, which ought, of course, to have occurred to her before. And for a moment shame and compunction were strong in her.

"I am so glad," she said. "It is far more suited to her voice than mine: and I want so much to hear her sing it. Please, Mr Harcourt, go and ask her. I hadn't sung for ever so long before I came here," she added, apologetically, to the little circle round the piano, "and they made me begin again; and I never know when to stop—so that I have scarcely heard May. Isn't it a dreadful confession to make?" she said, with an embarrassed laugh.

"You have so strong a voice," said Miss Bampton, melting a little. "May's voice is a little thing after yours."

"May herself is a little thing beside me," said Mrs Brunton, sitting down apart from the piano. "I am almost old enough to be her mother!" She felt that in saying this she had made fully the *amende honorable* to May.

But May would not sing, though she was entreated by all the company. She had her little dignity. "Oh, no," she said, "I could not sing after Nelly — Nelly has so much stronger a voice than I have. Oh, please no!"

"There is nobody who sings so sweetly as you do," said young Harcourt, delighted with the opportunity.

But May would not be persuaded. I don't know that Mrs Brunton was altogether pleased to hear her voice described as so "strong." That is not always a complimentary adjective, and it gave her an amusement tempered with annoyance to hear her organ thus classified. She could not help a little half-angry smile, nor could she help meeting Fitzroy's eye, whose position at the piano, with no one to join him, was a little absurd. He was putting aside the music, looking exceedingly annoyed and rather fierce; but when their eyes met he, too, laughed. They understood each other at once, and when, after this little incident, the music was stopped altogether, he came and sat by her, anxious to communicate his feelings. "What a ridiculous business!" he said. "How silly! to put a stop to everything for the gratification of a little absurd jealousy!"

"Jealousy!" said Nelly; "that would be the most absurd of all — if there was any jealousy in it. There is very little reason for any one to be jealous of me."

"I do not think so," said Fitzroy, in a low voice.

And then Nelly felt again how very foolish it was to remark upon such simple incidents in this strain.

"You don't understand my cousins, I see," she said. "It is nothing of the kind; but it is extraordinarily foolish of me to have absorbed everything, and forgotten that May was not a child any longer. She always seems a child to me."

"She looks quite as old as you do," her companion said.

"Oh, nonsense! she is full ten years younger than I am. However, it does not matter so much, for I am going away."

"So soon?" murmured Fitzroy.

"Soon! I have been here a fortnight — away from my little children." Mrs Brunton found it expedient to quench his tone of devotion by putting all her disadvantages in the foreground. He looked at her with more meaning than he had ever felt in his life in his eyes.

"Would it be indiscreet to ask where you were going?" he said.

"Not at all; I am going home. I have a little house at Haven Green, where my children are."

"I am going, too," he said. "May I come and see you? I shall be for some time in town."

"Oh, if you are in the neighbourhood," said Mrs Brunton; and she turned aside to talk to some one on the other side, an old friend, with whom her colloquy was not conducted in such subdued tones. And soon the name of Haven Green, and the fact that her children were there awaiting her, and that she was going almost immediately, floated from one to another through the room. Miss Bampton heard it, and her heart rose; yet it smote her when she thought these incidents over to feel that she had herself been almost guilty of suggesting to Nelly that it would be better if she went away. As for May, she had seen the conversation, the two heads bent, the exchange of looks, the evidently subdued tone of the communications that passed between them. The poor girl scarcely knew how to behave when Fitzroy approached her some time after. She had been foolish about the song—she had shown her feelings, which is to a girl in such circumstances the worst of sins. Should she tell him she had a headache, or a sore throat, or anything that would excuse her? But he did not leave her the time to invent any excuse.

"I am so sorry," he said, carrying the war into the enemy's country, "that you would not sing with me to-night: for it will be, I fear, one of the last times, if not the very last, that I shall have the chance."

May's poor little heart seemed to cease to beat. What a sudden, dreadful punishment was this for her little gentle self-assertion! "The last time?" she cried. "Oh, are you going away?"

"I must, I fear," he said. "I have been idling too long, and I seem to have outstayed my welcome. I did think that you would have sung with me this last night."

"Oh, Mr Fitzroy!" was all that May could say. She had hard ado to keep the tears out of her eyes.

CHAPTER IV

Bampton-Leigh felt very blank and vacant when both these people who had troubled its peace went away. Had Nelly gone alone and Mr Fitzroy remained, it is possible that there might have been some consolation; indeed, May, in her inmost heart, had looked forward to that period as to a time of peace, when the disturbing element being removed—the "strong" voice of Nelly, and those amusing and enlivening social qualities in which it was natural that a matron of her age should excel a timid girl—things might return to their original condition, and Fitzroy once more hang over her, and encourage her exertions, and praise the sweetness of her voice, which "went" so well with his. Perhaps May had not been aware how eagerly she had been looking forward to this time: and the abyss into which she fell when her hopes came to an end so suddenly, the dull and dreadful vacancy, which was all that remained to her, was almost more than she could bear. It was her first experience of disappointment and deprivation. She had been the spoiled child all her life of her father's house. Whatever she had wanted had been got for her, had it been in any way possible to attain it: and May had never wished for anything that was quite unattainable, until she wished, yet would not for the world have expressed the wish, for the visits, the songs, the fascination of Percy Fitzroy's society, which had come to her without asking, without any action or desire of hers. This gives additional sharpness to the stab of such losses—that the thing which makes your life desolate when it is taken away, has come accidentally, as it were, unsought—to add to and then to annihilate the happiness of (as in this instance) a poor little girl, who had been quite happy without it, who had not wanted it when it originally appeared. Poor May felt that she had no share in bringing on this doom, which to her youthful consciousness seemed to have overwhelmed her for ever. She had not wanted Mrs Spencer-Jackson to invite him; she had not suggested to Julia to bring him to Bampton-Leigh; she had not even begun the singing, poor little May! She was a perfectly innocent victim. And now, alas! she could not bring back the happy unconscious state to which Percy Fitzroy was unknown. The afternoons did not return to her as they had existed before—full of cheerful occupations and amusements. They were blank, and vacant, and impoverished, full of a wistful longing. Oh, if he were but here! Oh, if she could but hear his voice, and join in his singing again! She spent hours at the piano, dreaming that he was by her side, murmuring over her part, recalling all the past delights. Poor little May! When the girls from the Rectory came to play tennis, which they did more often than usual, at Miss Bampton's instigation, instead of being glad to see them, May hated the sight of their well-known faces. She said to herself that she was sick, altogether sick, of her life.

And if May was thus miserable, it may be imagined how much more miserable was the elder sister, who suffered all that May suffered, and the additional burden of blaming herself for all the unthought-of steps that had brought it about. Why had she allowed Fitzroy to come at all? Why had she permitted all that singing, those constant attentions which stole May's heart away? Why, having done that, had she asked Nelly? Oh, what a fool, what a fool she had been all round! It was always she who was to blame whatever happened—she, with such a dear little sister to take care of!—she ought to be a dragon in respect to gentlemen, and never allow one to come near unless she knew his character and could trust him; and she knew nothing of Fitzroy's character. And then, when that harm was done by her fault, to think that she should go and invite Nelly, and throw everything into confusion! Was there ever so abominable, so wicked, a thing to do? Had she asked Nelly *at the first* (these italics were all Miss Bampton's, deeply, trebly underlined in her thoughts), everything would have been well; for then it would have been Nelly and this stranger, this unknown, untrustworthy man, who would have attracted each other, and May would have gone free. But no! if she had intended to make mischief, to make everything as bad as could be, she could not have managed better. It is all my fault, she said to herself—all, all, *my* fault. It was she, indeed, and not Percy Fitzroy, who had broken May's heart!

Thus it will be seen that these two persons left chaos and untold confusion behind them when they went away. Mrs Brunton looked very wistfully at her cousins when she took leave of them. She had the air of wishing to ask their pardon. But then it would have been an offence, an insult, to ask pardon—for what? for taking May's lover from her, for being preferred to May! Better to bear the stain of blackest guilt, to submit to an everlasting breach, than to insult May by suggesting that. And yet Nelly was very sorry and ashamed of herself, though supported underneath these two sentiments by a certain softening of complacence and gratified vanity, which she would not have acknowledged for the world. That she, poor Jack's widow, hardly out of her weeds (indeed she left Bampton-Leigh in the same crape bonnet, with the long veil, in which she had arrived), should have interfered with May's love affair, should have taken her place, and carried on something which she could not to herself deny to be very like a flirtation with her young cousin's admirer! How terrible, how treacherous, how shocking it was! At the bottom of her heart there remained that dreadful little guilty sense that there was pleasure in it; that to be still capable, amid all her disadvantages, of touching a man's heart, was something not disagreeable: but this she did not own to herself. She was very tender to May all that last morning, praising her and flattering her with the intention of making up a little for her fault; and she looked very wistfully in Julia's face, and would fain, very fain, have said something. But Miss Bampton was much on her dignity, and had a look which forbade all such effusions. "I hope you will like your new house," Miss Bampton said. "For my part, I think you would have been a great deal better in the country—not so near town."

"But it is quite in the country," said Nelly.

"Nothing which is within ten minutes of town by the railway can be called the country," said Julia, with great severity. "I *hope* it may be good for the children—of course it will be much livelier for yourself."

"Indeed, I don't see how it can be very lively for myself," cried Nelly, feeling this attack upon her. "I know nobody but the clergyman's family—and the society is not usually very lively in such places—if I wished for lively society," she added in an equally serious tone.

"Oh, my dear Nelly, you will wish for it!" cried her cousin. "It is not to be expected that you should shut yourself up for ever at your age. And then it will be so handy for town—you will have all your friends coming to see you from town."

And a look passed between these ladies which did away with the recollection of many years of love and friendship—a look which said on one side—You know that you have asked him to come to see you!—and on the other with a flash. Well! and what then!—notwithstanding that Julia's heart was full of charity, and Nelly's of compunction. But Mrs Brunton was stirred up to self-defence, and Miss Bampton had in her all the fury of the outraged dove.

"Well! she is gone," said Miss Bampton, coming back to May who stood at the window of the hall looking out very gravely at her cousin's departure. Julia did not recollect now how angry she had been with May for not driving to the station to meet Mrs Brunton. But neither of them thought of accompanying her when she went away. May stood at the hall window while Julia went out to the door, and they both looked after the disappearing carriage with a seriousness that was alarming to see. It might have been a funeral after which they were gazing, instead of Nelly in her mourning bonnet and with all her little boxes. "Well!" said Miss Bampton, "she is gone at last, and I am sure I am very glad. I never thought Nelly Bampton could have changed so in half a dozen years."

"Has she changed?" said May, with a quiet air of indifference, turning from the window. "And I don't see why you should say 'at last.' For, after all, she has only been a fortnight here."

"A fortnight too long," Miss Bampton said.

"You are such a very strange person, Julia, one never understands you," said her young sister. "Why in the name of wonder did you ask Nelly to come here, if she has been a fortnight too long? What absurdity that is! She thinks she had a most successful visit, I feel sure."

"If she calls that success!"

"What?" said May, looking fiercely into Miss Bampton's eyes.

But that was what the poor mother-sister dared not to say. If she had uttered the name of Percy Fitzroy, May would have turned upon her, with what angry disdain! "Mr Fitzroy! what could he possibly have to do with it?" May would have said. Miss Bampton did not venture to bring upon herself such a response as that.

"Oh, nothing!" she said. "I am always making mistakes. Nelly is—not at all what she used to be, dear. Matrimony is not good for some people, and ladies in India get dreadfully spoiled sometimes. They are accustomed to so much attention. There are not so many of them there as here, and they are never contented if they have not every man they see at their feet."

"I did not remark that in Nelly," said May, who was very pensive, and so wounded and sore in her poor little heart that it did her good to be disagreeable to Julia. "There was Bertie Harcourt, for instance, whom she took no notice of—and who, I am sure, was not at her feet."

"Ah, Bertie Harcourt!" cried Miss Bampton, "He"—she paused on the pronoun for greater emphasis, speaking with fervour—"He—is a heart of gold."

"Is he?" said May, indifferently; "you seem to imply that others are different—and indeed I think that it would be much more comfortable to have a heart like other people."

"Oh, May!"

"I wish you would stop all that," cried May, angrily; "when you get into one of your moods, Julia, you are intolerable. I wish you would let Nelly Brunton alone: I don't see anything remarkable about her," the girl said with a toss of her head, walking back into the drawing-room, where she flung the piano open, and began to sing in the most defiant manner. It was a wet day, the lawn swept by a white blast of rain, and all the trees cowering piteously as if running in for shelter. Poor Miss Bampton sat down in a deep chair to hide herself, feeling as if she had been the occasion of all that had happened, and that it was natural she should suffer accordingly. And when presently May ran singing up-stairs, and the door of her room was heard to shut upon her, poor Julia did not follow. She dared not follow; for the first time in her life poor little May, now finding out what it was to be grown up and a woman, had to bear her moment of bitterness by herself. I need not say that Julia cried silently all the time, sunk in the depths of the big chair, so that Mr Bampton when he came in, in quest of tea or something to break the dulness of the afternoon, saw nobody in the room, and went out again calling indignantly for Ju and Maysey, and demanding of the butler in angry tones whether this afternoon of all others, when no one could go out or do anything to amuse oneself, there was to be no tea.

CHAPTER V

Mrs Brunton was not, I think, at all comfortable in her mind as she left her cousin's house. It had been in some sort a trial visit. She had not gone anywhere, or seen anybody, except aunts and other uninteresting relations, since she had returned home. She had paid a long visit to her husband's family, with her children, where everything of course was mourning and seclusion, and where she was made more conscious of her widowhood than of any other condition in her life; then she had been in the country with her own people, where everything was subdued in order to be suitable for poor Nelly; and then she had been involved in the trouble of settling, finding a little house, which was nice and not too dear, which would be good for the children, and quiet, and yet sufficiently in the way to be accessible to those who were most interested in her. This had cost a great deal of trouble and kept her in full occupation, so that it was only when she had settled down, furnished the house, and arranged everything, and got her new address neatly printed upon her writing paper and her visiting cards (if she ever had any need for the latter, which she doubted), that she had consented to go for a fortnight to Bampton-Leigh, leaving the children under charge of their excellent nurse, who had assisted at their birth and was devoted to them—for her uncle Bampton could not bear children in the house. She had explained to her only friend at Haven Green, the clergyman's wife, and still more gravely she had explained to herself, that this was in every way a trial visit to see whether she could bear society again. Society, she said to herself, without Jack! without the consideration which is accorded to a woman who has her husband behind her. She did not know how it looked to a widow, who would naturally be shut out from some things, who might perhaps be pushed aside among the dowagers, who certainly would see everything from a different point of view. Should she be able to bear it?

Alas, Nelly had felt that she was but too able to bear society! She had gone into it with the elasticity and ease with which one glides into one's native element. The absence of Jack behind her, the position of a widow among the dowagers, had never once come into her mind. She had not even required time to bring her to the surface, but had risen at once to be, as she had always been, rather the ringleader than a follower—always in the front of everything, singing, talking. Nelly felt herself flush and burn all over, as she sat in the Bampton carriage on the way to the station with the windows shut between her and the pelting rain; and then she burst into a guilty yet irrestrainable laugh. Yes, she had proved to herself that she was quite able to bear society, and that the temptation to fall into her old ways was not in any way lessened by widowhood. She had done the same sort of thing before now, out of sheer high spirits and love of enjoying herself, when Jack was alive and looking on, and amused by his wife's pranks. She had always known that she was too fond of admiration, too fond of fun. It was not the first time, alas!—and this she had always known was wicked—that she had given some brother officer's *fiancée* a moment of alarm, a thrill of misery, by taking the man away, and boldly tying him to her own apron-strings for a week or so, for some occasion of festivity, "for fun," and to show what she could do, Nelly laughed, and then she cried, at some of the recollections thus evoked. Jack had even been brought to the point of scolding her—not on his own account, but on account of the lady on the other side. And then Nelly, as gaily as she had taken him up, had thrown over her prey.

All these naughty and wicked ways—of which she had been only able to say in self-defence that she meant no harm—were still in her, it appeared, though she was a widow and had believed that she never would be equal to society again. Oh, what a frivolous, unfeeling little wretch she must be! To think that she had plunged into it as if nothing had happened! The faces of her two cousins—one at the door, seeing her off with such warnings about her imprudence in settling so near town, and the other in such gloomy gravity at the window behind, watching her going—could not be remembered without compunction. And Nelly could not say to herself, as she had done before, that no harm was done, that the sinner would return and be forgiven. This man Fitzroy was different. He was not May's *fiancé*! Perhaps, Nelly said to herself, he never would have been. He was not a marrying man; he was a man who amused himself, and whom to expose and show in his true light was a good thing for the girl. But this was mere casuistry, as Nelly knew; for May had given the man her heart, or, if not her real heart, at least her imagination, and she, Nelly, had wickedly taken him away.

It is difficult, however, to see the full enormity of one's own guilt in such a conjuncture. There is always a certain amusement in it to the culprit. It is fun—though it is so little fun to the other persons concerned. Nelly did not, however, feel herself at all responsible so far as Mr Fitzroy was concerned. She had not inspired him with a hopeless passion; she had probably only afforded him the means of extricating himself from a situation in which things were going too far. When Nelly was safely established in the railway compartment, restored completely to her own independence and individuality, with all her packages around her, a modest tip administered to Johnson, and the Bampton carriage out of sight, May indeed floated out of her thoughts; but Percy Fitzroy did not so disappear. Should she ever meet him again? she wondered. Would he seek her out, as he had said, at Haven Green? She felt that it was quite likely he might do so, being a man who was fond of his amusement; and if so, Nelly promised herself that the situation should certainly not be permitted to become strained, or the fun go too far. She had been more or less irresponsible, a free lance, under Julia Bampton's eyes; but in her own little house she would always remember that she was Jack's widow, a householder, the head of a family, a personage in her own right, very different from a girl protected by home—very different from a young wife thinking of nothing but a little fun, and with Jack, who understood all her ways, behind—oh, very different! She had her dignity to keep up, her position, her place in life. If this man insisted on coming, he should be made at once to see that a flirtation was entirely out of place in these circumstances. He might make a call—there was nothing to prevent any man making a call—he might even sing a song, or she might join him in a single duet: but no more—upon no pretence any more.

No later than the first Sunday after Mrs Brunton's return these fine sentiments were put to the test: for Mr Fitzroy appeared in the afternoon, early, with the full intention, as was evident, of staying as long as he should be permitted to stay. Nelly had not forgotten him at all in that little interval. He had intruded into her mind a number of times, to her annoyance and discomfiture. Why should she keep wondering whether he would come? Better that he had come and gone, and Nelly had never thrown a thought after him. Why should she think about this man, or whether she should ever see him again? But she did, in spite of herself, perhaps because he was the only figure visible on her way, where there had been once so many. Her house was a nice little house, made in a sort of imitation of that country house which is the English ideal. In France and other countries the better houses of the village are built like town houses—high, with rows of shuttered windows and a big staircase. But in England it is always the country house that is copied—windows opening upon a little lawn, mimic trees, shrubberies, conservatories, the walls covered with climbing plants and roses.

Nelly's villa had a little verandah on one side, a little hall, with a tiger skin—one of poor Jack's trophies—spread out in it; a drawing-room full of Indian curiosities. She went and came by the drawing-room window oftener than by the door, and so did her intimates the clergyman's wife and daughters, who would run round through the garden and tap at the pane. Of course Mr Fitzroy did not do this. He came decorously through the hall, ushered in by the maid, and was received with a little state by Mrs Brunton, who had her two children with her—little Jack, aged five, and Maysey, aged three. These little people remained playing in the room during the greater part of the interview, in which scarcely a word was said about music. Mr Fitzroy took the little girl on his knee, and patted the boy on the head, and asked them their names. "Ah, Maysey," he said, "the same as your cousin, Miss May Bampton." "Yes, the same: for they are called after the same person, a great authority in the family," answered Mrs Brunton. This was the unexceptionable character of their talk.

But that was only the first of a series of continual visits, during which, as was inevitable, the intimacy grew. The piano was opened on the third or fourth occasion, and after that the children no longer formed part of Mrs Brunton's *mise en scène*. She did not any longer feel it necessary to keep them in the front, to keep herself and her visitor in continual remembrance of her widowhood and her responsibilities. When a friend comes two or three times in a week, you cannot be always in a state of preparation for him. You must occasionally fall off your guard, forget that there is anything in his presence that needs to be guarded against. The children came in whenever they pleased, but it was the hour for their walk, or they preferred to play in the garden, which was much better for them. And Nelly forgot: sometimes it seemed to her that she forgot everything, their very existence, and poor Jack who was dead, and India and all her experiences, and was for a moment now and then as she had been when Jack was a young lover, and she was nineteen—at home in the old days. It is curious how a woman, who has had a home of her own for many years, goes back to the time when her father's house was the only place that bore that name. "We used to do that at home," the matron will say, with a smile or a tear, realising in a moment the girl she used to be—with how much stronger reason when she is only parted from it by some half-dozen years. Nelly felt as if she were again a girl at home during many of those golden afternoons, as if nothing had ever happened, as if her life were as yet all to come. She forgot herself, and that position which had been so much impressed upon her by all her friends. Poor Nelly! It was very wrong for a woman who was a widow, and had been a widow not eighteen months; but she was young, and her heart was very light and elastic, rebounding from the deep gloom which was so unnatural to her character and to her age. For her character, I need not say, was not a solid and steady one, as that of the mother of these two little children ought to have been. And it was so sweet to be young again, to receive the homage which seemed so genuine, to have the companionship which was so entrancing, to sing with that other voice which was so suited to hers, to talk and smile, and be amused, and find the time fly. She did not know many people—nobody, indeed, but good Mrs Glynn and the girls, who were absorbed in parish work and mothers' meetings, in which they had hoped and expected Mrs Brunton would take her part. They had wanted her to take a district; they had set apart many things in which she ought to take an interest. But Nelly's interest had never been awakened in such things. She would have been dull, very dull, in her new home if it had not been for that very different kind of interest which was so much more in her way. It is impossible, when you have an excellent nurse who really knows much better what is right than you do, to occupy your whole time with a little boy of five and a little girl of three. Nelly gave Jack his little lesson every morning very punctually, and devoted to the children as much of the earlier part of the day as remained when they had taken their walk, and fulfilled the little routine of their existence. And then in the afternoon— —

Well, in the afternoon Mrs Brunton found it dull. She went across to the rectory, and often found that the girls were all out about their parish work, or else playing tennis at the house of some neighbour whom she scarcely knew, or who did not venture to ask the young widow to appear at a garden party—so soon. And then Nellie would take a rather mournful, lonely walk. Is it wonderful that when she saw Mr Percy Fitzroy coming her heart gave a jump of pleasure, and her face grew bright with smiles? Not at first because he was Percy Fitzroy—but because he was life and movement and pleasure and fellowship, and because this was the kind of occupation and entertainment which she had been most used to in her former career.

CHAPTER VI

There is nothing in the world, as all the world knows, that can go on for any time at a given point without developments, and those probably of an unforeseen sort, especially not a kind of intercourse like this—the "friendship," as Nelly to herself stoutly and steadily called it. It was much remarked upon, as may be supposed, but not in any unkindly way. Though her neighbours scarcely knew her as yet, they knew, or thought they knew, that the young widow about whom they were all prepared to be so much interested would not, as was said, be a widow much longer. And her husband not yet a twelvemonth dead, some said, who were of the class who always hear the wrong version of a story. Others, who had called upon her and liked her, explained to each other apologetically that young Mrs Brunton was a sweet young woman, and of course could not be expected to make a recluse of herself at her age. Thus it was with charity, though clear-sightedness, that the village saw Mrs Brunton and her "friend" from town, followed by the children and the nurse, walking across the fields towards the river one September afternoon, the gentleman in boating costume. Mr Fitzroy himself was not perhaps so much touched by that procession as were Nelly's neighbours. He had come early, and proposed that, as the river was not far off, Mrs Brunton should go for a row, to which Nelly had replied with delight—half naturally, half to cover her own pleasure; for are not all things mingled in this world?—that little Jack had been crying to go on the river, and that it would be such a treat for the children. Young mothers have a way of doing this, on much less moving occasions, when the delight of the children is the last thing in the world of which their entertainers are thinking. Fitzroy had to make a great gulp and swallow the children, though he did not like it. The nurse sat behind him in the boat, and Nelly kept the two little ones beside her in the stern, and they were very well behaved. But Fitzroy felt that, had any of his friends seen him on the river in this patriarchal guise, the joke would have rung through all the clubs where his name was known. Happily, however, in September there are few people about of the club kind. When he came down another time in his flannels Mrs Brunton said nothing about the children. She hesitated a little, and the colour fluttered in her face. Oh, if she only knew what was the right thing! There was no harm in it, certainly. It was like walking along a public street with him, which was a thing no one could object to. And if she refused to go, what would he think? or, rather, what would he think that she was thinking? He would probably imagine that she was afraid of him, that she was giving a character to his friendly attentions which did not belong to them, thinking that he was in love with her. How silly and vain that would seem; how he would laugh in his sleeve to see that this was what she thought, like any silly girl — she, a woman whom he only considered as a friend!

This was the argument which made Nelly finally decide to go. And she enjoyed that row beyond anything she could remember. It was as if she had made an escapade as a girl, with some one who perhaps one day — —But she never would have been allowed to make that escapade as a girl. Now, at her present age and in her position of dignity as a married person, what could there be wrong in it? And yet it was rather wrong. She was a little ashamed, a little self-conscious, hoping that nobody would see her. And the sunset was so glorious, and the river so golden, and the sense of a secret, intense companionship so sweet! There was very little said between them — nothing, Nelly protested to herself afterwards, that all the world might not have heard — but they came home across the fields in the misty lingering autumn twilight, with a bewildering sense of happiness and perfect communion. "I do not know," Fitzroy said, "when I have spent so happy an evening." "The river was so lovely," said Nelly, faltering a little. "Everything was lovely," he said. He was so delicate and considerate that he would not come in, but said good night to her at the gate, in the presence, so to speak, of all the world.

And this occurred a good many times, as long as the fine weather lasted. It would be such a pity, Fitzroy said, not to take advantage of it, and, indeed, Mrs Brunton thought so too. And once or twice he did come in, and there was a little supper, and he went off in good time for the half-past nine train. Nobody could say that was late: and then, to be sure, if any one did say so, Nelly was not responsible to anybody for her actions. She was herself the best judge of what was befitting. Perhaps she was not quite so sure now that nothing was ever said that all the world might not hear. Things were said — about philosophical subjects, about the union of souls, about affinities, about the character of love metaphysically considered, whether a man or a woman could love twice, whether sometimes in early youth it was not more imagination than love that moved the heart, whether it did not require a little experience of life to make you really acquainted with the force of that sentiment. "There is no passion in the love of girls and boys," Fitzroy said, and he almost convinced Nelly that passion was the salt of life, the only thing really worth living for. These discussions perhaps were a little dangerous. But they were not personal — oh no! abstractions merely, the kind of subjects which promote conversation and which draw out the imaginative faculties. The thing that proved this was that there was not a suggestion of marriage ever made, nothing which approached that subject. Love-making from the point of view of an Englishwoman means marriage as a matter of course. And Fitzroy had never in the most distant way said to Nelly, "Will you marry me?" "Is it possible that you should one day become my wife?" He had talked, oh! a great deal about love in the abstract. He had said hurried things, phrases that seemed to escape him, about a man's "passion." And Nelly had felt many times, with a trembling of all her faculties, that he and she were on the eve of a crisis, that the moment must soon come in which these decisive words must be said.

But that crisis never did come, though certainly the excitement of the intercourse grew daily, and the suspense bewildered and overwhelmed her so that she was entirely absorbed in it, and no longer her own mistress. She had let the stream carry her away. From the time when she went out first alone, with something of the secret delight of a girl making an escapade, upon the river with her kind visitor in the early September, till now, scarcely a month later, what a change had occurred! Then she obeyed a pleasurable impulse, partly that he might not think she thought of anything beyond the pleasant intercourse of an hour or two; now she felt her whole existence, her life, her happiness, her credit with the world, hanging as it were on the breath of his lips. Would he say, or would he not say, the words which would make all clear? For a time after every meeting she felt as if she had barely escaped from that supreme scene, holding it off, according to a woman's instinct; and then a chill began to creep over Nelly when he went away without a word: and life and everything concerning her seemed to hang in that suspense. Poor Nelly! poor, foolish, unsuspicious creature! If she had ever been a cruel little flirt in her heedlessness, never meaning any harm, she was punished now.

One night—it was early in October—Fitzroy stayed late and shared Nelly's supper, and lingered after it, going back to the drawing-room with her, not taking leave of her in the little hall as he was in the habit of doing; and thus he missed the half-past nine train. But what did that matter? for there were two later, and an hour's delay could not, after all, make much difference. They were both full of emotion and suppressed excitement, and Nelly felt that the crisis could not be much longer delayed. She made, however, that invariable effort to keep it at arm's length, to talk of other things, which is one evidence that things have come to an alarming pass. She chattered, she laughed, flushed with feeling, with suspense and excitement, thinking every moment that the passion (certainly there was what he called "passion") in his eyes must burst forth. But still the suspense went on. Nelly's nerves and spirit were almost on the point of breaking down when she was suddenly roused by the chiming of the clock. "Oh," she cried, "eleven! you must run, you must fly! You have not a moment to lose for your train—the last train!"

He looked at her for a moment with unutterable things in his eyes. "Is it so very indispensable that I should catch the last train? Nelly! how can I leave you? How can you send me away, when you know how I love, how I adore— —"

There came at this moment a sharp knock at the door.

"If you please, ma'am," said Nelly's excellent nurse, "there's just time for Mr Fitzroy to catch the last train."

And he had to go, seizing his hat, hurrying out with an apology for staying till the last moment, while Nelly, trembling, terrified, shrank back into the room where a little fire was still burning, though the night was warm. She went back to it with the chill of exhausted nerves, and held out her hands to the smouldering glow, while nurse locked and bolted the hall door with unnecessary noise and commotion. Then that excellent woman once more put her head into the room with a look which Nelly could not meet. "Is there anything I can get for you, ma'am, before I go to bed?" she said.

Nelly thanked her, hurriedly recalling her faculties. "How glad I am you came to warn Mr Fitzroy, nurse! I had told him, but he paid no attention. Gentlemen always think they can catch a train by a rush at the last moment." She felt that she was apologising to nurse, and was ashamed of doing so, though it was shame and uneasiness which had forced the words to her lips. Nurse did not commit herself to any approval or condonation of her mistress's behaviour. She said only "Yes, ma'am," and marched up-stairs with measured steps to bed.

Nelly sat down on a low chair in front of the smouldering fire. She was trembling all over, scarcely able to command herself, her cheeks burning with the heat of excitement, yet her teeth chattering with a nervous chill, her strength almost completely broken down. Now that she was alone the tension of her nerves gave way: the light went out of her eyes, her heart seemed to suffocate her, struggling in her breast. The agitation of her whole being prostrated her physically as well as mentally. She lay back upon her chair, as if its support were necessary to hold her together, and then she bent forward, holding her trembling hands to the fire. Had the crisis come, not as she had expected, but in a form that she did not understand? or was this strange interrupted climax a mere break in the stream, no end at all, a broken thread to be taken up again to-morrow and to-morrow indefinitely?

Nelly was not capable of forming these questions in her mind, but they swept through the whirlwind within her, with a horror and alarm which she did not understand and knew not how to explain. What had he said? Why had he said that and not something else? What had she done that he had looked at her so? No, she did not ask herself all this; these questions only went whirling about in the wild commotion of her soul. She did not know how long she sat thus, incapable of movement. The fire sank lower, and she felt, without knowing whence it came, a chill draught from her right hand where the window was, but took no notice, perceiving it only, not in a condition of mind to account for it. But Mrs Brunton suddenly sat up erect, and all that tempest stopped in a moment, at the sound of a footstep outside and a tap on the window. What was it? Oh, heaven! what was it? She suddenly remembered in a moment that the window had been unfastened because the room was too warm. The shutters had been almost closed upon it, leaving only the smallest opening to give a little air, and Nelly had forgotten all about it, in her agitation and trouble. She sat for a moment motionless in her panic, thinking of burglars and robbery, not daring to stir. Then there came another tapping, and a low voice. "Mrs Brunton, I have lost my train; I remembered that the window was open; may I come in?"

The next moment, without waiting for any reply—which, indeed, Nelly in her consternation was unable to give—he pushed open the window quickly and came into the room. She stood petrified, staring at him, feeling as if she must have gone suddenly mad, and that all this was a hallucination, as he entered with a glow of triumph in his face.

"Nelly," he said, coming forward to her, dropping down on his knee by the side of her chair. "Darling, you left it open for me! You knew I would come back."

It all happened in a moment, and in a moment Nelly had to make her decision: her life, her fate, her good name, everything in the world worth thinking of, was in the turn of the scale. If he had not made that suggestion, heaven knows, in this prostration of her whole being, what poor Nelly might have done. But it gave her a sting of offence too sharp to bear.

"I left it open for you!" she cried, starting up. "You must be mad, Mr Fitzroy! What do you want? What do you want? Why have you come back here?"

He was startled by the terror, yet almost fury, in her eyes. "Forgive me," he said, starting up also, facing her, "I have lost my train. You know it is the last. What could I do but come back to the only house where I am known? and I thought you would not refuse me shelter for the night."

"Oh," she said almost wildly, "shelter—for the night!"

"May I close the window? It's rather cold, and you are shivering. If I have frightened you, forgive me, forgive me! Rather than that, I would have walked to London or sat down on a doorstep."

"I am not frightened," said Mrs Brunton with a gasp. Her senses came back to her; she felt that she must keep very cool, and make no scene. "It was a little alarming to see a man come in," she said. "It is very unfortunate that you should have lost your train. I am afraid you will not be very comfortable, but we will do the best we can for you."

He caught her sleeve as she was turning to the door. "Where are you going?" he cried.

"Only to call one of the maids to make a room ready for you."

"I want no room," he said. "An hour or two on the sofa will be luxury; and I shall be off in the morning by dawn of day, and disturb no one. Nobody need know: and you are not the sort of girl to think of Mrs Grundy. Nelly, my darling! stay, stay with me a bit! what is the use of taking me in if you leave me like this? Half an hour, just half an hour, to finish our talk!"

"When I have given my orders, perhaps," said Nelly. She would not stop even to forbid the familiarity of his address. She walked out of the room with composed steps, but as soon as she was outside flew up the dark staircase to the nursery, where nurse, an anxious and troubled woman, was not yet asleep. Mrs Brunton went in like a ghost to the room in which the night-light was burning, where the children were breathing softly in their cribs. "Nurse," she said, with all the composure she could command, "Mr Fitzroy has come back; he has lost his train. I want you to get up and prepare the spare room for him. I am sorry: but what else can we do?"

Nurse looked fixedly at her mistress in the light of the candle which Nelly had just lighted, and which came to life in a sudden glare upon her agitated face. "Yes, ma'am," she said quietly, beginning to dress.

What a strange agitated scene in the middle of the silent night! The man below could not have been more dismayed by the appearance of a band of soldiers than he was by the quiet, respectable, respectful maid-servant who came in with a candle to show him to his room, and whose polite determination to get rid of him, to put out the lamp and see that everything was safe for the night, was full of the most perfect calm. "I'll go up-stairs presently; but you need not wait," he said. "Oh, sir, I don't mind waiting; but my mistress likes me to see the lights out. I'll be in the next room when you are ready, sir, to show you the way."

He was moved at last to ask impatiently, "Is not Mrs Brunton coming down-stairs again?"

"Oh dear no, sir; my mistress is passing the night in the nursery, for Master Jack is a little feverish, and he never will part with his mamma when once he sees her. If she offered to go away he'd scream so, he'd raise the whole house."

Fitzroy glared at this guardian of the little helpless household—a very respectful, very obliging maid-servant—making light of the trouble a nocturnal visitor gave. He could no more have resisted or insulted this woman than if she had been a queen. He followed her quite humbly to his room, not daring to say a word. He might as well have been in a hotel, he said bitterly to himself.

When nurse went back she found poor Nelly sitting on the floor between the two little beds, her head leaning on one of them, holding fast the rail of the other, and weeping as if her heart would break.

Next morning Mr Fitzroy left the cottage early, without asking to see Mrs Brunton. It was, indeed, too early to disturb the lady of the house.

CHAPTER VII

Mrs Brunton woke next morning with an aching head and a confused mind, not knowing for a moment what had happened to her. Was it a nightmare? a dreadful dream? She had not slept till morning, and then had fallen into an unrestful torpor, full of the broken reminiscences of the night. A nightmare! that was most like what it was—until she came to herself all at once, and remembered everything.

Everything! and yet did not in the least understand. What had been the meaning of it all? It was more like a nightmare than ever as all the different incidents come back upon her mind. The lingering, the wild talk—the question, "Must I go away?" The cry "I love you. I adore——" and nurse coming in to save her mistress perhaps from wilder utterances still. "Was it indispensable that he should go by the last train?" What a question! Was it not indispensable—more! exacted by every feeling, by every necessity? "I love you, I adore——" Oh yes, these words made poor Nelly's heart beat; but they were not words a man should have said in the silence of the night to a woman without any protection, with a wild heart leaping and struggling in her bosom, and to whose code of possible existence something else, something very different, was needful. Was it indispensable?—oh! it was not, it was not *that*, a man should have asked. He might love her, but what kind of love was it to humble a woman in her own esteem, to make her ask herself, "What have I done, oh what have I done, that I should be spoken to so?" Nelly did not think of her reputation, of honour, or, as he dared to suggest, of what people might say. Mrs Grundy! That was all very well for the light follies that mean nothing, the laughing transgression of a formal rule. But the shock of his look, the horror of his return, struck at her very being. It seemed to her that she could die of shame only to remember it. And what could he think of her? Was it indispensable? Had not she left the window open for him? Had she not known he would come back?

O God, O God! These words, that come to us by instinct at the most dreadful moments, were not profane exclamations in poor Nelly's case. She sat up in her bed, and wrung her hands, and uttered that wild appeal—not a prayer, for her brain was too distracted for prayer—but only an appeal, a cry. The words he had said kept whirling through her mind, till they came to have no meaning except the one meaning of horror and pain: "indispensable," and "Mrs Grundy," and "you knew I would come back." Oh, what kind of woman must he have thought her to think that she knew he would come back, to leave the window open for him? The last train, was it indispensable? and the window left open—and Nelly had to seize herself, as it were, with both hands, to keep her reason, to stop the distracted rush of those words over and over and over again through her brain. There was a lull when nurse came in—nurse, who had been her saviour from she did not know what, who had cut the dreadful knot, but who must not, not even she, know the tempest which was going on in Nelly's being. She stopped that nervous wringing of her hands, pulled herself together, tried to smile. "How dreadfully late I am! How did I come to be so late?" she cried.

"It was the fright, ma'am, last night."

"I—I—was just trying to recall that, nurse. Mr Fitzroy"—she could not say his name without flushing scarlet all over to the tips of her fingers—"lost his train, and came back?"

"He did, ma'am," said nurse, with severe self-restraint.

"He ought not to have done it, nurse."

"Indeed, ma'am, he ought not to have done it." Nurse shut up her lips firmly, that other words might not burst forth.

"He—gave me—a terrible fright, nurse. I had forgotten that the window was open."

"Yes, Mrs Brunton." Poor Nelly looked so wistfully in the woman's face, not explaining further, not asking her support in words, but so clearly desiring it, that nurse's heart was deeply touched. "I think, ma'am," she said, "if you'll not be angry——" Nelly's face was heartrending to behold. She expected nothing but condemnation, and how could she accept it, how defend herself against it, from her servant, her dependant, a woman who at least might have been expected to be on her side? If nurse had indeed condemned her, Nelly's pride might have been aroused, but now she sat with her eyes piteously fixed upon her, appealing to her as if against a sentence of death.

"If you won't be angry with me, ma'am," repeated nurse, "and if I may make so bold as to say it, I think you behaved just as a lady ought—not stopping to argue with him, but coming right away, and leaving the gentleman to me."

"O nurse!" cried Nelly, bursting into tears with a relief unspeakable. "O nurse! thank God that you think I did right."

"It was an awful trial for a lady, a young lady like you—oh, an awful trial, enough to drive you out of your senses!" Nelly had flung herself on the woman's shoulder and lay sobbing there, while nurse patted her tenderly, as if she had been one of the children. "Don't take on now, don't, there's a dear lady! Get up, ma'am, and dress quick, and don't spoil your eyes with crying. I saw Mrs Glynn at the Rectory door, looking as if she were coming here."

"O nurse! I cannot see her! You must say I have a headache."

"Not this morning, Mrs Brunton, oh, not this morning," cried nurse, "if I may make so bold as to say it. Come down and look your own self; and I would own to the fright, if I was you."

To say that Nelly was not half-angry at nurse's interference, which she had evoked, would scarcely have been true. She began to resent it the moment that she had most benefited by it, as was natural. But she also recognised its truth. And she dressed with as much care as possible, and did all she could to efface the signs of agitation and trouble from her face. Nelly was like most people in a dreadful social emergency; she forgot that Mrs Glynn was the kindest of women. She began to ask herself, with fictitious wrath, if this was indeed Mrs Grundy, the impertinent inquisitor, come to inquire into her private affairs, with which she had nothing to do—nothing! She immediately perceived, arrayed against her, an evil-speaking, evil-thinking world, making the worst of everything, accepting no explanation, incapable of understanding! When she walked down to the drawing-room it was not Nelly, the kind and confident girl-widow, nor was it Mrs Brunton, the young matron secure in her own right and the protection of her home and her children, feeble shields as these were against the world; it was rather an army with banners, spears flashing, and flags flying, which marched against the enemy, defying fate.

It was Mrs Glynn who looked pale and unhappy when Nelly went into the room. She was old enough to be Mrs Brunton's mother, and in the tenderness of her heart the Rector's wife felt something like it as the younger woman appeared. Her experienced glance showed her in a moment that Nelly was self-conscious and defiant, which meant, of course, that her information was correct, and that something dreadful had occurred. They bade each other good morning and kissed—as ladies do in the habit of intimacy, which generally means so little—Nelly meeting the salute with a little impatience, Mrs Glynn giving it with a marked and lingering tenderness, which also was to Mrs Brunton an offence; and then they talked for a moment or two about the beauty of the autumn morning, the health of the children, and various other small subjects of no immediate interest. Then Mrs Glynn was silent for a moment, and said softly, "Mrs Brunton!" and paused, hesitating, looking wistfully in Nelly's face.

"Yes."

"I am afraid you will be angry. I have come to say something—to ask you——Dear Mrs Brunton, you are very young—and I—knew your mother."

"Yes," said Nelly again, with an attempt at cheerfulness. "Please tell me at once what it is. Have I—done anything wrong?" She gave a little, nervous laugh. An altogether innocent person would have been frightened, but Nelly knew every word that was going to be said, and steeled herself for the ordeal.

"The Rector," said Mrs Glynn, "came home by the last train last night; and he saw some one—a gentleman—go in at your gate. He was frightened—for you, my dear; and he stood still and watched, meaning to call a policeman if anything was wrong; and then he saw who it was, recognising him in the moonlight. Dear Mrs Brunton! Mr Glynn came home to me in great distress. We have done nothing all night but think, and think, what we ought to do. Oh, my dear girl, hear me out! You are so young, and you have been used to such different ways in India, such hospitality, and all that. We know it, and we know that people there keep a sort of open house, that friends are constantly visiting each other. But it's not so here, and you don't know how people talk, and I thought you would, perhaps, let me speak to you, warn you——"

"Of what?" said Nelly, with white lips. All sorts of plans and thoughts had rushed through her mind while this address was made to her—quick impulses, bad and good, to overwhelm her visitor with scorn, to refuse to answer, to turn the meddling woman out of her house. But oh, on the other hand, she wanted help so much! to throw herself upon this kind woman's breast, at her feet. For a moment this battle raged fiercely in her breast, and she herself knew not which side would win. "Mrs Grundy," she said, at length, with a smile upon her parched mouth, not able to articulate any more.

"Mrs Grundy!" said the Rector's wife. "Oh, my dear, I am not Mrs Grundy; I am a very anxious friend, anxious to help you, to do anything. Oh, let me help you! We are sure there must be an explanation."

"No," cried Nelly, "you are not Mrs Grundy, I know; I was a fool to say that."

"Thank you, my dear. You are so young, and a stranger—a stranger to our village ways, Mrs Brunton!" The good woman took Nelly's hand in both of hers, and looked at her with appealing eyes.

"I will tell you precisely how it was," said Nelly, hastily, as quickly turned to the good as to the bad impulse. "Nobody was to blame. Mr Fitzroy——" She grew red at the name, and then felt herself chill all over—chill to her very heart, turning as pale as she had been red, as if some ice wind had blown over her. The sensation made her pause for a moment. "Mr Fitzroy stayed a little too late last night; he left himself scarcely time to catch the train—men are so apt to do that. They think they can rush in a moment."

"I know," said Mrs Glynn, pressing her hand.

"And he lost it," said Nelly, faltering. "He came back; and he remembered that the drawing-room window had been left a little open, and he thought it better to come round by the garden instead of—instead of rousing the house."

"Tell me," said Mrs Glynn, "one moment; are you engaged to him, my dear?"

Nelly drooped her head. "Not yet," she said. "You shall know everything. He was—saying that—when nurse came to tell him he must fly for his train."

"Ah!" cried Mrs Glynn, pressing Nelly's hand in both hers, "now I begin to see! And he came back to have it out! Oh, how glad I am I came! Now I can see all the excuses for him. It was an error of judgment, but it was very natural. My dear, my dear; and then?"

"There was no more," Nelly said, raising her head. With what relief she heard that—excuses for him! even for *him*. "I was very much frightened," she added, with new confidence, "for I had forgotten the window was open, and I thought—I don't know what I thought. I ran up-stairs at once to bid nurse prepare a room for him—and I did not see him again."

"God bless you, my dear," cried the Rector's wife, taking Nelly into her arms and giving her a kiss. "That was the very best thing you could have done; unless you had sent him over to us to the Rectory, but of course you did not think of that. Oh, how glad I am I came! Oh, how pleased my husband will be! It was what I would have wished you to have done if you had been my own child. But what a situation for you! what a moment, my poor dear! It was wrong—it was very wrong—of him; he ought to have known better: but yet, a young man! and interrupted at the very moment when— —He was wrong, but there were excuses for him, my dear."

Mrs Glynn stayed for some time, full of sympathy and consolation. "He has behaved very foolishly, my love. He ought not to have come, and, being here, he ought not to have gone away so soon. He ought to have left openly, like any other visitor, and settled everything before he went. But a young man in the height of passion— —" It was a comfort to Nelly that good Mrs Glynn said "passion," too. "Of course, he will come back in the afternoon, and you will have your explanation," she added. "And then you will come to the Rectory, and bring him to see us; you will—you will, promise me you will? And, oh, God bless you, and make it a happy change for you, my dear!"

CHAPTER VIII

There were excuses for him; he had been interrupted, and he had come back to have it out, to tell his tale, to make his declaration. Mrs Glynn, who was quite cool and impartial, not bewildered by excitement like Nelly, thought so. But then she had not that heavy sense of something else—some things said that ought not to have been said—which crushed Nelly's heart like a stone. "Was it indispensable that he should catch the last train? Had she not expected him back—left the window open for him?" If Mrs Glynn had known of these words, would she have still thought there were excuses? Nelly's heart lay in her breast like a stone. The scientific people may say what they will—that the heart is a mere physical organ; not those who have felt it ache, who have felt it leap, who have felt it lie like a stone. There seemed no beating in it, no power of rising. She said to herself that she was relieved and comforted, and thanked God that, to a calm spectator, there were excuses for him. But her heart did not respond; it lay motionless in her breast, crushed, heavy as a stone.

She did not, however, leave the house all that day, expecting, yet not expecting, the visit which should put everything right, of which her friend had been so confident; but he did not come. Next morning there arrived a letter, full of agitation and bewilderment to Nelly. It was not the apology, the prayer for forgiveness, which she had expected. The letter took a totally different tone. He accused Nelly—poor Nelly, trembling and miserable—of distrust, which was an insult to him. What did she think of him that she had fled from him, turned him over to a servant? What horrible idea had she formed of him? What did she expect or imagine?

"I have often been told," he wrote, "that women in their imaginations jumped at things that would horrify a man; but I never believed it, least of all of you. What could be more simple or more natural than to go back to the house of my only friend—to one more dear to me than any other friend—instead of walking to London, which was my only alternative? What dreadful things have people put into your head? for they would not arise there of themselves, I feel sure. And now here we have come to a crisis which changes our relationship altogether. How are we to get over it? My first thought was to rush off at once—to put the Channel between us—so that you might feel safe; but something tugs at my heart, and I cannot put myself out of reach of you whatever you may think of me. O Nelly! where did you learn those suspicions that are so insulting to me? How can I come again with the recollection of all that in my mind? Do you wish me to come again? Do you want to cast me off? What is to happen between us? After the insult you have put upon me, it is for you to take the next step. I am here at your orders—to come or to stay."

Nelly was struck dumb by this letter. She did not know what to think or to say. A simple-minded person, not accustomed to knavery, has always the first impulse of believing what is said to her (or him), whatever she may know against it. How could she tell, a woman so little acquainted with life, whether he might not be in the right—whether he had not cause to feel insulted and offended? If his motives were so transparent and his action so simple as he thought, he had indeed good reason to be offended—and for a moment there was a sensation of relief and comfort indescribable in Nelly's heart. Ah! that these vile things which had given her so much pain had not risen again like straws upon an evil wind, and blown about her, confusing all her thoughts. Not indispensable that he should catch the last train—he who treated this incident now as so inevitable, so simple an occurrence! And had she not expected him to come back—left the window open for his stealthy entry, which was to disturb nobody?—he who now took so high a tone, and explained his coming as so entirely accidental and justifiable. Nelly did not know what to think. She was torn in two between the conviction which lay heavy at the bottom of her heart, and the easier, the delightful faith to which he invited her with that show of high-toned indignation. And even now he said no more: a dear friend, the dearest of all—but not a word of that which would smooth away all doubt, and make it possible for her to believe that her ears had deceived her, that he had never said anything to make her doubt him. Poor Nelly was torn with trouble and perplexity. They had come to a crisis? Oh yes! and she had felt so long that the crisis was coming, but not—not in this guise! She sat all the evening alone, pondering how to reply, writing letter after letter, which she burned as soon as they were written. At last, after all these laborious attempts, she snatched her pen again, and wrote in great haste, taking no time to think: for the powers of thought were exhausted, and had nothing more to do in the matter. She wrote that it was best he should not come again—unless——And then, in greater haste still, with a countenance all glowing with shame, she scratched out that word "unless." Oh no, no!—not from her, whatever were the circumstances, could that suggestion come.

During the next two days a hot correspondence went on. Fitzroy wrote angrily that he respected her decision, and would not trouble her again.

Then, almost before the ink was dry—before, at least, she had awakened out of the prostration of misery caused by reading this letter—there came another imploring her to reverse her judgment, to meet him, at least, somewhere, if she would not permit him to come; not to cast him off for ever, as she seemed disposed to do. Poor Nelly had very little desire to cast him off. She was brought to life by this hot protest against the severance which she felt would be death to her. She began to believe that, after all, there was nothing wanting on his part—that all he had not put into words was understood as involved in the words which he did employ. Poor Nelly! "It must be so," she said to herself—"it must be so!" A man in whose thoughts there was nothing but love and honour might never think it possible that he could be doubted—might feel that his truth and honesty were too certain to be questioned. "Women in their imaginations jump at things that would horrify a man." Was this true? Perhaps it was true. At what horror had Nelly's imagination jumped on that dreadful night? Dared she say to any one—dared she to put in words, even to herself—what she feared? Oh no, no! She had not known what she feared. She had feared nothing, she said to herself, her cheeks burning, her bosom panting—nothing! All that she was conscious of was that this was not what he ought to have done—that he had failed in respect, that he had not felt the delicacy of the tie between them. Was that all? Surely that, after all, was not a matter of life and death.

Nelly went on reasoning with herself that had she been a man it would have been the most natural thing in the world that he should have come back, having lost his train. Had her husband been living, had she been in her father's or her mother's house, of course he would have done so; and why should she think herself less protected by her own honour and good faith, by the presence of the children, than by these other safeguards? Nelly began to be ashamed of herself. "Women in their imaginations jump— —" Was she so little sure of herself, she cried at last to herself with burning scorn, her heart beating loud, her countenance crimson, that she attributed to him ideas altogether alien to his thoughts—that she had fled to the help of nurse as if she wanted protection? After this argument with herself, which lasted long and went through more phases than I can follow, Nelly read Fitzroy's first letter over with feelings ever varying, ever deepening in force. Had she done him wrong? She had done him wrong—cruel wrong. He had acted with simplicity all through. She it was who had put meanings he never thought of into his mind. She it was— —Oh! and she had thought herself a good woman! What horrors were those that filled a woman's imagination—things that would confound any man?

The result was that, with many a confused and trembling thought, Nelly granted to Fitzroy the interview he asked for. Something in her heart—a sick sensation of giddiness and bewilderment, as if everything had gone wrong in her life—prevented her from receiving him again at home; but she consented to meet him (of all places in the world) at the railway station—the noisy, bustling place where no quiet could be secured, where anybody might see them, where, indeed, it was impossible that they should not be seen. I wonder if any other pair ever walked about Paddington, rubbing shoulders with the calmest suburban folk, and all the daily commotion of the little commonplace trains, with such a subject between them. But we never know how often we touch tragedy as we walk about the world unconscious. They met, these two people, with such a question between them, with all the confused and incomprehensible intermediate atmosphere which veils two individual minds from each other, in the midst of all the bustle and noise, in which, in their self-absorption, they were lost as in a desert. They walked about, round and round, in the darker corners of the great area, and at last, overcome with fatigue and excitement, sat down upon a bench a little out of the way, where few passengers came. I cannot tell what was in the man's mind—if he was conscious of wrong and acting a part, or conscious of right and only speaking as a man who felt himself to be under an unjust imputation might have a right to do. But it became very visible now if never before that he was a coarse-minded man, notwithstanding his outside of refinement, and that he no longer took the trouble to attempt to veil it as he had hitherto done. And Nelly, on the other hand, though keenly conscious of this, accepted it as if she had always known it. They had been together for nearly an hour, pacing up and down the gloomy background of the great noisy station, talking, talking; and yet she did not know with any more conviction than when they first met whether it was he or she that was in the wrong. Was he true—a man who had acted in all simplicity and honour—and she a woman with a bad imagination which, had jumped at something enough to horrify a man? Nelly's mind seemed to be enveloped in cobwebs and mists, so that she could make out nothing clearly, though sometimes there pierced through these mists a keen ray of light, like an arrow, which seemed to break them up for a moment and make all plain. Ah! but it came sometimes from one side, sometimes from another, that sudden arrow cleaving the confusion. Sometimes its effect was to make her heart leap; sometimes to make it drop, down, down into the depths. Oh, if she could but see into his heart! But there is no one who can do that—not into the heart of the dearest and most near our own—or be absolutely certain of those motives which bring the smile or the sigh.

There was one strange thing, however, that this strange incident had done—it had set the two upon a level of intimate acquaintance, of sincerity in speaking to each other, which all their previous intercourse had not accomplished. With what veils of flattering illusion that intercourse had been wrapped! It had never been mentioned between them that she expected or that he withheld any proposal, that the time had come for any decision, that there was any question between them greater than the question whether he might come again to-morrow. Now that pretence had blown away for ever. When they sat down upon that bench at the dreary end of the long platform, where once in a half-hour or so a railway porter went past, or a bewildered stray passenger, this was what Fitzroy said—

"The thing that has risen between us now is the brutal question of marriage, and nothing else, Nelly. Oh, you needn't cry out! I use the word 'brutal' in the French sense: all that belongs to the imagination or the fancy, all that's vague, seductive, and attractive is over. It *is* a brutal question——"

"Mr Fitzroy!" cried Nelly, springing to her feet.

"Don't 'Mr' me!" he cried, almost angrily, seizing her hand, drawing her to her seat again. "What good will all this commotion do? We must face the real question; and you know this is what it is. I should never have forced it upon you; but still, here it is, and there is nothing else for it now. Don't you think I see that as well as you do? It is the only thing, and I have made up my mind to it."

The colour that covered Nelly's face was more than a blush—it was a scorching fire. She drew farther from him, raising, with what pride she could, her abashed and shame-stricken head. "If you think that I—will permit any man to speak to me so—that to make up *your* mind is enough——"

Oh, the humiliation even of that protest, the deep destroying shame even of the resentment which was a kind of avowal! For here, at least, he was logically right and she helpless, dependent for so much upon the making up of his mind.

"I can't stop," he said, "after all that's past, Nelly, to pick my words. Here's the fact: I was an ass, I suppose, to go back that night. I was off my head; and you had not given me any reason to suppose you were a prude. I had not expected to find—the British matron up in arms, and an old witch of a duenna to watch over her mistress! What more harm is there in talking to a lady after midnight than before? I can't see it. But we needn't argue. After all this fuss, and the maid, and the vicaress, and so on, there's nothing, I say, but this brutal question of marriage. Can't you sit still, now, and hear me out?"

"You have no right," she said—"you have no right—to speak to me in that tone!"

"What tone? There is nothing particular that I know of in my tone. I haven't time to pick my tones any more than my words. Your train will be going soon, and the deuced affair must be settled somehow. Look here! it is horribly inconvenient for me to get married now. I have no money, and I have a lot of debts to pay. A marriage in St George's, published in the papers and all that, would simply make an end of me. These tradesmen fellows know everything; they would give each other the word: Married a widow with a family and with no money! By Jove! that would finish me."

"Mr Fitzroy!"

"I tell you not to 'Mr' me, Nelly. You know my name, I suppose. We are past all that. The question now is how to manage the one business without bursting up the other. Making a regular smash of my affairs can't do you any good, can it? We'll have to go abroad; and we can't, of course, take those chicks—dragging a nursery about with us all over the world. Keep still! you'll frighten that porter." He had seized and held her arm tightly, restraining her. "For goodness' sake be reasonable, now, Nelly. You don't suppose I mean you any harm? How could I?" he added, with a harsh laugh, "you're much too wide awake for that. Listen to what I say, Nelly."

"I cannot—I cannot endure this," she cried.

"We may neither of us like it," said Fitzroy, with composure, "but you ought to have thought of that a little sooner. There's nothing else for it now that I can see. Speak up if you know any other way. I don't want to ruin you; and you, I suppose, don't want to ruin me. There's no other way."

"There is the way—of parting here, and never seeing each other more!"

He held her fast, with her arm drawn closely through his. "That's the most impracticable of all," he said. "For one thing, I don't want to part and never see you more."

Oh, poor Nelly! poor Nelly! She was outraged in every point of pride and tenderness and feeling, and yet the softness of this tone sank into her heart, and carried, like a flood, all her bulwarks away.

"Well, and then it couldn't be done. You've gone too far, with your vicaress, and all that. I don't want to ruin you; and neither, I suppose, do you want to ruin me. Look here, Nelly: I've got a little money at present—by chance, as it happens. I'll buy a licence—it's all you'll have from me in the shape of wedding-present—and you'll run up to town to-morrow morning, and we'll be married at the registrar's office. Can't help it, Nelly; can't do anything better. It is no fault of mine."

There was silence for a moment. Nelly was not able to speak. Her heart was beating as if it would burst; her whole nature revolting, resisting, in a horror and conflict indescribable. At length she burst forth: "It is a brutal question, indeed, indeed—a brutal question!" she cried, scarcely able with her trembling lips to form the words.

"Well, didn't I say so? But we can't help it; there's nothing else left to do. I am not an infernal cad—altogether; and you're not—altogether—a fool. We may have been that—that last—both of us; but there's no use going over all that again. Nelly, compose yourself—compose yourself!"

"I cannot! I cannot!" she cried, struggling with that burst and flood of misery which is one of the shames and terrors of a woman. It had come to such a point that she could not compose herself, or resist the wild tide of passion that carried her away. Passion! ah, not of love—of shame, of horror, of self-disgust, of humiliation unspeakable. A woman who has had poor Nelly's experiences seldom retains a girl's dream of superlative womanhood, of the crown and the sceptre. But to endure to be spoken to like this—to feel the question to be not one between two lovers, but between a man who was not "an infernal cad" and a woman who was not "a fool"; to submit to all this because there was nothing else for it, to be obliged by her reason to acquiesce in it—was almost more than flesh and blood could bear. She kept in, by the exertion of all her strength, those heartrending sobs and cries within her own bosom as much as was possible. Even in the depth of her misery she was aware that to betray herself, to collect a crowd round, would be worse still, and must be avoided at any price. Finally, poor Nelly found herself, all wounded and bruised with the conflict, exhausted as if she were going to die, alone in the railway carriage in which Fitzroy had placed her, kissing her openly in sight of the guard as he left her, and bidding her remember that he would meet her at eleven o'clock to-morrow. At eleven o'clock to-morrow! It seemed to ring in her ears all the way down, like a bell going on with the same chime. Eleven o'clock! Eleven o'clock to-morrow!— for why? for why?

CHAPTER IX

Thinking, thinking all the long night through did not seem to do poor Nelly any good. She had arrived at home so exhausted in mind and body, so chilled to the heart, that she was good for nothing but to retire to bed. She was scarcely able to see the children—the children, whom perhaps in a day or two— —Oh! should she not secure every moment of them, every look of the innocent faces that were her own, lay up in her heart every innocent word, with that dreadful possibility before her? But the effect was exactly the reverse. The sight of them seemed to fill her with a sick horror. She could not meet their eyes, could not bear their caresses, turned from them with an awful sense that she had betrayed them. And then all the night through in the dark she lay awake thinking, thinking, listening to the clock striking— the vigilant clock, which watched and waited, measuring out the unhasting time, never forgetting, looking on whatever happened. It would strike eleven o'clock to-morrow in the calm little unalarmed house where nobody would suspect that the young mother, the smiling and loving guardian of the children, had come to her hour of doom. For a long time her mind held to this as if it were a sentence which had to be carried out. Eleven o'clock to-morrow, eleven o'clock! a thing which she could not alter, which had to be done. Then by-and-by, which was worse still, there flashed into her soul the thought that it was no sentence, but a thing subject to her own decision, which she might do—or not. Or not! She was free; it was for her to settle, to do it or not to do it. I don't know how to explain how much worse this was. To be held fast by a verdict, sentenced at a certain hour to do something which perhaps you would rather die than do, but which you must do, your dying or not dying being a matter of indifference—is a very terrible thing: yet even in this the *must* gives a certain support. But to be cast back again into a sea of doubt from which you have to get out as best you may, in which you must decide for yourself, choose—this or that, settle what to do, what not to do; the choice being not between pleasure and pain, between good and evil, as it used to be in the old days—but only of two tortures, which was the worst and which the best.

The result of this terrible night was at least to solve the question for eleven o'clock to-morrow: for she was too ill to stand, her limbs aching and her head aching when to-morrow came. It was dreadful to Nelly to have to call nurse, who already half knew so much, and to send her with the necessary telegram. "Too ill to move—postpone for a day or two" was, after long labour with her aching head and perturbed brain, all she could think of to say; and she had scarcely said it when it flashed upon her that the very word "postpone" was a kind of pledge, and committed her to an acceptance of everything he had settled upon, though even this did not hurt like the look which nurse gave her when she saw Fitzroy's name—a look, not of reproach, but of anxious curiosity. Before this time poor Nelly had begun to feel to her very soul the misery of having a confidant. It is a comfort in some cases: it relieves the full heart to speak, it sometimes gives support, the support of being understood in a difficult crisis. But it also gives to the person confided in a right to follow further developments, to know what happens after, to ask—to look. "You did not come as you promised, dear?" Mrs Glynn had said to her; "you did not bring him to see us." The Rector's wife doubted, but did not know certainly, that Fitzroy had not come. "No," Nelly had faltered, "I did not, I—could not." "But to-morrow! promise me, promise me faithfully that you will bring him to-morrow. Dear, let us have the comfort of seeing you two together." Nelly had only nodded her head, she could not trust her voice to speak. This was before the interview at Paddington. And Mrs Glynn had gone away sorrowing. She was very anxious about the poor young woman whose life was thus compromised by what might turn out to be a bad man. She could not comprehend why all was not settled by this time, and the lover ready to satisfy her friends. She took Nelly's hands in both hers, and kissed her, and looked wistfully in her face. Poor Nelly had felt as if she must sink into the ground. She could not meet her friend's eyes. She gave no sign of reply, no answering look: but dropped the kind hands that held hers, and turned back into the house, which was a refuge at least for the time.

But she was not safe even in her house, for nurse also had been her confidant, and had a half right to ask, an undoubted right to look. Her eyes when they flashed upon the name of Fitzroy in Nelly's telegram were terrible. Well-trained woman as she was, she raised those eyes instinctively to Nelly's face with a question in them before which Nelly's, hot with fever yet dim with tears, fell. Oh, if she had said nothing, if she had but kept the whole story to herself! But that had been impossible—he had made it impossible. When she had confided the telegram to nurse she gave instructions that she was not to be disturbed, and lay, with her blinds down, in the darkened room, trembling lest Mrs Glynn should force the *consigne*, and find the way to her bedside in spite of all precautions. It was bad enough to be questioned when she had nothing to reply; what would it be when her heart and mind were so full? Nelly lay there in the dark the whole day with her troubled thoughts. In an hour or two nurse came back, bringing the children from their walk, and told her mistress that they had walked as far as Deanham, a little neighbouring village, and that she had sent the telegram from that office, which she hoped would not matter. It mattered only so far as to send a fiery dart through Mrs Brunton, who divined at once that this was done to save her—that no local telegraph clerk might be able to betray the fact of her communication with Fitzroy. And Mrs Glynn called, and was repulsed, not without difficulty, and left her love, and a promise—which was to Nelly as a threat—of calling early to-morrow. And once more there came the night when all was silent, when there was no one even to look a question, when Nelly was left alone again to battle with her thoughts.

Alone, to battle with her thoughts. With this addition, that if she remained here and faced her trouble, and resolved to tread the stony path, to bear the penalty of her indiscretion, and cling to her children—she would have Mrs Glynn to meet in the morning, to explain to her that Mr Fitzroy had not come and was not coming, that all this stormy episode was over, and to endure her astonishment, her questions, perhaps her reproaches. And nurse, too, to nurse there would be due some explanation—nurse, who had seen everything, who had gone on the river with them, who had known of all his constant visits, before that last visit which had brought to a crisis the whole foolish, foolish story. Oh, how well everything had been before he ever came; how contented she had been with her children, how pleased with her little house, how much approved by everybody! Nelly believed in all good faith that she would have been quite contented and happy had Fitzroy never appeared to disturb her life, alone in her tranquillity with her children: but it may be doubted whether her confidence would have been justified. At all events, now, she shivered when she looked forward upon that life which would lie before her if this was to be the end. Alone, with the children. Oh, how dear the children were! But they were so little, such babies, not companions for a woman in the full tide and height of her life. Mrs Glynn would be kind, she knew, but a little suspicious of her. Nurse would watch her as if she were a giddy girl; she would not dare to open her doors to any one, to offer a curate a cup of tea! I don't say that Nelly was guilty of such thoughts as these in her musing—but they drifted through her desolate, solitary, abandoned soul, abandoned of all comfort and counsel. Whereas, on the other side——

In a great many histories of human experience it is taken for granted—and indeed, perhaps, before the reign of analysis began it was almost always taken for granted—that when man or woman of the nobler kind found that a lover was unworthy, their love died along with their respect. This has simplified matters in many a story. It is such a good way out of it, and saves so much trouble! The last great instance I can remember is that of the noble Romola and Tito her husband, whom, though he gives her endless trouble, she is able to drop out of her stronghold of love as soon as she knows how little worthy of it is the fascinating, delightful, false Greek. My own experience is all the other way. Life, I think, is not so easy as that comes to. Nelly understood a great deal more of Mr Fitzroy now than she might have done in other circumstances had she been married to him for years. She had seen him all round in a flash of awful reality and perception, and hated him — yet loved him all the same. She did not attempt to put these feelings in their order, to set so much on one side and so much on the other. She knew now, as she had never done before, what love could mean in some natures. How it could be base, and yet not all base, and how a man who was only not altogether a cad, to use his own description, apprehended that passion. And yet it did not matter to her, it did not affect the depth of her heart, any more than it would have affected her had he lost his good looks or his beautiful voice. Ah yes! it did matter. It turned her very love, herself, her life, into things so different that they were scarcely recognisable. The elements of hate were in her love, an opposition and distrust ineradicable took possession of her being: and yet she belonged to him, and he to her, almost the more for this contradiction. These are mysteries which I do not attempt to explain.

Yet, notwithstanding all this terrible consciousness, when Nelly awoke next morning (for she was tired out and slept notwithstanding everything) and remembered all that lay before her, and the decision she had to make, the two things which immediately flashed upon her mind — small things of no real importance — were, the look which nurse would fix upon her, trying to read her thoughts, and the inevitable call of Mrs Glynn. They were not Mrs Grundy — oh, how little, how petty, how poor was anything that the frivolous call Mrs Grundy! They were women who were fond of her, who would stand for her and defend her, women who, alas! were her confidants. They had a right to know. Of all that stood in her way and made the crisis dreadful, there was nothing at this moment so dreadful as the glance of suppressed anxiety, the question, that did not venture to put itself into words, of nurse's look, and the more open, more unconcealed gaze of Mrs Glynn. She felt that she would not, could not, bear these, whatever she might have to bear.

I do not pretend to say that this was what finally turned the scale. Was there any doubt from the beginning how it would turn? She came down-stairs very early on that dreadful morning and breakfasted with the children, and dressed them with her own hands for their walk, fastening every little button, putting on each little glove. She kissed them again and again before she gave them over to nurse, who was waiting—and stood at the door looking after them until they had disappeared beyond the garden gate. Then she, who had seemed so full of leisure, all at once became nervous and hurried. She called the housemaid to her, who was busy with her work. "Mary," she said, "I have to run up to town by the half-past ten train. I have not a moment to lose; if Mrs Glynn should come you must tell her that I am gone, and I will slip out by the back door—for if she comes in I know I shall miss my train." "Yes, ma'am," said Mary, making no remark, but thinking all the more. Happily, however, Mrs Glynn did not come, and Mrs Brunton left the house in good time for the train, carrying her dressing-bag. "It is possible I may not get home again to-night," she said. "Give this to nurse, Mary. I forgot to give it to her; and if any one inquires, say I have gone to town for a few days." Mary never knew how she could have made so bold. She cried out: "Oh, ma'am, I hope as you are not going to leave us." "To leave you!" said Nelly. "What nonsense you are speaking! How could I leave you?" But she was not angry; she gave the girl a look which made Mary cry, though she could not have told why.

What was left for nurse was a letter with a cheque enclosed, imploring her to take the greatest care of the children till she could send for them. "I may tell you to satisfy you that I am going to be married," Nelly wrote. "We want to have no fuss. And I could not take the children; but as soon as—as we are settled I shall send for you to bring my little darlings. Oh, take care of them, take care of them!" And that was all; not an address, not an indication where she had gone. Nurse did not say a word to any one as long as her courage held out. When Mrs Glynn, after receiving her message from the housemaid, asked to see the more important servant, nurse made her face like a countenance cut out of wood. She could give no explanation. Mrs Brunton had gone to town for a few days. Perhaps she might be detained a little longer. It was on business she had gone. "But it was very sudden?" cried Mrs Glynn. "Yes, ma'am," said nurse. "And you don't know what day she will be back?" "No, ma'am," replied the faithful servant. There was nothing more to be learned from her.

She kept this up as long, I have said, as her courage held out; and indeed a week strained that courage very much. The servants all grew frightened left in the house alone. They did not know how to contain themselves, or to bear up in the unusual leisure and quiet. I think that nurse held out for ten days. And then she wrote to Mrs Brunton's married sister—for Nelly's mother was an old lady, and not to be disturbed. After this there ensued a whirl of agitation and trouble, in which the cook and the housemaid found much satisfaction. The sister came, and then her husband, and after them a brother and uncle, all in consternation. Nelly's letter to nurse was read over and over, and much of what had passed before was elicited by anxious questioning. "Depend upon it, she has gone off with this man," said the uncle solemnly, and nobody contradicted him, the fact being self-evident. "Fitzroy—of what Fitzroys I wonder?" said the brother, who thought he knew society. Finally, Nelly's brother, who was young and impetuous, started off for the Continent in search of her, and the married sister took the children home.

Poor little children! they were so forlorn, and so ignorant, crying for mamma, such little things. Consoled by a box of chocolate, treated very kindly, oh very kindly! but not kings and queens, nurse said with tears, as in their own home. And the poor mother, poor Nelly—where was she? She was discussed by everybody, all her affairs, whether she were really married, or what dreadful thing had happened to her: how she could go away, for any man, and leave her children. All that she had kept most private to herself was raked up and gone over, and her conduct at Bampton-Leigh, and how all this had begun. Poor Nelly! all the world was in her secret now.

CHAPTER X

The children had been but a week at the house of Mrs Evans, Nelly's sister, when a letter arrived, first sent to Haven Green, then by various stages to their present habitation, to nurse, asking for news of them. It was rather a melancholy letter. "I cannot send for my darlings yet, and it is dreadful to be without any news. Mr Fitzroy and I are moving about so much that I can scarcely give you an address; but write at once, and if we are no longer here, I will leave word where we are going, and your letter can follow me;" and again a cheque was enclosed, signed with the name of Helen Fitzroy. "Say, if anybody inquires, that we may come back any day," she added in a postscript. It was evident that she had overestimated nurse's courage, that she had calculated upon her remaining quietly at home, until further orders: and the assumption made nurse feel exceedingly guilty, as if she had betrayed her mistress. A short time after, information came from the family solicitor that he had received Nelly's orders to sell all the property that Mrs Brunton had in her own power, and forward the money to her at another address, different from that given to nurse. It was not a sum which represented very much in the way of income, yet it was a large sum to be realised without a word of explanation, and roused the worst auguries in everybody's breast. Needless to say that both addresses were telegraphed at once to the impetuous brother who was roving about Europe, looking under every table in every hotel for Nelly. Needless also to add that she was found at last.

But here exact information fails. Her brother Herbert never described how he found her, or went into any unnecessary details. The pair, who were henceforward spoken of in the family as the Fitzroys, were at Monte Carlo when he came up with them; and it was evident enough that "my new brother-in-law," as Herbert called him, awakened no enthusiasm in the young man's breast. He acknowledged that he thought the fellow was in his proper place among the queer society there, though it was not much like Nelly; and there it appeared they meant to remain, on the ground that Nelly had showed some symptoms of delicate health, and it was thought expedient that she should winter in the south of France, which made it impossible for her to have the children with her, as she had intended. "So far as that goes, Nelly was silly," Herbert said; "how could she expect a fellow newly married to have another man's children dragging after him all over the place? And she knew they'd be safe with Susan." Susan Evans took this very quietly; but she knew that Nelly had not intended the children to be with her, but had meant to send for them, or to come back to them, leaving the issue to the decision of after events. Poor Nelly, she looked delicate, Herbert allowed. She was not like herself. He confessed, when he was alone with his sister, and had become confidential, walking about the room in the twilight when the changes of his countenance could not be remarked, that perhaps Nelly had made a mistake, and he was not sure that she had not found it out.

"Do you mean that he is unkind to her?" cried Susan, all aflame.

"I should just like," said Herbert, grimly, "to have seen any man unkind to her while I was there."

"Isn't he fond of her, then? Then why did he marry her? Do you mean that they're unhappy, Herbert? So soon, so soon!"

"Now, look here," said Herbert, "I won't be cross-examined; I say that I think Nelly has made a mistake, and I fear she thinks so too. I can't go into metaphysical questions why people did that, or why they did this. I'm not fond myself of Mr Percy Fitzroy—and we are not done with him yet," Herbert said.

"Done with him? and he Nelly's husband; I should hope not, indeed!" Mrs Evans cried.

"Then I promise you you'll have your wish," her brother replied.

And, indeed, for the next year or two there was a great deal heard of Mr Percy Fitzroy. One thing that developed itself in the further history of poor Nelly was a chronic want of money. She disposed of everything over which she had the least power. Her little house was, of course, sold and everything in it. What was the good of keeping it up? and even the Indian curiosities, the little stock of plate, all the things of which Nelly Brunton had been proud. What did all that matter now? These trifles served to stop the wolf's mouth for a very short time, and then Herbert began to receive letters by every post, which he showed to nobody. He was the head of the family, and he was the only one who was fully acquainted with the affairs of the Fitzroys. He gained a prominent line on his forehead, which might have been called the Fitzroy wrinkle, from this constant traffic and anxiety, and nobody knew but himself how far these claims and applications went.

Meanwhile the poor little children remained in the nursery of Mrs Evans; not poor little children at all—much benefited, at least in Mrs Evans' opinion, by the superior discipline of a large family. Susan was of opinion that whoever suffered by Nelly's second marriage, to little Jack and Maysey all things had worked together for good. How much better it was for them to be brought up with a little wholesome neglect among a great number of nice children, who were very kind to their little cousins, than spoiled to the top of their bent by Nelly, who gave them everything they wanted, and kept up no discipline at all? And, indeed, there could not be a doubt that it was far better for them to be in the wholesome English nursery than dragging about through a series of hotels after their mother and their mother's husband. It was against her judgment that Mrs Evans kept nurse devoted to their special service; but she did so, for, though she thought a great deal of her own system, she was a kind woman, and very sorry for poor Nelly, thus separated from her children, though at the same time very angry and indignant with her for submitting to it. "I should like to see Henry, or any other man, try to keep me from my children!" Susan cried. But then Henry Evans, good man, had no such desire, nor naturally, in his lifetime, had any other man the right.

It need scarcely be said that the subject was discussed in all its aspects at Haven Green, where nobody knew anything, and there was the widest field for conjecture. Mrs Glynn, who never would allow an unkind word to be said of Mrs Brunton, now Mrs Fitzroy, in her hearing, blamed herself very much that she had not watched Nelly more closely and that the Rector had not interfered. "For if my husband had married them, even if it had been by special licence in her own drawing-room—though I disapprove of that sort of proceeding very much—yet not a word could have been said." "I suppose it was done at a registry office," said some ill-natured person. "We have none of us any right to suppose such a thing," Mrs Glynn replied. Well! there were dark whispers in corners that it might have been even worse than that—though, of course, now that the family had taken it up, it was clear that all must be right; but these whispers were not uttered in the presence of the Rector or of Mrs Glynn, who avowed boldly that she had been in Mrs Brunton's confidence all the time. You cannot do much harm, it may be proudly asserted, when you unbosom yourself to your clergyman's wife!

Among all poor Nelly's sympathisers and anxious supporters there was no one more anxious—no one, it may be said, so compunctious—as Julia Bampton. She said that she could never forgive herself, for it was she who had introduced dear Nelly to Percy Fitzroy. She it was, all unwitting of evil, who had thrown them together. Mrs Spencer-Jackson, indeed, had brought him into the county, but it was at Bampton-Leigh that he had been taken up most warmly and made most of. It was because of his voice—such a beautiful baritone voice; and Julia herself—Julia, who spoke with tears in her eyes, had thrown them together, made them sing together, brought it all on. She could never forgive herself for this, though she hoped with all her heart that poor Nelly, though she had been so imprudent, was happier than people said. By this time May had married Bertie Harcourt, and was the brightest of young matrons, with a handsome house and an adoring husband, and nothing but happiness about her. She, too, was very sorry for Nelly, and said she had always thought there was something queer, like a man in a book, about Mr Percy Fitzroy.

And thus it came about that the poor little Brunton children were a great deal at Bampton-Leigh, where there was no discipline at all, and which seemed to them the most delightful place in the world. They called Julia aunt, *en attendant* the arrival of Harcourt children who would have a right to address her by that title, and made up to her in such a surprising way for the absence of May that their visits were the happiest portions of her life. Julia was seated with them in the drawing-room on an evening in October about two years after these events, telling them stories, Maysey's little figure buried in her lap (for the good Julia began to grow stout), and Jack leaning closely against her knee. It was growing dark, but the fire was bright and filled the room with ruddy gleams and fantastic shadows and reflections. She had come to a very touching point in the story, and Maysey had flung her arms round aunt Julia's neck in the thrill of the approaching catastrophe which the children both knew by heart, yet heard over and over again with undiminished delight and horror. They all heard the door open, but paid no attention, supposing it was the tea; and Julia had told the tale all out, and the nervous clasp of the child's arms had loosened, when, looking up, Miss Bampton saw — not in actual reality, but in the great mirror over the mantelpiece — a shadowy figure standing over them, a woman in a travelling cloak, with a great veil like a cloud hanging over her face. Julia gave a shriek that rang through the house, and the veiled figure dropped down upon the hearthrug on its knees, and encircled the whole group with eager arms. "O Nelly, Nelly, Nelly!" Julia cried, thinking at first that it was a ghost.

When the lights came it was visible that both things were true — that it was Nelly, and that she was little more than the ghost of herself. It was some time before the frightened children — who had forgotten her, and who were terrified by her paleness, and her cloak and her veil, and her sudden arrival — would acknowledge their mother. Oh, how different from the Nelly who had arrived there on that summer afternoon, and stopped the singing at the piano, and diverted (as Julia in the profoundest depths of her heart was aware) from May's path an evil fate. She bore all the traces of that evil fate upon her own worn countenance. She was very pale, worn, and thin:

she was not like herself. But when she had rested from her journey, and recovered the confidence of her children, then the old house of her kindred became aware of another Nelly, who was not like the first, yet was a more distinct and remarkable personage than Nelly Brunton. She was dressed in all the elegance of the fashion, and she had an air which the country lady did not understand. Was it natural stateliness and nobility? Or was it only the tragedy of her unknown fate?

Nelly stayed and lingered in the calm of Bampton-Leigh. It seemed as if she never could separate herself from the children. It was with reluctance that she allowed them to be put to bed, or to go out for their play. She could not bear them out of her sight, and she never spoke of Mr Percy Fitzroy except when questions were put to her. When Mrs Spencer-Jackson came to see her, with effusive welcome, she received that lady with extreme coldness, holding her at arm's length. "My husband is quite well," was all she answered to a thousand inquiries. Letters came to her "from abroad" at rare intervals, and she herself wrote very seldom. She never looked as if she wanted to hear anything except about her little boy and girl.

And for anything I have heard she is there still, much wondered at, yet very kindly cherished, good Julia asking no questions, at Bampton-Leigh.

QUEEN ELEANOR AND FAIR ROSAMOND

CHAPTER I
THE FAMILY

Mr and Mrs Lycett-Landon were two middle-aged people in the fulness of life and prosperity. Though they belonged to the world of commerce, they were both well-born and well connected, which was not so common, perhaps, thirty years ago as it is now. He was the son of an Irish baronet; she was the daughter of a Scotch laird. He had never, perhaps, been the dashing young man suggested by his parentage, though he rode better than a business man has any call to ride, and had liked in moderation all his life the pleasures which business men generally can only afford themselves when they have grown very rich. Mr Lycett-Landon was not very rich in the Liverpool sense of the word, and he had never been very poor. He had accepted his destination in the counting-house of a distant relation, who was the first to connect the name of Landon with business, without any heartbreak or abandonment of brighter dreams. It had seemed to him from the beginning a sensible and becoming thing to do. The idea of becoming rich had afforded him a rational satisfaction. He had not envied his brothers their fox-hunting, their adventures in various parts of the world, their campaigning and colonising. Liverpool, indeed, was prosaic but very comfortable. He liked the comfort, the sensation of always having an easy balance at his bankers (bliss, indeed! and like every other kind of bliss, so out of reach to most of us), the everyday enjoyment of luxury and well-being, and was indifferent to the prosaic side of the matter. His marriage was in every sense of the word a good marriage; one which filled both families with satisfaction. She had money enough to help him in his business, and business connections in the West of Scotland (where the finest people have business connections), which helped him still more; and she was a good woman, full of accomplishments and good-humour and intelligence. In those days, perhaps, ladies cultivated accomplishments more than they do now. They did not give themselves up to music or to art with absorbing devotion, becoming semi- or more than semi-professional, but rather with a general sense that to do lovely things was their vocation in the world, pursued the graces tenderly all round, becoming perhaps excellent in some special branch because it was more congenial than the others, but no more. Thus while Mrs Lycett-Landon was far from equal to Mozart and Beethoven, and would have looked on Bach with alarm, and Brahms with consternation, in dance music, which her children demanded incessantly, she had no superior. The young people preferred her to any band. Her time was perfect, her spirit and fire contagious—nothing under five-and-twenty could keep still when she played, and not many above. And she was an admirable mistress of a house, which is the first of all the fine arts for a woman. What she might have been as a poor man's wife, with small means to make the best of, it is unnecessary to inquire, for this was fortunately not her *rôle* in life. With plenty of money and of servants, and a pretty house and everything that was necessary to keep it up, she was the most excellent manager in the world. Perhaps now and then she was a trifle hard upon other women who were not so well off as she, and saw the defects in their management, and believed that in their place she would have done better. But this is a fault that the most angelic might fall into, and which only becomes more natural and urgent the more benevolent the critic is, till sometimes she can scarcely keep her hands from meddling, so anxious is she to set the other right. It was to Mrs Lycett-Landon's credit, as it is to that of many like her, that she never meddled; though while she was silent, her heart burned to think how much better she would have done it. Her husband was somewhat of the same way of thinking in respect to men in business who did not get on. He said, "Now, if So-and-so would only see——" while his wife in her heart would so fain have taken the house out of the limp hands of Mrs So-and-so and set everything right. It is a triumph of civilisation, and at the same time a great trial to benevolent and clear-sighted people, that according to the usages of society the So-and-so's must always be left to muddle along in their own way.

Lycett, Landon, Fareham, & Co. (Mr Lycett-Landon combined the names and succession of two former partners) had houses in Liverpool, Glasgow, and London, and a large business. I think they were cotton-brokers, without having any very clear idea what that means. But this will probably be quite unimportant to the reader. The Lycett-Landons had begun by living in one of the best parts of Liverpool, which in those days had not extended into luxurious suburbs as now, or at least had done so in a very much less degree;

and when the children came, and it was thought expedient to live in the country, they established themselves on the other side of the Mersey, in a great house surrounded by handsome gardens and grounds overlooking the great river, which, slave of commerce as it is and was, was then a very noble sight, as no doubt it continues to be. To look out upon it in the darkening, or after night had fallen, to the line of lights opposite, when the darkness hid everything that was unlovely in the composition of the great town and its fringe of docks, and to watch the great ships lying in midstream with lights at their masts and bows, and the small sprites of attendant steam-boats, each carrying its little lamp, as they rustled to and fro, threading their way among the anchored giants, crossing and recrossing at a dozen different points, was an endless pleasure. I do not speak of the morning, of the sunshine, shining tranquil upon the majestic stream, flashing back from its miles of waters, glowing on the white spars and sails, the marvellous aërial cordage, the great ships resting from their labours, each one of them a picture, because that is a more common sight. But there are, or were, few things so grand, so varied, so full of interest and amusement, as the Mersey at night. There were times, indeed, when it was very cold, and rarer times when it was actually dangerous to cross the ferry; when the world was lost in a white fog, and a collision was possible at every moment. But these exciting occasions were few, and in ordinary cases the Lycett-Landons, great and small, thought the crossing a pleasant adjunct both to the business and pleasure which took them to vulgar Liverpool. Vulgar was the name they were fond of applying to it, with that sense of superiority which is almost inevitable in the circumstances, in people conscious of living out of it, and of making of it a point of view, a feature in the landscape. But yet there was a certain affection mingled with this contempt. They rather liked to talk of the innumerable masts, the miles of docks, and when their visitors fell into enthusiasm with the scene, felt both pleasure and pride as in an excellence which they had themselves some credit from—"A poor thing, sir, but mine own"; and they felt a little scorn of those who did not see how fine the Mersey was with its many ships, although they affected to despise it in their own persons. These were the affectations of the young. Mr Lycett-Landon himself had a solid satisfaction in Liverpool. He put all objections down at once with statistics and an intimation that people who did not respect the second seaport in the kingdom were themselves but little worthy of respect. His wife, however, was like the young people, and patronised the town.

At the time when the following incidents began to happen the family consisted of six children. These happy people had not been without their griefs, and there was more than one gap in the family. Horace was not the eldest, nor was little Julian the youngest of the children. But these times of grief had passed over, as they do, though no one can believe it, and scarcely disturbed the general history of happiness looking back upon it, though they added many experiences, made sad thoughts familiar, and gave to the mother at least a sanctuary of sorrow to which she retired often in the bustle of life, and was more strengthened than saddened, though she herself scarcely knew this. Horace was twenty, and his sister Millicent eighteen, the others descending by degrees to the age of six. There was a great deal of education going on in the family, into which Mrs Lycett-Landon threw herself with fervour, only regretting that she had not time to get up classics with the boys, and with great enthusiasm throwing herself into the music, the reading, all the forms of culture with which she had already a certain acquaintance. These pursuits filled up the days which had already seemed very fully occupied, and there were moments when papa, coming home after his business, declared that he felt himself quite "out of it," and lingered in the dining-room after dinner and dozed instead of coming up-stairs. But there is nothing more common than that a man of fifty, a comfortable merchant, after a very comfortable dinner, should take a little nap over his wine, and nobody thought anything of it. Horace was destined for business, to take up the inheritance of his father, which was far too considerable to be let fall into other hands; and though the young man had his dreams like most young men, and now and then had gratified himself with the notion that he was making a sacrifice, for the sake of his family, of his highest aspirations, yet in reality he was by no means dissatisfied with his destination, and contemplated the likelihood of becoming a very rich man, and raising the firm into the highest regions of commercial enterprise, with pleasure and a sense of power which is always agreeable. Naturally, he thought that his father and old Fareham were a great deal too cautious, and did not make half enough of their opportunities; and, that when "new blood," meaning himself, came in, the greatness and the rank of merchant princes, to which they had never attained, would await the house. He had been a little shy at first to talk of this, feeling that ambition of a commercial kind was not heroic, and that his mother and Milly would be apt to gibe. But what ambition of an aspiring youth was ever gibed at by mother and sister? They found it a great and noble ambition when they discovered it.

Milly's cheeks glowed and her eyes shone with the thought. She talked of old Venice, whose merchants were indeed princes, generals, and statesmen, all in one. There are a great many fine things ready existing to be said on this subject, and she made the fullest use of them. The father was rich and prosperous, and able to indulge in any luxury; but Horace should be great. A great merchant is as great as any other winner of heroic successes. Thus the young man was encouraged in his aspirations. Mr Lycett-Landon did not quite take the same view. "He'll do very well if he keeps up to what has been done before him," he said. "Don't put nonsense into his head. Yes; all that flummery about merchant princes and so forth is nonsense. If he goes to London with that idea in his head, there's no telling what mischief he may do."

"My dear," said Mrs Lycett-Landon, "it must always be well to have a high aim."

"A high fiddlestick!" said the father; "if he does as well as I have done, he'll do very well." And this sentiment was perhaps natural, too; for though there are indeed parents who rejoice in seeing their sons surpass them, there are many on the other side who, feeling their own work extremely meritorious, entertain natural sentiments of derision for the brags of the inexperienced boy who is going to do so much better. "Wait till he is as old as I am," Mr Lycett-Landon said.

"So long as he is not swept away into society," said the mother. "Of course, when he is known to be in town, he will be taken a great deal of notice of, and asked out— —"

"Oh, to Windsor Castle, I daresay," said papa, and laughed. He was in one of his offensive moods, Milly said. It was very seldom he was offensive, but there are moments when a man must be so, against the united forces of youth and maternal sympathy with youth, in self-defence. Unless he means to let them have it all their own way he must be disagreeable from time to time. Mr Lycett-Landon asserted himself very seldom, but still he had to do it now and then; and though there was nothing in the world (except Milly) that he was more proud of than Horace, called him a young puppy, and wanted to know what anybody saw in him that he was to do so much better than his father. But the ladies, though they resented it for the moment, knew that there was not very much in this.

It was to the London house that Horace was destined. He was to spend a year in it "looking about him," picking up an acquaintance with the London variety of mercantile life, learning all the minutiæ of business, and so forth. At present it was under the charge of a distant relative of Mr Fareham's, who, as soon as Horace should be able to go alone in the paths of duty, was destined to a very important post in the American house, which at present was small, but which Fareham's cousin was to make a great deal of. In the meantime, Mr Lycett-Landon himself paid frequent visits to town to see that all was going well, and would sometimes stay there for a fortnight, or even three weeks, much jested at by his wife and daughter when he returned.

"Papa finds he can do a great deal of business at the club," said Milly; "he meets so many people, you know. The London cotton-brokers go to all the theatres, and to the Row in the morning. It is so much nicer than at Liverpool."

"You monkey!" her father said with a laugh. He took it very good-humouredly for a long time. But a joke that is carried on too long gets disagreeable at the last, and after a while he became impatient. "There, that's enough of it," he would say, which at first was a little surprising, for Milly used, so far as papa was concerned, to have everything her own way.

CHAPTER II
THE LONDON OFFICE

"Again—so soon!"

This is what Mrs Lycett-Landon and Milly said in chorus as the head of the house, with something which might have been a little embarrassment, announced a third visit to London in the course of four months. There was an absence of his usual assured tone—a sort of apologetic accent, which neither of them identified, but which both were vaguely conscious of, as expressing something new.

"Robert," said his wife, "you are anxious about young Fareham; I feel sure of it. Things are not going as you like."

"Well, my dear, I didn't want to say anything about it, and you must not breathe a syllable of this to Fareham, who would be much distressed; but I am a little anxious about the young fellow. Discipline is very slack at the office. He goes and comes when he likes, not like a man of business. In short, I want to keep an eye upon him."

"Oh, papa," cried Milly, "what a dear you are! and I that have been making fun of you about the club and the Row!"

"Never mind, my dear," said her father, magnanimously; "your fun doesn't hurt. But now that you have surprised my little secret, you must take care of it. Not a word, not a hint, not so much as a look, to any of the Farehams. I would not have it known for the world. But, of course, we must not expose Horace to the risk of acquiring unbusiness-like habits."

"Oh, and most likely fast ways," cried Mrs Lycett-Landon, "for they seldom stop at unbusiness-like habits." She had grown a little pale with fright. "Oh, not for the world, Robert—our boy, who has never given us a moment's anxiety. I would rather go to London myself, or to the end of the world."

"Fortunately, that's not necessary," he said with a smile, "and you must not jump at the worst, as women are so fond of doing. I have no reason to suppose he is fast, only a little disorderly, and not exact as a business man should be—wants watching a little. For goodness sake, not a word to Fareham of all this. I would not for any consideration have him know."

"Don't you think perhaps he might have a good influence? he has been so kind to his nephew."

"That is just the very thing," said Mr Lycett-Landon. "He has been very kind (young Fareham is not his nephew, by the way, only a distant cousin), and, naturally, he would take a tone of authority, or preach, or take the after-all-I've-done-for-you tone, which would never do. No, a little watching—just the sense that there is an eye on him. He has a great many good qualities," said the head of the house with a little pomp of manner; "and I think—I really think—with a little care, that we'll pull him through."

"Papa, you are an old dear," said Milly with enthusiasm. Perhaps he did not like the familiarity of the address, or the rush she made at him to give him a kiss. At least, he put her aside somewhat hastily.

"There, there," he said, "that will do. I have got a great many things to look after. Have my things packed, my dear, and send them over to Lime Street Station to meet me. You can put in some light clothes, in case the weather should change. One never knows what turn it may take at this time of the year."

It was April, and the weather had been gloomy; it was quite likely it might change, as he said, though it was not so easy to tell what he could want with his grey suit in town. This, however, the ladies thought nothing of at the moment, being full of young Fareham and his sudden declension from the paths of duty. "And he was always so steady and so well behaved," cried Mrs Lycett-Landon. She saw after her husband's packing, which was a habit she had retained from the old days, when they were not nearly so rich. "He was always a model young man; that was why I was so pleased to think of him as a companion for Horace."

"These model young men are just the ones that go wrong," said Milly, with that air of wisdom which is so diverting to older intelligences. Her mother laughed.

"Of course your experience is great," she said; "but I don't think that I am of that opinion. If a boy is steady till he is five-and-twenty, he is not very likely to break out after. Perhaps your father's prejudice in favour of business habits——"

"Mamma! It was you who said a young man seldom stopped there."

"Was it? Well, perhaps it was," said Mrs Lycett-Landon, with a little confusion. "I spoke without thought. One should not be too hard on young men. They can't all be made in the same mould. Your father was always so exact, never missing the boat once—and he cannot bear people who miss the boat; so, I hope, perhaps it is not so bad as he thinks."

"It would never do," said Milly, still with that air of solemnity, "to have Horace thrown in the way of any one who is not quite good and right."

At this her mother laughed, and said, "I am afraid he must be put out of the world then, Milly. I hope he has principles of his own."

Notwithstanding this sudden levity, Mrs Lycett-Landon fully agreed—later in the day, when the portmanteau had gone to the Lime Street Station, and she and her daughter had followed it and seen papa off by the train—that it was very important Horace should make his beginning in business under a prudent and careful guide; and that if there was any irregularity in young Fareham, it was very good of papa to take so much pains to put it right. Horace, who went home with them, was but partially let into the secret, lest, perhaps, he might be less careful than they were, and let some hint drop in the office as to the object of his father's journey. The ladies questioned him covertly, as ladies have a way of doing. What did the office think of young Mr Fareham in London? Was he liked? Was he thought to be a good man of business? What did Mr Pearce say, who was the head clerk and a great authority?

"I say," said Horace, "why do you ask so many questions about Dick Fareham? Does he want to marry Milly? Well, it looks like it, for you never took such notice of him before."

"To marry me!" said Milly, in a blaze of indignation. "I hope he is not quite so idiotic as that."

"He is not idiotic at all; he is a very nice fellow. You will be very well off if you get any one half as good."

"I think," said the mother, "that papa and I will make all the necessary investigations when it comes to marrying Milly. Now make haste, children, or we shall miss the first boat."

It was an April evening, still light and bright, though the air was shrewish, and the wind had some east in it, blighting the gardens and keeping the earth grey, but doing much less harm to the water, which was all ruffled into edges of white. The ten minutes' crossing was not enough to make these white crests anything but pleasant, and the big ships lay serenely in midstream, owning the force of the spring breeze by a universal strain at their anchors, but otherwise with a fine indifference to all its petty efforts. The little ferry steam-boat coasted along their big sides with much rustle and commotion, churning up the innocent waves. It was quite a considerable little party of friends and neighbours who crossed habitually in this particular boat, for the Lycett-Landons lived a little way up the river—not in bustling Birkenhead. They were all so used to this going and coming, and to constant meetings during this little voyage, that it was like a perpetually recurring water-party—a moment of holiday after the work of the day. The ladies had been shopping, the men had all escaped from their offices; they had the very last piece of news, and carried with them the evening papers, the new 'Punch'—everything that was new. If there was any little cloud upon the family after their parting with papa, it blew completely away in the fresh wind; but there was not, in reality, any cloud upon them, nor any cause for anxiety or trouble. Even the mother had no thought of anything of the kind, no anticipation that was not pleasant. Life had gone so well with her that, except when one of the children was ailing, she had no fear.

Mr Lycett-Landon on this occasion was a long time in London. He did not return till nearly the end of May, and he came back in a very fretful, uncomfortable state of mind. He told his wife that he was more uneasy than ever; he did not blame young Fareham; he did not know whether it was he that was to be blamed; but things were going wrong somehow. "Perhaps it is only that he doesn't know how to keep up discipline," he said, "and that the real fault is with the clerks. I begin to doubt if it's safe to leave a lot of young fellows together. It will be far safer to keep Horace here under my own eye, and with old Fareham, who is exactitude itself. He will do a great deal better. I don't think I shall send him to London."

"Of course, Robert, I should prefer to keep him at home," she said, "but I am afraid, after all that has been said it will disappoint the boy."

"Oh, disappoint the boy! What does it matter about disappointing them at that age? They have plenty of time to work it out. It is at my time of life that disappointment tells."

"That is true, no doubt," said the mother; "but we are used to disappointment, and they are not."

He turned upon her almost savagely. "You! What disappointments have you ever had?" he cried, with such an air of contemptuous impatience as filled her with dismay.

"Oh, Robert!" She looked at him with eyes that filled with tears, "Disappointment is too easy a word," she said.

"You mean the—the children. What a way you women have of raking up the departed at every turn. I don't believe, in my view of the word, you ever had a disappointment in your life. You never desired anything very much and had it snatched from you just when you thought— —" He stopped suddenly. "How odd," he said, with a strange laugh, "that I should be discussing these sort of things with you!"

"What sort of things? I can't tell you how much you astonish me, Robert. Did you ever desire anything so very much and I not know?"

Then he turned away with a shrug of his shoulders. "You are so matter of fact. You take everything *au pied de la lettre*," he said.

This conversation remained in Mrs Lycett-Landon's mind in spite of her efforts to represent to herself that it was only a way of speaking he had fallen into, and could mean nothing. How could it mean anything except business, or the good of the children, or some other perfectly legitimate desire? But yet, in none of these ways had he any disappointment to endure. The children were all well and vigorous, and, thank God, doing as well as heart could desire. Horace was as good a boy as ever was; and business was doing well. There was no failure, so far as she was aware, in any of her husband's hopes. It must be an exaggerated way of speaking. He must have allowed the disorder in the London office to get on his nerves; and he had the pallid, restless look of a man in suspense. He could not keep quiet. He was impatient for his letters, and dissatisfied when he had got them. He was irritable with the children, and even with herself, stopping her when she tried to consult him about anything. "What is it?" or "About those brats again?" he said, peevishly. This was when she wanted his opinion about a governess for little Fanny and Julian.

"What between Milly's balls and Fanny's governess you drive me distracted. Can't you settle these trifles yourself when you see how much occupied I am with more important things?"

"I never knew before that you thought anything more important than the children's welfare," she said.

"If there was any real question of the children's welfare," he answered, with more than equal sharpness.

It came almost to a quarrel between them. Mrs Lycett-Landon could not keep her indignation to herself. "Because the London office is not in good order!" she could not help saying to Milly.

"Oh! mamma, dear, something more than that must be bothering him," the girl said, and cried.

"I fear that we shall have to leave our nice home and settle in London. It is like a monomania. I believe your father thinks of nothing else night and day."

Mrs Lycett-Landon said this as if it were something very terrible; but, perhaps, it was scarcely to be expected that Milly would take it in the same way. "Settle in London!" she said; and a gleam of light came into her eyes. The father came into the room at the end of this consultation and heard these words.

"Who talks of settling in London?" he said.

"My dear Robert, it seems to me it must come to that; for if you are so uneasy about the office, and always thinking of it— —"

"I suppose," he said, "it is part of your nature to take everything in that matter-of-fact way. I am annoyed about the London office; but rather than move you out of this house I would see the London office go to the dogs any day. I don't mind," he added, with a little vehemence, "the coming and going; but to break up this house, to transplant you to London, there is nothing in the world I would not sooner do."

She was a little surprised by his earnestness. "I am very glad you feel as I do on that point. We have all been so happy here. But I, for my part, would give up anything to make you more satisfied, my dear."

"That is the last thing in the world to make me satisfied. Whatever happens, I don't want to sacrifice you," he said, in a subdued tone.

"It would not be a sacrifice at all; what fun it would be: and then Horry need never leave us," cried Milly. "For my part, I should like it very much, papa."

"Don't let us hear another word of such nonsense," he said, angrily; and his face was so dark and his tone so sharp that Miss Milly did not find another word to say.

CHAPTER III
ALARMS

It was rather a relief to them all when the father went away again. They did not say so indeed in so many words, still keeping up the amiable domestic fiction that the house was not at all like itself when papa was away. But as a matter of fact there could be little doubt that the atmosphere was clear after he was gone. A certain sulphurous sense of something volcanic in the air, the alarm of a possible explosion, or at least of the heat and mutterings that precede storms, departed with him. He himself looked brighter when he went away. He was even gay as he waved his hand to them from the railway carriage, for they had gone very dutifully to see him off, as was the family custom. "Papa is quite delighted to get off to his beloved London," Milly said. "He feels that things go well when he is there," her mother replied, feeling a certain need to be explanatory. The household life was all the freer when he was gone. The young people had a great many engagements, and Mrs Lycett-Landon was very pleasantly occupied with these and with her younger children, and with all the manifold affairs of a large and full house. As happens so often, though the fundamental laws were not infringed, there was yet a little enlarging, a little loosening of bonds when the head of the house was not there. Mamma never objected to be "put out" for any summer pleasure that might arise. She did not mind changing the dinner-hour, or even dispensing with dinner altogether, to suit a country expedition, a garden-party, or a picnic, which was a thing impossible when papa's comfort was the first thing to be thought of. It was June, and life was full of such pleasures to the young people. Horace, indeed, would go dutifully to the office every morning, endeavouring to emulate the virtue of his father, and never miss the nine o'clock boat; though as this high effort cost him in most cases his breakfast, his mother was much perplexed on the subject, and not at all sure that such goodness did not cost more than it was worth. But he very often managed to be back for lunch, and the amusements for the afternoon were endless. Mr Lycett-Landon wrote very cheerfully when he got back to London: he told his wife that he thought he saw his way to establishing matters on a much better footing, and that, after all, Dick Fareham was not at all a bad fellow; but he would not send

Horace there for some time, till everything was in perfect order, and in the meantime felt that his own eye and supervision were indispensable. "I shall hope by next year to get everything into working order," he said. The family were quite satisfied by these explanations. There was nothing impassioned in their affection for their father, and Mrs Lycett-Landon was happy with her children, and quite satisfied that her husband should do what he thought best. So long as he was well, and pleasing himself, she was not at all exacting. Marriage is a tie which is curiously elastic when youth is over and the reign of the sober everyday has come in. There is no such union, and yet there is no union that sits so lightly. People who are each other's only confidants, and cannot live without each other, yet feel a half-relief and sense of emancipation when accidentally and temporarily they are free of each other. A woman says to her daughter, "We will do so-and-so and so-and-so when your father is away," meaning no abatement of loyalty or love, but yet an unconscious, unaccustomed, not unenjoyable freedom. And the man no doubt feels it perhaps more warmly on his side. So it was not felt that there was anything to be uncomfortable about, or even to regret. The letters were not so frequent as the wife could have wished. She sent a detailed history of the family, and of everything that was going on, every second day; but her husband's replies were short, and there were much longer intervals between. Sometimes a week would elapse without any news; but so much was going on at home, and all minds were so fully occupied, that no particular notice was taken. Mrs Lycett-Landon asked, "How is it that you are so lazy about writing?" and there was an end of it. So long as he was perfectly well, as he said he was, what other danger could there be to fear?

There are times when the smallest matter awakens family anxiety, and there are other times when people are unaccountably, inconceivably easy in their minds, and will not take alarm whatever indications of peril may arise. When real calamity is impending how often is this the case! Ears that are usually on the alert are deafened; eyes that look out the most eagerly, lose their power of vision. Little Julian had a whitlow on his finger, and his mother was quite unhappy about it; but as for her husband, she was at rest and feared nothing. When he wrote, after a long silence, that he felt one of his colds coming on and was going to nurse himself, then indeed she felt a momentary uneasiness. But his colds were never of a dangerous kind; they were colds that yielded at once to treatment. She wrote immediately, and bade him be sure and stay indoors for a day or two, and sent him Dr Moller's prescription, which always did him good. "If you want me, of course you know I will come directly," she wrote. To this letter he replied much more quickly than usual, begging her on no account to disturb herself, as he was getting rapidly well again. But after this there was a longer pause in the correspondence than had ever happened before.

On one of these evenings she met her husband's partner, old Fareham, as he was always called, at dinner, at a large sumptuous Liverpool party. There was to be a great ball that evening, and Mrs Lycett-Landon and her two eldest children had come "across" for the two entertainments, and were to stay all night. The luxury of the food and the splendour of the accompaniments I may leave to the imagination. It was such a dinner as is rarely to be seen out of commercial circles. The table groaned, not under good cheer, as used to be the case, but under silver of the highest workmanship, and the most costly flowers. The flowers alone cost as much as would have fed a street full of poor people, for they were not, I need scarcely say, common ones, things that any poor curate or even clerk might have on his table, but waxy and wealthy exotics, combinations of the chemist's skill with the gardener's, all the more difficult to be had in such profusion because the season was summer and the gardens full of Nature's easy production. Mr Fareham nodded to his partner's wife, catching her eye with difficulty between the piles of flowers. "Heard from London lately?" he said across the table, and nodded again several times when she answered, "Not for some days." Old Fareham was usually a jocose old gentleman, less perfect in his manners than the other member of the firm, and of much lower origin, though perhaps more congenial to the atmosphere in which he lived; but he was not at all jocose that evening. He had a cloud upon his face. When his genial host tried to rouse him to his usual "form" (fcr what can be more disappointing than an amusing man who will not do anything to amuse?) he would brighten up for a moment, and then relapse into dulness. As soon as he came into the drawing-room after dinner he made his way to his partner's wife.

"So you haven't been hearing regularly from London?" he said, taking up his post in front of her, and bending over her low chair.

"I didn't say that; I said not for a few days."

"Neither have we," said old Fareham, shaking his white head. "Not at all regular. D'ye think he is quite well? He has been a deal in town this year."

She could scarcely restrain a little indignation, thinking if old Fareham only knew the reason, and how it was to save his relative and set him right! But she answered in an easy tone, "Yes, he has thought it expedient—for various reasons." If he had the least idea of his nephew's irregularities, this, she thought, would make him wince.

But it did not. "Oh, for various reasons?" he said, lifting his shaggy eyebrows. "And did you think it expedient too?"

"You know I enter very little into business matters," she replied, with the calm she felt. "Of course we all miss him very much when he is away from home; but I never have put myself in Robert's way."

"You've been a very good wife to him," said the old man with a slight shake of the head, "an excellent wife; and you don't feel the least uneasy? Quite comfortable about his health, and all that sort of thing? I think I'd look him up if I were you."

"Have you heard anything about his health? Is Robert ill, Mr Fareham, and you are trying to break it to me?" she said, springing to her feet.

"No, no, nothing of the sort," he said, putting his hand on her arm to make her reseat herself. "Nothing of the sort; not a word! I know no more than you do—probably not half or quarter so much. No, no, my dear lady, not a word."

"Then why should you frighten me so?" she said, sitting down again with a flutter at her heart, but a faint smile; "you gave me a great fright. I thought you must have heard something that had been concealed from me."

"Not at all, not at all," said the old man. "I'm very glad you're not uneasy. Still it is a bad practice when they get to stay so long from home. I'd look him up if I were you."

"Do you know anything I don't know?" she said, with a recurrence of her first fear.

"No, no!" he cried—"nothing, nothing, I know nothing; but I don't think Landon should be so long absent. That's all; I'd look him up if I were you."

Mrs Lycett-Landon did not enjoy the ball that night. For some time indeed she hesitated about going. But Milly and Horace were much startled by this idea, and assailed her with questions—What had she heard? Was papa ill? Had anything happened? She was obliged to confess that nothing had happened, that she had heard nothing, but that old Fareham thought papa should not be so long away, and had asked if she were not uneasy about his health. What if he should be ill and concealing it from them? The children paled a little, then burst forth almost with laughter. Papa conceal it from them! he who always wanted so much taking care of when he was poorly. And why should he conceal it? This was quite unanswerable; for to be sure there was no reason in the world why he should not let his wife know, who would have gone to him at once, without an hour's delay. So they went to the ball, and spent the night in Liverpool, and next morning remembered nothing save that old Fareham was always disagreeable. "If he knew your father's real object in spending so much time in London!" Mrs Lycett-Landon said. It was her husband's generous wish to keep this anxiety from the old man; and how little such generous motives are appreciated in this world. It was evening before they returned home—for of course with so large a family there is always shopping to do, and the ladies waited till Horace left the office. But when they reached the Elms, as their house was called, there was a letter waiting which was not comfortable. It was directed in a hand which they could scarcely identify as papa's; not from his club as usual, nor on the office paper—with no date but London. And this was what it said:—

> "My dear,—You must not be disappointed if I write only
> a few words. I have hurt my hand, which makes writing
> uncomfortable. It is not of the least importance, and you
> need not be uneasy: but accept the explanation if it should
> happen to be some days before you hear from me again.
> Love to the children.—Yours affectionately,
>
> R. L. L."

Mrs Lycett-Landon grew pale as she read this note. "I see it all," she said; "there has been an accident, and Mr Fareham did not like to tell me of it. Horace, where is the book of the trains? I must go at once. Run, Milly, and put up a few things for me in my travelling-bag."

"What is it, mother? Hurt his hand? Oh, but that is not much," Horace said.

"It is not much perhaps; but to be so careful lest I should be anxious is not papa's way. 'If it should happen to be some days— —' Why, it is ten days since he wrote last. I am very anxious. Horry, my dear, don't talk to me, but go and see about the trains at once."

"I know very well about the trains," said Horace. "There is one at ten, but then it arrives in the middle of the night. Stop at all events till to-morrow morning. I will telegraph."

"I am going by that ten train," his mother said.

"Which arrives between three and four in the morning!"

"Never mind, I can go to the Euston, where papa always goes. Perhaps I shall find him there. He has never said where he was living."

"You may be sure," said Horace, "you will not find him at the Euston. No doubt he is in the old place in Jermyn Street. He only goes to the Euston when he is up for a day or two."

"I shall find him easily enough," Mrs Lycett-Landon said.

And then a little bustle and commotion ensued. Dinner was had which nobody could eat, though they all said it was probably nothing, and that papa would laugh when he knew the disturbance his letter had made. At least the children said this, their mother making little reply. Milly thought he would be much surprised to see mamma arrive in the early morning. He would like it, Milly thought. Papa was always disposed to find his own ailments very important, and thought it natural to make a fuss about them. She wanted to accompany her mother, but consented, not without a sense of dignity, that it was more necessary she should stay at home to look after the children and the house. But Horace insisted that he must go; and though Mrs Lycett-Landon had a strange disinclination to this which she herself could not understand, it seemed on the whole so right and natural that she could not stand out against it. "There is no occasion," she said. "I can look after myself quite well, and your father too." But Horace refused to hear reason, and Milly inquired what was the good of having a grown-up son if you did not make any use of him? Their minds were so free, that they both tittered a little at this, the title of grown-up son being unfamiliar and half absurd, in Milly's intention at least. She walked down with them to the boat in the soft summer night. The world was all aglow with softened lights—the moon in the sky, the lamps on the opposite bank, reflecting themselves in long lines in the still water, and every dim vessel in the roadway throwing up its little sea-star of colour. "I shouldn't wonder," said Milly, "if it is a touch of the gout, like that he had last year, and no accident at all."

"So much the more need for good nursing," her mother said, as she stepped into the boat.

Milly walked back again with Charley, her next brother, who was fifteen. They went up to the summer-house among the trees and watched the boat as it went rustling, bustling through the groups of shipping in the river, and made little bets between themselves as to whether it would beat the Birkenhead boat, or if the Seacombe would get there first of all. There were not so many ferry-boats as usual at this hour of the night, but one or two were returning both up and down the river which had been out with pleasure-parties, with music sounding softly on the water. "It is only that horrid old fiddle if we were near it," said Milly, "but it sounds quite melodious here,"—for the soft night and the summer air, and the influence of the great water, made everything mellow. The doors and windows of the happy house were still all open. It was full of sleeping children and comfortable servants, and life and peace, though the master and the mistress were both away.

CHAPTER IV
GOING TO LOOK HIM UP

They reached London in the dawn of the morning, when the blue day was coming in over the housetops, before the ordinary stir of the waking world had begun. Of course, at that early hour it was impossible to do anything save to take refuge in the big hotel, and try to rest a little till it should be time for further proceedings. They found at once from the sleepy waiter who received them that Mr Lycett-Landon was not there. He remembered the gentleman; but they hadn't seen him not since last summer, the man said.

"I told you so, mamma," said Horace; "he is in Jermyn Street, of course. If he had been anywhere else, he would have put the address."

They drove together to Jermyn Street as soon as it was practicable, but he was not there; and the landlord of the house returned the same answer that the waiter at the Euston had done. Not since last summer, he said. He had been wondering in his own mind what had become of Mr Lycett-Landon, and asking himself if the rooms or the cooking had not given satisfaction. It was a thing that had never happened to him with any of his gentlemen, but he had been wondering, he allowed, if there was anything. He would have been pleased to make any alteration had he but known. Mrs Lycett-Landon and her son looked at each other somewhat blankly as they turned away from this door. She smiled and said, "It is rather funny that we should have to hunt your father in this way. One would think his movements would be well enough known. But I suppose it's this horrid London." She was a little angry and hurt at the horrid London which takes no particular note even of a merchant of high standing. In Liverpool he could not have been lost sight of, and even here it was ridiculous, a thing scarcely to be put up with.

"Oh, we'll soon find him at the club," Horace said; and they drove there accordingly, more indignant than anxious. It was still early, and the club servants had scarcely taken the trouble to wake up as yet. Club porters are not fond of giving addresses, knowing how uncertain it is whether a gentleman may wish to be pursued to their last stronghold. The porter in the present instance hesitated much. He said Mr Lycett-Landon had not been there for some time; that there was a heap of letters for him, which he took out of a pigeon-hole and turned over in his hands as he spoke, and among which Horace (with a jump of his heart) thought he could see some of his mother's; but nothing had been said about forwarding them, and he really couldn't take upon himself to say that he knowed the address.

"But I'm his son," said Horace.

The porter looked at him very knowingly. "That don't make me none the wiser, sir," he said with great reason.

The youth went out to his mother somewhat aghast. "They don't know anything of him here," he said; "they say he hasn't been for long. There's quite a pile of letters for him."

"Then we must go to the office," Mrs Lycett-Landon said. "He must have been very busy, or—or something."

That was an assertion which no one could dispute. When the cab drove off again she repeated the former speech with an angry laugh. "It is ridiculous, Horace, that you and I should have to run about like this from pillar to post, as if papa could slip out of sight like a—like a—mere clerk." The mercantile world does not make much account of clerks, and she did not feel that she could find anything stronger to say.

"Nobody would believe it," said Horace, "if we were to tell them; but in the City it will be different," he added, gravely.

In Liverpool it must be allowed the City was not thought very much of. It had not the same prestige as the great mercantile town of the north. The merchant princes were considered to belong to the seaports, and the magnates of the City had an odour of city feasts and vulgarity about them; but in the present circumstances it had other attractions.

"The name of Lycett-Landon can't be unknown there," said the lad.

His mother was wounded even by this assertion. She drew herself up. "A Lycett-Landon has no right to be unknown anywhere," she said. "We don't need to take our importance from any firm, I hope. But London is insufferable; nobody is anybody that comes from what they are pleased to call the country 'here.'"

There was an indignant tone in Mrs Lycett-Landon's voice. But yet she too felt, though she would not acknowledge it, that for once the City would be the most congenial. They drove along through the crowded, noisy streets in a hansom, feeling, after all, a little more at home among people who were evidently going to business as the men did in their own town. The sight of a well-brushed, well-washed, gold-chained commercial magnate in a white waistcoat with a rose in his button-hole did them good. And thus they arrived at "the office," that one home-like spot amid all the desert of unaccustomed streets.

"Perhaps," the mother said, "we shall find him here, ready to laugh at us for this ridiculous expedition."

"Well, I hope not," said Horace, "for he will be angry. Papa doesn't like to be looked after."

This speech chilled Mrs Lycett-Landon a little, for it was quite true; and for her part she was not a woman who liked to be found fault with on account of silly curiosity. As a matter of fact, few women do. So that it was with a little check to their eagerness that they got out at the office door among all the press of people coming to their daily labour. Horace, though he had been intended to work there, scarcely knew the place; and his mother, though she had driven down three or four times to pick up her husband on the occasions when they were in town together, was but little better acquainted with it. And the clerks did not at all recognise these very unlikely visitors. Ladies appeared very seldom at the office, and at this early hour never.

"Your father, of course, would not be here so early," Mrs Lycett-Landon said as they went up-stairs; "and I don't suppose young Mr Fareham either is the sort of person—but we must ask for Mr Fareham."

Remembering all that her husband had said, she did not in the least expect to find that young representative of the house. How curious it was to wait until she had been inspected by the clerk, to be asked who she was, to be requested to take a seat, till it was known if Mr Fareham was disengaged! An impulse which she could scarcely explain restrained her from giving her name, which would at once have gained her all the respect she could have desired; and for the first time in her life Mrs Lycett-Landon realised what it must be to come as a poor petitioner to such a place. The clerks made their observations on her and her son behind their glass screen. They decided that she must want a place in the office for the young fellow, but that Fareham would soon give her her answer. These young men did not think much of the personal appearance of Horace, who was clearly from the country—a lanky youth whom it would be difficult to make anything of. Their consternation was extreme when young Mr Fareham, coming out somewhat superciliously to see who wanted him, exclaimed suddenly, "Mrs Landon!" and went forward holding out his hands. "If I had known it was you!" he said. "I hope I have not kept you waiting. But some mistake must have been made, for I was not told your name."

"It was no mistake," she said, looking graciously at the young clerk, who stood by very nervous and abashed. "I did not give my name. We shall not detain you a moment, we only want an address."

While she spoke she had time to remark the perfectly correct and orthodox appearance of young Fareham, of whom it was almost impossible to believe that he had ever committed an irregularity of any description in the course of his life. He led the way into his room with all the respect which was due to the wife of the chief partner, and gave her a chair. "My time is entirely at your service," he said; "too glad to be able to be of any use."

Mrs Lycett-Landon sat down, and then there ensued a moment of such embarrassment as perhaps in all her life she had never known before. There was a certain surprise in the air with which he regarded her, and not the slightest appearance of any idea what she could possibly want him for at this time in the morning. And somehow this surprised unconsciousness on his part brought the most curious painful consciousness to her. She was silent; she looked at him with a kind of blank appeal. She half rose again to go away without putting her question. She seemed to be on the eve of a betrayal, of a family exposure. How foolish it was! She looked at Horace's easy-minded, tranquil countenance, and took courage.

"Do you expect," she said, "Mr Landon here to-day?" with a smile, yet a catch of her breath.

"Mr Landon!" The astonishment of young Fareham was extreme. "Is he in town? We have not seen him since May."

"Horace," said Mrs Lycett-Landon, half-rising from her chair and then falling back upon it. "Horace, your father must be very ill. He must have had — some operation — he must have thought I would be over-anxious — —"

She became very pale as she uttered these broken words, and looked as if she were going to faint; and Horace, too, stared with bewildered eyes. Young Fareham began to be alarmed. He saw that his quick response was altogether unexpected, and that there was evidently some mystery.

"Let me see," he said, appearing to ponder, "perhaps I am making a mistake. Yes, I am sure he was here in May — he had just come back from the Continent. Wasn't it so? Oh, then, I must have misunderstood him. I thought he said — — Now I remember, he certainly was here in town. Yes, came to tell me something about letters — what was it?"

"Perhaps where you were to send his letters," Mrs Landon said quickly. "That is what we want to know." While she was listening to him, her mind had been going through a great many questions, and she had brought herself summarily back to calm. If it should be serious illness, all her strength would be wanted. She must not waste her forces with foolish fainting or giving in, but husband them all.

Then there arose an inquiry in the office. One clerk after another was called in to be questioned. One said Mr Lycett-Landon's letters were all forwarded to the Liverpool house, or to the Elms, Rockferry, his private address; another, that they were sent to the club; and it was not till some time had been lost that one of the youngest remembered an address to which he had once been sent, to a lodging where Mr Landon was staying. He remembered all about it, for it was a pretty house, with a garden, very unlike Jermyn Street.

"It was just after Mr Landon came back from abroad," the youth said; and by degrees he remembered exactly where it was, and brought it written down, in a neat, clerkly hand, on an office envelope. It was a flowery address, a villa in a road, both of them fanciful with a cockney sentiment.

Mrs Lycett-Landon took the paper from him with a smile of thanks; but she was so bewildered and confused that she rose up and went out of the office without even saying good-morning to young Fareham.

"Mamma, mamma," cried Horace after her, "you have never said— —"

"Oh, don't trouble her," said young Fareham; "I can see she is anxious. You'll come back, won't you, and let me know if you've found him? But I hope there is some mistake."

He did not say what kind of mistake he hoped for, nor did Horace say anything as he followed his mother. He, like Milly, thought it impossible that papa would have hidden himself thus to be ill. He was a little nervous of speaking to his mother when he saw how pale and preoccupied she looked.

"Shall I call a cab?" he said. "Mother, do you really think there is so much to fear?"

"He has never been on the Continent," was all his mother could say.

"No; that's true. They just have got that into their heads. It was no business of theirs where he went."

"It is everybody's business where a man goes—a man like him. I think I know what it is, Horace. He has been fretful for some time, and restless; he must have been ill, and he has been going through an operation. Don't say anything; I feel sure of it. Perhaps there was danger in it, and he feared the fuss, and that I should be over-anxious."

"We always thought as children that papa liked to be made a fuss with," said simple Horace.

"You thought so in the nursery, because you liked it yourselves. Yes, we had better have a cab. How full the streets are! one cannot hear oneself talking."

Then she was silent a little till the hansom was called. It was a very noisy part of the City, where the traffic is continual, and it was very difficult to hear a woman's voice. She paused before she got into the cab.

"Now I think of it," she said, "you had better go and telegraph to Milly, for she will be anxious. Go back to the hotel and do it. Tell her that we have got to town all safe, and that you will send her word this evening how papa is."

"But, mother, you are not going without me! and it will be better to telegraph after we know."

"That is what I wish you to do, Horace. It might upset him. I think it a great deal better for me to go by myself. Just do what I tell you. Milly will want to know that we have arrived all right; and wait at the hotel till I send for you."

"You had much better let me come with you, mother."

The noise was so great that she only made a "No" with her mouth, shaking her head as she got into the cab, and gave him the address to show the cabman. Then, before Horace had awakened from his surprise, she was gone, and he was left, feeling very solitary, pushed about by all the passers-by upon the pavement. The youth was half angry, half astonished. To go back to the hotel was not a thing that tempted him, but he was so young that he obeyed by instinct, meaning to pour forth his indignation to Milly. Even in a telegram there is a possibility of easing one's heart.

CHAPTER V
THE HOUSE WITH THE FLOWERY NAME

Mrs Lycett-Landon drove off through the crowded City streets in a curious trace of excited feeling. She had a sense that something was going to happen to her; but how this was she could not have told. Nor could she have told why it was she had sent Horace away. Perhaps his father might not wish to see him, perhaps he might prefer to explain to her alone the cause of his absence. She felt the need of first seeing her husband alone, though she could not tell why. It was a very long drive. Out of the bustling City streets she came to streets more showy, less encumbered, though perhaps scarcely less crowded, and then to some which showed the lateness of the season by shut-up houses and diminished movement, and then to line after line of those dingy streets, all exactly like each other, which form the bulk of London. There are so many of them, and they are so indistinguishable. She looked out of the hansom and noted them all as she drove on—but yet as if she noted them not, as if it were they that glided by her, as in a dream. Then she reached the suburbs, the roads with the flowery names, houses buried in gardens, with trees appearing behind the high enclosing walls. This perhaps was the strangest of all. She could not think what he could want here, so far out of the world, until she recalled to herself the idea of an illness and an operation which had already faded out of her mind—for that, like every other explanation, was so strange, so much unlike all his habits. Her heart began to beat as the cab turned into the street, going slowly along to look for the special house, and she found herself on the point of arriving at her destination. Though she was so anxious to find her husband, she would now, if she could, have deferred the arrival, have called out to the driver that it was not here, and bidden him go on and on. But there could not be any mistake about it—there was the name of the house painted on the gate. It was a little gate in a wall, affording a glimpse of a pretty little garden shaded with trees inside. She would not let the cabman ring the bell, but got out first and paid him, and then, when she could not find any further excuse, rang it—so faintly at first that no sound followed. She waited, though she knew she could not have been heard, to leave time for an answer. Looking in under the little arch of roses to the smooth bit of lawn, the flowers in the borders, she said to herself that there was not very much taste displayed in the flowers—red geraniums and mignonette, the things that everybody had, and great yellow nasturtiums clustering behind—not very much taste or individuality, but yet a great deal of brightness, and the look as of a home; not lodgings, but a place where people lived. There were some garden-chairs about, and on a rustic table something that looked like a woman's work. How natural it all seemed, how peaceable! It was curious that he should be living in such a place. Perhaps, she said to herself, it was the house of some clerk of the better sort—some one who had known him in his early years, and had wished to be kind: and in good air, and out of the noise of the streets. She made all these explanations as she stood at the door waiting for some one to answer a ring which she knew very well could not have been heard—unable to understand her own strange pause, and the manner in which she dallied with her anxiety. But this could not last for ever. After she had waited more than the needful time she rang again, and presently the door was opened by an unseen spring, and she went in within the pretty enclosure. How pretty it was—only red geraniums and nasturtiums, it was true, but the soft odour of the mignonette, and the sunshine, and the silence—all so peaceful and so calm. There came over her a certain awe as she stepped across the threshold and closed behind her the garden-door. The windows were all open, the house-door open. Under the trees on the little lawn were two basket-chairs, and a white heap of muslin, which some woman must have been working at, on the table. Mrs Lycett-Landon felt like an intruder in this peaceful place. She said to herself at last that there must be some mistake, that it could not be here.

A housemaid, wiping her arms on her apron, came to the house-door—a round-faced, ruddy, wholesome young woman, just the sort of servant for such a place. No doubt there were two, cook and housemaid, the visitor said to herself, just enough for needful service. The young woman was smiling and pleasant, no forbidding guardian. She did not advance to meet the stranger, but stood waiting, holding her own place in the doorway. Her honest, open face confirmed the expression of peace and comfort that was about the house. The intruder came up softly, not able to divest herself of that sense of awe.

"Does Mr Lycett-Landon live here?" she said, almost under her breath.

"Yes, ma'am, but he's rather poorly this morning," the housemaid said.

"He is at home then? Will you take me to him, please — —"

"Oh, I don't think I can do that, ma'am. He's rather poorly; he's keeping his room. The doctor don't think that it's anything serious, but as master is not quite a young gentleman he says it's best to be on the safe side."

"Is Mr Lycett-Landon your master?"

"Yes, ma'am," with a little curtsey.

"Has he been ill long?"

"Oh, bless you, not at all. He has his 'ealth as well as could be wished; only a little bilious or that now and then, as gentlemen will be. They ain't so careful in what they eat and drink as ladies—that's what I always say."

"He is only bilious then—not ill? not long ill? there has been no—operation?"

"Oh, bless you, nothing of the sort!" the young woman said, with the most evident astonishment.

Mrs Lycett-Landon put all these questions in a kind of dream. Something kept her from saying who she was. She felt a curious anxiety to find out all the details before she announced herself.

"I think he will see me," she said, a little faintly. "I have come a long way to see him. Take me to him, please."

"Is it business, ma'am?" said the girl.

"Business? yes; you may say it is business. I am his— —Take me to him at once, please."

"Oh dear, I can't do that. I ask your pardon, but the last thing the doctor said was that he mustn't be troubled with no business."

"But I must see him," Mrs Lycett-Landon said.

"You can't, ma'am, not to-day—it's not possible. To be sure," the girl added with a pleasant smile, "if Mrs Landon would do as well."

"Mrs— —, whom— —?"

"Mrs Landon—Mrs Lycett-Landon, that's her full name. Oh, didn't you know as he was married? She'll be down in a moment if you'll step inside."

The woman outside the door felt herself turned to stone. She said faintly, "Yes, I think I will step inside."

"Do, ma'am: you don't look at all well; you've been standing in the sun. Missis will be fine and angry if she knows as I let you stand like that. Take a chair, ma'am, please. She'll be here in a moment," the cheerful maid-servant said.

She did not ask for the visitor's name—she was evidently not accustomed to visits of ceremony—but went up-stairs quickly, with her solid foot sounding on every step.

The visitor for her part sat down, not feeling able to keep upon her feet, and faintly looked round her, seeing everything, understanding nothing. What did it all mean? The room was furnished like that of a newly-married pair. Little decorations were about, newly-bound books, a new little desk all ormolu and velvet; albums, photograph-frames, trifles from Switzerland, carved and painted, like relics of a recent journey. Nothing was in absolute bad taste, but the fashion of the furnishing was not of the larger kind, which means wealth. It was slightly pretty, perhaps a little tawdry, yet not sufficiently worn to acquire that look as yet. Mingled with all this decoration, however, there was something else which had a curious effect upon the intruder, something that reminded her of her husband's library at home, a chair of the form he liked, a solid table or two, strangely out of place amid the little low sofas and *étagères*. She saw all this, and took it into her mind at a glance, without making any of these observations upon it. She made no observations. She was unable even to think; the maid's words went through her head without any will of hers—"Didn't you know as he was married?" "If Mrs Landon would do as well." Mrs Landon! Who was this that bore her own name—who was the man up-stairs? She was not in any hurry to be enlightened. She seemed to herself rather grateful for the pause; glad to hold off any discovery that there might be to make with both hands, to keep it at arm's length. She sat quite still in this strange room, not thinking or able to think, wondering what was about to happen—what strange thing was coming to her.

At last she heard a footstep, a light step very different from the maid's, coming down-stairs. She rose up instinctively and took hold of the back of a chair to support herself. The door opened, and a young woman, pretty, timid, tall, in a white flowing gown, with a little cap upon her dark hair, and a pair of appealing eyes, came in. She had an uncertain look, as if not wholly accustomed to her position. She said with a pretty blush and shyness, "They tell me that you want to see my husband on business—but he is not well enough for business. Is it anything that I could do?"

"Will you tell me who you are?"

The new-comer looked a little surprised at the voice, which was hoarse and unnatural, of her visitor. She answered with a little dignity, drawing up her slight young figure. "I am Mrs Lycett-Landon," she said.

CHAPTER VI
PERPLEXITIES

What was she to do?

It is not often in life that a woman is brought to such an emergency without warning, without time for preparation. She did nothing at all at first, and felt capable of nothing but to stare blankly, almost stupidly, at her supplanter. She did not feel capable even of rising from the chair into which she had sunk in the utter blank of consternation. She could only gaze, interrogating not the face before her only, but heaven and earth. Was it true? Could it be true?

The young woman was evidently surprised by this pause. She too looked curiously at her visitor, waited for a minute, and then advancing a step, asked, with a tone in which there was some surprise and a faint shadow of impatience, "Is it anything that I can do?"

"Have you been married long?" This was all the visitor could say.

A pretty blush came over the other's face. "We were married in the end of April," she said. It still seemed quite natural to her that everybody should be interested in this great event. "We went abroad for a month. And we were so lucky as to find this house. You know my husband?"

"I think so—well; his Christian name is——"

"Robert is his Christian name. Oh, I am so glad to meet with any one who has known him!" She drew a chair with a pretty vivacious movement close to that on which her visitor sat. "I feel sure," she said, "you are a relation, and have come to find out about us."

There was something in the young creature's air so guileless, so assured in her innocence, that if there had been any fury in the other's heart, or on her tongue, it must have been arrested then; but there was no fury in her heart. After the first unspeakable shock of surprise there was nothing but a great pang, and that almost more for this young life blighted than for her own. "It is true," she said, "that I am a—connection. Is your mother alive?"

"Mamma?" cried the girl, with a laugh. "Oh yes, and she is here to-day. She does not live with us, you know. She would not. She says married people should be left to themselves, though I always told her Mr Landon was far too sensible to believe in that trash about mothers-in-law. Don't you think it is rubbish? Young men may believe it; but when a gentleman is experienced and knows the world— —"

"Perhaps I could see your mother," said the old wife. She felt herself growing a little faint. The day was warm, and she had been travelling all night. Was not that enough to account for it? And this happy babble in her ear made her heart sick, which was more.

"Mamma? Oh yes, certainly she will be very glad to see you. She always wanted to see some of the relations. She said it was not natural; though, to be sure, at his age— —Shall I go and tell her you want to see her—her and not me? But you must not take any prejudice against me. Don't, please, if you are his relation: and you look so nice too. I know I should love you if you would let me."

"Let me see your mother. I have no—prejudice." She scarcely knew what she was saying. The room was swimming in her eyes, the green of the closed blinds waving up and down, surrounding her with an uncertain mist of colour, through which she seemed to see a half-reproachful, wondering look. And then the white figure was gone. Mrs Lycett-Landon leant her head upon the back of the chair, and for a minute knew nothing more. Then the greenness became visible again, and gradually everything wavered and circled back into its place.

The little house was very still; there were hurried steps overhead, as if two people were moving about. It was the mother hastily being put in order for a visitor—her cap arranged, a clean collar put on, the young wife dancing about her in great excitement to make all nice. This process of decoration occupied some time, and as it went on the visitor came fully to herself. What should she do? As she recovered full command of herself she shrunk from inflicting such a blow even upon the mother. Should she go away before they came down?—disappear like a dream, take no notice, but leave the strange little drama—what was it, comedy or tragedy?—to work itself out? Why should she interfere, after all? If he liked this best—and all the harm was now done that could be done—the best thing was to go away and take no more notice. She had risen with this intention to slip away, to let herself out, not to interfere, when another sound became audible—the sound of a door opening in the back part of the house. Then a voice called "Rose"—a voice which, in spite of herself, made the visitor's brain swim once more. She had to stop again perforce. And then a step came towards the room in which she was; a heavy step, with a little gouty limp in it—a step she knew so well. It came along the passage, accompanied by a running commentary of half-complaint. "Where are you? I want you." Then the door of the little drawing-room was pushed open. "Why don't you answer me?" He paused there in the doorway, seeing a stranger—with a quick apology—"I beg your pardon." Then suddenly there came from him a cry—a roar like that of a wounded animal—"Eleanor!"

Neither of the two ever forgot the appearance of the other. She saw him with the little passage and its stronger light opening behind him, his large figure relieved against it; the sudden look of consternation, horror, utter amaze in his face. Horror came first; and then everything yielded to the culprit's sense of unspeakable downfall, guilt self-convicted and without excuse. He fell back against the wall; his jaw dropped; his eyes seemed to turn upon themselves in a flicker of mortal dismay. The entire failure of all force and self-defence did not disarm his wife, as might have been supposed, but filled her with a blaze of sudden vehemence, passion which she could not contain. She had said his name as he said hers, in a quiet tone enough; but now stamped her foot and cried out, feeling it intolerable, insupportable. "Well!" she cried, "stand up for it like a man! Say you are sick of me, of your children, of living honestly these fifty years. Say something for yourself. Don't stand there like a whipped child."

But the man had nothing to say. He stood against the wall and looked at her as if he feared a personal assault. Then he said, "She is not to blame. She is as innocent as you are."

"I have seen her," said the injured wife. "Do you think you need to tell me that? But then, what are you?"

He made no reply. And the sight of him in the doorway was unbearable to the woman. If he had stood up for himself, made a fight of any kind, it would have been more tolerable. But the very sight of him was insupportable—something she could not endure. She turned her head away and went quickly past him towards the open door. "I meant to tell her mother." She scarcely knew whether she was speaking or only thinking. "I meant to tell her mother, but I cannot. You must manage it your own way."

Next moment she found herself out in the street, walking along under the shadow of the blank wall. She was conscious of having closed both doors behind her, that of the house and that of the garden. If she could but have closed the door of her own mind, and put it out of sight, and shut it up for ever! She hurried away, walking very quickly round one corner after another, through one street after another, of houses enclosed in walls and railings, withdrawn among flowers and trees. You may walk long through these quiet places without finding what she wanted—a cab to take her out of this strange, still, secluded town of villas. When she found one at last, she told the driver to take her back to the Euston, but first to drive round Hyde Park. He thought she must be mad. But that did not matter much so long as she was able to pay the fare. And then there followed what she had wanted, a long, endless progress through a confusion of streets, first quiet, full of gardens and retired houses; then the long bustling thoroughfares leading back into the noisy world of London; then the quiet streets on the north side of the park, the trees of Kensington Gardens, the old red palace, the endless line of railings and trees on the other side; the bustle of Piccadilly, so unlike the bustle of the other streets. Naturally the hansom could not go within the enclosure of the park, but only by the streets. But she did not care for that. She wanted movement, the air in her face, silence so that she might think.

So that she might think! But a woman can no more think when she wills than she can be happy when she wills. All that she thought was this, going over and over it, and back and back upon it, putting it involuntarily into words and saying them to herself like a sort of dismal refrain. At fifty! After living honestly all these fifty years! Was it possible? was it in the heart of man? At fifty, after all these years! This wonder was so great that she could think of nothing else. And he had been a good man—kind, ready to help; not hard upon any one—fond of his family, liking to have them about him. And now at fifty! after living honestly——She did not think of it as a matter affecting herself, and she could not think of what she was to do, which was the thing she had intended to think of, when she bade the man drive to the other end of the world. When she perceived, as she did dimly in the confusion of her mind, that she was approaching the end of her long round, she would but for very shame have gone over it all again. But by this time she had begun to see that little would be gained by staving it off for another hour, and that sooner or later she must descend from that abstract wandering, which had been more like a wild flight into space than anything else, and meet the realities of her position. Ah heavens! the realities of her position were—first of all, Horace, her boy—her grown-up boy: no longer a child to whom a family misfortune could be slurred over, but a man, able to understand, old enough to know. Her very heart died within her as this suddenly flashed upon her deadened intelligence. Horace and Milly—a young man and a young woman. How was she to tell them what their father had done? At fifty! after all these years!

She was told at the hotel that the young gentleman had gone out—for which she was deeply thankful—but would be back immediately. Oh, if he might but be detained; if something would but happen to keep him away! She came up the great vulgar common stairs which so many people trod, some perhaps with hearts as heavy as hers, few surely with such a problem to resolve. How to tell her boy that his father—oh God! his father, whom he loved and looked up to; his kind father, who never grudged him anything; a man so well known; a good man, of whom everybody spoke well—to tell him that his father——She locked the door of her room instinctively, as if that would keep Horace out, and keep her secret concealed.

It was one of those terrible hotel rooms, quite comfortable and wholly unsympathetic, in which many of the sorest hours of life are passed, where parents come to part with their children, to receive back their prodigals, to look for the missing, to receive tidings of the worse than dead; where many a reconciliation has to be accomplished, and arrangement made that breaks the heart. Strange and cold and miserable was the unaccustomed place, with no associations or soothing, no rest or softness in it. She walked about it up and down, and then stopped, though the movement gave her a certain relief, lest Horace should come to the door, hear her, and call out in his hearty young voice to be admitted. She had not been able to think before for the recurrence of that dismal chorus, "At fifty!" and now she could not think for thinking that any moment Horace might come to the door. She was more afraid of her boy than of all the world beside: had some one come to tell her that an accident had happened, that he had broken an arm or a leg, it seemed to her that she would have been glad,—anything rather than let him know. And yet he would have to know. The eldest son, a man grown, after his father the head of his family, the one who would have to take care of the children. How would it be possible to keep this from him? And how could it be told? His mother, who had prided herself on her son's spotless youth, and rejoiced in the thought that a wanton word was as impossible from the lips of Horace as from those of Milly, reddened and felt her very heart burn with shame. How could she tell him? She could not tell him. It was impossible; it was beyond her power.

And then she shrank into the corner of her seat and held her breath: for who could this be but Horace, with a foot that scarcely seemed to touch the ground, rushing with an anxious heart to hear news of his father, up the echoing empty stair?

CHAPTER VII
EXPLANATION

"Mother! are you there? Let me in. Mother! open the door."

"In a moment, Horace; in a moment." It could not be postponed any longer. She rose up slowly and looked at herself in the glass to see if it was written in her face. She had not taken off her bonnet or made any change in her outdoor dress, and she was very pale, almost ghastly, with all the lines deepened and drawn in her face, looking ten years older, she thought. She put her bonnet straight with a woman's instinct, and then slowly, reluctantly, opened the door. He came in eager and impatient, not knowing what to think.

"Did you want to keep me out, mother! Were you vexed not to find me waiting? And how about papa?"

"No, Horace, not at all vexed."

"I went a little farther than I intended. I don't know my way about. But, mother, what of papa?"

"Not very much, my dear," she said, turning away. "It must be nearly time for lunch."

"Yes, it is quite time for lunch; and you had no breakfast. I told them to get it ready as I came up. But you don't answer me. Of course you found him. Is he really ill? What does he mean by it? Why didn't he come with you? Mother dear, is it anything serious? How pale you are! Oh, you needn't turn away; you can't hide anything from me. What is the matter, mamma?"

"It is serious, and yet it isn't serious, Horace. He is not ill, which is the most important thing. Only a little—seedy, as you call it. That's a word, you know, that always exasperates me."

"Is that all?" the youth said, looking at her with incredulous eyes.

She had turned her back upon him, and was standing before the glass, with a pretence of taking off her bonnet. It was easier to speak without looking at him. "No, my dear, that is not all. You will think it very strange what I am going to say. Papa and I have had a quarrel, Horace."

"Mother!"

"You may well be startled, but it is true. Our first quarrel," she said, turning half round with the ghost of a smile. It was the suggestion of the moment, at which she had caught to make up for the impossibility of thinking how she was to do it. "They say, you know, that the longer one puts off a thing of this kind the more badly one has it, don't you know?— measles and other natural complaints. We have been a long time without quarrelling, and now we have done it badly." She turned round with a faint smile; but Horace did not smile. He looked at her very gravely, with an astonishment beyond words.

"I cannot understand," he said, almost severely, "what you can mean."

"Well, perhaps it is a little difficult; but still such things do happen. You must not jump at the conclusion that it is all my fault."

Horace came up to her with his serious face, and put his arm round her, turning her towards him. "I was not thinking of any fault, mother; but surely I may know more than this? You and he don't quarrel for nothing, and I am not a child. You must tell me. Mother, what is the matter?" he said, with great alarm. For she was overdone in every way, worn out both body and mind, and when she felt her son's arm round her nature gave way. She leant her head upon his young shoulder, and fell into that convulsive sobbing which it is so alarming to bear. It was some time before she could command herself enough to reply—

"Oh, that is true—that is true! not for nothing. But, dear Horry, you can't be the judge, can you, between your father and mother? Oh no! Leave it a little; only leave it. It will perhaps come right of itself."

"Mother, of course I can't be the judge; but still, I'm not a child. May I go, then, and see papa?"

"Oh no," she cried, involuntarily clasping his arm tight—"oh no! not for the world."

The youth grew very grave: he withdrew his arm from her almost unconsciously, and said, "Either it is a great deal more serious than you say, or else— —"

"It is very serious, Horace. I don't deceive you," she said. "It may come to *that*—that we shall never—be together any more. But still I implore you, don't go to your father—oh! not now, my dear. He would not wish it. You must give me your word not to go."

She could not bear the scrutiny of his eyes. She turned and went away from him, putting off her light cloak, pulling open drawers as if in a search for something; but he stood where she had left him, full of perplexity and trouble. A quarrel between his parents was incredible to Horace; and the idea of a rupture, a public scandal, a thing that could be talked about! He stood still, overwhelmed by sudden trouble and distress, though without the slightest guess of the real tragedy. "I can't think what you could quarrel about," he said. "It seems a mere impossibility. Whatever it is, you must make it up, mother, for our sakes."

"My dear, anything that can be done, you may be sure will be done, for your sakes."

"But it is impossible, you know. A quarrel! between you and papa! It is out of the question. Nobody would believe it. I think you must be joking all the time," he said, with an abrupt laugh. But his laugh seemed so strange, even to himself, that he became silent suddenly with a look of confusion and irritation. Never in his life had he met with anything so extraordinary before.

"I am not joking," she said; "but, perhaps, after a while——Come and have your luncheon, Horace. I know you want it. And perhaps after a time——"

"You are worn out too, mother; that is what it is. One feels irritable when one is tired. After you have eaten something and rested yourself, let me go to papa. And we'll have a jolly dinner together and make it all up."

And she had the heroism to say no more, but went down with him, and pretended to eat, and saw him make a hearty meal. While she sat thus smiling at her boy, she could not but wonder to herself what *he* was doing. Was he smiling too, keeping up a cheerful face for the sake of the unfortunate girl not much older than Horace? God help her whom he had destroyed! She kept imagining that other scene while she enacted her own. Afterwards she persuaded Horace with some difficulty to let everything stand over till next day, telling him that she had great need of rest (which was true enough) and would lie down; and that next evening would be time enough for any further steps. She insisted so upon her need of rest, that he remembered that Dick Fareham had asked him to dine with him at his club, and go to the theatre if he had nothing better to do—a plan which she caught at eagerly.

"But how can I go and leave you alone in a hotel?" he said.

"My dear, I am going to bed," she replied, which was unanswerable. And after many attempts to know more, and many requests to be allowed to go to his father, Horace at last yielded, dressed, and went off to the early dinner which precedes a play. He had brought his dress clothes with him, though there had been so little time for feasting, confident that even a few days in London must bring pleasure of some kind. And already the utterly absurd suggestion that his father and mother could have had a deadly quarrel began to lose its power in his mind. It was impossible. His mother was worn out, and had been irritable; and his father, especially when he had a touch of gout, was, as Horace well knew, irritable also. To-morrow all that would have blown away, and they would both be ashamed of themselves. Thus he consoled himself as he went out; and as the youth never had known what family strife or misfortune meant, and in his heart felt anything of the kind to be impossible, it did not take much to drive that incomprehensible spectre away.

Mrs Lycett-Landon was at length left alone to deal with it by herself. What was she to do? She had a fire lighted in the blank room, though it was the height of summer, for agitation and misery had made her cold, and sat over it trembling, and trying to collect her thoughts. Oh, if it could be but possible to do nothing, to say no word to any one, to forget the episode of this morning altogether! "If I had not known," she said to herself, "it would have done me no harm." This modern Eleanor, who had fallen so innocently into Rosamond's bower, had no thought of vengeance in her heart. She had no wish to kill or injure the unhappy girl who had come between her and her husband. What good would that do? Were Rosamond made an end of in a moment, how would it change the fact? What could ever alter that? The ancients did not take this view of the subject. They took it for granted that when the intruder was removed life went on again in the same lines, and that nothing was irremediable. But to Mrs Lycett-Landon life could never go on again. It had all come to a humiliating close; confusion had taken the place of order, and all that had been, as well as all that was to be, had grown suddenly impossible. Had she not stopped herself with an effort, her troubled mind would have begun again that painful refrain which had filled her mind in the morning, which was perhaps better than the chaos which now reigned there. So far as he was concerned she could still wonder and question, but for herself everything was shattered. She could neither identify what was past nor face what was to come. Everything surged wildly about her, and she found no footing. What was to be done? These words intensify all the miseries of life—they make death more terrible, since it so often means the destruction of all settled life for the living, as well as the end of mortal troubles for the dead—they have to be asked at moments when the answer is impossible. This woman could find no reply as she sat miserable over her fire. She was not suffering the tortures of jealousy, nor driven frantic with the thought that all the tenderness which ever was hers was transferred to another. Perhaps her sober age delivered her from such reflections; they found no place at all in the tumult of her thoughts; the questions involved to her were wholly different: what she was to do; how she was to satisfy her children without shaming their youth and her own mature purity of matronhood which had protected them from any suggestion of such evil? How they were ever to be silenced and contented without overthrowing for ever in their minds their father and the respect they owed him? This was the treble problem which was before her—by degrees the all-absorbing one which banished every other from her thoughts. What could she say to Horace and Milly? How were they to be kept from this shame? Had they been both boys or both girls, it seemed to their mother that the question would have been less terrible; but boy and girl, young man and young woman, how were they ever to be told? How were they to be deceived and not told? Their mother's powers gave way and all her strength in face of this question. How was she to do it? How was she to refrain from doing it? That pretext of a quarrel, how was it to be kept up? and in what other way—in what other way, oh heaven! was she to explain to them that their father and she could meet under the same roof no more? She covered her face with her hands, and wept in the anguish of helplessness and incapacity; then dried her eyes, and tried again to plan what she could do. Oh that she had the wings of a dove, that she might flee away and be at rest!— but whither could she flee? She thought of pretending some sudden loss of money, some failure of fortune, and rushing away with the children to America, to Australia, to the end of the world; but if she did so, what then? Would it become less necessary, more easy to explain? Alas! no; nothing could change that horrible necessity. The best thing of all, she said to herself, if she were equal to it, would be to return home, to live there as long as it was possible, with her heart shut up, holding her peace, saying nothing— as long as it was possible!—until circumstances should force upon her the explanation which would have to be made. Let it be put off for weeks, for months, even for years, it would have to be made at last.

Thus she sat pondering, turning over everything, considering and rejecting a thousand plans; and then, after all, acted upon a sudden impulse, a sudden rising in her of intolerable loneliness and insufficiency. She felt as if her brain were giving way, her mind becoming blank, before this terrible emergency, which must be decided upon at once. Horace was safe for a few hours, separated from all danger, but how to meet his anxious face in the light of another day his mother did not know. She sprang up from her seat, and reached towards the table, on which there were pens and ink, and wrote a telegram quickly, eagerly, without pausing to think. The young ones were in the habit of laughing at old Fareham. She herself had joined in the laugh before now, and allowed that he was methodical and tedious and tiresome. He was all these, and yet he was an old friend, the oldest friend she had, one who had known her father, who had seen her married, who had guided her husband's first steps in the way of business. He was the only person to whom she could say anything. And he was a merciful old man: when troubles arose—when clerks went wrong or debtors failed—Mr Fareham's opinion was always on the side of mercy. This was one of the reasons why they called him an old fogey in the office; always—always he had been merciful. And it was this now which came into her mind. She wrote her telegram hastily, and sent it off at once, lest she should repent, directing it not to the office, where it might be opened by some other hand than his, but to his house. "Come to me directly if you can. I have great need of your advice and help. Tell no one," was what she said. She liked, like all women, to get the full good of the permitted space.

CHAPTER VIII
EXPEDIENTS

His mother was in bed and asleep when Horace returned from his play—or at least so he thought. He opened her door and found the room dark, and said, "Are you asleep, mamma?" and got no answer, which he thought rather strange, as she was such a light sleeper. But, to be sure, last night had been so disturbed, she had not slept at all, and the day had been fatiguing and exciting. No doubt she was very tired. He retired on tiptoe, making, as was natural, far more noise than when he had come in without any precaution at all. But she made no sign; he did not wake her, where she lay, very still, with her eyes closed in the dark, holding her very breath that he might not suspect. Horace had enjoyed his evening. The play had been amusing, the dinner good. Dick Fareham, indeed, had asked a few questions.

"I suppose you found the governor all right?" he said.

"I didn't," said Horace; "the mother did."

"And he's all right, I hope?"

"I can't tell you," said Horace, shortly; "I said I hadn't seen him."

The conversation had ended thus for the moment, but young Fareham was too curious to leave it so. He asked Horace when he was coming to the London office. "I know I'm only a warming-pan," he said, "keeping the place warm for you. I suppose that will be settled while you are here."

"I don't know anything about it," said Horace. "We heard you were all at sixes and sevens in the office."

"I at sixes and sevens!"

"Oh, I don't mean to be disagreeable. We heard so," said Horace, "and that the governor had his hands full."

"I'd like to know who told you that," said the young man. "I'd like to punch his head, whoever said it. In the first place, it is not true, and your father is not the man to put such a story about."

Now Horace had not been told this as the reason of his father's absence, but had found it out, as members of a family find out what has been talked of in the house, the persons in the secret falling off their guard as time goes on. He was angry at the resentment with which he was met, but a little at a loss for a reply.

"Perhaps you think I have put it about?" he said, indignant. "It has not been put about at all, but we heard it somehow. That was why my father——"

"I think I can see how it was—I think I can understand," said young Fareham. "That was what called your father up to London. By Jove!"

And after that he was not so pleasant a companion for the rest of the evening. But the play was amusing, and Horace partially forgot this *contretemps*. When he found his mother's room shut up and quiet, he went to his own without any burden on his mind. He was not so anxious about "the governor" as perhaps Milly in his place might have been. It was highly unpleasant that the mother and he should have quarrelled, and quite incomprehensible. But Horace went to bed philosophically, and the trouble in his mind was not enough to keep him from sleep.

Young Fareham, on his side, wrote an indignant letter to his uncle, demanding to know if his mind too had been poisoned by false reports. The young man was very angry. He was being made the scapegoat; he was the excuse for old Landon's absence, who had not been near the office for months, and he called upon his own particular patron to vindicate him. Had his private morals been attacked he might have borne it; but to talk of the office as at sixes and sevens! this was more than he could bear.

Next morning, before anybody else was awake, an early housemaid stole into Mrs Lycett-Landon's room, and told her that a gentleman had arrived who wanted to see her. The poor lady had slept a little towards the morning, and was waked by this message. She thought it must be her husband, and after a moment of dolorous hesitation got up hastily and dressed herself, and went to the sitting-room, which was still in the disorder of last night, and looking, if that were possible, still more wretched, raw, and unhomelike than in its usual trim. She found, with a great shock and sense of discouragement, old Mr Fareham, pale after his night's journey, with all the wrinkles about his eyes more pronounced, and the slight tremor in his head more visible than ever. He came forward to meet her, holding out both his hands.

"What can I do for you?" he said. "What has happened? I came off, you see, by the first train."

"Oh, Mr Fareham, I never expected this! You must have thought me mad. I think, indeed, I must have been off my head a little last night. I telegraphed, did I?—I scarcely knew what I was doing——"

"You have not found him, then?"

She covered her face with her hands. To meet the old man's eyes in the light of day and tell her story was impossible. Why had not she gone away, buried herself somewhere, and never said a word?

"I have seen Mr Landon, Mr Fareham; he is not—ill: but Horace knows nothing," she said, hastily.

"My dear lady, if I am to do anything for you I must know."

"I don't think there is anything to be done. We have had a—serious disagreement; but Horace knows nothing," she repeated again. He looked at her, and she could not bear his eyes. "I am very sorry to have given you so much trouble——"

"The trouble is nothing," he said. "I have known you almost all your life. It would be strange if I could not take a little trouble. I think I know what you mean. You were distracted last night, and sent for me. But now in the calm of the morning things do not look so bad, and you think you have been too hasty. I can understand that, if that is what you mean."

She could not bear his eye. She sank down in the chair where she had sat last night and talked to Horace. *In the calm of the morning!* It was only now, when she felt that she had begun to live again, that all her problems came back to her, full awake, and fell upon her like harpies. *Things do not look so bad!* There passed through her mind a despairing question, whether she had strength to persuade him that this was so, and that there really was nothing to appeal to him about.

"My dear lady," he said again, "you must be frank with me. Is it a false alarm, and nothing for me to do? If so, not another word; I will forget that you ever sent for me. But if there is something more——"

How much was going through her mind, and how many scenes were rising before her eyes as he spoke! There appeared to her a vision of duty terrible to perform; of going home, putting on a face of calm, speaking of papa as usual to the children, living her life as usual, keeping her secret: and then of the universal questions that would arise, Where was he? what had become of him? why did he never return? Or she seemed to see herself going away, making some pretext of health, of education, she could not tell what, carrying her children, astonished, half unwilling, full of questions which she could not answer, away with her into the unknown. These visions rolled upward before her eyes surrounded with mists and confusion, out of which they appeared and reappeared. When her old friend stopped speaking her imagination stopped too, and she came to a pause. And then the impossibility of all these efforts came over her and overwhelmed her—the mists, the clouds, the chaos of helplessness and confusion in which there was no standing-ground, nor anything to grasp at, swallowing her up. She did not know how long she sat silent while the old man stood and looked at her. Then she burst forth all at once,—

"I cannot tell the children! How is it possible? Horace and Milly, they are grown up; they will want to know. How can I tell them? I want you to help me to keep it from them—to think of something. I would rather die than tell them," she said, starting up wringing her hands.

"My dear lady! my dear lady!—--"

"Mr Fareham, Robert—has married—again!"

The old man gave a loud cry—almost a shriek—of surprise and horror. "You don't know what you are saying," he said.

"That sounds as if I were dead," she said, calmed by the revelation, with a faint smile. "Oh yes, I know very well what I am saying. He is married—as if I were dead—as if I had never existed. I went to see him, and I saw—her!"

Old Fareham caught her hands in his; he led her to her seat again, and put her in it, uttering all the time sounds that were half soothing, half blaspheming. He stood by her, patting her on the shoulder, his old eyebrows contracted, his lips quivering under their heavy grey moustache. He was more agitated now than she was. The telling of her secret seemed to have delivered her soul. When he had recovered himself he asked a hundred questions, to all which she answered calmly enough. The room, with its look of disorder—the litter of last night, the fresh morning sunshine streaming in disregarded, emphasising the squalor of the ashes in the grate—surrounded with a fitting background the strange discussion between these two—the old man fatigued with his night journey, the woman pale as a ghost, with eyes incapable of sleep. She told him everything, forestalling his half-said protest that it must be another Lycett-Landon with the fact of her personal encounter with her husband, forgetting nothing. The facts of the case had by this time paled of their first importance to her eyes, while they were everything to his. They no longer agitated her; while that which convulsed her very soul seemed to him of but little importance. "I cannot tell the children. How am I to tell the children?" He became weary of this refrain.

"We can think of the children later. In the meantime, this other is the important question. He has brought himself within the range of the law; you can punish him."

"Punish him?" she said, with a strange smile—"punish him?"

"Yes; you may forgive if you please, but I can't forgive. He deserves to be punished, and he shall be punished—and the woman——"

"He said she was as innocent—as I am."

"He said! he is a famous authority. One knows what kind of creature——"

"I have seen her," said Queen Eleanor, with a sigh, "poor child. He said nothing but the truth; she is not in fault. She is the one who is most injured. I would save her if I could."

"Save her! You would let this sweet establishment go on," he said, with fine sarcasm, "and not disturb them?"

"Yes," she said. "It may be wrong, but I think I would if I could."

"You are mad!" cried the old man. "You have lost all your good sense, and your feeling too. What, your own husband! you would let him go on living in sin—happy——"

She stopped him with a curious kind of authority—a look before which he paused in spite of himself.

"Happy!" she said; "I suppose so; at fifty, after living honestly all these years!"

He stopped and shook his grey head. "I have known such a thing before. It seems as if they must break out—as if common life and duty became insupportable. I have known such a case once before."

She cried out eagerly, "Who was it?" then stopped with a half-smile. "What does it matter to me who it was? The only thing that matters now is the children. What is to be done about the children? I cannot tell them; nor can you, nor any one. Mr Fareham, let him alone; let him be—happy, as you call it—if he can. But the children—what am I to say to the children?" She rose up again, and began to walk about the room, unable to keep still. "Horace, who is a man, and Milly. If they were little things it would not matter; they would not understand."

"And is it possible," said old Fareham, looking at her almost sourly, "that this is the only thing you can think of?—not your own wrongs, nor his abominable behaviour, nor——"

She paused a little, standing by the table. "Oh, you do wrong," she said, "you do wrong! A woman has her pride. If his duty has become—insupportable; it was you who used the word—and life insupportable, do you think a woman like me would hold him to it? Oh, you do wrong! I have put that away. But the children—I cannot put them away! And he was a good father, a kind father. Think of something. If only they might never find out!"

Here her voice gave way, and she could say no more.

"Horace will have to know," he said, shaking his head.

"Why? You could tell him there was some difficulty between us, something that could not be got over. That we were both in the wrong, as people always are in a quarrel. And no doubt I must have been in the wrong, or—or Robert would never have gone so far—so far astray. No doubt I have been wrong; you must have seen it—you with your experience—and yet you never said a word. Why didn't you tell me?—you might have done it so easily. Why didn't you say, 'You make life too hum-drum, too commonplace for him. He wants variety and change?' I would have taken it very well from you. I am not a woman who will not take advice. Why did you never tell me? I could have made so many changes if I had known."

He took her hand again, with a great pity, and almost remorse, in his old face. "It is too early," he said, "to do anything. Tell me where I shall find him, and go back to your room and try to rest. Say you are too tired to see the boy, if that is all you are thinking of; and go to bed—go to bed, and try and get a little sleep. I have a great deal of experience, as you say. Leave it to me. I will see him, and then we will talk it over, and think what is best to be done."

"You will see—him? What will you say to him, Mr Fareham? Why should you see him? Is not the chapter closed so far as he is concerned?"

"Closed? He will come home when he is tired of—the other establishment—is that what you mean him to do?"

She blushed like a girl, growing crimson to her hair. "Oh yes," she said, "I know you have a great deal of experience; but, perhaps, here you do not understand. That—that would not be necessary. He is not a man who would—Mr Fareham, you don't suppose I wish him any harm?"

"You are a great deal too good—too merciful."

"I am not merciful; it is all ended. Don't you know, since yesterday the world has come to an end. Life has become impossible—impossible! that is all about it. I am not angry; it is too serious for that. I would not harm him for the world. God help him! I don't know how he can live, any more than I know how I can live. It is—no word will express what it is. But he will not come back. He is not that kind of man."

"Do you think if you had not seen him yesterday, if he did not know that you had found him out—do you think," said old Fareham, deliberately, "that he would not have come back?"

She looked at him for an instant, and then hid her face in her hands.

"I have no doubt on the subject," said the old man, triumphantly. "But when a man has put himself within the reach of the law he is powerless, and we have him in our hands."

CHAPTER IX
THE REVELATION

She woke suddenly with the sense that somebody was by her, and found Horace seated by her bed. She had fallen asleep in the brightness of the morning, overcome with fatigue, and also partly calmed by having confided her secret to another: even when it is painful, when it is indiscreet, it is always a relief. The bosom is no longer bursting with that which it is beyond its power to contain. She woke suddenly with that sense of some one looking at her which breaks the deepest sleep. She was still in her dressing-gown, lying upon her bed. "Horace!" she said, springing up.

"I am so glad you have had a sleep. Don't jump up like that; you look so tired, mother, so worn out."

"Not now, my dear; I feel quite fresh now. Did you enjoy your evening?"

"What does it matter about my evening?" he said, almost sternly. "Mother, do you know that old Fareham came up by the night train?"

"Yes, Horace," she said, turning her head away.

"You knew? Do you think you are treating me fairly—I that am more interested than any one? What *is* the matter? The business has gone wrong. Do you mean to say that my father—*my* father——?"

Poor Horace's voice faltered. That it should be *his* father was the extraordinary thing, as it always is full of mystery to us how misfortune, much less shame, should affect us individually. He looked at his mother with a look which was imperative and almost commanding, not perplexed and imploring, as it had been before. Mr Fareham's arrival had thrown light, as Horace thought, on the mystery—light which to him, as a young man destined to be a merchant prince, and to convey to the world higher ideas of commerce altogether, was more dreadful than anything else could have been. He thought he saw it all; and that as no one would be so deeply affected as he, his mother had been weakly trying to hide it from him. Horace felt that his spirit would rise with disaster, and that he was capable of raising the house again and all its concerns from the ground.

And for a moment she caught at this new idea. To her own feminine mind disaster to the business was as nothing in comparison with what had happened. If others could make him believe this, it would be a way out of the worse revelation. This was how she contemplated the matter. She said, "It was I who sent for Mr Fareham. He is a very old friend, and his interests are all bound up with ours."

"Then that is what it is. He has been speculating. Oh, how could you conceal such a thing from me? How could you keep me in the dark? Mother, I don't mean to be unkind, but this is nothing to you in comparison with what it is to me. You don't care for a man's credit," said Horace, rising and striding about the room, "or the reputation of the firm, or anything of real importance, in comparison with his health or his comfort or some personal matter. His health—of what consequence is that in comparison? Mother, mother, I shall find it hard to forgive you if you have let our credit be put in danger without warning *me*."

This reproach was one that she had not looked for, and that took her entirely by surprise. She looked up at him, still feeling that what there was to say was worse, far worse than anything he could imagine, yet startled and confused by his vehemence. "I—I—don't think the credit of the house will suffer," she said, faltering a little.

"It is not so bad as that? But then why did you send for old Fareham? You ought to have taken no step without consulting me. I understand this sort of thing better than you do," he said, with an impatience which he could not suppress. "Mamma, I beg your pardon; everything else I am sure you know better—but the business! Don't you know I have been brought up to that? I mind nothing so much as the credit of the house."

"Nothing, Horace?" she said, faintly.

"Nothing," he repeated with vehemence, "nothing! Of course," he added after a moment, "if papa were ill I should be very sorry: but he must not play with our credit, mother—he must not; that is the one thing. What has he been doing? Surely not anything to do with those new bubble companies?"

"Oh, Horace, how can I tell you? Wait till Mr Fareham comes back."

"He has gone to see papa, then? I thought it must be that; but why, why not tell me? I am not very old, perhaps, but I know about the business, and care more for it than any one else. I would make any sacrifice, but our credit must not be touched—it must not be touched."

"Compose yourself, Horace; it need not be touched, so far as I can see."

This calmed him a little, and he sat down by her, and took pains to explain his views to her. "You see, mamma," he said kindly, but with a little natural condescension, "ladies have such a different way of looking at things. You think of health and comfort and good temper, and all that, when a man thinks of his affairs and his reputation. You would be more distracted if the governor" (at home Horace never ventured on this phrase, but it suited the atmosphere of town) "had a bad accident, or got into a snappish state, than if he had pledged the credit of the firm. It is nice in you to think so, but it would be silly in a man."

"You think then, Horace, that nothing can be so bad as trouble to the firm. You think that loss of money— —?"

"Loss of money is not everything," he said, testily. "I hope Lycett-Landon's could lose a lot of money without being much the worse. The fact is, you don't understand. It is always the personal you dwell upon. I am not reproaching you, mamma; it is your nature." He patted her hand as he said this, and looked at her with a half-smile of boyish wisdom and superiority, very kindly compassionating her limited powers.

This silenced her once more: and so they remained for some time, he sitting thoughtfully by her, she reclining on the bed looking at him, trying to read the meaning in his face. At last she said tremulously, "I am not quite so bad as you think: but perhaps a matter that touched our family peace, that sundered us from each other—disunited us— —"

He kept on patting her hand, but more impatiently than before. "Nothing could do that—permanently," he said. And he asked no more questions. He was a little, a very little, contemptuous of his mother. "I ought to have gone along with old Fareham. We should have talked it over together. I suppose now I must have patience till he comes back. When do you think he will come back? Can't I go and join him there? Oh, you think papa wouldn't like it? Well, perhaps he might not. It is rather hard upon me, all the same, to wait on and know nothing."

"Don't you think if you were to take a walk, Horace, or go and see the pictures— —?"

"Oh, the pictures! in this state of anxiety? Well, yes, I think I will take a walk; it is better than staying indoors. And don't you make yourself unhappy, mother. It can't have been going on very long, and no doubt we shall pull through."

Saying this with a cloudy smile, Horace went away, waving his hand to her as he went out. She then got up and dressed with a stupefied sensation, taking all the usual pains about her toilet, though with a sense that it was absolutely unimportant. She could not remember what day it was, or what month, or even what year. She was conscious of having received a remorseless and crushing blow, but that was all; when she had left home or whether she would ever go back to it, she could not tell; neither could she form the least idea of what was going to happen when old Mr Fareham came back. She forgot that she had not breakfasted, and even, what was more wonderful, that to save appearances it was necessary to make believe to breakfast. Everything of the kind was swept away. She went into the sitting-room and sat down at the window like an abstract woman in a picture. It was very strange to her to do nothing; and yet she never thought of doing anything, but sat down and waited—waited for something that was about to happen, not knowing what it might be.

She had not waited long when one of the hotel servants knocked at the door, and, opening it, admitted a stranger whom she had never seen before—a small, thin woman in a widow's dress, who stood hesitating, looking at her with a pair of anxious eyes, and for the first moment said nothing. Mrs Lycett-Landon was roused by the unlooked-for appearance of this visitor. She rose up, wondering, at such a moment, who it was that could have come to disturb her. The stranger was very timid and shy. She hung about the door as if there were a protection in being near it.

"I beg your pardon," she said, "I don't even know by what name to speak to you. But one of my daughter's maids saw you yesterday get into a cab, and then we heard you had come here."

"I think I understand; your daughter is — —?"

"Mrs Landon, madam, where you called yesterday. You asked for me, and then went away without seeing me. I could not help feeling anxious. You may think it presuming in me to track you out like this, but I do feel anxious. We were afraid perhaps that my son-in-law — —"

She had a wistful, deprecating look, like that of a woman who had not received much consideration in the course of her life. She watched the face of the person she addressed with an anxiety which evidently was habitual, as if to see how far she might go, to avoid all possible offence. Mrs Lycett-Landon returned the look with one which was full of alarm, almost terror. It seemed impossible that she could get through this interview without revealing everything; and the small, anxious, hesitating figure looked so little able to bear any shock.

"Will you sit down?" she said, offering her a chair.

The stranger accepted it gratefully, with a timid smile of thanks. She seemed to take this little civility as a good omen, and brightened perceptibly. She was very carefully, neatly dressed, but her crape was somewhat rusty, and the black gown evidently taken much care of. She twisted her hands together nervously.

"We were afraid," she repeated, "that perhaps Mr Landon—had got himself into trouble with his own family because of his marriage; and that you had come perhaps—to see. We were so delighted that you should have come; and then when we found you had gone away——"

Her voice trembled a little as she spoke. She watched every movement of the face which regarded her with such strange emotion, ready to stop, to modify any word that displeased.

"Then did you let him—did you give him your daughter—without any inquiries, without knowing anything——?"

"Oh, madam," the widow cried, clasping and unclasping her nervous hands, "perhaps I was imprudent. But at his age one does not think of the family approving. If he had been a younger man——But who could have any right to interfere at his age?"

"That is true—that is very true!"

"And you see it came upon me, you might say, unexpectedly. I saw that he was getting fond of Rose; but I never thought, if you will excuse me for saying so, that she would marry a gentleman so much older—and then it was so sudden at the last. He had leave from his office, and the opportunity of getting away——"

"Leave from his office!" The listener could not help repeating this with a curious cry of indignation. It gave her a shock, in the midst of so many shocks. As for the widow, this interruption confused her. She trembled and stumbled in her simple tale.

"And so—and so—it was settled at last in a hurry. I have not very strong health, and I was very glad that Rose should be settled. Oh yes, I was glad that she should have some one to take care of her in case anything happened. I had confidence that you could feel for me as a mother; perhaps you are a mother yourself."

The widow stopped short when she had made this suggestion, with a momentary panic; for Rose's idea had been that the lady who had appeared and disappeared so suddenly was a sister, perhaps a maiden sister. Her mother judged otherwise, but then paused, afraid.

"Yes, I am a mother myself."

"I thought so—I thought so! and I felt sure you would feel for me as a mother. It was Rose I had to think of. As for his family, at his age, you will understand— —But it makes my poor girl very unhappy to think she may have been the means of separating him from his relations. I tell her a wife is more to a man than any other relation. But still, if it could be possible to make a reconciliation—if you would be so kind as to help us— —"

The nervous hands clasped together; the little hesitating woman looked with a face full of prayer and entreaty at the lady who sat there before her, like an arbiter of fate. If she could have known how the heart was beating in that lady's breast! Mrs Lycett-Landon did not speak for some time, not being able to command her voice. Then she said, tremulously, but with a great effort to be calm—

"You don't know what you ask. I am the last person— —"

"Oh, madam!"

She had an old-fashioned, over-respectful way of using this word. And there was no fear or suspicion of the truth, though much anxiety, in her eyes.

"Oh, madam! you have a kind face; and who should be the one to make peace but such as you, that can feel for a young creature, and knows what is in a mother's heart?"

The words were scarcely out of her lips when Horace entered hastily, asking, before he saw that any stranger was present—

"Mother, has Fareham come back?"

"No, Horace; but you see I am engaged."

"I beg your pardon," he said, surprised by the look of agitation in the stranger's face. But he was terribly excited. "I won't stay a moment; but do please tell me papa's address. I cannot wait and knock about all day. Old Fareham is so tedious; he will take hours about it. Tell me my father's address."

Horace was not without wiles of his own. He thought it more likely that he should extract this address when somebody was there.

"Horace, I am engaged, as you can see."

"Only a moment, mother; it was something flowery—Laburnum, or Acacia, or something. If I go to the office I can get it in a moment."

The little widow rose up; something strange and terrible came over her face.

"Young gentleman," she said, "are you any relation to Mr Lycett-Landon? You will tell me if no one else will."

"Relation?" said Horace, with a laugh, "oh yes; only his son, that is all!"

"And this lady? This lady is——?"

"My mother; who else should she be?" the youth said.

There was a moment during which the two women stood gazing at each other in an awful suspension of all sound or thought. And there the visitor uttered a great and terrible cry, and fell down at their feet upon the floor.

CHAPTER X
THE END

The Lycett-Landons went home to the Grove that night. Horace asked his mother no questions. He helped her to lift up and place upon a sofa the visitor whose strength had failed her so strangely; but how much he heard from Mr Fareham, or how much he guessed, she never knew. He was anxious to go home at once, and, instead of making any objections as she had feared, facilitated everything. He was very kind and tender to her on the journey, taking care of her and of her comfort, saving her from every trouble. This had not heretofore been Horace's way. He was still so young that the habit of being taken care of was more natural to him than that of taking care of others; but he had learned a new version apparently of his duty on that strange and agitating day. It was late when they reached the Mersey again, and the great river was full of shooting fireflies, little steamers with their sparks of glowing colour flitting and rustling to and fro among the steady lights of the moored ships. The sky was pale with the rising moon, the stars appearing languidly out of the clouds. As they crossed the river to their home, sitting close together on the deck, saying nothing to each other, avoiding in the darkness all contact with the other passengers, two or three little steam-boats rustled past, full of music and a crowd of merrymakers going home noisy and happy after a day's pleasure. The sky was stained all round the horizon behind them by the smoke of the great town, but before them was soft and clear with fringes of dark foliage and outlines of peaceful houses rising against it. Everything was full of quiet and peace, no false or discordant note anywhere; even the fiddles and flutes of the bands harmonised by the air and water and magical space about, and the dew dropping, and the moon rising. It was only forty-eight hours since they had left their home almost under the same conditions, but what a change there was!

Milly was full of questions and surmises. How was papa? Why did they leave him? When was he coming home? Why did they return so soon? She supposed the season was over, and nothing going on, not even the theatres. She never thought it possible they would come back directly. She poured a flood of remarks upon them as they walked from the boat to the house. Fortunately it was dark, and their faces gave her no information; but their brief replies, and a something indefinable, a restraint in the atmosphere about them, a something new which she did not understand, began to affect the girl after the first abandon of her surprise and her interrogations. As soon as Mrs Lycett-Landon entered the house she announced that she was very tired and going to bed. "I am growing old; travelling affects me as it never used to do, and I have got a headache. I shall go to bed at once, Milly. No, I don't want anything to eat; quiet and rest—that is all I want. Give Horace his supper, dear; and you need not come into my room to-night. I shall put out my light and get to sleep."

"Not even a cup of tea, mamma? Mayn't I come and help you to take off your things? Let me send White away, and undress you myself."

"I want no one, my darling, neither you nor White. My head aches. I want darkness and quiet. Good night. To-morrow morning I shall be all right."

She kissed them, her veil still hanging over her face, and hurried up-stairs. Milly watched her till she had disappeared, and then turned upon her brother. "What does this mean?" said the girl; "what has happened to mamma, and where's papa, Horry? Tell me this very moment, before you have your supper or anything. I know something must be wrong."

"Something is wrong," said Horace, "but I can't tell you what it is. I don't know what it is. Now, Milly, that is all I am going to say. You need not go on asking and asking, for you will only make me miserable. I can't tell you anything more."

"You can't tell me anything more?" She was struck, not dumb indeed with amazement, but into such a quiver and agitation that she could scarcely speak. Then she regained her courage a little. "Where's papa? He can't be ill, or you would not have come home."

"I have not seen him," said Horace, doggedly.

"You have not seen him?"

"Mother did, and then old Fareham. I can tell you this: it isn't speculation, or anything of that sort. The firm is all right. It's nothing about that."

"The firm—speculation!" cried Milly, with wild contempt; "who cares for business? What is the matter? and why doesn't he come home?"

"Who cares for it? I care for it. I thought at first that was what had happened; but we may make our minds quite easy—it's not that." Horace was really comforted by this certainty, though not perhaps so much as he pretended to be. "I was very much frightened at first," he said. "It was a great relief to find that, whatever it is, it is not that."

Milly stood looking at him with scared eyes. "Do you mean to say that papa is not coming home? Oh, Horry, for goodness' sake tell me something more. Has he done anything? What has he done? Papa! It is impossible, impossible!" the girl cried.

"So I should have said too," said Horace, who had now had a long time in which to accustom himself to the idea. "Perhaps the mother will tell you something; she has not said a word to me. I don't know, and therefore I can't tell you. It has been a horrid sort of day," said the lad, "and perhaps you'll think it unfeeling, Milly, but I'm hungry. I'd like to have something to eat, and then I'd like to go to bed. I'm horribly tired, too; wandering about, and always waiting to hear something and never hearing, and imagining all sorts of things, is very fatiguing, and I don't think I've eaten anything to-day."

Milly despised her brother for thinking of eating, but yet it was a relief to superintend his supper and get him all he wanted. They had a great deal of talk over this strange meal, and though Horace gave his sister no information, they yet managed to assure themselves somehow that a terrible catastrophe had happened, and that their father had gone out of their lives. Milly wept bitterly over it, and even Horace could not keep the tears from his eyes; but somehow they recognised the fact between them, far more easily than their mother above stairs or any bystander could have imagined possible. Two days ago what could have been more impossible to them? And Milly did not know even so much as Horace knew, nor had any insight at all into how it was; and yet she, too, in the course of an hour or so, had accepted the fact. To youth there is something convincing in certainty, an obedience to what is, which is one of the most remarkable thinks in life. They acknowledged the mystery with wonder and pain, but they did not rebel or doubt. Their mother thought nothing less than that they would struggle, would be incredulous, would rebel even against her for their father's sake. But there was nothing of all this. They submitted almost without a struggle, though they did not understand.

And then the quiet days closed down upon this family, upon which so mysterious a loss had fallen. It need not be said that there was great discussion as to the cause of Mr Lycett-Landon's disappearance, both among the merchants in Liverpool and among their wives and daughters on the other side of the water. The explanations that were given at first were many and conflicting; and for a long time people continued to ask, "When do you expect your husband?" or "your father?" And then there came the time, not less painful, when people pointedly refrained from asking any questions, and changed the subject when his name was mentioned, which was, perhaps, almost less tolerable. Then, gradually, by degrees it became an old story, and people remembered it no more. Ah, yes! they remembered it whenever any incident happened in the family—when Horace took his place as one of the partners in the office, when Milly married—then it all cropped up again, with supposititious details; but when nothing was happening to them the family escaped into obscurity, and their circumstances were discussed no longer. Old Mr Fareham had a very bad cold after he returned from London, and was for some time confined to the house, and would see nobody. And then other things happened, as they are continually happening in a mercantile community. A great bankruptcy, with many exciting and disgraceful circumstances, followed soon after, and the attention of the community was distracted. The Lycett-Landon business remained a mystery, and after a while the waters closed tranquilly over the spot where this strange shipwreck had been.

Milly never heard till after her marriage what it was that had happened, and at no time did Horace ask any questions: how much he divined, how much he had been told, his mother never knew. And she herself never was aware how the other story ended: if the poor Rose, her husband's unfortunate young wife, died of it, or if she abandoned him; or if the poor mother lacked the courage to tell her; or if between them the young woman was kept in her poor little suburban paradise deceived. Mrs Lycett-Landon made many a furtive effort to ascertain how it had ended; but she was too proud to inquire openly, and though she wondered and pondered she never knew.

Years, however, after these events, when Horace had begun to be what he had determined upon being, a merchant prince, and the house of Lycett-Landon & Co. (old Mr Fareham being dead, and young Mr Fareham at the head of the American branch, Landon, Fareham, & Co.) was greater than ever, Mr Lycett-Landon suddenly appeared at the Grove. He came to make a call in the morning, sending in his name; for the old butler was dead, and the new one did not know him, and he was admitted like any other stranger. His wife even did not know who he was—for she had come down expecting a distant relation—until she had looked a second or third time at the stout, embarrassed old gentleman, looking very awkward and deprecating, who stood up when she came into the room, and shrank with a certain confusion from her inspection. After the first shock of the recognition they sat down and conversed calmly enough. He inquired about the children with a little affectation of ease.

"I know about Horace, of course," he said, "and I saw Milly's marriage in the papers. But I should like to hear a little about the others."

She accepted his curiosity as very natural, and gave him all the particulars very openly and sedately. He sat for nearly an hour, sometimes asking questions, sometimes listening, with a curious air of politeness, like a man on his best behaviour, in the society of a lady a little above him in station, and with whom his acquaintance was far from intimate, and then took his leave.

With what thoughts their minds were full as they sat there, in the old home equally familiar to both, where every article of furniture, every picture on the walls, had the same associations to both! But nothing was said to betray the poignant sensation with which the woman, compunctious, though she had never been revengeful, or the man, so strangely separated and fallen from all that had been habitual to him, beheld each other, sat by each other, after these years. He smiled, but she had not the strength to smile. After this, however, he came again at intervals, always asking with interest about his children, but not caring to see them.

"I suppose they don't remember anything about me," he said.

His visits were not frequent, but he became, in the end, acquainted with all the family, and even resumed a certain intercourse with Horace and Milly, his first meeting with whom was accidental and very painful. To see him elderly, stout, and (but perhaps this was one effect of some refinement of jealous and wounded feeling on the part of Mrs Lycett-Landon) oh so commonplace! and fallen from his natural level, shuffling his feet, reddening, smiling that confused and foolish smile, conciliating his children, gave to his wife almost the keenest pangs she had yet suffered. She could not bear to see him so lowered from his natural place. Tragedy is terrible, but when it drops into tragi-comedy, tragi-farce at the end, that is the most terrible of all. Pity, shame, something that was like remorse, though she was blameless, was in his wife's heart. The impulse in her mind was to go away out of the house that was his, and leave him in possession. But, to do him justice, he never, by look or word, reminded her that the house had been his, or that he was anything but a visitor.

And what was the explanation of the strange passion which made him, at fifty, depart from all the traditions of his virtuous life—whether it was a passion at all, or only some wonderful, terrible gust of impatience, which made duty and the rule of circumstances, and all that he was pledged and bound to, insupportable—she never knew; nor whether he found that this poor game was even for a moment worth the blazing flambeau of revolution which it cost; or whether it cost him still more than that candle—the young life which he had blighted; whether Rose lived or died; or where he came from when he paid these visits to his old home, and disappeared into when they were over: all this Mrs Lycett-Landon lived in ignorance of, and so, in all probability, will die.

MADEMOISELLE

CHAPTER I

She was not altogether French, notwithstanding her name: indeed her nationality was the most dubious thing in the world, unless any assault was made upon either of the countries to which she owed her parentage. She had a way of thus becoming intensely English at a moment's notice, and intensely French the next—the latter, perhaps, with still greater warmth than the former, as became the constitutional difference between French and English. She was a woman in the full flower and prime of life—that is, approaching thirty-five: a period, however, at which few people will acknowledge a woman's prime to be. According to the vulgar notion, indeed, beauty has begun to fade at this period, when it ought to be in fullest, gorgeous flower. There are some liberal minds which will confess that a woman who is married is in all her magnificence at this age; but for those who are unmarried it is always, in England at least, considered a time of decadence. Thirty-five means fading—the state of the *délaissée*— the condition of the old maid. Mademoiselle had come to this age. She had been a governess for a great part of her life, since she was twenty: fifteen long years, but it seemed a hundred as she looked back upon it. She had developed in that time from a raw girl—weeping passionate tears over a great many things which she scarcely noticed now, feeling herself abandoned, miserable, left in the background, left out of everything, humiliated in her unaccustomed position, injured by life and all that happened to her—into a rational, calm woman, who had made up her mind to the path she was compelled by necessity to tread, and had acquired a dignity of her own which no little slights or scorn could touch. The number of people who are absolutely unkind to their governesses and dependents is small, and yet it can scarcely be, except in very exceptional cases, a comfortable position. To be as good as, or perhaps better than, your employers and superiors—as good and yet so very much worse; to live in a house, and yet not to belong to it; to sit alone and hear the echoes of life going on all round—sounds of voices, of doors opening and shutting, of people coming and going, which you cannot help hearing, and yet have nothing to do with; to be contented and independent alone, not showing too much sympathy nor too much zeal, interfering with nothing, making no remark,—can anything be more difficult? A woman can scarcely do this without deteriorating in some way; and there is a state of mind which is born of the condition—its most common development—a state in which the faculties are on the alert to interpret all the echoes, to catch at every whisper, to make out everything that is concealed or under the surface. The back-stairs at Court do not afford an edifying sphere of study, but still there are notable persons coming and going, and a faint reflection of history in their chance words and looks. But the back-stairs in an ordinary house, in Belgravia, in Bloomsbury, in the suburban villas, are so much less elevating that there is nothing notable or historical in them. And yet how can a woman, all alone in a schoolroom, keep from hearing what floats upward, keep from that curiosity which all human creatures share, in respect to the people whom she is meeting every day? The pitiful little records that form the chief interest of so many starved and impoverished lives afford often one of the saddest spectacles in existence. And the woman who is able to resist this tendency runs the risk of growing stoical, cynical, harsh, and contemptuous. A girl may go through a few years of it without suffering. If she is happy at the end, and is able to live her own life, she forgets the difficulties of the probation, and probably the strongest feeling in her mind is the sense of being neglected, justly or unjustly, which is very bitter yet evanescent. But a woman who goes on with it for life has a hard lot.

Mademoiselle had carried on this profession for fifteen years, and she had no prospect but to continue it all her life. It had developed in her a sort of self-denied and reserved quietude, which was strangely out of accord with the natural vivacity which she had inherited from her French father, and which all the subduing influence of an English mother had not brought under. A foreign governess is so much worse than a native that she has not even possession of an independent and distinctive name. Miss Smith or Miss Jones is better off than the impersonal Mademoiselle or Fräulein, whose title is generic and official, to be transferred to her successor with an indifference to any individuality in it which, were it not the mere growth of unthinking custom, would be brutal. Perhaps the ladies thus officially addressed do not, among their many grievances, count this; but the special personage of whom we speak, who was in her soul a very proud woman, and possessed, as it happened, a *beau nom*, a fine, and ancient, and high-sounding name, did feel it, though she was one who never owned to any grievances, nor showed her dislike of any of the peculiar methods of English politeness in dealing with governesses. Her name was De Castel-Sombre, an old name of Béarn, from whence her family came: but her father had been the last of his branch of the house, and had fallen off from its spirit by becoming an artist, which, as he had no money to begin with, had cut him off entirely from the favour of the noble cousins who might have helped him on had he been without tastes of his own. Mademoiselle's pride, therefore, was purely visionary, and had nothing vulgar embodied in it. It was the refuge of a high mind, longing for everything that was excellent, yet attached by straitest bonds of necessity to the common soil. When Monsieur de Castel-Sombre died he left his wife with scarcely any money, two girls, and a number of unsold pictures, for which nobody cared. Naturally, at that moment these women believed that he was one of the greatest of unappreciated painters, and that it was the cruelty and envy of the world which had deprived him of the fame which was due to him. At least Madame de Castel-Sombre clung to this belief, which her daughters held hotly until experience taught them better. Mademoiselle (she had really a Christian name also of her very own, and was called in her family Claire) knew now as well as any one that these cherished pictures, with which her mother's little rooms were darkly hung, were of small merit, and that there was nothing at all remarkable in the fact that they had not found anybody to buy them; but that, too, was a discovery which it took time and experience to make.

Thus she had come through a great many illusions, and discovered the falsehood of them before the time at which our story begins. She no longer felt that she was left out of life when the family in which she lived received company or returned their visits. She no longer believed that it was intended as a slight to her, or neglect of her, when she was left behind, but perceived that it was the commonest necessary arrangement, a thing which she herself approved. Instead of being always offended, always conscious of injury, she perceived now all the difficulty of circumstances, and that the presence of a stranger in the house was often as great an inconvenience to the people of the house as it was a humiliation to the governess. She learned to look upon the circumstances in general with those "larger, other eyes" which the poet has attributed to the dead. In one sense Mademoiselle felt that she was dead. She had died to, or rather had outlived, many things in which the chief charm of life seemed once to lie. She no longer expected, as young people do, that life would change sooner or later, and that one time or another she should have what she wanted. This is an illusion that some people pursue as long as they live, and which even age does not cure. "Hope springs eternal in the human breast." They think, however unlikely, that it is not possible but things must improve, and the good they desire come to them before they die. Mademoiselle had got over that. She expected nothing but to go on as she was doing for the rest of her life. It was not, perhaps, an exhilarating prospect. She had thought it over in every way, but she could not make anything better of it. She had thought of taking up a school, which was the highest possibility in the future of a governess, and getting her mother under the same roof, and her sister to help. But to set up a school required capital, and Mademoiselle had none. She had a little—a very little—laid by in case of illness, or to bury her if she died, which is a forlorn provision often made by lonely proud women, who even in death would be indebted to no one; but to furnish a house and live till pupils came would require what would have appeared a fortune to Mademoiselle—a thousand pounds, or something of that sort. As well say a million at once. She had learned, among her many experiences, that to rise to the height of independence like that it was necessary to begin on a large scale—to have a good house, and gardens, and servants, and pretensions. The little bit of a house in a little street, with half-a-dozen little daily pupils drawn from the neighbourhood, meant beggary and misery and endless struggles. When the time should come that the mother wanted her children's care and tendance, and could not be left alone, then it might come to that; but a mother who was only sixty, and full of activity, required no such sacrifice. Therefore Mademoiselle had arrived at the conviction that there was no change to be expected in the tenor of existence—no change for the better—nothing but decadence and downfall. When the present pupils grew up she would go on to another family. She would have little difficulty in finding another situation. It gets very speedily known in any profession what people are worth, and she would find another place easily enough; but she would be older, and when another change came older still. By the time she was fifty she would have finished her present pupils, and probably another set, and then she would be old, and the young mothers of growing girls would not care to have her. They would fear that she would not be strong enough, that she would be unable to take the walks that were necessary, and to be up sufficiently early in the morning. They would be alarmed lest she should fall ill on their hands. She looked forward, seeing this prospect very clearly before her, not deceiving herself, thinking it all over with a sort of cheerful despair. She kept cheerful—for what good would it do her to be gloomy?—and it was altogether foreign to her temper, in which there was a natural horror of dulness and monotony, and an elasticity which astonished even herself; but yet, no doubt, the outlook was one of despair: to labour on, always with a kind of personal luxury, living and lodging more or less as people who are very well off lodge and live, yet with so little money—money which, when she sent a share to her mother, and looked to her modest, serious wardrobe, her dark gowns, which were so thrifty, and lasted for ever, left so little over—sometimes a few pounds, sometimes only shillings! Great is the power of saving, as we have all heard, and many littles make a mickle, the proverb says; but you may think how slow a process saving is when all that it permits to be laid by is, perhaps, ten pounds a-year. In ten years a hundred pounds! which was a great comfort, and made her feel that she might have a long illness and die of it, and be laid in the bosom of the mother-earth without being indebted to anybody—a consolation unspeakable; but yet, when you come to think of it, one which means despair, though always a cheerful despair. Alas! no chance of ever getting a Rosebank, a Sunnyside, a dignified mansion that would pay, for such a sum as that: it would, however, be enough for the expenses of a last illness (if not too long), and of her burial after, which was a great relief to think of, and gave her the power of looking without fear in the face of fate.

Mademoiselle was at present in the family of Mr Leicester Wargrave, who was in the City, but who lived in an old-fashioned house in the Bayswater district—a house with beautiful rooms and a delightful garden, though not within the lines of fashion. He was the junior partner in the business to which he belonged, a rising man making a great deal of money, but also with many demands upon him in the shape of a large family and a hospitable, cheerful disposition, which his wife shared fully. They both liked to see their friends, to have their house full, to enjoy their life. Though Mrs Leicester Wargrave was in the habit of declaring with some ostentation that she and her husband were quite outside the fashionable world, yet they loved to entertain people from Belgravia, to show their fine rooms, their beautiful old-fashioned decorations, their large shady garden—a thing so unusual in London. "We don't pretend to be fashionable, but we have something to show for ourselves," said the lady, who was fond of asserting that she was nothing but a City lady; "City people, *pur et simple*"—people with no pretensions to be anything better. There are many ways in which pride shows itself, and this mock humility was one of these ways. Mrs Wargrave had a number of vanities, though she was, on the whole, a nice woman. She liked to speak French with the governess in the presence of people not, perhaps, quite conversant with any language but their own, which is so often the case in the best society; and she liked to say that her governess was "a great swell—far finer, you know, than anything we can pretend to—a *fille de Croisé*, and that sort of thing." But if there was one thing more than another of which she was proud, it was the influence which she allowed she had over her cousin-in-law, the head of the firm, who was a bachelor, a man about town, a fashionable person. "I don't know, I'm sure, what he sees to make such a fuss about in us," Mrs Leicester Wargrave said; "I suppose ours is the only house, poor fellow, in which he finds real family life. There is nothing he wouldn't do for me. Leicester and he have always been like brothers, but my husband says I can do more with Charlie than he can. I don't think myself that he will ever marry. I know as a fact that many and many a set has been made at him, but he only comes and tells me and laughs over it. He had a disappointment, you know, in early life, before he settled to the business. Oh, he has not settled much to it now. He came in in his father's place, which makes him nominally the head; but my husband is really the first working partner. *He* is not too fine for City life. It is a little absurd, isn't it, that a man who never does anything should get the lion's share, and the real workers come off second best?"

"It is a question of capital, I suppose," said the friend to whom she was telling this story of the family fortunes.

"Oh, to be sure! he has the capital which the old gentleman worked for, so now he doesn't require to do much, and everybody toils for him. But I don't think he will ever marry—all his habits are against it. And he says why should he, when we have been so kind as to provide an heir for him as well as a home? He refers to little Charles, of course. You may imagine I don't build much on what a young man like that says; but I really don't, myself, believe he will ever marry. He is too happy with us here."

"He is very young to come to such a decision," was the remark of the listener, whose private opinion was that Mrs Leicester Wargrave was far too self-important, and ought to be taken down.

"Oh, yes, not much over thirty. Of course it's ridiculous: but I have my own ways of knowing, and you'll see it'll come true."

Whether Mrs Leicester Wargrave believed that a hopeless platonic attachment for herself lay at the bottom of Mr Charles Wargrave's determined celibacy it would be difficult to say. She was certainly very proud of his devotion to her, of the dutiful way he appeared at all her parties, and the familiar manner in which he haunted her house. It was a very pleasant house, unlike other London houses, in the depths of the quaint little square of which it formed one side—with its great wide staircase showing a sublime disregard of space, its stuccoed roofs and walls, fine garlands of delicate white against a pale green not quite so faded as the last novelty of asceticism, though a hundred and fifty years old, and its windows opening upon a genuine garden—a garden in which you could lose yourself, in which there were shady walks and great trees, in which it was impossible to believe that at the other side of the house omnibuses were standing, and that a hansom could be called to the door by a whistle almost at any hour of the night or day. This gave it a quaint and paradoxical character, adding a charm to the large pleasant rooms, which were not shrouded in curtains and blinds as London houses usually are, but saw clear sky out of every window—clear sky and waving trees. And Mrs Leicester Wargrave had a choice of very good society, mixed and more original than is usual. She had a number of law people, a few who were simply society people, an occasional literary person, and a certain contingent from the City. The City makes a good mixture when it is carefully done. It brings in the practical, it brings a kind of intelligence always entertaining to the other classes, and a kind of prejudice and narrowness all its own, which is, as people say, "full of character" and amusing to the enlightened. This sort of thing is, perhaps, more practicable in Bayswater than it is in Belgravia. Need less to say that Mrs Leicester Wargrave cultivated relations also in the world of artists, meaning the musical and dramatic professions, especially the former, for it was necessary to amuse her guests. An Academician now and then is a feather in one's cap, but it is not exactly amusing. This, however, was the society which Charles Wargrave found sufficiently agreeable to bring him across the Park whenever his cousin's wife held up her little finger. He thought it more amusing than anything he found in Mayfair or St James's. I do not suppose he was fortunate enough to be anything but an occasional guest in the very greatest houses of all, which are the Elysian fields of society.

Such were the assemblies which Mademoiselle heard arriving and departing as she sat up-stairs in the schoolroom, thinking her own thoughts or reading her book. Sometimes she was invited to be one of the guests; more often she was not wanted or was forgotten. She kept up on the outside a serene indifference, and really believed that she did not at all care one way or the other. As a matter of fact, some remnant of the old passionate sense of being left out would occasionally revive in her mind; but, on the other hand, Claire de Castel-Sombre did not like to be introduced to strangers as "Mademoiselle," so that there was a good deal to be said on both sides.

–

CHAPTER II

One summer evening Mademoiselle was seated in her schoolroom as usual, which was a very pretty room though at the top of the house, a room with a balcony overlooking the garden, and refreshed by all the air which was kept up by the fanning of the trees and the open space. It was covered with fresh cool matting, and lighted by a reading-lamp, which scarcely added to the heat, and diffused a mild light. The large window was wide open. The balcony with its seats seemed to form part of the room, and Mademoiselle had put herself into a white dressing-gown. The children were in bed, and a grateful stillness filled this part of the house. The rest, the quiet, and the coolness were very refreshing after the intolerable heat and noise of the day. There had been a dinner-party down-stairs, and, as usual, the carriages coming and going had been heard in the schoolroom. The children had brought up a description, as they generally did, of the splendour of the ladies, for they had been in the drawing-room in all their finery when the guests arrived. Mademoiselle had listened to their remarks and criticisms, but she had not regretted her own absence. She had accomplished all her little tasks after Edith and Dorothy had gone to bed—corrected their exercises, looked over their lessons for next day—and then she had put on her dressing-gown, and concluded to put off certain mendings that were necessary till next evening, as it was so hot, and had taken up her book.

She was thus seated in great luxury when the sound of some one running and stumbling up-stairs startled her—evidently a maid in great haste, her foot catching in her gown. She put down her book and listened, feeling that she was about to be called upon for some service. Then came a hurried knocking and a cry of "Mademoiselle!" "Oh, if you please, come down-stairs; Mrs Wargrave has gone off quite dead-like, and they don't know what to do. O Mademoiselle, come quick, for the gentlemen is off their heads," cried the messenger, continuing in her excitement to drum against the door. Mademoiselle sprang up, and only pausing to take a bottle of eau-de-cologne and a fan from a table, hurried down-stairs. "It will be a faint," she said. "I don't know what it is, but she looks like death," said the maid. The governess had forgotten her dressing-gown, her loosened hair, her aspect altogether informal and out of character with her position.

She rushed into the drawing-room to find Mrs Wargrave lying on the floor, her husband slapping her hands and calling to her, half in fright, half in anger, "Marian, Marian! wake up; what's the matter? Wake up, dear!" Charles Wargrave had gone to fetch some water, and came in with it ready to discharge it upon the head of the poor lady. When something white descended between them, shedding odours of some perfume and raising a sudden air with the fan, the two men were more startled than ever. Neither of them had ever had to do with a woman in a faint before.

"It will be nothing," said Mademoiselle. "She has fainted. It is the great heat. She has not been well all day." She took the command of the situation quite simply, taking the water from Charles Wargrave's hand without even looking at him, and sending the aggrieved husband out of the way. The men ran about quite humbly, obeying the orders of Mademoiselle, who knew what to do, setting the door open to make a draught, bringing cushions, doing everything she told them. It is doubtful for the moment whether even Mr Leicester Wargrave, though he was her employer, said good morning to her every day at breakfast, and gave her a cheque every quarter, was at all clear as to who she was; and Mr Charles Wargrave did not know her at all. She did not look like Mademoiselle, a mere official without any name of her own. In her loose white dressing-gown, her hair falling out of its very insecure fastenings, her mind entirely occupied with her patient, she looked like one of those beings whom men call angels, when they come in unexpectedly and save a great deal of trouble. This was the position which Mademoiselle had suddenly taken. They had been about to send for the doctor, to do all sorts of desperate things. Mademoiselle in a moment took everything out of their hands.

By-and-by, when Mrs Wargrave had recovered consciousness, the white figure with the falling hair disappeared as suddenly as she had come. When the lady came to herself she had looked up and asked, "What is the matter? Where am I?" and then she had breathed out with a faint vexation, "Oh, is it you, Mademoiselle?"

"She ought to go to bed," said Mademoiselle to the husband.

"I feel as if I had been ill," said Mrs Wargrave. "Where am I? Where is Jervis? I want Jervis. O Jervis, send these gentlemen away and let me get to bed."

Mademoiselle had disappeared. She had slightly shrugged her shoulders with a gesture which was not British; and suddenly, no one knew how, had stolen away. To have her services of kindness so repulsed and the maid called for—the maid who had been too frightened to do or think of anything while her mistress lay insensible—was painful enough. No, she said to herself, not painful—nothing so tragic—only disagreeable; for, after all, it was not gratitude nor tenderness which she looked for from Mrs Wargrave. She had not done any great thing—only the most common good offices of one human creature to another. Why should Mrs Wargrave be grateful? And, naturally, she liked the services of her maid, to whom she was used, best. There was nothing in it to resent, nothing to be pained by. And just then Mademoiselle had caught sight of herself with the white dressing-gown and her hair hanging loose, in the great dim mirror between the windows, and this had so quickened the effect upon her of Mrs Wargrave's cry for Jervis that in a moment she was gone. She flew up-stairs like an arrow from the bow. She was horrified by the sudden sight of her own negligent apparel, of which till now, in the necessity of the moment, she had not thought.

When Mademoiselle arrived again in the shelter of the cool schoolroom, with its windows open to the night and its mild lamp burning steadily, she was panting with the haste and slight excitement of the moment, and still more with her hurried rush up-stairs; but she was not excited in any other way, and she would have laughed, or, at least, smiled to scorn the idea that anything had happened in those few minutes which could in any way affect her life. Nevertheless, she was a little struck by the sight of herself which suddenly appeared to her in the glass which was over the mantelpiece of the schoolroom, straight in front of her, as she came hurriedly in. The white figure seemed to fill the mirror with light. Her hair had not got completely detached, but hung loosely, forming a sort of frame round her face, which, naturally pale, had now a slight rose-flush; and her eyes, generally so quiet, were shining with the commotion produced in her physical being by the accelerated throbbing of her heart and pulses—due, as much as anything else, to her rapid flight, first down- and then up-stairs. Everything had passed in the course of a few minutes; and, of course, the hasty movement, the momentary thrill of alarm and anxiety, had made her heart beat; but it was curious that it should have produced the change in her appearance which she could not but perceive as she caught the reflection of her own face in the glass. She half laughed to herself with amusement and surprise, and no doubt a little pleasure too. She looked (she thought) as she had done when she was a girl of twenty. The reflection passed through her mind that white was very becoming, *très flatteur*. It is not *flatteur* to everybody, but it certainly was to Mademoiselle. She laughed to herself at the young, bright figure which she saw in the glass, and then shook her head with a sort of amused melancholy. No, Claire! no white gowns for you to make you look young and fair. Why should you look young and fair, not being either? White dresses, like other illusory pleasures, are not adapted for a governess of thirty-five. With this thought she shook back those loose locks, thrusting them behind her ears. Many people have grey hair at her age, but not a thread of white was in that dark-brown *chevelure*, which was so abundant and vigorous. Mademoiselle had always been a little proud of her hair—a small and innocent vanity. She pushed it away, and sat down again to her book, which, somehow, did not arrest her attention after that very brief, very insignificant episode. Mrs Leicester Wargrave was a pretty woman in her way. As she lay on the floor in her faint, Mademoiselle had admired her straight features, her fine shoulders, partially uncovered, the dazzling whiteness of her complexion. She was a year or two older than the governess, but her circumstances were very different. She had a devoted husband, nice children, a beautiful house, plenty of money. Why did she faint, *par exemple*? This question, however, did not produce in Mademoiselle any conjectures of mystery or mental trouble. She concluded, more sensibly and practically, that it was the heat, the thunder in the air, or that something had gone wrong in the unromantic regions of the stomach. Faints come from these reasons rather than from the non-ethereal causes to which they are attributed in dramatic art. If it is true that men die and worms eat them, but not for love, it is also true that women faint, in most cases, from anything but mental trouble. Mademoiselle did not attempt to hunt out any mystery. She did not dwell upon the enormous difference between the woman to whom she had just been ministering, and who did not want her ministrations, and herself. With one of those exercises of the philosophy of experience which were habitual to her, she said to herself that nobody would willingly change their own identity for that of another, however much they might like the advantages belonging to the other, and that she herself would certainly rather be Claire de Castel-Sombre than Mrs Leicester Wargrave: though she added also to herself that this, too, was a delusion, and that there was nothing so delightful in Claire de Castel-Sombre that a reasonable mind should prefer her personality in this decided way. However, Mademoiselle was wise enough to see that there was little progress to be made by entering into the region of metaphysics in this way; so that, with a smile at herself, she returned to her book in earnest, and found the thread of interest in it again. The one result which remained from the incident of the evening was a sensation of pleasure, at which she mocked, but which was quite real, in her own momentary return to her youthful brilliancy—a sensation expressed in the passing reflection that white was *très flatteur*, and that she was not too old to look well in it, but yet— —

"Who is the angel and minister of grace that you keep in your house, ready for any emergency?" said Mr Charles Wargrave to his cousin, when the mistress of the house had been transported to her room and left in the care of her maid.

"Eh?" said Mr Leicester Wargrave, dully; but his mind was occupied with other questions. "I wonder what made my wife faint?" he said; "there was nothing in what we were talking of that could have made her faint." He was of the romantic opinion that mental shocks were the causes of such disturbances, and not the weather or the digestive organs. He had not the least suspicion or jealousy of his wife, but he was a man of some temper, and took such a performance as more or less an offence to himself.

"I have no doubt it was the heat."

"Oh, the heat! in this cool room? And why to-night, specially? It has been as hot for the last three days."

"I suppose that having borne it for three days would make one all the more likely to succumb on the fourth," said Charlie.

Leicester Wargrave shook his head. "Suppose we had been out," he said; "suppose it had been in somebody else's house. What a nuisance it would have been—making everybody talk! I shall have to speak to Marian seriously——"

"You don't suppose she fainted to annoy you?" said Charles.

"Oh, you never can tell what a woman will do," said the husband. "If I could only remember what we were talking of when she went off in that ridiculous way——"

"We were talking of nothing of the least importance, Leicester."

"Ah, you don't know. A wife's a great comfort in some circumstances, I don't deny, and Marian's a good wife; still, there's nobody can make a man look so ridiculous—when she chooses."

"Poor Marian! It must have been very unpleasant for herself: she couldn't have done it on purpose, you know."

"You can never tell," said the aggrieved master of the house. He looked so rueful and so annoyed that the young man burst into a laugh. He was aware that his cousin was prone to blame some one for every accident that occurred, but it seemed a new way of dealing with a fainting-fit. After a minute of silence, during which Leicester Wargrave kept walking up and down the room in an impatient way, Charles repeated his previous question. "I say, old fellow, who was the angelic being in white?"

"Eh?" said the other again, with half attention; then he added angrily, "Don't be such a fool—the angelic being was simply Mademoiselle."

"Mademoiselle! the governess? That's nonsense, Leicester."

"What is nonsense? I hope I know as much as that: and there is no doubt about it. She was in a nightgown, or something; that woman Jervis, who is good for nothing, fetched her, I suppose. I'll tell Marian to send that useless fool away. She's no good."

"Mademoiselle," said Charlie, "the governess? I thought she was a dowdy, elderly person—but this one was a beautiful girl. Are you sure you are not making a mistake?"

"Girl!" said Mr Leicester Wargrave; "she's nearer forty than thirty. She's not a bad-looking woman—there's a good deal in her: I've often said as much to Marian. But Marian says she's very French—though that's what we have her for, I suppose."

"I don't mind what country she is of. She's——" But here Charles Wargrave seemed to check himself, and said no more.

"You—don't mind? No, I don't suppose so. Between ourselves, I don't see what you've got to do with it," said Leicester, with a laugh.

Charles, who had been sitting with his hands in his pockets, thrust deeply down, and his head bent as if in deep consideration, here roused himself a little, and gave his head a shake as if to chase some cobwebs away. "No," he said, after a moment's pause, "I don't suppose I have got anything to do with it—as you say."

This being granted, and his grievance in respect to his wife's faint beginning to subside a little, Mr Wargrave unbent. "Yes," he said, "I noticed she looked very well to-night. She had a little colour; that's the drawback of Frenchwomen, they have so little colour—except what they put on themselves, don't you know."

The two men laughed at this, though it was not very funny. "By Jove! they do make up!" said the elder. "There's plenty of that in the Park, but still Englishwomen have complexions. The French like it—they talk of *blanc mat*, though there's not much *blanc* either, by nature, any more than red—except what's put on."

The joke failed the second time, and did not even elicit a smile from Charlie Wargrave, who sat with a perfectly grave face staring straight before him and swinging his leg. He was seated on the arm of a sofa—not the legitimate part to sit upon—and either he did not care to discuss the charms of Frenchwomen or he was fatigued by the discussion. He got up suddenly and held out his hand.

"You want to get up-stairs, I'm sure, to see after Marian. I think I'd better go."

"Oh, don't hurry yourself, Charlie. I could go up and come back to you again if I was so anxious as that."

"Anyhow, I must go, it's getting late," said the visitor, getting up. He paused a moment, as if he were trying to recall something as he stood in the middle of the room, where his cousin's wife had lain fainting with Mademoiselle bending over her. To think that it was only Mademoiselle! He felt a sort of dazzle in his eyes, not thinking, as she had done, that white was becoming, but wondering how it was that a sort of light seemed to diffuse itself from the white figure—healing and consolation. She had scarcely spoken at all; she had not so much as looked at him or taken any notice of his existence. She had taken the water out of his hands as if he had been a servant—more than that, as if he had been the table on which it stood—without looking at him. She had said "Get me a cushion" with the same non-recognition of him or his existence. And the moment that the necessity for her presence was over she had disappeared like a vision. It was curiously disappointing, tantalising, provoking to hear that she was only Mademoiselle. Charles Wargrave was not a man whom ladies generally—women much more imposing than any governess—passed over without notice. He reflected that of those he knew very few, even in a similar emergency, would have treated him with that calm and absolute indifference. There would have been a glance in recognition of the fact that he was he, never an unimportant person. There would have been something in the shape of a smile of thanks, or of apology. But this lady had taken no more notice of him than if he had been a wooden figure made to hold things in his hands, like the grinning negro candelabras of Venice. One would not say "thank you" to the painted and gilded blackamoors, and neither did she say "thank you" to him. He could think of no fitter image. As if he were made of wood! Charles Wargrave was not used to this sort of treatment. He laughed to himself softly at the thought of it—laughed, yet was piqued and a little rueful. And all the time it was only Mademoiselle!

CHAPTER III

Mrs Wargrave made next morning a very pretty little speech of mingled gratitude and apology to Mademoiselle. "I can't imagine," she said, "what made me so silly as to faint last night. It is a thing I've always been subject to, but it's always a stupid thing to do. I hear you were so good, coming down directly when Jervis lost her head, and doing everything that was kindest and best. I am so much obliged to you, Mademoiselle. Of course I was not conscious of what was going on, so I couldn't show you any gratitude then."

"De rien," said Mademoiselle, "à votre service, as my country-folk say."

"Your country-folk are always polite," said Mrs Wargrave, and then she laughed a little meaning laugh. "I hear the gentlemen were quite impressed by the sight of you in your dressing-gown."

Mademoiselle coloured a little. She had forgotten that reflection of hers that white was becoming, and only felt the horror of having been seen in *déshabillé*. "I did not stop to think," she said, "how I was dressed: and it was so hot. I had no idea that I should be called down-stairs."

"No, how could you? I shall not do anything so absurd again if I can help it. I have told that foolish creature Jervis what she ought to have done. Yes, I feel all right this morning, thanks. The heat was tremendous last night, there was not a breath of air, but this morning it's quite cool again. Don't let me delay the lessons. I only came to say again 'Thank you,' Mademoiselle."

"De rien," said Mademoiselle again. Edith and Dorothy were sitting very demurely all the time with their books quite ready, waiting to begin. They were two nice little girls, and they learned their lessons very creditably. Mademoiselle sat and heard their little dull, expressionless voices running on glibly enough, giving forth the knowledge of the schoolbooks, the information, cut and dry, which had nothing to say to any circumstance round them, and remained in its concrete state, never dissolved or assimilated as long as memory held out—and wondered to herself what was the good of it, and wherein these unexceptionable children were the better for the pills or stores of knowledge which they thus swallowed dutifully. But this was not a reflection to be followed, since it would go to the root of much that is called education, and drive many honest persons out of the occupation by which they made their living. It was Mademoiselle's vocation, as it is of so many other people more pretentious, head-masters and classical tutors, and all the high-priests of the schools, to superintend the swallowing of these pills, which might be digested or otherwise, as it pleased Providence. The brother of the little girls was disposing of many more such doses at Eton with much the same result. It is, however, perhaps rather a pity when the teachers of youth are disturbed by such thoughts. It is much better to believe entirely in the advantage of what one is doing, as some happy people do,—to believe that you are determining the character of children when you administer boluses of knowledge, and that it is for the eternal gain of your parishioners that they should go to hear you preach. Mademoiselle did not believe that the little girls in the nursery would be at all changed out of their natural bent by anything she could do—and this, perhaps, took something from the fervour of her teaching, though everybody said she was so conscientious. Perhaps the thing which Edith and Dorothy retained most clearly from the day's lessons was their mother's laugh and assertion that the gentlemen had been "so impressed" by the appearance of Mademoiselle in her dressing-gown. What gentlemen? and why were they impressed? and which was it, the white one or the blue one? These were questions in which they took more interest than in the Merovingians and the divisions of the Continent under Charlemagne. Mademoiselle herself took the reference as a little prick on the part of Mrs Wargrave—a reminder that even to succour the sick it is indiscreet and unladylike to come down-stairs in a dressing-gown, and she felt it was a reproof to which she had perhaps justly laid herself open. She resolved that, until she was certain that everybody was in bed, nothing should induce her to put on a dressing-gown again.

Mr Charles Wargrave, however, was moved by very different feelings. He could not get that white figure out of his head. Perhaps he was piqued to think that there was a woman, and she a dependant, who could look at him as if she did not see him, and take a thing from his hand without, so to speak, being conscious of his existence. He came in one day to luncheon without any warning, apologising for taking advantage of the invitation so often given him, and making a very lame explanation of how he had been passing through the Square and had heard the bell ring for the nursery dinner. He was made to sit down with the little fuss and commotion of laying a new place, at Mrs Wargrave's right hand, and then cast his eyes about with great anxiety to discover who was there. The sunblinds were down and the room in a sort of rosy twilight, shutting out as much of the light and heat as possible. But he recognised Mademoiselle at the other end of the table. She was in a dark dress, and her hair was more tidy than words could say. She sat with Dorothy at one side of her, paying more attention to the little girl's dinner than to anything else, taking a slight share in the conversation now and then, only enough not to be remarkable—a true governess, knowing her place, not taking too much upon herself, or asserting her right to be treated as one of the company. After luncheon she left the room immediately with a child on each side. It would be difficult to describe the disappointment with which Charles Wargrave looked after her, the curious revulsion of feeling that had taken place within him! He felt angry that such a person should have cheated him out of so many thoughts—a mere nobody—a person evidently quite suited to her circumstances, nothing but a governess. He gave himself a shake, and threw off the ridiculous impression which had been made upon him, he supposed, by the mere situation—the helpfulness of the woman, and the dress, which had produced a false air of gracefulness and youth. Youth! She was no doubt, as Marian said, five-and-thirty if she was a day—and not particularly handsome; a fine sort of *air noble* about her, a nice way of carrying herself—but that was all. What a fool he had been to be taken in so easily by appearances! He was obliged to confess to himself, however, that the deception was not Mademoiselle's doing—that she had no hand in it. She was a sensible person of middle age, devoted to her own duties, giving herself no airs. If he was taken in, it was entirely his own fault.

As for Mademoiselle, she knew as little that she had disappointed Charles Wargrave as she knew that she had excited his imagination. She thought nothing at all about it—did not try to look dowdy, or to limit her remarks to the most formal subjects, any more than she had tried to excite his interest. He was just the same to her as one of the pictures which Mr Leicester Wargrave called family portraits which hung on the walls.

However, the matter did not end there, though Charles Wargrave hoped it would. He went away from the Square feeling quite light, and released from a burden that had been weighing on him—for, to be sure, he had no desire to attach himself to a governess, however beautiful and charming she might be—and it was a real relief to find that he could shake off the visionary yoke, and that she was not either charming or beautiful. He left the house in the Square quite at his ease, saying to himself that it would be a joke indeed, after having passed harmless through all the snares which every man about town believes to be laid for him, should he fall a victim at last to the delusive angelic presence of old-fashioned poetry—

"When pain and anguish wring the brow,
A ministering angel thou."

That was all very well, and women were good sick-nurses in general, and Mademoiselle in particular might be very kind and ready, he made no doubt. It might be reasonable enough to fall subject to an angelic nurse who had ministered to yourself; but when it was only your cousin-in-law who was the object of the ministrations! He laughed, and said to himself that it was a good joke, as he went away, and shook off the recollection, which was a sort of hallucination, a deceptive effect of the lights, and the white dress, and the extreme consolation of having a woman in a faint taken off his hands. He had no doubt Mademoiselle was quite a superior article of her kind, a nice woman, and all that. He was glad he had seen her in her everyday garb, and convinced himself what a nice, commonplace, ordinary governess she was. He went out feeling quite emancipated and much pleased to have altogether regained his independence. Good heavens! what a business it would have been had he, acquainted with the finest women in London, fallen a victim to a governess! It was too ludicrous to be considered for a moment—and yet it was certainly an escape.

But next morning Mademoiselle, by some inexplicable caprice, had regained her unconscious ascendancy. The governess in the dark gown disappeared and the white figure came back. He could not get it out of his eyes. He said to himself that it was a mere vision, and had no existence at all, but all the same it haunted him, and he could not get it out of his mind. It was with an effort that he kept his feet from moving towards the Square. He felt that he must see her again and convince himself that she was merely the governess, a dowdy and elderly person, nothing at all like his imagination. It was with the utmost difficulty that, reasoning with himself, and pointing out the consequences that must result if he were to be seen constantly at his cousin's in the middle of the day when there was no occasion for his presence, he persuaded himself not to go again to luncheon till several days were past. The second time he appeared was on Sunday, when Mr Leicester Wargrave was at home, and his appearance more natural. But Mademoiselle was absent. He thought at first she was only late, and kept watching the door, expecting her to come in, and almost disposed to find fault, as an employer might have done, at her tardy appearance and want of punctuality. But the meal went on without remark from any one, and the governess did not appear. It was not till something was said about Mademoiselle that he, with his embarrassing consciousness of having come there to see her, and her alone, ventured to ask a question.

"Oh!—Mademoiselle! what has become of her?" he said at last.

"She has a friend she goes to on Sundays—not every Sunday, but a day now and then. It is a great loss for me," said Mrs Wargrave, "for there are so many people that call on Sunday afternoon, and I have the children on my hands."

Charles Wargrave received this explanation very unsympathetically. He relapsed into silence, not taking the trouble to make himself agreeable, and he took a long walk afterwards, during which his curiosity and interest grew higher and higher. He tried all the means in his power to put out of his mind this unwelcome visitor: for she was unwelcome. Of all people in the world, persons in her position were the least likely to occupy this man of fashion. He began to feel it something like a calamity that he had been present on that unlucky occasion when Marian was so silly as to faint. No more absurd seizure of the fancy had ever happened. What was Mademoiselle to him, or he to Mademoiselle? And yet the unlucky fellow could not get her out of his head.

About a week later he went to the Square in the afternoon, whether wishing to see her or wishing not to see her it was difficult to say. He was told that Mrs Wargrave had gone up to have tea with the young ladies in the schoolroom, but could be called at once. It was a wet day, and probably she expected nobody. "With the young ladies in the schoolroom?" he repeated; "is there any one else?"

"There's only Mademoiselle," said the butler—"the governess, sir."

Charles Wargrave felt disposed to knock the fellow down for his impertinence; he had scarcely patience to desire him to show the way. How dared he speak of a lady so—a lady better than any one in the house, the pampered menial? He made the man an impatient sign to get out of the way when they came to the top of the house to the schoolroom door, which was sufficiently pointed out by the sound of cheerful voices within. He knocked, smiling to himself at the little Babel of noise, two or three speaking together; and was bidden to come in by a voice with a faint little *parfum* of foreignness in its sound, so faint as to be only discernible by the sharpest ears. A sudden flush came to his face as he heard it. It was not a voice, he thought, like the others. It was full of sweetness and yet of power—a voice round and harmonious like the notes of an organ, with nothing shrill or thin or common in it; a voice which suddenly brought before him again, not the dowdy governess, but the white-robed ministering angel. He felt himself flush with pleasure and expectation as he opened the door.

Mademoiselle was sitting opposite pouring out the tea. She had her back to the light, and he saw her in a kind of relief against the large window—the shape of her head, her hair a little loosened, not quite smoothed upon her brow, in the shining perfection of the other day. He saw her face in a luminous shadow, clear yet dusky, her eyes looking down, somewhat deeply set, the oval of their form and the hollow under the eyebrow clearly defined. She had not perceived him, nor did she even look up to see who was coming in in obedience to her invitation. It was only when the children made a sudden pause in their chatter with a cry of, "O Uncle Charles!" that

Mademoiselle raised her eyes and stopped, with teapot in hand, to see who it was.

"Yes, it's me," he said, more cheerfully than grammatically. "I heard you were here, and I thought I'd ask Mademoiselle's permission to come in—and, perhaps, get a cup of tea——"

"Oh, come in, Charles," said Mrs Wargrave; "I'll answer for it you shall be welcome: we are all glad of anything to break the monotony of a long day."

Mademoiselle made no movement, gave no sign, except the faintest, scarcely perceptible bow of recognition. She found a clean cup for him and filled it with tea, calling one of her pupils to present it to him. She withdrew a little into the seclusion of her subordinate place while Mrs Wargrave took up the talk. It did not occur to the governess that she had anything to do with it. She had no great interest even in the visitor. The monotony of the long day was her natural atmosphere. She had no recognised need of anything to break it. Mrs Wargrave went on talking, and Mademoiselle heard and assisted now and then to keep the speakers going when she found that from the stranger, to whom the discourse was addressed, there was little response. And the children resumed their chatter *sotto voce*. As for Charles Wargrave, he sat still, saying very little, watching them all, but especially Mademoiselle, wondering how it was that such a woman could pass under a generic name, and bear, so far as the people around her were aware, no individuality at all. She withdrew from the centre of the scene, so to speak, in order to let the chief personages, Mrs Wargrave and her visitor, occupy it. Then, when it became necessary that there should be a response, or chorus, she disclosed herself by moments out of the background, just enough to keep up the action. He sat and watched them, watched her under his eyelids. Mrs Wargrave found Charlie more than usually taciturn, but felt that she was entertaining him—helping him to overcome his dulness, whatever might be the occasion of it. It never occurred to any one that he had another object, still less that his object could be in any way associated with Mademoiselle.

CHAPTER IV

It was not at once remarked in the Square that Mr Charles Wargrave had changed his habits in respect to his visits there,—that he came in the afternoon and at the hour of luncheon, and often declined invitations for the evening, which had previously been the time he generally spent with his cousins. This was partially accounted for, when it was noticed, by the reflection that during the height of the season the evenings of a young man who was to some extent a man of fashion and "went everywhere" were not his own. "He comes as much as he can," Mrs Leicester Wargrave said; "he comes when he can: of course he's full of evening engagements—three or four every night." She was, indeed, on the whole, pleased with the demonstrations of pleasure in her society, as she thought, which the young man showed. "He takes us just as he finds us. We have no inducements to offer him. He has such simple tastes. There is nothing he is so fond of as family life. He comes to me and the children just as if he were one of the family. Of course he is one of the family, but you would think he was either a son or a brother to see how that young fellow, to whom every smart house in London is open, comes and spends his afternoons with the children and me!" Mrs Wargrave was a little proud of the good influence which she felt she was exercising over her husband's cousin. He was becoming so domestic, so fond of home! He even sometimes met the children on their walks, and had taken them over to the Natural History place, and another time to the Kensington Museum. It was really too kind of him to think of the little girls.

During all this time, except on those two occasions when he had met the children, Charles Wargrave had not been able to secure any personal communication with Mademoiselle. She accompanied her charges with the greatest calm—a calm which was not at all complimentary to the young man who thus made himself her companion whether she would or not. She showed no signs whatever of embarrassment, or of supposing that his attentions might be misconstrued. If he had been eighty she could not have been more at her ease. And Edith and Dorothy had seized upon him on both sides, each clinging to an arm, which was not at all what he intended. He was so entirely discomfited, indeed, by the too much *empressement* of the little girls and the too little of Mademoiselle, that after these two accidental encounters he gave up attempting anything of the sort. However domestic he might be, it did not suit him to expound the Kensington Museum to Edith and Dorothy, each clinging to an arm. And was she made of stone, that woman? Was she made of vulcanite or some such impervious material, white to the sight but tough and unyielding to the touch? He was so much disgusted after that second expedition that he turned violently round upon himself and declared that he would have nothing more to say to Mademoiselle. What was Mademoiselle that she should exact such service? To be sure, it could not be said that she exacted any service; she smiled and ignored it with a perfect composure which was still more aggravating. And why should a man take all that trouble for a woman who took no notice, who never seemed to see anything, neither his civilities nor his impatience? He said to himself that it was in every way a mistake, that to pursue a person of that class was the height of folly, that to marry her would be madness itself. To marry a governess! a woman almost middle-aged, as Mrs Leicester Wargrave assured him so often—a foreigner—a nobody—above all, one who showed no appreciation of his attentions, and probably would not marry him! Oh, it was too much. He would break off at once and think of such folly no more.

This decision Charles Wargrave emphasised by going out of town for a whole week. But when he returned the first place he went to was the Square, just to see whether she was as composed as ever, he said to himself. As it happened it was in the afternoon, after the hour of luncheon and before that of tea, that he presented himself at Leicester Wargrave's house, and Mrs Wargrave was out. He paused a moment to think what he was to do; then, hearing the voices of the children, asked if they were in the garden.

"Yes, sir, with Mademoiselle," replied the servant.

"Then," said Charles, "I'll go out there, and you can let me know when your mistress comes in."

The garden was large and shady, and there was always something *banal* to say about the wonder of finding such a place in London, with omnibuses and hansom cabs on the other side of the house. He found Mademoiselle walking slowly round under the trees while the children played, and he felt sure that she gave a start when first she saw him—a quiver of astonishment and dismay. She might be dismayed and astonished for anything he cared. She might look all round for a way of escape; this time she should find none. Edith and Dorothy were in the middle of a game at tennis, and the governess was at some distance from them, taking a meditative walk. She was in a white dress, the first he had seen her wear since that night. It was a very still afternoon, the borders flaring with their late summer show of geraniums and all the foliage in full green, untouched as yet even by the heat and dust of London summers. He saw her before she saw him, walking along with her head bent a little, and an air of meditation and thought about her. She had a book in her hand, as if she had intended to read, but the soft stillness, the green shadiness, the warm, soft, drowsy air, had vanquished that intention. And then she perceived him and started with a slight glance round, as if she would have run away. No, no; not this time. He felt a kind of revengeful exultation in the suggestion of alarm which was in her startled movement. She was afraid then, after all her imperturbable airs!

It was, however, with the greatest composure that they met. She began at once to tell him how sorry she was that Mrs Wargrave was out.

"Oh, I can wait," he said; "I am in no hurry. She will come in by-and-by, no doubt."

"Not for some time, I fear," said Mademoiselle.

"Oh, I am in no hurry," he repeated, and, turning, walked with her. It was so sweet and still, and he found it so satisfactory to have at last got this impenetrable person to himself, with leisure to speak to her and nobody looking on, that for a time Charles Wargrave said nothing at all. It was pleasant to walk by her, to be conscious of the white figure by his side, so perfectly quiet and tranquil, not betraying by so much as a quiver of her dress anything of that alarm which he had divined in her at the first sight of him. For a minute or two he was quite satisfied with this; and it was to his surprise Mademoiselle herself who burst into those usual *banal* sentences about the strangeness of this garden in London, so secluded, so perfectly quiet, as if there was not a house or a vulgar sound within miles, while all the time the omnibuses were running, &c. He knew the words exactly, and had indeed meant to say them himself if other means of conversation failed.

"Yes," he said, "it is wonderful; but not so wonderful as some other things—for instance, to find you here, waiting upon the amusements of these two little——Mademoiselle, will you do me a favour?"

She looked up surprised—alarmed, too, this time, he felt sure—but said with a smile, "If it is anything in my power."

"It is quite in your power. It is very simple. Do you know that I have known you all this time without knowing you by anything else than the absurd official (if I may call it so) generic name of Mademoiselle?"

She coloured a little and laughed. "That is allright," she said, with one of the few slips she made in English, running the last two words into one. "It is an official title, and I am Mademoiselle. You would refuse to let an Englishwoman be called Miss, but with a Frenchwoman it is allright."

"I don't think it all right; I dislike it very much. Will you permit me the pleasure of being able to call you by your name?"

Mademoiselle paused a little. She was evidently doubtful which was the more dignified—debating between a reluctance to reply and a reluctance to permit it to be seen that she had any objection to reply. A denial, it appeared to her, might seem coquettish—a sort of challenge to a playful struggle. So she raised her head and answered, "I am Claire de Castel-Sombre," with the air of a queen.

"Ah," said Wargrave, "I thought as much. Is it out of pity for us as nobodies, with a name never heard of till our grandfathers went into business, that you have concealed, Mademoiselle de Castel-Sombre, *un si beau nom*?"

"I have not concealed it," she said with a smile. "Mrs Wargrave knows my name; but why waste breath upon so many syllables when Mademoiselle answers every purpose just as well?"

"That is a little scoff at us as industrials—not willing to waste anything, even our breath."

She shook her head. "I will not be tempted into an argument."

"No?" said Wargrave, changing rapidly from one language into the other. He knew French well, which is not too common with young men about town, and he was proportionately pleased with his own acquirement, and glad to note the little start of light and colour in Mademoiselle's face. "You are too proud to argue or even to assert the difference between an old noble name of Béarn and a common English one which, on the foundation of a little money, sets itself up as something, and condemns a woman like you, such a woman as you, to give up every attribute of real life and waste all your gifts and become an abstraction for the benefit of two——"

"Stop, stop!" she cried; "you are going a great deal too far. I am not compelled to anything. I am doing only what it is my business to do, in circumstances which are unusually comfortable and favourable. I do not know what can have put such an idea of my situation into your mind."

"It is very easy to explain that," he said. "My indignation has been growing since ever I made your acquaintance. As if you did not know very well that there is nobody in this house at all your equal, either in family and breeding—which are, perhaps, accidental advantages, for, of course, to have them you had only to give yourself the trouble of being born—but also in mind, in heart——"

She put up her hand to stop him. "Mr Wargrave, you are under some strange delusion. I am neither very clever nor very highly instructed, nor capable of anything above what I have to do. As for breeding, I was trained to be a governess as I am. Oblige me by giving up this subject, which can lead to nothing but misunderstanding. I possess nothing but that *beau nom* of which you form so great an idea. Of all visionary things to stand upon, is not birth the most visionary? Certainly it is so in my country: and ought to be still more in yours, which is so practical— —"

"Mine is not practical at all," said Wargrave; "that is one of the mistakes you make. You are far less affected by romantic reasons than we are. I have always thought so, and more than ever now."

She said nothing, but with a little movement of her hand seemed to wave his argument away. "These things are beyond discussion," she said.

"That may be; but you cannot imagine that one can look on and see such a sacrifice, and not earnestly protest against it?" Wargrave said.

Mademoiselle laughed—half pleased, half provoked. "You force me into a discussion," she said. "I don't know what to say to convince you that I am very well off, and desire no better. If I was not doing this, what should I do?"

She turned and looked him in the face as she put this question, half angry, half flattered, amused also at the young man's curious earnestness and excitement. The look was unexpected, and caught him full in the eyes. He made a hurried step backwards, and uttered an unconscious exclamation.

"There is nothing," she said, quickly—"nothing else that I could do. Do not disturb with such suggestions a woman working for her bread. One might have had other dreams when one was young. But life is very different from one's dreams. I am very well off; and there is nothing else that I could do."

"Yes," he said, drawing a long breath, "there is something else. I must say it—you could marry me."

She looked at him again with consternation, falling back a little, drawing away, her eyes opening wide with amazement, and made no answer for a moment. Then she said in a soothing tone, "Mr Wargrave, don't you think you had better go home?"

Charlie was piqued beyond measure by this speech. "I believe she thinks I am out of my mind," he said.

"It looked like it for a moment." She gave a little, low, uneasy laugh. "You have given me a great fright. Pray go in at least, and lie down upon the sofa till Mrs Wargrave comes in."

"Do you think me mad?" he said.

Her eyes dwelt upon his face with a serious doubt. "I think—the sun has been too much for you. Your head is a little confused, Mr Wargrave. Don't let us talk of it. I am quite sure that you did not mean to be rude."

"Rude!" he cried; "Mademoiselle de Castel-Sombre, you are very cruel to me; you wound me deeply. I made you a very serious proposition, and you treat me as if I were insane."

"Temporarily," she said. And at this moment there came an interruption unexpected on his part. The two little girls had finished their game, and they came with a rush, both together, upon Uncle Charlie, as they called him, pushing between him and Mademoiselle, and breaking up the situation in a moment. Edith and Dorothy seized him and clung to him, hanging one on each arm. "O Uncle Charlie, where have you been? What are you doing in the country? Why, everybody is in London at this time of the year."

"Ask this lady what I was doing—she knows," he replied, not without an effort to cast them off: but the children held fast.

"Ask Mademoiselle! How does Mademoiselle know? Was that what you were telling her in French? I didn't know you could speak French, Uncle Charles. O mamma! Here he is, and he's been here all the time waiting for us till the set was over and talking French to Mademoiselle."

"Well, I am sure I am very glad to see you, Charles. I hope you're better for your change," said Mrs Wargrave, sailing up to the group across the grass in all her finery. "And so you were talking French to Mademoiselle? Well, of course, I understand it, and read it and all that, but I'm not good at talking. Mademoiselle must have been quite pleased to have a chat in her own language. Come in; there's tea in the drawing-room, and it is cooler there than out of doors. Edith and Dorothy, don't hang on to your uncle so."

"Oh, he doesn't mind!" cried the children, hanging on more closely than ever. He was led in thus helpless to the cool drawing-room, unable even to gain a look from Mademoiselle. She fell back in her habitual way, leaving Mrs Wargrave to take her place. He was himself forced forward in advance when she dropped behind. And the last he saw of her was the sweep of her white dress across the grass as she went another way. He turned his head to look after her, but she did not vouchsafe him a glance. And the family loudly called for his attention, and dragged him over the sill of the great window which opened on to the lawn.

As for Mademoiselle, she went hastily up-stairs and reached the schoolroom almost at a flying pace; nor did she pause then, but went into her own room, which opened from it, shutting the door behind her. She was in great agitation, she who was always so calm. She tore her dress, stumbling and treading upon it as she made that breathless run up-stairs. Her breath came quick, and she turned the key in the door as if she were afraid of being pursued, which, of course, was nonsense. But Mademoiselle was not in a state of mind to weigh possibilities. The question was, what had happened to her? Had she been insulted, or had some new thing too strange to be comprehensible entered into her life?

CHAPTER V

Claire de Castel-Sombre reached her room in a condition of mind in which, though this was quite unusual, she forgot altogether that she was Mademoiselle and became herself, a woman of strong feelings, great personal pride, and a temperament impassioned and imperious rather than subdued and calm. It was subdued under the burden of all those necessities which made her natural impetuosity almost a crime, so out of place was it, and out of keeping with every circumstance around her; but such subjugation, being artificial, is always at the mercy of an emotion or an impulse too strong for manufactured bonds, and at this moment the natural flood had swelled beyond all restraint. Her usual paleness was flushed with angry colour. Her eyes shone, her whole figure thrilled with an excitement which was beyond all restraint. A curious consequence, one would suppose, of a proposal of marriage made by a young man considered eligible in every way in circles much more exacting than Mrs Leicester Wargrave's daughters or sister, much less her governess. But Claire was roused by emotions which would not have influenced these young ladies. It was not that there was anything in the English language which prevented her full understanding of what was said to her, or in the habits of Englishmen; but perhaps something of French breeding, and something of the involuntary depression and susceptibility which are fostered by such a position as hers, turned her from the natural interpretation of such an overture to a strained and false one. She thought that she had been insulted by a light proposal which meant nothing, which was not intended to mean anything, which was a sort of jibe and no more; and every sentiment in her mind, as well as every drop of blood in her veins, seemed to rise up again. "You might marry *me*;" it meant contempt, or suggestive of an impossible escape from the subdued state which, in the first place, it was insulting for any man to remark upon. A woman who does her duty in the position which her circumstances compel her to accept, whose pride lies in accepting those circumstances as not alone the only possible, but as the most natural and dignified, is not a woman to be insulted, she said to herself, passionately stamping her foot upon the floor in her paroxysm of wounded pride and feeling. In her usual condition Mademoiselle would have been bitterly ashamed of that stamp upon the floor. She was even now, in the fumes of her passion, and blushed for herself, clenching her hands, which was a noiseless operation, to stay in herself any possible repetition of that *bêtise*. All good feeling, all honour, all justice even, forbade that a woman should be jeered at for circumstances she could not help, circumstances which her strength lay in making the best of, in taking the sting out of by a dignified acceptance of them, in which there should be neither question nor assumption of injury, nor the pose of a person wronged. Above all things that pose of wrong was abhorrent to Claire. It went against her pride to acknowledge that she was in an inferior position, a dependant, and in the cold shade. Her pride had been to ignore all that, to define her place as clearly as possible, and make it fully comprehensible that it was the place which she chose and that pleased her best. To remark upon it at all, as Mr Charles Wargrave had done, even though in a way that was intended to be flattering, was very bad taste, to say the least; but to end these remarks by such a suggestion, by an offensive jest, was an insult in every sense of the word. Her blood boiled in her veins. She walked up and down the room to wear out as far as she could the exasperation that possessed her, not stamping her foot any more, which was a humiliating confession of weakness, but pacing up and down because she was incapable of keeping quiet. A woman who had always avoided any folly of so-called sensitiveness, who had accepted everything with a smiling face, never murmured, never taken offence, consented to be Mademoiselle, and to dignify the title by the perfect philosophy of her self-adaptation to it—and after all these years, after all these heroisms, after her proud self-denials and self-subjugation, to be thus insulted! a sneer flung full in her face, a dart of contempt to her heart! Mademoiselle felt as if that sneer had struck her like a blow. Her face burned with the smart of it: she had the sensation of the physical shock as well as of the rush of blood to the brain which is its result.

And there was this special smart in it, that she had been beginning to find in Charles Wargrave a friendly figure, a sympathetic look. He had not been so often in the schoolroom, so often at the luncheon-table, without exchanging now and then a word with herself which had made her feel that he was more akin to her than his relations were, more able to understand. The people under whose roof she had lived for a year had not the faintest beginning of understanding, nor were they likely to have it should she remain there for five years more, which was very likely if she continued to "give satisfaction." But he had looked at her now and then as if he recognised that she was an individual, and not merely Mademoiselle. He had asked her opinion on one or two subjects on which he and she were in accord against the other stolid couple whose point of view was so different. Mademoiselle had not been able to deny to herself—nay, had done so with serious pleasure—that she liked to see M. le Cousin; that he was one of the few people whose entrance was agreeable to her. The fact that he was young made no impression upon this well-trained stoic. She herself was old, she was on the level of men ten years her senior, according to a well-understood chronology current in society. There might not be, perhaps, much actual difference between them in point of years, but, according to this system, she was at least ten years in advance of her male contemporaries. It is difficult, perhaps, to know the reason why, but it is perfectly understood by everybody. She was "old enough to be his mother," and she had no feeling that it was otherwise. She regarded him as so completely out of her sphere, in character and in age, as well as in circumstances, that it had never occurred to the imagination of Claire that he and she should meet anywhere save as they sometimes did, on the ground of a mutual opinion, a common taste. But this was enough to make her feel that it was an outrage greater and more painful than usual, that scorn or insult should come from him.

There was a knock at the door while Claire had as yet scarcely regained any of her usual composure. "Please, Mademoiselle, mother wants to know if you're coming down for tea?"

She paused a moment to master herself, and then opened the door. "Not this afternoon, Edith. As you are going out with your mother I am going to begin my mending, do you see?" There were some garments laid out upon the bed that supported her plea. The little girl cast a glance upon the high colour, so unusual in her governess's cheeks, and ran off, with a vague sense of something which she did not understand.

"She's not coming; she's going to mend her things; and, oh! mamma, she's got such a red face, like she does when she's furious with us!"

"To hear these little monkeys," said Mrs Wargrave, "you would think Mademoiselle had the temper of a fiend. But she hasn't, Charlie; don't take up a false impression. She is really one of the best-tempered women I ever knew."

If any one had looked at Charles Wargrave at that moment it would have been seen that he had "a red face" too; but he said nothing, and presently went away.

That evening, sitting alone in the schoolroom, having so exercised the power over herself which she had acquired by the practice of many years as to banish the unusual colour from her face, to subdue the over-beating of the heart and pulses, and to present to the eager eyes of the children, when they returned from their drive, the same calm countenance with which they were acquainted, Mademoiselle received a letter which made her glad that she was alone, with nobody to spy the changes of her face. It was very short, and, though she had never seen his handwriting before, she knew that it was from Charles Wargrave before she had taken it from the attendant housemaid's tray. It was as follows:—

> "I feel that I have offended you, though I scarcely know why. I spoke hastily, without considering the form of words I used. If you had been an Englishwoman you would perhaps have thought less of that: but as you are you are the only woman in the world for me. My hasty proposal was not hasty in meaning, and it was made in all reverence and respect, though I fear you did not think so. Forgive what has seemed to you careless in the expression, but believe in the love that made it. Say I was rude, and punish me as you please, but reply; and oh! if you can, accept.—Yours ever and only,
>
> "C. W."

Mademoiselle read this letter over three times, almost without breathing, and then she laid it down on the table before her, and grew, not red, but pale. Her lips dropped apart with a long-drawn breath which seemed to come from the very depths of her being; the blood seemed to ebb away from her heart; she grew white like marble, and almost as chill, with a nervous shiver. She was terrified, panic-stricken, dismayed. If all the anger had gone out of her it had been replaced by something else more trying still. Astonishment in the first place, dismay, a panic which impelled her to rise and flee. But this it was impossible to do out of this well-regulated house, where all went on with such unfailing routine, and there were no breaches either of decorum or of hours. To have gone out after dinner, unless for an understood engagement, would have scandalised every inmate, as well as Mademoiselle herself, who also had far too much good sense to allow for a moment, even to herself, that it was possible to run away. No; she had, as is usual, something much worse to do—to remain; to meet the man who, she thought, had insulted her, who, instead of insulting her, had done her the greatest honour in his power, who had attracted her sympathy and liking, and now had made himself one of the most interesting of all mankind in her eyes—to meet him without betraying by a sign that anything had ever passed between them more than good-night or good-morrow, to discourage and dismiss him summarily at once, yet to be always ready to receive him when he deigned to converse with her, as though never a word had been said between them which all the world need not hear. Mademoiselle's first impulse was absolute dismay; the embarrassment of the situation struck her above everything else. Everything about it was embarrassing. She would have to answer his letter, yet she must put her answer in the post herself, keeping it away from all prying eyes: for why should she write to Charles Wargrave, the cousin of the house? Supposing that the housemaid saw it, that Edith or Dorothy saw it? Though she was utterly blameless, how could that be proved,—how could she keep their untutored minds from drawing their own conclusions? She had nothing whatever to blush for, and yet she blushed instinctively, involuntarily, at the idea of being found out in a correspondence with Charles Wargrave. How much more, she said to herself with fright, had she accepted his offer (wild thought which sent all her pulses beating!). And then she must meet him absolutely unmoved; not only without a look or word, but without the suspicion of a breath that could have any meaning. The air must not move a fold of her dress or lock on her forehead, lest it might be supposed that she trembled. These were difficulties of which he would never think—how should he?—of which nobody would think who was not in her position. And though nothing else came of it, this must come of it. Nothing else! What else? She paused, with a shock of abrupt cessation in her thoughts, as one does who suddenly stops running. What else? Nothing else except this—that she could never be at her ease, but must always seem to be at her ease, in Charles Wargrave's presence again.

In the meantime, the first thing to be done was to answer his letter: that was a thing that could not be delayed, that must be accomplished at once. And yet it took a long time even to begin it. Mademoiselle arranged the paper upon her desk a dozen times before she was satisfied. She did more than this. She shut up the schoolroom writing-table, where all her usual writing was done, and fetched from her bedroom a little old desk, a relic of girlish days, once pretty in its inlaid work and velvet lining, now sadly shabby in faded finery. She did not even say to herself what freak of fancy it was which made her produce this old toy, this treasury of girlish souvenirs, for the serious purpose she had in hand. It gave her a great deal of trouble, for there was no ink in the minute ink-bottle, no pens in the tray, nothing she wanted. She had to bring the paper from the writing-table, and all the other accessories. Even after she had surmounted these obstacles there was still a considerable delay. She wrote a letter in French, and then one in English, and tore them both into small pieces, and it was not till almost midnight, after all the other members of Mr Leicester Wargrave's family were in bed, that Mademoiselle succeeded in producing the following, which, though it did not please her, she sent, as being the best she could do: —

"I am very thankful, sir, that it is not as I at first supposed: and indeed I ought to have known better, and never to have believed that an English gentleman would insult a woman in my position. I thank you that you have not done so; but, on the contrary, complimented and indeed flattered me to a very high degree.

"In return I send you a very direct answer, as you have a right. There can be no question, sir, of my accepting a gift far too great, which I had never anticipated, to which my thoughts were never directed at all. It would be a poor compliment in return for your goodness if I should take what you offer as carelessly as if it were a cup of tea you were offering me. Oh, no! no! I respect you too much to do so. A moment's thought will also show you how very unsuitable in every way it would be. You are young, you are rich, you have all the world can give. I am old—a middle-aged woman. I have nothing at all but the *beau nom* you were so good as to recognise. It does not mean even what it would mean in England—it means nothing; in my own country, being poor, I would not even carry it. My mother calls herself in Paris only Madame Castel. And, chief of all, I am more old than you, middle-aged; it is therefore a thing beyond the possibility of even taking into consideration at all.

"Adieu, monsieur, je vous remercie de tout mon cœur; vous ne m'avez pas insultée, vous m'avez flattée; je réponds avec une vive reconnaissance. Que le bon Dieu vous donne tous ce que vous pouvez désirer hors la pauvre et obscure créature qui s'appellera toujours,—Votre obligée,

"Claire de Castel-Sombre."

She wrote this in great haste at last, and, without even trusting herself to read it over, fastened it hastily into its envelope. She was so frightened lest anybody should see it—lest it should fall under the eyes of any youthful observer, whether pupil or attendant—that she put it by her bedside unaddressed until the morning, when she concealed it in her pocket until, in the course of the morning's walk, she could put it into the nearest post-office. Perhaps it was her sense of wishing to conceal which made the children's chatter so significant to her. "Oh, Mademoiselle," said Edith, "why didn't you send your letters out for the early post with mother's?" "And why didn't you give it me to carry?" cried Dorothy; "you know I'm always the postman." "Mother would say it was to somebody, and you didn't want us to see the address," said the one little importunate. "And you needn't have been so careful, Mademoiselle," said the other, "for I would never have told who it was." "There is no question of telling," said Mademoiselle, very gravely, to stop further discussion; but as she turned away from the post-office another dreadful and unforeseen accident happened. Charles Wargrave came up to the group. She felt her heart leap from where it was, very low down in her being, up, up to her throat. The children seized upon their cousin as usual, while she walked along by their side with downcast head. They told him all the story, how Mademoiselle had been posting a letter and would not let any one see the address. "And I always put the letters in the post," said Dorothy, aggrieved. Mademoiselle kept her eyes down, and would not meet the look which she divined.

CHAPTER VI

It would not be easy to find a more difficult position than that in which Mademoiselle now found herself. She had just put into the post-box a letter to the man who came up at the moment, almost before it had disappeared, and before she had returned his bow and evaded the hand held out to her in greeting. The children had informed him of this almost clandestine letter, which the governess would intrust to nobody, which she had posted with her own hands. He gave her a rapid look of inquiry, which she saw without making any response to it. She could even see, somehow, without looking, the flush that rose to his face on this intimation. He knew as well as she knew that the letter was to himself, and, perhaps, perceived for the first time, in a sudden flash of unconsciously communicated feeling, how it was that she had posted it herself, and the reluctance she must feel to allow the fact of her communications with him to be known. The flush on his face was partly pain at this discovery, and partly suspense on his own part, and the tantalising consciousness that, though she was so near him, and a word— even a look—might enlighten him, neither word nor look was to be had from her. She had completely relapsed into Mademoiselle—the careful guardian of the children, a member of a distinct species, an official personage, not Claire de Castel-Sombre, nor any mere individual. She was at her post like a sentinel on duty, to whom the concerns of his personal life must all be thrown into the background. There was no place in the world where she would not rather have been than walking along the road towards Kensington Gardens by Charles Wargrave's side, though with the potent interposition of Edith and Dorothy between. But, though he felt this, he went on, with a curious fascination, prolonging the strange thrill of sensation in himself, and glad to prolong it in her, to keep up in her the excitement and whirl of feeling which he knew must exist in the strange, concealed circumstances which, for the moment at least, bound the two together. To think that they should be walking thus, not speaking, she, at least, never turning her head his way, who possibly might be destined to spend all their lives together, to be one for the rest of their days! Charles felt, with a sickening sensation of failure, that there was little prospect of this; but yet that moment could never, whatever happened, pass from the memories of either for all their lives to come. He liked to prolong it, though he was aware it must give her pain, though it made himself giddy and dazed in the confusion and suspense. There was a cruel kind of pleasure in it—a pleasure that stung, and smarted, and thrilled every nerve. They walked thus, with the children chattering, along the side of Kensington Gardens towards Hyde Park, all the freshness of morning in the air, the sounds softened by summer and that well-being and enjoyment of existence which warmth and sunshine bring. When at last he left them, he would not let Mademoiselle off that touch of the hands which she had the excuse of French habit for eluding, but he the settled form of English use and wont to justify his insistence upon. It was another caprice of the excitement in his mind to insist upon shaking hands: but the hurried, reluctant touch taught him nothing, except that which he did not desire to learn.

Mademoiselle reached home much exhausted by her walk, and retired to her room, complaining of headache, which was very unusual; but not before the whole history of the morning had been reported to Mrs Wargrave—the mysterious letter put in the post, the meeting with Uncle Charlie, and all the rest. Happily, no member of the Wargrave family required any reason, save his devotion to themselves, for Charles Wargrave's appearance. "He is so devoted to the children; it is quite beautiful in a young man!" their mother said. But she felt, at the same time, that Mademoiselle's behaviour required looking into. A mysterious letter transferred from her pocket to the post-office, though Dolly was always the postman, and loved to be so employed—as if she did not want the address to be seen! and then the mysterious headache, so unusual in Mademoiselle, who, in delightful contrast to other governesses, never had headaches, never was ill, but always ready for her duties. Mrs Leicester Wargrave was divided between the fear of any change which might deprive her of so admirable a governess, and that interest which every woman feels in the possibility of a romance going on under her eyes, and of which she has a chance of being the confidante. She graciously consented that Mademoiselle should not come down-stairs to luncheon, but paid her a visit afterwards in her room, with every intention of finding out what was the matter. She found Mademoiselle in her dressing-gown—that famous white dressing-gown—retired into her own chamber, but with nothing the matter, she protested; no need for the doctor—only a headache, the most common thing in the world.

"But not common with you, Mademoiselle," Mrs Wargrave said, drawing a chair near, and putting her hand on the governess's wrist to feel if she were feverish,—for, of course, she knew, or thought she knew, something of nursing, as became a woman of her time.

"No, it is not usual with me: I am glad, for it is not pleasant," said Mademoiselle.

"I am very glad, too, I assure you; for a person in the house with a continual headache is the most horrid thing! It is always such a pleasure to find you ready for everything—always well."

Mademoiselle smiled, but said nothing. She was not without sympathy for the employers of governesses who had perpetual headaches: at the same time it is, perhaps, not exhilarating to be complimented on your health as a matter of convenience to another—though quite reasonable, as she was ready to allow.

"That is what makes me think," said Mrs Wargrave, "that you must have something on your mind."

This assault was so entirely unexpected that Mademoiselle not only flushed to her very hair, but started from her half-reclining attitude in her chair.

"Ah," said Mrs Wargrave, "I thought as much! I don't call myself clever, but it isn't easy to deceive me in that sort of a way, Mademoiselle. I have noticed for a long time that you were not looking like yourself. Something has happened. The children—they are such quick observers, you know, and they tell me everything, poor things!—said something about a letter. You know, I am sure, that I don't want to pry into your affairs, but sometimes it does one good to confide in a friend—and I have always wished my governesses to consider me as a friend—especially you, who give so little trouble. I thought it might, perhaps, be a comfort to you to speak."

Mademoiselle, during this speech, had time to recover herself. She said only, however, with the most polite and easy way of evasion, "I know that you are always very kind."

"I am sure that I always mean to be," her patroness said, and she sat with her eyes fixed upon the patient, expectant—delighted with the idea of a sentimental confession, and yet rather alarmed lest this might lead to an intimation that it would be necessary to look for a new governess. Mrs Leicester Wargrave meant no harm to anybody, and was, on the whole, an amiable woman; but, as a matter of fact, the thing that would have truly delighted her, real pleasure without any penalty, would have been the confession from Mademoiselle of an unhappy love.

And now there suddenly occurred an idea, half mischievous, half humorous, to Claire, who, in her own personality, had once been *espiègle*, and was not now superior to a certain pleasure in exposing the pretences of life. She scarcely understood how it was that, having finally and very seriously rejected the curious proposal which certainly, for a day or two, had done her the good service of quickening the monotony of life, she should have the sudden impulse of taking advice about it, and asking Mrs Wargrave, of all persons in the world, what she ought to do. Caprices of this kind seize the most serious in a moment without any previous intention, and the thought that to get a little amusement out of Charles Wargrave's proposal was permissible, seeing how much embarrassment and annoyance she was sure to get out of it, came to her mind with a flash of amused impulse: she said, "I did not think I had betrayed myself; and, indeed, it is only for a day or two that I have had anything on my mind."

"Then there *is* something?" cried Mrs Wargrave, delighted, clasping her hands. "I was sure of it: I am a dreadful person, Mademoiselle; there is no deceiving *me*."

"So it would appear," said Claire, with a gleam of humour which was a little compensation, she felt, for her trouble. And she added, casting down her eyes, "I have had a—very unexpected—proposal of marriage."

"I knew it!" Mrs Wargrave said. She added, more warmly than she felt, "And I hope it is a good one—and makes you happy. Tell me all about it, my dear."

It was not that she had never called Mademoiselle "my dear" before, for this is a word which glides very easily to some women's lips: but once more it made Claire smile.

"It makes me neither happy nor unhappy," she said, "though it is a very good one; for it is not a possible thing: except the trouble of vexing some one, it can do nothing to me."

"You can't accept it?" Mrs Wargrave felt a momentary relief, and then a stronger sentiment seized her. She could not bear to have sport spoiled in the matrimonial way. "But why?" she said. "Why? Do tell me all about it. If it is a good offer, and there is nothing against the man, why shouldn't you accept it, Mademoiselle?"

"I have many reasons, Madame; but the first is, that I do not care for him at all. You do not accept an offer which you have never expected, never thought of as possible."

"Oh, if that is all!" said Mrs Wargrave. "Good heavens! nobody ever would be married if that was to be the rule. Why, I never was more surprised in my life than when Mr Wargrave proposed to me! That's nothing—nothing! If it is a good match——"

"It is much too good a match. The gentleman is not only much, much richer than I—that is nothing, for I am poor—but he is better in the world in every way. His family would consider it a *mésalliance*: and it would be so completely to my interest— —"

"But, good heavens!" cried Mrs Wargrave again, "what does that matter? Let his family complain—that's their affair. You surely would never throw up a good match for that? Is there anything against the man?"

"Nothing!" said Mademoiselle, with some earnestness.

"Then, what does it matter about his family? I suppose he's old enough to judge for himself? And he could make nice settlements, and all that?"

"Very likely—I do not know. He is rich, I am aware of that."

"You surprise me very much," cried Mrs Wargrave. "I have always heard that the French cared nothing for sentiment—that it was always reason and the *dot*, and all that, that was considered. Yet, here you are, talking like a silly girl. Mademoiselle, if you will be guided by me, you will not let any romantic nonsense stand in the way of your advancement. Dear me! you don't disapprove of married life, I suppose? You don't want to set up as superior to your neighbours? And, only think what your position is—Mr Wargrave and I are very much satisfied with you, and I had hoped you would stay with us as long as Edie and Dolly require a governess; but you must reflect that you won't be any younger when that time comes. We are all growing older, and the time will come when ladies will think you are not lively enough to take the charge of young children; they will think you are not active enough to go out for their walks. Many people have a prejudice against old governesses. I want to put it quite clearly before you, Mademoiselle. Think what it is to go on slaving when you are an old woman. And you will never be able to earn enough to keep you comfortable if you should live to be past work; and what will you do? Whereas, here is, apparently, an excellent chance, a certain provision for you, and a far more comfortable life than any governess could ever expect. Goodness! what do you look for? You must accept it; you must not throw such a chance away. I can't hear of it; and any one that had your real interests at heart would say the same."

Mrs Wargrave spoke like a woman inspired. She reddened a little in her earnestness, she used little gestures of natural eloquence. All selfish thoughts of retaining so good a governess for Edith and Dorothy had gone out of her mind. She could not endure that such a piece of folly should be perpetrated under her eyes.

"All that I know very well," said Mademoiselle. "I have gone over it too often not to know."

"And yet!" cried Mrs Wargrave, with a sort of exasperation. "Come, come," she added with a laugh, "you are only playing with my curiosity. Of course you can't possibly mean to do such a silly thing as refuse. Poor man! when everything is in his favour and nothing against him! I never heard of such a thing. I can't have it! Your friends *must* interpose."

"But his friends will be most indignant—they will be in a state of fury—they will say I am an adventuress, a schemer, a designing woman— everything that can be said."

"Let them say!" cried Mrs Wargrave in her enthusiasm; "what have you to do with that? Of course they'll say it. Men's friends always do: but what is it to you what they say? that's their concern, not yours. I suppose he is old enough to judge for himself."

"That is the last and greatest objection of all," said Mademoiselle. "He is quite old enough to judge for himself: but he is younger than I am. If all the rest could be put right, there is still that."

"Oh!" said Mrs Wargrave, making a pause. "Well, that is a pity," she added, slowly. "I don't much fancy these marriages myself. But," she said, pausing again, "it can't be denied that they turn out very well. I have known three or four, and they've all turned out well. And, besides, that's the man's own affair. If he is pleased, I don't see why *you* should object. Is it much?" she asked, with a little hesitation.

"I am sure as much as—two or three years," said Mademoiselle, firmly.

Mrs Wargrave was so indignant that she sprang from the chair and all but stamped her foot. "Two or three years!" she cried. "Do you mean to laugh in my face, Mademoiselle? I thought you were going to say a dozen at least. I supposed it must be some boy of twenty. Two or three years!"

"No, not twenty, nor thirty, but still younger than I am."

"This is quite absurd," said Mrs Wargrave, sharply; "a year or two makes *no* difference, and you must let me say that it will be not only foolish but wicked, *criminal*, to let such an opportunity slip. How can you think of doing it, you who have a mother, and nothing but your own work to look to? How do you know how long you may be able to work? how can you tell what may come upon you if you slight a distinct interposition of Providence like this? I can't imagine what you are thinking of. Do I know the gentleman? Is he a Frenchman? I hope, when you have thought it over, you will not be such a fool as to send such a man away."

"No, he is not a Frenchman. He is English," said Mademoiselle, eluding the other question. "And do you think I could bear it that his family should call me all the names and turn against him?"

"His family!" repeated Mrs Wargrave with fine scorn. "What have his family to do with it? It will be the most dreadful folly in the world to give up your own happiness for anything his family can say."

She had no patience with Mademoiselle. She preached quite a clever little sermon upon the necessity and duty of thinking of herself, and of the ingratitude not only to Providence, which had afforded this chance, and to the man who had given it, but even to the people under whose roof she was, and who had her best interests at heart, should she neglect such a means of securing her own comfort and independence. Mrs Wargrave ended by feeling herself aggrieved. Mademoiselle's culpable sentimentality, her rejection of the best of advice, her obstinacy and wrong-headedness would, she felt sure, recoil upon herself—but in the meantime Mrs Wargrave could not conceal that she was wounded, deeply wounded, by seeing her advice so slighted—"Though it is yourself who will be the chief sufferer, Mademoiselle," she said, with almost vindictive vehemence. And it was in this mood that she left the room, leaving, so to speak, a prophecy of doom behind her. Mademoiselle, she said, would repent but once, and that would be all her life.

Mademoiselle tried to laugh when Mrs Wargrave was gone, but the effort was too much, and she astonished herself very much by suddenly bursting into tears instead. What for, she could not tell. It was, she supposed, a case of overstrained nerves and bodily exhaustion, for she felt herself curiously worn out. But afterwards she grew more calm, and it was impossible for her not to go over Mrs Wargrave's arguments, and to find in them many things which she could not gainsay. The smile that came over her face at the thought of her own little mystification, the snare which had been laid without intention, and into which her adviser had fallen so easily, was very transient; for, indeed, the oracle which she had so lightly evoked had spoken the words of truth and soberness. Claire asked herself whether, on the whole, this matter-of-fact and worldly woman was not right. Poor, solitary, and, if not old, yet within sight of the possibility of growing into what was old age for a woman in her position, had she any right to reject the chance of comfort and advancement thus held out to her? Had she any right to do it? She asked herself this question so much more at her ease that she had already rejected it, and Charles Wargrave must already have accepted her decision, so that she said to herself it was only a hypothetical case she was considering. The question was, under such circumstances, a mere speculation. What should a woman do? Poverty before her on one side and wealth on the other—obscurity, helplessness, the absence of all power to succour or aid, and possibly want at the end—while with a word she could have all that a woman could desire, every possibility of helpfulness, comfort for her family, freedom for herself, the freedom from all cares and personal bondage. And it was not as if there was anything wrong involved. Mademoiselle knew herself not only to be a woman who would do her duty, but one who would have no thought beyond it or struggle against it. If she married a man she would be a good wife to him, one in whom his soul might trust. Was it necessary to reject the overture which would bring so much, because she had not that one ethereal thing—the sentiment above duty, the uncertain errant principle called Love, to justify the transaction? She asked herself the question, with all the French part of her nature and breeding urging her towards the common-sense view. Marriage meant a great deal more than mere loving. It meant the discharge of many duties which she could undertake and faithfully do. It meant a definite office in life which she knew she could fulfil. It meant fellowship, companionship, the care of joint interests, the best advice, support, and backing up that one human being could give another. She felt, though she would not have said it, that all this she could give, far better, perhaps, than a girl could, who would be able to fancy herself in love. Ah! but then——The other side of her character turned round and cut her short in her thinking, but with an abruptness that hurt her. She gave an almost sobbing sigh of regret and something like pain.

Then another part of Mrs Wargrave's argument came to her mind. Let his family say what they pleased, that was their concern. After all there, too, was the teaching of common-sense. Mademoiselle had felt as if it would be something like treachery to live in the Wargraves' house and allow their relation to make such overtures to her. Why? The Wargraves were kind enough, good enough, but not more to her than she to them. They gave her the food and shelter and wages they had engaged to give, and she gave to them a full equivalent. They never considered her but as their children's governess. On what rule should she consider them as something more than her employers, as people to whom she owed a higher observance beyond and above her duty? Gratitude?—there was no reason for gratitude. There is a curious prejudice in favour of being grateful to the people under whose roof you live, however light may be the bond, however little the bargain may be to your advantage. Mademoiselle knew that the day she ceased to be useful to the Wargraves they would tell her so, and arrange that she should leave them, not unkindly but certainly, on the common law which exists between employers and employed. And why should she abandon any hope of improving her condition through a visionary sentiment of treachery to them? Ah! she said to herself again, but then——What was it that stopped her thoughts in both these cases? In neither was there anything wrong—no law of man, none even of God would be broken. She would wrong no one. And yet——She ended her long course of thinking with a sigh. An invisible barrier stood before her which she regretted, which was unreal, which was, perhaps, merely fantastic—a folly, not a thing to interfere with any sensible career. But there it stood.

What a good thing that the case was merely hypothetical, everything being in reality quite fixed and decided, to be reopened no more!

CHAPTER VII

That night late there came a note by the last post—that post which sometimes adds horrors to the night in London, with missives which interfere hopelessly with the quiet of the hour. In it Charles Wargrave thanked her that she did not accept his heart carelessly, as if it were a cup of tea. He thanked her for her decided answer, but he thought she would at least understand him when he said that, so far as he was concerned, it could not stop there. Next time it would not at least be a question which she had not anticipated, and he would still hope that her prayer for his welfare might be accomplished without the condition she put upon it—with which there could be no welfare for him at all. It cannot be said that, though her heart beat at the sight of it, this letter was a great surprise to Claire. Notwithstanding her conviction that it was a hypothetical case which she was putting to herself, she felt now that she had not indeed really imagined or believed that Charles Wargrave, a man who had got his own will all his life, was now to be thwarted in so important a matter without resistance or protest. She felt at once that this was what was to be expected. The letter, however, piqued her a little—annoyed her a little. It would have been reasonable that he should have met her arguments one way or other. It would have been civil to have protested, and declared that she was not old, though she pleased to call herself so. Though Mademoiselle was herself so full of common-sense on this subject, as on most others, she had a feeling that it was a failure of politeness on the part of Charles Wargrave not to have said something about it. When she discovered this sentiment in her own spirit she was a little ashamed of it, but still it was there. And the note in general said so little that it piqued and interested her. It was skilfully done; but Mademoiselle did not see this—neither, perhaps, did the writer. Perhaps Mademoiselle was momentarily vexed, too, that there was no need to answer it. If there is one weakness which is common to human nature, it is the pleasure which people take in explaining themselves, especially on emotional subjects, so as to leave their correspondents in no doubt as to their real meaning. Claire had written very hurriedly the first time, with a genuine desire to sweep such a troublesome episode out of her life. She felt now that it would be pleasant to fill out and strengthen all these arguments, and especially to bring out that point of age of which he had taken no notice.

He might, perhaps, from what she had herself said, think her forty or more, seeing that he did not object to her statement about her age; and she would have liked, while reiterating that, to have made it quite clear what her age was—not, after all, so much as he might think. But her good sense was sufficiently effective still to make her feel that no answer was needed to his letter. She put it away in the little faded desk, which, perhaps, was doing it too much honour. There the matter would end, notwithstanding what he said. He should find it impossible to get any opportunity of speech; nothing would induce her to listen to him in his cousin's house—nothing, though she had felt all the force of Mrs Wargrave's arguments about the family. In short, it must be allowed that, in respect to the question, in this, its second phase, Claire de Castel-Sombre did not carry with her all the prudence and experience of Mademoiselle, but was sometimes in her thoughts more like a petulant girl than was at all consistent with her character of a philosopher or a mature woman of the world.

And then there occurred what can only be called a pause in life. Everything, of course, went on quite as usual; but in this particular matter there was silence in heaven and earth. Life came to a pause, like that pause in music which gives so much expectancy to what precedes it, so much emphasis and effect to what follows. It is easy to notice the advantage of a pause in music, but not so much in life, where perhaps the occurrence of an interval, whether agreeable or disagreeable, is, while it lasts, exceedingly tedious, involving many stings of disappointment and blank moments of suspense. Claire would not have allowed even to herself that she wanted the sensation, the new condition of affairs to go on, which had suddenly brought a shock of interest and novelty into her monotonous existence. But, all the same, she suffered when it stopped. The monotony to which she had so well schooled herself seemed more monotonous than ever. A restless desire that something should happen dawned within her; not so much that another incident in this history should happen, as that something should happen—an earthquake, a great fire, even a thunderstorm if nothing more. But this desire was in vain, for nothing happened. There was a time of very brilliant yet mild weather, not even too hot, threatening nothing, and all went on in its usual routine. Mr Charles Wargrave came occasionally to luncheon, as he had been in the habit of doing, but Mademoiselle had always the best of reasons for withdrawing immediately that the meal was over—lessons that required instant attention, or letters that had to be sent off by the afternoon post. Sometimes she caught a look from him which reproached her, or questioned her, or merely assured her, as a look can do, that he saw through her artifices, yet was not moved by them. She felt the strain upon her nerves of these meetings, which were not meetings at all, and in which no word was exchanged on any private subject; but when he was absent, and did not appear for about a fortnight, strangely enough Claire felt this still more. She said to herself, with a smile, that he was at last convinced and saw the futility of the pursuit; but though the smile ran into a laugh, there was no sense of absolute pleasure in her mind. When an exciting story stops, even when it is only a story in a book, and there are no more accidents and adventures to anticipate, it leaves a dulness behind. And Claire felt a dulness. The story of Charles Wargrave stopped. She did not want it to go on—oh! far from that, she said quickly, with a hot blush; but it left a dulness—as much as that a woman might allow.

The season was just about coming to an end, and Mrs Leicester Wargrave's engagements were many in the rush of the final gaieties. She had gone out one afternoon, taking the little girls with her, to a garden-party, a thing which did not happen often, but when it did come was a holiday to Mademoiselle. It was the beginning of July, still and warm, and Claire went out with her work to the garden, to a shady corner in which she could be quiet and undisturbed. She had no fear of any interruption: a visitor for herself was the rarest possible occurrence (for people naturally do not like the governess's visitors about, who might be mistaken for visitors of the house), and none of Mrs Wargrave's visitors were likely to penetrate to the garden, the mistress of the house being absent. Claire had brought out her mending, which was her chief work in her brief moments of solitude. It was in a trim little covered basket, not to offend anybody's eye; and, as a matter of fact, she did more thinking than sewing. The happiness of thinking is when you think about nothing in particular, thinking without an object: and the sense of unusual leisure and quiet, and the soft influences of the air outdoors—which she could enjoy without any anxiety as to Edith exposing herself to the sun, or Dorothy running too fast—had filled Claire's mind with this soft atmosphere of musing without definite thoughts. Stray fancies went flitting through her mind like the little white clouds upon the sky. She was Claire de Castel-Sombre through and through, she was not Mademoiselle at all. She had forgotten to remember about Charles Wargrave, and the story which had come to a pause.

For once in a way to have got rid of all that, and then to lift your eyes quickly at the sound of a step on the gravel, and to see him, walking out quietly from under the shadow of the trees! Her heart gave a leap as if it had somehow got loose, but she rose to meet him with a countenance which was no longer that of Claire de Castel-Sombre, but the well-trained face of Mademoiselle.

"I am sorry," she said, "Mrs Wargrave and the children are gone out. There is a garden-party at the Merewethers'."

"I know," he said, "and hoped to find you alone."

"They were kind enough to ask me too," said Mademoiselle.

"I am very glad you did not go; I have been watching for this opportunity so long! I suppose you don't think what it is to see you across the table, and never have a chance of a word?"

"Monsieur Wargrave," said Mademoiselle, "might avoid that by coming—to dinner, for example, when I am not there."

"It is malice that makes you say so," he replied. She had changed into French and he followed her lead. "You know the purpose for which I come. No, I cannot consent to lose my small opportunity, my holiday from observation, by not speaking of what is nearest my heart."

"Monsieur does not care, then, for spoiling mine?"

"Ah!" he said, "Mademoiselle de Castel-Sombre, you think you can silence me with that. So you can. If it is, indeed, to take anything from you, to spoil your quiet, of course there cannot be any question on the subject, and I will go away."

Thus it would have been easy to finish the conversation. No doubt it would have been rude—and to be rude was very abhorrent to all Mademoiselle's notions—still, on such an important issue, and to secure that he should go away! But Mademoiselle evidently would rather suffer than be so impolite, for she answered not a word.

"I must take advantage when I can," he said, "or otherwise how am I to make myself known to you—how prepare the way? I will talk on any subject you please. I have not come here to worry you, to press myself upon you like an ice or a cup of tea. How I thank you for that simile! I do not want you to take me, when you take me, as if I were a cup of tea."

Mademoiselle once more was silent. If she had combated the assumption of that *when*, it might have reopened the whole discussion, she said to herself.

"There are certain mistakes about myself I should like to correct," he said. "You seem to have thought I was twenty or twenty-five, and I am thirty-four. It is not of much importance, but I should like you to know it. I wonder Mrs Wargrave, who knows everybody's age, did not inform you of that."

"She does not care about the ages of men," said Mademoiselle with an effort. Like many other people, when there was a desperate occasion for keeping up the conversation, she plunged into sarcasm as the easiest way. "To keep women from going wrong about their age is what she wishes. You know we are sometimes accused of taking off a year or two."

"Unless when you add a year or two," he said. She had ventured on a glance upward at him over her work, and he caught the glance, being on the watch, and made a point on his own side by that which replied to it. "I suppose both have their uses," he added, "to attract or to repel."

"If you think," said Mademoiselle hastily, "that all women think of is either to attract or repel— —! But even were it so, it is but a small number of women who are within that circle. In youth it may be the object of too many thoughts, but when a woman is in the midst of life, do her thoughts dwell on such arts more than a man's? No, Mr Wargrave, it is not just to say so."

"Mademoiselle de Castel-Sombre," he said with great gravity, pronouncing every syllable, till she smiled at the formality in spite of herself, "I am not superior to such arts, if I knew how to use them. And, man or woman, I think the desire to please is of itself a great charm."

"It must be kept within bounds," she said, vaguely, scarcely knowing what it was she said.

"There would be no bounds in mine if I had the luck to succeed," he said, "or even the hope of succeeding." Then he stopped himself with a little abruptness, and there was a silence during which the birds came in singing, and the leaves rustling in a curious little interlude which Mademoiselle never forgot. At last he said: "The opportunity of speaking with you alone goes to my head. And I run the risk of wearying you, I know, of pressing prematurely. I wish you would tell me—anything you would like me to do."

"Yes," she said, suddenly putting down her work and looking up at him. She saw against the trees, for a moment, his head bent forward, his look of profound pleasure, the expectation in his face. "If you wish to please me," she said, "you will go away."

It was cruel, and she felt it to be cruel,—an insult flung full in his face when he looked for it so little. He sprang suddenly to his feet as if he had been shot. His countenance changed. Mademoiselle bent her head again, not to see what she had done.

"Mademoiselle!" he cried, with a pang in his voice, then composing himself. "If that is really what you wish—if it is the only thing I can do for you, to relieve you of my presence— —"

"Forgive me!" said Mademoiselle, very low. She added more distinctly: "Monsieur Wargrave will see that here, in the home of his family, who would resent it so much, is the last place in the world— —"

"Confound my family!" he cried, then begged her pardon hastily; "they are not my family—a cousin, to whom I am no more responsible than to his gardener."

"But I am responsible," she said. "She is my—mistress. Ah! whatever glosses we put upon it, that is the case. I will not be dishonourable to listen to what would enrage her and shock her, here."

"Then I may speak—elsewhere?" he said, eagerly.

"There is no elsewhere; we are here. It is the only place where we meet. Monsieur Wargrave must not take advantage of what I say. There is but one good thing and true that can be done."

"And that is to leave you?" he said, despondently. "Mademoiselle, it is yours to command and mine to obey—but it is cruel. Surely at the most, with all your delicacies and precautions, you cannot think a man's honest love, and wish to commend himself to her, is any shame to a woman?"

"Not if she were a queen!" Claire could not have said otherwise had she died for it; but she did die, or rather put herself to death, and Mademoiselle came back to her place. "But there are times and seasons, and there are places in which what was honourable becomes profane. If Monsieur Wargrave will put himself in my place, instead of thinking of his own."

Mademoiselle did not know whether she was most elated or depressed by her victory. When he had left the garden she hurried indoors, feeling that all the peacefulness of her previous mood was gone. The afternoon quiet had been sweet to her, but it was so no more, and all that had made her position endurable seemed to have gone with it. Why should the life, which she had so carefully shaped into the limitations in which she believed it must be bound for ever, be thus disturbed? She thought with almost resentment that it was for a caprice, for a little additional pleasure to a man who had all the pleasures of life at his command, that this had been done, and that he had thought of himself, and not of her, when he thus took in hand the unsettling of all her views, the disturbance of every plan. It would have been little had he been satisfied with her first reply, had he left her to herself when he saw that there was no response in her to his proposition; but to continue to push on, in spite of her prohibition! She went in angry in her annoyance and trouble, for it was now no use to say to herself, as she had done at first, that it was nothing, a passing folly, to-morrow to be numbered among the follies of the past. Now she knew very well that her life had been disturbed, that the interruption was not a nothing; that the calm had been broken up, and all her rules displaced. And all this by no doing of hers, at the caprice of a young man, who wanted for nothing, to whom, perhaps, it was but one of many diversions! She was very indignant with him as she gained the refuge of her room; but milder thoughts came in, relentings, a curious rueful sense of the interest and variety which he had brought into her monotonous life. She had been contented after a sort. She had fully adapted herself to her fate, and learned to think it not an ill fate, better than so many. But now! And yet there had been a certain pleasure in the disturbance all the same.

Mademoiselle did not see Mrs Wargrave till next day, when she asked to speak to her, and to that lady's great astonishment put forward a request for a holiday—leave to go to Paris to see her mother, who was ailing and wanted her. Mrs Wargrave grew pale with astonishment and dismay. "A holiday, Mademoiselle! to go to Paris! You could not have chosen a more inconvenient time. You know we shall be going to the country in about a month, and how do you suppose I can take the charge of the children, with all I have to do?"

"I will come back before that time," said Mademoiselle.

"Then it is now directly you want to go? But that is worse and worse, for I have numbers of engagements; and what is to happen to the girls if you are away?"

"I am very sorry," said Mademoiselle, "but my mother——"

"Your mother cannot be more important to you than my children are to me. And you must recollect you have not yet been two years with us, Mademoiselle. I don't expect any governess to ask for a holiday till after the second year."

"I am very sorry," said Mademoiselle again; "but it is very important for me to go away. I—am not well: I must go—I cannot continue now. It is *plus forte que moi*."

"Mademoiselle! it is not your mother, it is this business about your marriage."

"Not my marriage; I shall never marry."

"Oh, nonsense, nonsense!" cried Mrs Wargrave. "I am sure you want to have him all the time. It will be too ridiculous if for a set of foolish romantic scruples you go and throw a good match away."

Mademoiselle made no reply. She stood uneasily moving from one foot to another, clasping and unclasping her hands. "I must, I must get away," she said, quietly, almost under her breath. "It must come to an end. I can do no good while I am kept in agitation. Ah, Mrs Wargrave, let me go."

"I wish you would be frank and tell me who he is," said Mrs Wargrave. "I wish you would let me speak to him. Going away is the very last thing you ought to do. To throw away a good match at your age, and with your prospects! I told you before it was criminal, Mademoiselle."

Mademoiselle said something under her breath, in her agitation, which sounded like "You do not know," and Mrs Wargrave grew angry. "I don't know? Who knows, then, I wonder? I tell you that for you, in your position, with your mother to think of, it is simple wickedness. If the man were an ogre I'd marry him if I were in your position. Goodness, what have you to do with his family? You make me so impatient I could shake you. You should marry him, whoever he is, if he can give you a good home."

"If Madame Wargrave could but spare me for a month—for three weeks!"

"I am sure it's not for your own good. You should be proud to stay and marry him, for your own good. Mademoiselle! I tell you, whoever he is, if he were an ogre——"

Mademoiselle suddenly laid her hand upon the arm of her patroness. There was a gleam of desperation in her eyes. "You would not say so were I to tell you his name."

"I would say so, whatever is his name, for your own good. What *is* his name?"

They stood looking at each other for a moment, both of them excited, Mrs Wargrave full of curiosity, and Claire carried away by the passion of the moment, feeling it the only way to clear herself, to throw off the shadow of double-dealing which she felt upon her: but the crisis was a desperate one, and calmed her in spite of herself. She took her hand from the other's arm. "It is Mr Charles Wargrave," she said.

Mrs Wargrave received the shock in all its force, being wholly unprepared for it. She was so startled that her sudden movement shook the very walls. "Mr Charles Wargrave!" she repeated, with a voice of horror. "It can't—it can't be true! Is it true?"

To this question Mademoiselle did not answer a word.

"Charles Wargrave!" repeated the lady, with a mixture of consternation and incredulity. "And you're not ashamed to tell me that?" she cried. "You can stand and look me in the face?"

Claire had not looked her in the face, but at these words she raised her head and met Mrs Wargrave's angry eyes. She was pale, but she did not flinch. Now it was all over, she knew. This house, which might have been more or less hers for five years, the salary which had helped to maintain her mother, the freedom from care for so long,—all was over! When she went out of these doors it would be to face the world again, to find another means of subsistence, to begin anew.

Mrs Wargrave turned and left the room, and Mademoiselle saw nothing of her till next day, when in the morning, before the lessons had begun, she was summoned down-stairs. To her surprise she found Mr Leicester Wargrave, as well as his wife, awaiting her in the room which they called the library. He was seated at the writing-table with some papers before him, she standing beside him. With some ceremony a chair was placed for her, and she was asked to sit down. "We will not detain you long, Mademoiselle," Mr Wargrave said, clearing his throat; and Mrs Wargrave, too, coughed and cleared hers before she began.

"Mademoiselle, you will not wonder that I thought it right to consult my husband about what you said last night. He thinks you must have made a mistake. His cousin is not at all that kind of man."

Claire's countenance lighted up with sudden indignation. "I have made no mistake," she said.

"Ladies are apt to think, when a young man is just amusing himself, that he means something. Anyhow, of course we can't pass it over."

"Pass it over!"

"I mean—that we think your going to Paris a very good plan; and perhaps, if you could find something there that would suit you, it would be better for you—to be within reach of your mother."

"You mean that I am not wanted here again?"

"It is not so decided as that. I'm sure we're both very sorry that any unpleasantness should have arisen, and both Mr Wargrave and I think you have behaved very well, Mademoiselle. You have nothing to reproach yourself with, and we'll be delighted to answer any inquiries. But, on the whole, I think, if you could find something in Paris, or thereabouts—where you could be nearer your mother—I do think you would find it—a relief to your mind."

"You are, no doubt, right, Mrs Wargrave," said Mademoiselle, rising from her chair.

"Yes, I'm sure I'm right: and Mr Wargrave has written a cheque—for the difference, you know. And if you would like Sarah to help you with your boxes—we thought you might, perhaps, like to go by the night train."

CHAPTER VIII

It is needless to add that Claire did not say a word in remonstrance or objection. She was startled and unprepared for such summary measures. And yet she said to herself that she had fully expected it, and was not surprised that her employer should take energetic measures to stop such a *mésalliance*. A *mésalliance*! But she reflected with her usual philosophy that it would be so, that her *beau nom* meant nothing—less even in her own country than here. If she had been a man who could confer that *beau nom* in return for some romantic nobody's money, then perhaps there might have been some value in it; but to her, a woman, an old maid, a governess! She was far too proud to ask for an hour's delay, even for so much as would enable her to travel by day instead of by night; yet there was no doubt that it was with a very strange sensation that she felt herself dismissed from the recognised place in which yesterday she had expected to remain for years, and facing once more a blank world, in which she knew not where to go, or what her next standing-point might be. It is true that she was in no way destitute or without a refuge. She had her mother's house to go to, the little shabby apartment in Paris, where she could scarcely hope to be triumphantly received, seeing that her return meant a diminution of its slender resources, besides the inference which old Aunt Clotilde at least would be so ready to draw, that Claire had left her good situation in disgrace. This suggestion made her blood boil, and it was one which was inevitable. But still there was nothing hopeless or even terrible in her position. She was sufficiently well known in the circles where people of her class are known to have little fear of finding another situation. And she had already known so many new beginnings that another did not appal her. No, there was nothing desperate, nothing tragical in her circumstances. A little additional humiliation, a shock, perhaps a reproach, but no more. And perhaps it was the best thing that could have happened. It put a stop summarily to an episode that never would have come to anything, which was well; surely from any point of view it was well. When she found herself on the Channel, looking somewhat wistfully at the clear sky overhead, full of the softness of the summer stars, and at the dim whiteness of the cliffs she was leaving behind, it is possible that Claire saw them blurred yet amplified though the medium of a tear. In front of her the other coast was lost in the distance and darkness of night, so that while what was past was still clear, what was future was wholly invisible, which was a perfect symbol of life itself. She noted the similitude with that love of imagery which is natural to a soul in trouble, with forlorn interest. How little she had expected last night to be crossing the Channel thus! how suddenly her existence had changed!

But these are vicissitudes which must occur in the life of a governess, for whom more than for most human creatures there is no continuing city; and by the time Mademoiselle had left behind her that dark and mystic interval of the Channel, with all its suggestions, she had begun to be able to indulge in a rueful smile at the transformation scene which had been played for her (doubtful) amusement in her late home in the Square. Mrs Wargrave's indignation at her fastidious and romantic objection to marry a man who could make a provision for her turned in a moment into swift horror and alarm lest such a catastrophe should occur, and the acknowledgment that Mademoiselle had "behaved very well" in the reluctance which half an hour before she had denounced as folly! Claire had known how it would be from the first, and it was an amusing exhibition of human inconsistency. But yet she was not so much amused after all. Exhibitions of this kind, perhaps, fail of their effect when they are too closely connected with ourselves. The spectator must not be too much involved in them if he would retain his power to smile.

When Charles Wargrave next appeared at the Square he was greeted by his two small cousins with rapture. They had great news to tell him. Mademoiselle had gone away. "Oh, Uncle Charles, only think what has happened!" The information was so unexpected that he was off his guard, and his consternation was evident. "Mademoiselle de Castel-Sombre!" he said, in tones of dismay. Mrs Wargrave kept her countenance very well, and maintained a close watch upon him under her eyelids, without betraying herself; but Leicester Wargrave, who was at home, as it was Sunday, was exceedingly uneasy, and hewed away at the roast-mutton before him, though everybody had been helped, to conceal the agitation he felt.

"Oh, you know her name? It is such a funny name, like a name in a novel. I never could keep it in mind; but, of course, to introduce her to any one, in her position, it was enough to say Mademoiselle."

"Do you think so? It is scarcely like your usual good breeding," said Charles, concealing his agitation too as best he could under a tone of high and somewhat acrid superiority. "And perhaps you don't know that Castel-

Sombre is a historical name, and one of the best in Béarn—which makes a difference."

"Oh, if you go so far as that," said Mrs Wargrave, with a slight quaver in her voice. She did not resent what he said; indeed, she felt very humble before him, and deprecated any argument. "We did not know, of course, when she came, that she was any one—in particular. I mean, any one out of the ordinary."

"And has it been long settled that she was to go away?" said Charles Wargrave in his most formal voice, addressing his cousin grandly from an eminence: which he had a right to do, as at once a man of fashion and the principal partner in the firm—a right, however, which he very seldom exercised.

"Oh, it was only on Friday," cried Edith; "she never said a word till then."

"And she went away the same night, oh! in such a hurry," added Dorothy, breathless to bring forth her part of the news before she could be frustrated. "She went by the night train."

"After she had that talk in the morning, mother, with you and papa in the library," Edith burst in.

"Yes, poor thing!" said Mrs Wargrave. "She had told me on Monday night her mother was ill; and, of course, in the circumstances, I spoke to Leicester, and we did what we could to make it easier for her." Leicester paused in his destruction of the leg of mutton at this speech, and gave his wife an astonished look; but Charles was too much preoccupied to note these signs of excitement, and he had to defend himself from observation at the same time.

"That was kind of you," he said, though with a certain haughtiness. He was angry that they should have given her aid, that she should have accepted it; but this was a sentiment impossible to express. "Then I suppose you little ones have holidays now, and no lessons?" he said, attempting a lighter tone.

"Only till the new governess comes," said Edith; "and oh! mother went out that very day to ask about another," cried Dorothy, in an aggrieved tone.

"Oh!" he said; "then Mademoiselle de Castel-Sombre is not coming back?"

"She is so anxious about her mother," said Mrs Wargrave, "we thought—that is, she made up her mind—that it would be better to look for something in Paris, that she might be near her mother. You know," added the lady, seeing a chance of administering a return blow, "her mother must be quite an old lady, for Mademoiselle herself is far from young."

Charles Wargrave gave her a keen look. But the pudding had been placed before her, and she was busy serving it, an occupation quite inconsistent, surely, with any unkind meaning. Leicester was a great deal more likely to betray himself, and was indeed very uneasy, looking and feeling very guilty, wondering how his wife should be able to tell such lies, yet not venturing to contradict her; for he had been as strong as she was on the necessity of parting Charlie (if he was really such a fool) from Mademoiselle.

Little more, however, was said. Charles was so much confused by this sudden catastrophe that it took him some time to collect his thoughts. And he felt it quite possible that Claire might have fled from him, and not by any means the worst omen for his success. If she had fled it was that she was afraid of yielding. His heart rose as he reflected that, by going home, she had freed herself from all hindrance to their intercourse; that he might go and see her without having to watch for an opportunity; that he might gain partisans in her family, make himself friends. These reflections cleared his brow, and made this alarming explanation, which had hung like a thunder-cloud over Mrs Leicester Wargrave, pass over with more ease than could have been hoped. The pair exchanged a look of congratulation as they rose from the table. The danger for the moment was past, or so at least they thought.

"By the way," said Charles, when his cousin and he strolled out into the garden to smoke the inevitable cigarette, "I suppose you can give me Mademoiselle de Castel-Sombre's address in Paris?" He took his cigarette from his mouth and blew away a long pennon of smoke, as if it had been the most simple question in the world.

"Mademoiselle's address!" said Leicester Wargrave, with open eyes and mouth.

"Yes. I've—I've got a book of hers which I should like to send back."

"You'd better send it to my wife," said Leicester. "Women have ways of managing these things. You had much better send it to my wife."

"Women have ways! One would think it was some mystery you were talking of."

"I say, Charlie, I'm older than you are, and I've seen more of the world. Don't you go after that Frenchwoman. They're not to be trusted. Marry if you like, but marry an English— —"

"What are you talking of?" cried Charles, red with wonder and wrath.

"Well, I don't know. Perhaps it's only the silly way women have of looking at a thing. They said, you know—but I don't generally mind them for my part.

"I should like very much to know what they said."

Mrs Wargrave was seized with a panic when she saw the two gentlemen together. She had no confidence in her husband. "He will go and spoil everything," she said to herself; and the consequence was that she hurried out to join them, arriving just at this critical point in the conversation. "What who said?" she asked, lightly. "I believe you are talking gossip, you two."

"Leicester tells me that somebody, whom he calls the women, have been talking—apparently about me. I want to know what they said."

"You are a pair of regular old gossips," said the lady, though she grew a little pale. "They said, and he said, and she said! You need not be afraid, dear Charlie; nobody says any harm of you."

"It is to be hoped so," he replied, shortly. "Perhaps you will tell me, Marian, the address of Mademoiselle de Castel-Sombre in Paris; Leicester does not seem to know."

"Mademoiselle's address!" cried Mrs Leicester, startled like her husband.

"Is there anything so wonderful in my question? I may have something to send her. I may know some one who wants—her help."

"Dear Charlie," said Mrs Wargrave, "I know you'll think it strange when I tell you—just as if she had something to conceal!—she left no address."

He turned upon his cousin, who was gazing at his wife, and caught him unawares. Seizing his arm: "Is that true?" he said.

"Charlie, don't!" said Leicester Wargrave. "My good fellow, don't do it. You'll never repent it but once, and that will be all your life."

"What does he mean?" said Charles, turning from the husband to the wife.

"How can I tell what he means?" cried that lady. "You are very uncivil to ask him if what I say is true. It is perfectly true. He may talk as much nonsense as he pleases, but it is the plain fact that I don't know Mademoiselle's address."

Charles Wargrave looked her in the face sternly. "I do not believe you!" he said, as if every word had been a stone; and, flinging his cigarette among the bushes, he turned round and left the garden and the house. It startled him a little as he went out to receive the same answer from the butler to whom he repeated his question. "The young lady, sir, went off in a great hurry. I asked her where I should send her letters, but she said she expected no letters. And she went off without leaving an address."

Was it a conspiracy against him, framed by her? or was it some interference of Marian's? or was it true, which would almost be worst of all?

It is a bad thing not to leave an address, but it is not such an effectual shield of privacy as might be wished. What with directories and other aids, it is very difficult for any one who does not belong to the hopelessly nomadic portion of the population to conceal their whereabouts for long. Charles Wargrave had all his wits about him, and he knew his Paris as well as foreigners ever succeed in knowing that wonderful city. The result of his investigations was that before a fortnight had passed he knocked at a door on the second floor of a house in one of the smaller streets near the Arc de Triomphe, and asked to see Madame Castel. He was shown into a tiny salon, looking out upon a narrow court,—a little room full of traces of a larger life, which did not make it more attractive now, with furniture too large, pictures which seemed to overshadow its small dimensions like clouds—relics evidently of a time when the family life was not pinched and restrained as now. A photograph of Claire was on the mantelpiece among other household treasures, at sight of which the visitor gave an exclamation of relief: for, though he had come in so boldly, he had been quite uncertain whether this was or was not the place he was seeking. He was standing before the little picture which had given him the welcome assurance that he was right, when the door opened and an old lady came in. She was, as Mrs Leicester Wargrave had suggested, quite an old lady, with, a cap made of black lace covering her rusty grey hair. Keen curiosity and an almost hunger of earnestness were in her blue eyes, which kept their colour and brightness, though the countenance was so faded. She had the air of one who had kept asking, "What is it? what is it?" for weary and unsatisfied years. She was dressed with that curious neglect which characterises so many Frenchwomen indoors, in garments indescribably dingy, of the colour of poverty, a well-ascertained and understood hue—the same, with variations,

which was visible in the carpets and curtains and all the old furniture—
but had so much intelligence in her face that her age and shabbiness had
nothing in them that was disagreeable. Charles Wargrave made her his bow,
like an Englishman, not like a Frenchman, and the old lady, though her
nationality had been partly washed out by long acquaintance with Parisian
shabbiness and mannerisms and formality, the reverse of the medal of
which the brighter side only is visible to visitors, noted the difference with
a favourable impression. There was a certain witchlike ruggedness in her
features and look which betrayed the old Scotch stock, never uncongenial
with the French, from which she sprang.

"You have a daughter, Madame," said Wargrave, who felt as shy as a
schoolboy before the keen old lady, who measured him from head to foot
with her penetrating eyes.

"Two," she replied, quickly. "That is Claire, at which you are looking;
and that is Leonore, who is away, who is in a situation. My eldest daughter
came home about a fortnight ago. She has gone out to see some people who
put an advertisement in 'Galignani.' Perhaps you wish to see her—about an
engagement?"

"That is exactly what I wish," said Wargrave, with an uneasy smile.

"Ah! will you take a seat? She may come back at any moment; and if I
could in the meantime give you any particulars——"

"Madame de Castel-Sombre——"

"No, no," said the old lady, putting away the double-barrelled name, as
it were, with a wave of her hand. "Plain Castel, if you please; that is enough
for us now."

"Madame," repeated Charles Wargrave, "it is not the kind of engagement
you think of, which I wish to propose to Mademoiselle Claire."

"Ah!" cried the mother with a sudden start; "is it, well—what is it? I
may misunderstand you. Please to speak plainly. You are——?" She gave a
quick glance at his card, which she held in her hand. "It is the same name as
Claire's employers in London. Perhaps I am making a mistake. Is she called
back?"

"The people in London are my relations. I saw your daughter there; you
will not wonder, perhaps, that I admired her, that I did all I could to make
myself known to her—that I loved her."

He made a pause, feeling his story somewhat embarrassing to tell under the close inspection of the mother's eyes.

"No," she said, after a moment's pause, "I am not surprised. I have always thought Claire a very interesting woman; but, pardon me, I should have thought her a little too old for you."

"What does that matter?" he cried, vehemently angry to have this objection produced against him from the last quarter in the world where it could have been expected.

"Well, nothing, if you don't think so," said this reasonable old lady. "I only mentioned it as a fact, you know. I am afraid it will weigh with Claire herself."

"Madame Castel, I have come to throw myself upon your protection. Would it not be better for Claire to be the mistress of her own house, and that a good one, to have her own life, and that a prosperous one, even though weighted with a husband, than to live and work as she is doing now?"

"Perhaps I should think the husband the best part of it," said Madame Castel. "Your appeal is a little bewildering, seeing that I never saw you before; but I agree with you, if it is as you say. My protection, however, is not of much importance. What would you have me to do?"

"Mademoiselle de Castel-Sombre is French, and in France a mother's power is supreme."

"Ah," said the old lady, shaking her head, "don't flatter yourself. A mother's power is seldom supreme over a daughter of thirty-five; and," she added, "I would gladly secure these good things for my Claire; but she is more able to judge than I am. Does she know?"

"I have done all I could to make her aware of my respectful devotion," said the young man, with a certain formality which came to him in the air of the unaccustomed foreign place; "but, indeed, I have no reason to flatter myself. My hope is that the objections which she thought valid in my cousin's house might not exist here."

"Ah, it was in your cousin's house. Then that explains— —" Madame Castel said. She gave a sigh of relief. "I had been fearing something, I know not what. She came so suddenly, without any warning but a telegram. I see it now."

"Mother, what is it you see now?"

Claire came into the room, bringing the air of the morning with her, a fresh waft of outdoor atmosphere. She was not the Mademoiselle of the Square. There was a freedom in her movements—the freedom of a woman at home—not the enforced sobriety of an official. Her look was alert and bright; she had found pleasure in her native air, in the surroundings she loved: and yet there was a line of anxiety in her forehead. She was emancipated for the moment, and keenly felt the warm thrill of independence; but she was anxious for her future, and that of her mother, and full of care. Pleased, yet anxious and full of care—it seemed a contradiction in words—and yet Charles Wargrave saw all that, and read more, written in her face. She had not seen him as he sat within the shadow of the door, and, he thought, he had never seen her before, free to express any emotion, free to come and go as she pleased, carrying her heart in her face.

"I have not been successful," she said. "Never mind; better luck will come to-morrow. They say I am quite sure to hear of something before— — Mr Wargrave!" she cried, with a sudden step back. The blood rushed to her face and then forsook it. Her brow clouded, her countenance fell.

"Yes, Mademoiselle Claire." He had risen to his feet, and stood before her with a painful, whimsical consciousness that he could not bow like a Frenchman, which, perhaps, was the sort of thing to please her, shooting through his mind even in the excitement of the moment, and all the eager rush of feeling roused by seeing her again in this new phase.

Claire was too much startled to know what she was saying. A flood of strange feelings seemed to carry her away. Her head, which she had carried with such airy grace, drooped; something seemed to dazzle her eyes. "I did not expect," she said, faltering, "to see you here."

"I have come—to seek the protection of your mother," he said. It was said in English, but the meaning was French. And there was something so strange in the idea of Madame Castel's protection—the shabby, eager, old lady—extended to this young man, who had everything that life could bestow, that Claire, after a hard effort to restrain herself, and with something hysterical climbing in her throat, suddenly broke the embarrassment of the situation by the most inappropriate thing in the world—a burst of unsteady laughter, which returned again and again, and would not be quieted. "My mother's protection!"

It was the ridiculous which follows so close upon the heels of the sublime. But though she laughed, Claire foresaw how it would be: Madame Castel's protection threw such a weight into the scales on Charles Wargrave's side that there was scarcely anything more to say. He was not sent away again. He remained, and found the little shabby apartment divine. It was his turn to laugh when they compared notes and found that even the obstacle of age meant nothing more than a few days. And thus this little drama, so exciting while it lasted, came to a speedy and satisfactory end. It is the penalty of a happy *dénoûment* that it is not half so interesting as the painful steps that sometimes lead to it; and Claire, in all the brilliancy of her late but perfect good fortune, was too happy to mind or to attract that sympathy which attended Mademoiselle.

The Leicester Wargraves found it a bitter experience when Mademoiselle returned as Madame, with a finer house, finer carriages, more social honours, than themselves. They said everything which she had herself predicted to Mrs Wargrave that they would say, calling her a designing woman, an artful adventuress, and half-a-dozen slanders more. But if anybody was harmed by their proceedings it was themselves, and not Claire.

THE LILY AND THE THORN

CHAPTER I

The Murrays of Overbeck, in the parish of Waterdale, among the hills, were nothing but a family of peasants. Nevertheless they were the cause of so much trouble and confusion that no ducal house could have done more to excite and interest the neighbourhood, which is the reason why we now attempt to give a sketch of their earlier story. The later part of it has, alas, by other means and in other ways, been blazoned before all the world.

Elizabeth Murray, the mother, was always considered a woman out of the common. She was tall and strong and handsome even in her old age, and in her youth it was said she had been as powerful as a man, doing many feats of strength altogether beyond the power of either men or women of ordinary calibre. She it was from whom the children took their beauty. It was not beauty of the full-blown rustic kind, but that of finer quality, the only true beauty, perhaps, in the formal meaning of the word: that which involves regularity and nobleness of features rather than the evanescent charms of complexion and colour. Elizabeth was not even exalted enough in position to be called Mrs Murray. She was addressed by everybody by her Christian name. She was a woman who drove her beasts to the field, milked her cows and churned her butter with her own hands, and would hoe and dig her potatoes without flinching, had there been need. But she had the carriage and bearing of a queen, and a majestic style of form and feature such as few queens possess. When she stood in the little market-place in Waterside, with her eggs and chickens for sale, she might have been a Roman matron—Portia, stately in old age, or the mother of Coriolanus. It was said that there was Gipsy blood in her veins, and no one knew where she came from, or how it was that a peaceable countryman like Abel Murray should have wanted to marry her. There were many who did not hesitate to say that she had driven the poor man to death. But it is easy to say such things, and very difficult to prove them. If her strength, high spirit, and imperious temper were too much for him, Abel Murray was not the man to say it; but he died, nevertheless, leaving her open to such accusations, as he might have done had he married a white maiden with no character at all. But he left all he had in her hands, with the three little children, who were as yet too young to be anything but encumbrances; and Elizabeth had worked for her children like a slave, like a heroine. All that they had in the world was a little house among the hills, far from all other habitations of men, and a few bare, unproductive fields, less profitable than they were sacred, as having been "in the family" for generations. Here the widow toiled and struggled alone, telling nobody of her privations and indebted to nobody, making out of her few cows and her poultry-yard enough to support her children and bring them safely through the simple dangers of childhood. From dangers more serious, however, where is the mother, however exalted, who can defend her sons and daughters? She was absolutely and passionately devoted to them, and during all the best years of her life toiled for them night and day; and if afterwards, when those perils befell them which she could not guard them from, Elizabeth, used to sacrifice everything in her own person, became selfish for her children and exacted sacrifices from others, such as she herself felt it natural to make, may not a little pity mingle with the blame her fault deserved? The passion of motherhood does not bear so high a place among human passions as it once was supposed to do, being set down now as a sort of animal instinct merely, we are told. But high or low, it is a very great and strong and overwhelming sentiment, and now and then works harm enough as well as good.

She had three children, all dark and handsome like herself. The eldest boy, Abel, was a young Hercules, stronger and taller for his age than any boy in the neighbourhood; and his little sister Lily, almost as soon as she reached her teens, had been talked of far and near as the beauty of Waterdale. Abel had other qualities besides. When he was about twelve years old his mother deprived herself of his services, then just becoming valuable, in order to send him to school. He went through storms and sunshine, never missing a day, whatever might be the weather, and in a year had driven the parish schoolmaster to despair, who had no more to teach him. He was as clever as he was handsome, and he was more ambitious than either, and full of that intellectual curiosity which is the making of a scholar. It was a fatal day for Elizabeth when she sent the boy to school, as all who knew them said. He could read and write very well before he went there at all, and what does a country boy want more? But after he had begun there was no getting him to care for anything else but learning. He borrowed all the schoolmaster's store of books, which was not great, and devoured them; then interested the clergyman and got admission to his library; then, best and worst of all, so caught the attention of a visitor that his whole lot in life was changed. This stranger took the boy and sent him to a school where he could learn more than was possible in Waterdale; then finding him worth the trouble, sent him to the university and made "a gentleman" of him. Thus, instead of labouring upon the tiny miserable farm, cultivating the late little patch of corn and working among the "beasts," and taking his share in the labours which his mother had carried on since he was a child, the boy carried his handsome face and keen intellect into the world, and throve, as was supposed, though the little house at Overbeck heard little of him. In one point of view, it was hard that he should thus deprive his mother of his legitimate assistance and leave her to toil alone; but then she, of all others, was the one most anxious that he should improve his position and rise into a higher place than that in which he was born. If she felt a pang at his complete desertion of her, she never put it into words, but rejoiced that he had made his way to better things, and exulted with the whole force of her being in the consciousness that her boy was "a gentleman." She bore the additional labour without grudging, and toiled on with a high heart, never fearing work. The work was sweet so long as Abel went on prospering and progressing; and the proud mother, rejoicing in his advancement, never betrayed to any one how soon this boy for whom she had toiled forgot all about his home.

By-and-by, however, it became necessary to think how Lily, her only daughter, was to set out in life. Lily had grown to be seventeen amid the silence of the hills. She had the education of her class, could read well enough, and write decently, though without any clear principles as to spelling, and she was no doubt in her turn a help to her mother, who was still strong and vigorous bodily, and in the prime of her days. Lily had plenty to do at home, and might have gone on there, never venturing upon the world, if she had chosen. But in that humble class it is recognised that a lass as well as a lad may naturally desire to see something of the world and to try her wing and her fortune even out of the cosiest nest. It never occurred to Elizabeth Murray to question this law of nature; indeed, had Lily chosen to remain under the shelter of her mother's shadow for ever, it is probable that the mother would have held it her duty to send her forth to try her own powers and strength. The only question was, what was Lily to do? To go to service was the first thing they thought of, and indeed tried; and the beautiful girl, looking like a half-savage princess, full of natural dignity, but untrained to conventional "manners," sometimes rude in youthful ignorance, if always sweet in natural temper, marched down from her native hills where all was wild and solitary and free, into the restraint of a little genteel home in a little gossiping village, and there made, as was very natural, a disastrous failure in her first place. Lily did not understand the many restraints nor the unceasing scoldings; and the minute and constant supervision to which she was subjected drove her wild with indignation and resentment. What was she, the daughter of a woman who sold butter and eggs in the market, to "speak back" to a lady—and to be as fond of her own way as if she had been a lady too? Elizabeth was sent for, and there were storms and passions; but the upshot was that Lily, after having been smoothed down and calmed on Saturday by her mother's representations and remonstrances, overcome by home-sickness and love of freedom, and general disgust with the world which was so contrary, ran away secretly on Sunday evening, and got home at midnight, to the great scandal of the gossips in the village she had left, who were very eager to find out who had been with her. But no one had been with her. Lily had not learned enough by that time either of herself or others to be vain. She was as yet more annoyed and angered by the stare of wondering admirers than pleased by their admiration. All life was still before her, a vague sweet chaos, undiscerned and undivined.

But after this it became more impossible still that Lily should tamely stay at home and help her mother. Though "the town" had been disagreeable to her while she was in it, it had a certain charm when recollected in the fields at Overbeck, where she never saw any one. The excitement of a carriage passing now and then, a party of tourists—strangers, perhaps foreigners— or of great people of the county, lords and ladies like those in the story-books: the wild exhilaration of a show or pedlar's van, the errand to a shop where countless desirable things were to be seen at least, if not to be had— all these sweetnesses, once tasted, leave a want, a void, when they have passed away, that nothing else can fill up. Lily felt this, though she did not wish to feel it. The remembrance of the constantly exacted obedience, the unrelaxing rule, and all the crosses of her first "service," were very distasteful to her. Home at a distance had seemed heaven. But, if the flaming sword had been swept aside, and Adam and Eve had found the entrance to Paradise reopen to them after the excitement of the struggle with barren earth, would they have gone back, one wonders? Home was (theoretical) Paradise to Lily; but how gay and how exciting, if not pleasant, looked now the little Purgatory below, which had seemed no better that an Inferno to the girl cribbed and cabined and confined! The very gleam of the light in the shop window, the lamp over the inn door—what a sense of dissipation and gaiety was in them! There was nothing like this on the hills, where the stars were the only lamps, and the tinkling of the beck all the music; whereas on the other hand sometimes an organ-grinder would come into the town, and once there had been a German band! The silence and the loneliness overcame Lily after that taste of the excitements of life. She was sick of her old familiar mountains; and the horizon on the landward side, a horizon which was contracted within the limits of a tree or two and a village steeple—that was the best of all.

Then there came sinkings of heart, and fitful ill-temper upon the part of the girl, who did not know what she would be at. But Elizabeth was learning wisdom, and knew. She said, "Lily, my lass, you must not bide here. It's fine to have you, but when I'm dead and gone, what would you do up on the fells? You would have to dig potatoes like me. Service is no heritage, but to have a good trade at your fingers' ends, what a thing that would be! I think I will speak to Miss Prentice on Saturday; that's lively. You could see whatever's going on out of her windows, and folks passing by to the castle; the young squire is at home, and there's balls, and I don't know what. I'm 'most sure you will like that, Lily, my dear."

Lily was too wild to respond with immediate approval, but her heart jumped. She had seen the young ladies and the young gentlemen out riding, and what a sight it was! They filled the streets, the horses' hoofs ringing like soldiers, and the ladies' long habits sweeping down, and the horses arching their shining necks. And when there was a ball, if you knew one of the servants you might be let in to see the ladies in their beautiful dresses, and to hear the music; and sometimes Miss Prentice would be sent for with one of her girls to hold the pins. Lily's heart danced at the thought of these delights. Miss Prentice was the dressmaker in Waterside, and lived in the street which was nearest to the gate of the castle, and where everything could be seen that was going on.

Here Lily went accordingly, after there had been various consultations between her mother and the dressmaker. "My Lily is a good lass; there's no harm in her," Elizabeth said. "You may think I'm partial; but who should know her like me; and who so anxious to see if there's ill in her? She's a good lass, but she's fanciful: she takes things into her head."

"Most folks does," said Miss Prentice; "especially them that is good for something. So long as she is not taken up with lads and nonsense——"

"Never such a thought has been in her head," said Elizabeth, with some heat.

"Ah! that's more than I would say of a saint. I'm not fond of the pretty ones, for my part; they're fine to try things on, for all looks well on them; but they seldom settle to the business as I could like. Lads are the destruction of the business; but you're an honest woman, Elizabeth Murray, and you've had a fight to bring up your bairns. I'll take her and I'll try her, to show my respect for her mother; and that's as fair as I can say."

Elizabeth made her acknowledgments like a duchess, with conscious dignity. "I cannot think a bairn of mine will ever shame me," she said; "if you take her canny, you'll never get a saucy word from my Lily. It's the unmannerly that make bad manners. If I saw her with a good business at her finger-ends I think I could die happy."

"Die! not you! You're not of the dying kind," said Miss Prentice, briskly; "and as for the business, if she will stick to the business, it will never forsake her: if she be not too bonnie for the business," the dressmaker added with a sigh. She was an enthusiast for her profession, as all artists should be, and sighed at the thought of those temptations of intrusive life which tempt the neophyte astray.

Thus it was that Lily came to Waterside to learn the dressmaking. She was a great deal too pretty for the business. Miss Prentice, who was a wise woman in her way, and who felt the advantage of having a girl (in such lonely places not yet called a young lady) upon whom every garment looked well, took great precautions in her treatment of the mountain Lily, and grew fond of her, and made much of her. And by-and-by Lily became enlightened as to the sweetness of admiration. She learned after a time why it was that the young squire rode past so slowly, staring at the dressmaker's window, and why other young men of less high degree passed the same way so often. She pretended even to herself that she was very angry with them all, for staring at her thus. But in her heart she soon ceased to be angry, and began to find the universal homage not unsweet. When she heard the horse's hoofs she was not averse to being visible or half-visible behind the fashion-book in the window. How handsome he looked on his horse, handsomer than the lads on foot—the town-lads who went and came, and saw nothing but the book of fashions! Lily's heart began to beat a little quicker at certain hours of the day when (she began to divine) he was likely to pass. He! of course; who could any one mean by that but the chief gentleman of the place, young Squire Ridley, who up the water and down the water was better known than any other man?

Meanwhile, Elizabeth had to help her with the beasts and the potatoes, and all her work, only the other boy, the youngest, of whom nothing has been said. No one thought it necessary to say anything about him. He was only Dick—he was the man of all work, though he was but sixteen. He was Elizabeth's prop, her right hand, whom she could always depend upon; but she did not make much account of Dick, any more than other people did. He never gave any trouble,—whatever anxiety came, it would not be by his means.

CHAPTER II

When Lily began her dressmaking in the Waterside village, her brother Abel had just attained the highest object of his ambition. He had become a fellow of his college, and thus was provided at once with the means of living, and with a position which was doubly dear to him, in that it supplied his greatest want, a recognised standing-ground and social rank, such as it is. Nothing could be more honourable to a man than thus to have gained, by his own exertions, a position so entirely satisfactory; but there were elements involved which made his success very different from that of most of his contemporaries. He did not announce it to his family, or indeed give them the least hint of this new step in life, with all the advantages it brought. This was not because he wanted to be unkind, or from any mean desire to keep his prosperity to himself. Could he have sent to them anonymously, without risk of inquiry, a share of his income, he would have been glad to do so; but he did not know how to resume his intercourse with them in his changed circumstances. What pleasure could there be in any meeting now, he asked himself? It seemed to him that any contact with the rude homely habits of his own class would be intolerable: all the more intolerable that he could not deceive himself on the subject, or deny that the honest, thrifty peasant folk were a credit to him, as he, were he as good as they, would be a credit to them. It must be allowed in his defence that a young University man of distinguished talents and prospects, to whom the best society in the country might be open, and who was already on intimate terms with many young great people and dawning notabilities, had need be of heroic strain to be capable of confessing that his mother was a woman who sold eggs and butter in the market. And Abel was not heroic. He was excitable, susceptible, nervous, and visionary, doing little credit, so far, to his mountain breeding. Perhaps it was because the fact of his dependence, and the extreme goodness of the patron who had done so much for him, had been unduly impressed upon his young mind, that he was so anxious now to conceal his origin entirely, and shrank from his family and kind with so much dread and horror. But it is more difficult to explain how, doing this, he should yet have accepted the invitation which young Charley

Landale, a much humbler member of his college, pressed upon him eagerly yet timidly. The Landales were well known to Abel, though they knew him only as a great scholar and "rising man," of whose friendship their son was proud. They were gentry of Waterdale, and it was thus to his own district, the very parish in which he had been brought up, that he was invited to go. It was madness to do so; yet he did it with rash excitement in consciousness of the danger, and foolish hankering after his birthplace: a kind of loyalty in disloyalty, very strange and unusual. Though the idea that his parentage might be found out alarmed him beyond measure, yet the thought of going "home" was sweet, in the most inconsistent way. Discovery would be death; but to dare discovery, to push danger to the very verge of ruin, was excitement, and made his heart beat. He liked the thrill of feeling, though it was pain, and might be destruction. His entire being seemed to be quickened with that mixture of pleasure, and wretchedness, and fear. And so it came to pass that just as Lily began to enter into the secret delight of having a lover who was "a gentleman," Abel reappeared in Waterdale, as the honoured guest of one of the best families in the district—he who had been a shepherd boy, a rough-shod, unkempt urchin, when he left the place. He was even told of the beauty of the village as he was driven through it, and directed to Miss Prentice's window. "There is such a pretty girl there!" Charley said, pointing with his whip as he drove past. How little he knew! Thus the brother and sister, unknown to each other, were brought together by the mysterious entanglements of fate.

The two greatest houses in the district were those of the Ridleys, who lived in the Castle, and were the oldest and furthest descended of all the gentry of the county; and the Featherstonhaughs, who, though probably of as old descent (for do not we all derive from Adam?), had come into importance only within the last four or five generations. Sir Richard, the present representative of the latter family, was still young, a man of five-and-thirty, and divided the suffrages of the district with Roger Ridley, the eldest son of the Squire, who was, though much younger, his natural rival in almost every way. Roger was the most popular of the two with the countryside generally, being what it is usual to call thoroughly English: a young man who threw himself into the popular life, was a bold rider, a fair shot, and ready to take his part in all the sports of his contemporaries, small or great. Sir Richard had his partisans more chiefly in his own class. He was not so frank and friendly, not so open to all comers as the young squire, but he was master of his own house and goods, whereas Roger Ridley was only second, and dependent on his father; and he was rich and entertained largely, which the family at Waterside Castle were not wealthy enough to do. This rivalry, however, had been apparently brought to an end by the betrothal of Sir Richard to Roger's sister, Mary Ridley, a young lady of whom Waterdale was proud. Mary was too good for Featherstonhaugh, the partisans of the Ridleys said; but it was a marriage so entirely suitable in every point of view, that no reasonable person could find a word to say against it, and all social difficulties and family contentions were settled by it. These details of local history Charley Landale told to his visitor when they strolled out, soon after Abel's arrival, "to see the neighbourhood," with which the stranger was so anxious to show no acquaintance. The Landales were within the charmed circle of county people, and highly esteemed in Waterdale, but they had no claim to approach the greatness of the Ridleys and Featherstonhaughs.

Landale took his friend to the water, and showed him with pride the beautiful lake, fringed by low hills, with lines of greater peaks in the distance. "There's the Castle on the right hand. I'll ask Ridley to show you all over it some day. It's a wonderful old place; and that is the chase, spreading along to the west. They have some of the finest oaks in the county there. The village lies lower down, but we passed through it, don't you remember? That's the beck, as they call it, meandering down from the hills. Do you see the road, like a white line, above the bridge? There's a most glorious view from that point. Oh yes, I suppose you who have been in Switzerland may despise it perhaps—but we are of a different opinion. I don't think anything in the world can be much finer—the lake in the foreground, and all the hills behind."

"You may be sure I shan't despise it," said Abel. How well he knew every point his good-humoured companion showed him!—Not a curve of the shore, not a little bay or inlet that was not far more familiar to him than to Charley. He had gone bird's-nesting in the chase before he was breeched. He had fished in the lake almost before he could speak. He had roamed out and in of all the wonders of the Castle, and could have guided the Ridleys themselves, not to say Charley Landale, about all its holes and corners. But nothing of this dared he to say. He stood and gazed like a man in a dream, feeling that it was unsafe to open his lips, and that even his eyes alone must betray him. But no one suspected him. The good Landales would as soon have believed he came from Jupiter as that he came under false pretences; and Charley believed in him as he believed in the British constitution or any of the other standards which are unquestionable by men of his simplicity of faith.

"Now look out," said Charley as they turned homeward, the dinner hour being near. They had made a long round to see the country, and had dropped in at the house of another college acquaintance five miles off for lunch. "Now look out—for if we have luck we may see the Lily, and she is worth looking at. It's an uncommon kind of face—not pink and white, like the usual village beauty; she's dark, as dark as you are, with eyes like two stars; you never saw such eyes. Come this way, it is not so dusty as the high road. This is the lover's lane—there's always a lover's lane close by a village; and by Jove, Murray, look out—here's a pair of lovers in it; bad luck for them, but rather fun for us. Why should two people always look so caught? They might put the best face upon it; they might have met by accident— they might be talking business. But they always betray themselves and look guilty. Hallo! upon my word; it is Lily herself—and," he added, with a low whistle of wonder and dismay, "Ridley, I do believe!—what an ass, in broad day!"

Murray looked at the two figures in the distance with strange intensity of interest. He remembered the young squire well, and all about him,—his lordly good-nature and liberality—the sixpences he would toss at a poor boy who held his horse, though himself very little older than that boy. He was interested to see him again, to note whether time had changed him much, even to run the risk of recognition; but how could Roger Ridley see in young Landale's companion the boy who had held his horse, and to whom he had chucked sixpences? Abel pressed on, somewhat eagerly, not listening to Charley, who had begun to think of retreat. "If we turn back they'll think no one has seen them," Charley was saying; "it's not a pleasant thing to be caught like this; suppose we turn back?"

"Is that your Lily?" said Abel. A great sudden flush had come to his face. They were not near enough to see her features distinctly, but there was something in her general air and aspect that struck him. Instead of paying any attention to Charley's suggestion, he went on with great strides. And by this time the pair had seen them, and Landale's precautions were of no further avail. Good-natured Charley did not perceive at the first moment that it was his friend's fault. He was compunctious as to his own share in it; but it was too late now to turn or go back.

"It is I that am an ass," he said; "a lover's lane ought to be sacred: but never mind, Murray, come along, there is no good in looking conscious now. Come along, as if it were the most natural thing in the world. Oh, yes, it's Lily, sure enough. There, she's off, poor little dear! I dare say she hates you and me. See how ceremoniously he is taking off his hat to her; met by accident, of course. Hallo, Ridley! you have come this way, like ourselves, to avoid the dust, I suppose?"

"That is so," said Roger, coming up to them with the portentous gravity of a man who has something to conceal. "It is the short cut from Grimston, where I've just been for my father. He is in full cry after some excavations they have been making. You know his antiquarian turn; and look here—I dare say it's some new manufactured antiquity from Brummagem direct—no, not that," he said, with confusion, "I don't mean that," dropping a little gold locket of very modern form and resplendent newness. Murray stooped to pick it up, but was forestalled by the owner, who snatched at it, raising a flushed and excited countenance as he hid the toy in his hand. "It is this I mean," he cried, taking an old coin out of his waistcoat pocket. Then he stood facing the two young men uneasily. "I think it is the hottest day we have had this season," he said.

It was not Abel's part to speak. He was himself too much agitated to do so. He would have known the young squire anywhere, if he had met him at the end of the world, he felt; and the sudden shock of recognition drove out of his mind the more important question who the girl was. He bent his head over the coin which Ridley held out in his hand. Why should not he be recognised as easily as the other? He dared not face the defiant yet abashed eyes with which the young squire stared at him, responding with a hurried bow to Landale's introduction. But the coin was safe ground; he peered at it, bending towards it as if he had been short-sighted, and glad of the little learning that gave him something to say. "Have you Roman remains here?" he said. "I think the coin is genuine." Roger Ridley started slightly at the sound of his voice.

"That will please my father," he said, and looked at Murray again. There was some thrill of likeness in the voice—a tone which recalled to him the other voice which as yet had scarcely died out of his ear—a fantastic likeness, no doubt suggested by his own imagination, which was full of Lily. "I will tell him you vouch for it," he added, with a smile, "and if he agrees with you (which he is sure to do, for one always believes in Roman remains on one's own land), he will think you an oracle. Bring Mr Murray to see the Castle, Charley. And good-bye, for I must hurry home."

"Ay, ay, he'll hurry home now we have parted him from Lily," said Charley, nodding his head. "You see for yourself. That is what I told you. He will commit himself and do something foolish if he doesn't mind."

"Who is she?" said Abel: his heart was thumping against his side with many emotions. To have looked the young squire calmly in the face, whom he knew so well, and to have borne his gaze, was surely enough for one day.

"Oh, a country lass, I believe; the daughter of a woman up on the fells. By the way, her name's Murray, like yours. It's partly a Gipsy name, you know."

"Is it?" said Abel. This time he could not hear his own voice, so loud was his heart beating. But he added, "All Scotch names have a democratic wideness; the clan includes both high and low." This was what he meant to have said. And as Charley looked quite unmoved it is to be supposed he got it safely uttered; but his blood was running at such a force through his veins, and his heart going like the piston of a steam-engine, with such tumult and riot of sound, that whether he said these words or not, or said some others in place of them, he never knew.

CHAPTER III

Lily had met the young squire many times already in the Lover's Lane. The back-door of Miss Prentice's little house was near of access, and the girl had been too much dazzled by her conquest to think of right and wrong. Besides, had she been put to defend herself, she had, you may be sure, enough to say. There is no harm in meeting your sweetheart when you have no reason to be ashamed of him; and she was a free-born lass of the fells, and what if she did meet Mr Ridley and talk to him? Did that harm any one? She herself was proudly indifferent to being badly spoken of. "Those that know me," said Lily, "know me—and that's enough." She was proud, she meant no harm, and why should there be any danger in talking to a civil-spoken gentleman? Only ridiculous people with prejudices could see harm in it. It was a scolding from Miss Prentice which made Lily accord the first interview to the young squire. "It means no good to a lass like you when a gentleman comes after her," the dressmaker had said, and Lily had blazed into fury. "Them that speaks civil to me, I'll speak civil to them," the hot-headed girl said in all the pride of conscious purity. That was not the way to take a lass, the forewoman remarked, shaking her head; and she took the rustic beauty aside and whispered to her that however pleasant a gentleman's ways might be, the like of them kept honest lads away. "And to lose a good honest man that would give you a good house of your own, all for a laugh with the young squire, that would be little to your advantage." "Am I thinking of a man, or of what would be for my advantage?" said Lily, bursting away from this second counsellor, stung with vexation and shame. And it was in this mood that she rushed out, all tears and wrath, her eyes sparkling, her cheeks glowing, almost into young Ridley's arms. There were ladies of his own rank in the countryside for whom he had a general admiration, and any one of whom, if thrown in his way, might have absorbed the thoughts of the light-hearted young man; but Lily blazed upon him in her agitation, more beautiful, and far more engaging, than any of them. She wept to him, and stormed and laughed and bid him go, yet let him stay, with all the caprice which is more captivating than good sense and virtue.

He had never been so much amused, so charmed out of himself; no one had ever before so thrown open to him the doors of her inner being: and all these changes and fluctuations reflected in the most lovely eyes he had ever seen, and touched and modified and softened by reference to himself, how could he be otherwise than overcome? As for Lily, his manners, so different from all the rural lads, his respect and delicacy which touched the finer fibres in the girl's heart, even his clothes and external graces, and the princely way in which he would take off his hat to her—the swains of the fells did not think it necessary to take off their hats—subdued her wholly. Perhaps she was in love with the gentleman even before she was in love with Roger; but that warmer sentiment had already sprung up when she was startled and fled off like a frightened dove at the sudden apparition of these two strange figures strolling down the Lover's Lane. Two *men*! what business had they there? Another pair would have comprehended, would have been full of fellow-feeling; but the harsh unsympathetic appearance of the two dark figures shutting out the light felt like discovery, like a judicial sentence. Lily fled, though the moment was so interesting. He had just shown her a locket, which he was going to give her—the little glistening golden toy had been held up for her admiration, and her hand was timidly put forth to take it, "only to look at it," with rising tears and compunctions, when these two heaved in sight, and Lily turned and fled. As she rushed away with her heart beating, it seemed to her that Providence itself had interfered. To "speak to" any one so civil and so kind, to speak when you were spoken to, was of the very alphabet of rustic politeness. Who could find fault with that? no one—not even her mother. But even Lily, already half-beguiled, felt that when she took a present from the young squire another link would be riveted. Ornaments were not so common then as now, and the trinket was a temptation to her, as well as the still more delightful thought of having thus a link between them, and something of his which it would make her heart jump to receive and to look at. But a present—it was not right to take a present,—it seemed to bind her to something, it seemed like a promise given.

The path of the girl who has wandered into those dazzling forbidden ways, and has "a gentleman coming after her," is full of thorns and difficulties, if also of pride and dazzling hopes. When Miss Prentice and her girls were about to sit down to their homely supper, the little maid-of-all-work mysteriously whispered to Lily that there was "one wanting to speak to her," an intimation which set the girl's heart once more beating. Who could it be? She was half disappointed, half relieved, to find that it was only an old woman, who gave her a little parcel and had nothing to say; but when the enclosure, being opened, was found to contain the locket and a letter, Lily's whole being was suddenly penetrated with excitement and surprise, and that delicious self-consciousness which is made up of vanity and delight and gratitude. She read only a few words in the letter, words which seemed to fill her veins with a subtle warmth, expanding her whole being, and thrust it into her pocket, that she might obey the call of Miss Prentice, hungry for her supper, who was calling at the foot of the stairs for Lily. Lily had run to her own room to see what the communication was. She came down-stairs so rapidly as to account for the colour in her cheeks; but how account for the dazzle in her eyes, which were so shining, yet misty with the excess of light in them? Miss Prentice could not tell what to make of her: "You're thinking of something?" she said, with quickly awakened suspicion. "Most folks think of something—except them that's stupid," was Lily's reply; and what answer could be made to it? Yet, though it was a truism, Miss Prentice's query had a just meaning; something that had nothing to do with the bread and cheese, something very different from Miss Musgrave's petticoat and Mrs Armstrong's new mantle, something that was beyond the dressmaking, was in Lily's eyes. "I wish that girl was with her mother. I wish she had never darkened my door. I wish she were safe away, and no harm done," Miss Prentice said to her forewoman. "Hoot! there's no harm in her," said that functionary, who did not think her employer knew what way to take a lass. But the dressmaker shook her head. "Them that have little harm in themselves are sometimes the cause of plenty of harm to others," she said, sententiously. But how could she let the mother know, when all she had to tell of was that dazzlement in Lily's eyes?

And what a business it was for Lily to get her letter read and her beautiful locket looked at! She was not so happy as to have a room to herself, and there was "something to finish," which the girls had to return to, and which kept them stitching till it was late. When she tried to get away for a moment her comrades looked black at her, as one who was evading her share of the work, and Miss Prentice called her back, with something which sounded like a taunt. "You'll not go out, young woman, again, to-night," she said. "I was not going out, nor thinking of going out," said Lily, instantly on the defensive. "I was wanting—to look out, and see what kind of a night it was." So that it was not till the morning dawned, and showed her room companion fast asleep, that Lily ventured to finish reading that beautiful letter which was like nothing she had ever heard of before. She had not been able to sleep for thinking of it, and she had held her locket in her hand, and put it on a ribbon to try how it felt on her neck in the dark, not venturing to light her candle. In the blue dawn, as it gradually made everything visible, she did not venture on so much as this; but folded it away in its paper, after once making acquaintance with it, under cover of her little bit of curtain. Her companion slumbered soundly, unmoved by her restlessness. It was a grievance to Lily generally that this companion snored, but how glad she was that Sarah should snore this morning, showing herself fast asleep! She read her letter thus over and over, her young bosom swelling with pride and happiness, her heart afloat on a vague sea of imaginative delight. How his praises and his protestations seem to fill her very veins with sweetness, smoothing away all fear or trouble! The sensation was so exquisite that Lily did not know how to contain it. She, a country lass and no more, was it she that was that queen among women, that lily among all the meaner flowers, that angel on earth? She did not understand it, nor did she believe it. But the incredulous confusion of wonder and almost amusement in her mind only enhanced the happiness. Lily had never thought it of any serious importance what was said to her by any "lad"; lads talked to lasses like that always from the beginning of time; meaning—yes, something, no doubt— to make themselves agreeable, to gain a little amusement for themselves. But no one thought anything more of it: a stroll through the Lover's Lane, a laughing and a talking, a grip of her hand, or attempt, never successful, for Lily was *farouche* in shy pride, at a kiss—that was nothing, and meant nothing,—but this— —?

For the truth was that the young squire had been much more seriously affected than Lily by the events of the evening. He had been caught in his love-making, and convicted of it even, for had not the stranger seen the little locket which he had bought for his Lily? Through the eyes of that stranger he seemed to see—what? His beautiful Lily, a mere village belle, to be flirted with by any one—by the stranger's self, perhaps, when his, Ridley's, back was turned. This thought irritated him in the wildest way. Perhaps he divined that Lily was not yet "in love with" himself, and therefore had no defence against the overtures of another; and real love is always modest, thinking every other adventurer more likely of success than itself. This idea had been more than he could bear. He had been a careless fellow enough, harming no one, indeed, but no way specially on his guard as to the looks he might send hither or thither, the words he might say; was this the retribution for many a light flirtation? The idea that Lily was but one of the others, and would lend as willing an ear to Charley Landale, for instance, or Charley Landale's friend, stung him to the quick. In an instant all the difference came home to him. Lily!—there was but one Lily in the world, and she was his, or else, as all poetry and romance said, he was no more his own. Nothing like this had happened to him in his life before. The idea of another man talking of love to Lily, perhaps gaining her attention, that was not to be endured. It was this that made him write the letter which she read in the blue morning before even the birds were awake. "My Lily, my darling! you hold my life in your hands," he said. Was it true? There was no reason for saying it if it were not true. Nothing could he gain but Lily, except the loss of all that it was possible to lose. His father, who was no dainty gentleman indeed, but proud as Lucifer, proud of his moss-trooping ancestors and old descent, was capable of excommunicating his son for such a crime, though he could not disinherit him; and Roger knew very well from what a height of scorn his sister, she who was to marry young Featherstonhaugh, would look down upon such a plebeian bride. All these things were food for thought before he committed himself, but his heart leapt beyond all thought when he wrote that letter pouring forth his impassioned heart to the soft, unawakened creature, who as yet knew no more how she was expected to respond than she understood any other mystery.

And there had been another stimulant to his rising passion administered that same afternoon. When Lily fled, Roger had stood still, thrilling in every nerve, and talked to the new-comers, longing all the time to pick a quarrel with them, little suspecting who one of them was; and when, having got rid of them, he turned, excited and irritated, homeward, whom should he meet but Featherstonhaugh, his brother-in-law that was to be. Sir Richard's engagement to his sister Mary had not been much to Roger's taste. The fellow had but half a heart, he always thought, and he was not worthy of Mary Ridley. Mary had thought otherwise, however, and it was she who had to decide. But when the young squire met his rival potentate in the moment of his own discomfiture, when all his nerves were jarring and thrilling, it is impossible to describe the causeless irritation that seized him. He felt more like a quarrel than he had ever felt before in his life.

"Going home?" the one said to the other, with all the dulness of a man who has nothing else to say.

"Yes; are you dining with us?" said Ridley, equally commonplace.

"Not to-day; I have still my house full. Did you meet any one as you came along? I have just seen a—vision—a—I don't know who she was—a wonderful creature to behold upon the road to Waterside."

"Here is enthusiasm!" said Roger, laughing harshly. "If it were not Mary—Mary, I think, has reason to complain."

"Mary!—oh, it was not a lady at all!" cried Sir Richard, with some eagerness. "It was—a girl—a—somebody of the lower classes. Mary! She would have admired as much as I did, had she been here."

"I would not advise you to trust to that," said Roger, growing less and less pleasant in tone. Featherstonhaugh looked at him surprised. He did not feel guilty in respect to Mary; in fact, he had not thought of Mary at all, and the suggestion annoyed him a little. Surely he was not compelled to shut his eyes in future to every beautiful face because of Mary! He looked at Roger curiously. The incipient rivalry and enmity between the two had not gone so far with him as with the other, but yet he felt it also. Roger was not of his species, a rough fellow, given to sports and rural dissipation, who did not know a Claude from a Poussin, or a Hobbema from a Ruysdael (in Sir Richard's day the worship of the early Italians was for the moment in abeyance, so he did not swear by Botticelli). The thought came upon him then strongly, as he stood confronting his neighbour and future relation, that to go through the world with this fellow always near would take a great deal of the pleasure out of life.

"And what was the goddess like?" Roger added in his own despite. He was so wroth and so sore that the smile he forced grew into a sneer without any will of his. Had the lout been drinking? was the question which, with some disgust, Sir Richard asked himself.

"I daresay it is some beauty of the village," he said, keeping his temper; "but since you did not see her, it is not worth while talking about it. I asked for mere—curiosity—because it is rare to see so perfect a face." Then he added, after a pause, "You met those other men, I suppose? I hear Charley Landale had a great scholar with him. Who is it, do you know? A known man? or only one of the lesser lights who may represent great scholarship here?"

"I never knew we were so ignorant in Waterdale," said Roger, finding it very difficult to master himself, "but I daresay you're right enough," he added, forcing a smile. "I saw Charley Landale with some owl or other, but I did not pay much attention. Scholars don't lie much in my way. I leave all that sort of thing to you, Featherstonhaugh; there may as well be some division of labour, you know."

"What will be your share?" said the other, not intending any insult; for indeed, it seemed to him, a man who knew nothing about art and did not care for knowledge, what could be his share of anything worth thinking of? Roger coloured to his hair, and said something that was not pious under his breath.

"I'm off," he said. "It is pleasant to know that you entertain so good an opinion of me." And with a wave of his hand he turned away. On the whole Sir Richard had the best of it. Roger went home with an additional sting in his heart: for it was true enough that Featherstonhaugh knew much more than he did, and could take advantage of all he knew, and probably a little more. And he was Mary's betrothed lover, confound him, and yet had noticed *her*! But of that, indeed, who could say anything? Could there be on the face of the earth a clod so heavy, a lout so insensible, as to see her and pass her by without wondering worship? A perfect face! Yes, indeed, it was a perfect face, but not one that would ever smile for Dick Featherstonhaugh.

·

CHAPTER IV

A few days afterwards, Charley Landale and his friend went to the Castle by special invitation to see the old squire's books and antiquities, and himself. "Don't stay talking to the girls; I would as soon keep the Queen waiting for luncheon," said Charley, on the way down-stairs, "as the old squire. He is an old Turk if ever there was one. They dare not say their souls are their own. Even Mary—but of course you don't know anything about Mary?"

"No. I suppose not; unless perhaps I may have met her in society," said Murray, with a faltering in his voice which he could not quite steady. It was not in him to say boldly that he knew nothing about Mary—Mary, whom he remembered, from her floating hair to her dancing feet, a vision of delight. Her name thrilled through him, though he had only a boy's recollection of her to move him. Once, when he was just on the edge of the ascent which had led to fortune, Mary had been at the Vicarage, when he in his new clothes, the *protégé* of the Vicar's friend, had been there also, and they had shared the nursery tea together and made friends. The children had all patronised Abel, but Mary had been kind. She had taken a fancy to the common boy whom the young people at the Vicarage considered beneath them, and that perhaps was why he remembered her so tenderly; though by this time a little sentimental haze of fancy and distance encircled that meeting, and Abel was of opinion that he had entertained a boyish passion for the young lady who was so much his superior. With the strangest tremor at his heart he went to meet her now. He knew he should recognise her wherever he met with her—would not she know him also? The sense of danger excited him. He had his nerves strung for self-defence, not remembering what other uglier words might apply perhaps to what he said—Lies! in strict fact it might be so; but it is very seldom at Abel's age that one has boldness to characterise the little fictions that may be necessary to give the world a true impression of one's dignity boldly as lies: they are, perhaps, inventions, little flights of the imagination; or he who tells them is "led into them," not by premeditation, unconsciously, by accident; lies are told by other people, seldom by ourselves. If they asked him point-blank whether he was Abel

Murray, why then, to be sure—but they were not likely to ask that question in so many words, and for the rest it should be as his stars ordained.

Roger Ridley met them at the gate, and led Murray to the library where his father was. "Find your way to the drawing-room, Charley; no one expects you or me to know anything," he said. "This is the way to my father's sanctum," and he pushed back the curtains and opened the oak door. The passages were panelled oak, dark, with a glistening of reflection about, while heavy curtains were hung here and there to shut out draughts and noise from the squire's sanctuary. Murray, who was used to the serious luxury of old wainscot and pictures, followed him silently, with less sense of the incongruity of the position than if they had taken the other turn which led to Miss Ridley's presence-chamber, the heart of the house. The squire in his library was not necessarily more awe-inspiring than the head of a college. Yet when he found himself in the old lofty room, clothed with books, Abel felt that to himself no head of a college could be so alarming as this old gentleman, whose keen eyes seemed to search through and through him, with suspicion in them, or so at last it seemed to his guilty soul. He remembered being brought there once before for some supposed offence to endure the inspection of the squire's keen eyes. It seemed the very same look which pierced him to the midriff now, and Mr Ridley's words were not reassuring. "How do you do, Mr Murray?" he said; "I am very glad to see you. Such visitors as you are rare in a country place. But God bless me, your face is familiar! I think I must have seen you before?"

Abel's cheeks grew crimson again, but he answered bravely with a smile, "I do not think I have ever had that honour; but we are always knocking up against each other, the Americans say, in this little island."

At this gentle pleasantry the squire laughed, or pretended to laugh. "A curious people the Americans," he said—"very odd people. I have had one or two of them down here. This is the sort of thing they don't understand. It's a sad puzzle to them; existing for so many centuries and yet not much of a thing after all," said the squire, waving his hands towards his surroundings. He kept a corner of his eye upon Abel to watch how he responded to this challenge.

"No, not much of a thing," said Murray, looking round upon it with veneration,—"only the most perfect old house in England. It may not be a very great matter, as you say, but there is nothing else like it in the world."

"Ah!" said the squire, rubbing his hands, "I perceive you know what you are talking of. I have a few old books here to show you, which I think will please you. We are not rich, but we have never been tempted, like some people, to turn all our treasures into money. We have a few old pictures still and old books to enrich the old walls. I wish my son was more interested in them, but Roger cares for none of these things. He has not my tastes. 'A primrose by the river's brim, a yellow primrose was to him'—Well, well, Mr Murray, we are not all made alike. You are one of the Scotch Murrays, I suppose?"

This question came in so suddenly that Abel, though he ought to have been on his guard, was startled. "By origin, yes, no doubt," he said; then added, with more self-command, "But I have been brought up by a—friend. I know more about my adopted family than my own."

"Ah!" the squire said, with a momentary stare; then he opened a glass case and plunged into the congenial occupation of showing his treasures. Roger, who knew them all by heart, after a time went quietly away, leaving the stranger alone with his father. What a strange sensation it was! and how clear and distinct was the recollection of standing in this same room a dozen years before, his head drooping, his heart beating as loudly as now. If the squire should turn upon him, and charge him with his real origin—if he should demand to know on what pretext the son of Elizabeth Murray, of Overbeck, had found his way among the Ridleys, what could the intruder say? But Mr Ridley asked no such questions, made no uncomfortable suggestions. On the contrary, he took down all the treasures of which he was most proud, and the illuminated MS. which (he said) the British Museum had bid for, to show to the only person, with an air of knowing anything about it, who had visited him for years. Abel, for his part, did not much believe in that story about the British Museum. But he examined the treasures with understanding, and said all that could be said in praise of them, and to the glory of the family who possessed them, listening even patiently to the squire's account of his grandfather, who was a collector, though with so much buzzing in his ears, and curious bewilderment of suppressed feeling, that he scarcely could follow the story. Abel had been in greater houses than this, and had talked familiarly to men more notable than Squire Ridley; but he could not forget the abashed boy, whom he seemed to see standing there, in his rough country clothes, listening to the squire's objurgations with a beating heart. He could not forget him. He was two people, not one, in that haunted place. "You little rascal, if I hear anything of the kind again I'll have you soundly whipped to show you what your duty is"—was that what the squire was saying?—or was it this, "My grandfather came just in time to make a good bargain with the superior of the convent: the poor monk had ceased to care for what was once the glory of their house," &c. Instead of sobbing audibly, with his fists rammed into his eyes, was it an ingratiating smile and look of deferential attention which Abel was turning upon the rural potentate? "How lucky that some one was there who knew the value," he said. Was it a dream? There was something unusual in the very sound of his own voice.

"Bless me! there is the luncheon bell. I must not detain you longer," said the squire. "I fear I have bored you already; and my daughter will upbraid me for keeping you all the morning over my toys, as she calls them. Ah, well! I suppose we old people can't expect the young ones to take after us or adopt our tastes. You have given me a very pleasant morning, Mr Murray. I don't know when I have enjoyed a couple of hours so much. It is not every one who has the good taste to admire, but there are still fewer who understand as you do. It has been, I assure you, a real pleasure."

"You are very good to say so—after having given me such true enjoyment," said Abel, confused, and feeling ready to stumble on the stairs, as at his previous interview, and to hear, "That way, you little wretch. John, look after this boy, and see him off the premises." He could have laughed as he felt himself ushered with ceremonious politeness by the squire himself towards the drawing-room, where the very John, who had then dismissed him with a kick, was standing now, grown somewhat elderly and imperative, to remind Miss Ridley that the bell had rung five minutes since. Abel could have laughed, but not because he was amused. The sight of John sent a chill and then a rush of hot blood over him. He thought John looked at him keenly. But, indeed, this was a mere illusion of conscience. John only glanced with disapproval at the strange gentleman who had kept his master too late for lunch.

And then Miss Ridley rose up, stately and fair, to receive him. Miss Ridley! was that the little Mary who had been so kind to him in the Vicarage at the nursery tea? He faltered, he felt, as he spoke to her, and made her the same kind of lumpish bow as little Abel made when they all laughed at him, all except Mary. But even in those days, when everything in the new life was strange to him, Abel had not been so dazzled by the little lady as he was now. Then she took his part; now she beamed down serenely upon him, like the moon out of the sky. Perhaps it was Miss Ridley's fault to be too stately; but when a girl is five feet ten in height, how can she help being stately?—it is so much the worse for her if she is not so. She had beautiful hair in great quantity, blue eyes, a Saxon beauty, in all the milk and roses peculiar to that complexion. Her features, perhaps, would not bear so close an inspection; but her smile was as bright as a sunny morning, and warmed and lighted up everything. "A daughter of the gods divinely tall, and most divinely fair." It was his arm she took to go down-stairs. He was the stranger, and a stranger of distinction, much more important than young Charley Landale, whom they had all known from his cradle. And John standing by said nothing. John did not interfere. He did not break in upon the talk of the gentlefolks, to say, in his gruff voice, "Please, squire, that's little Abel Murray down from the fells. I know him well. He's as stubborn as a brute beast, but his mother's a decent woman." None of these things happened or were said. Abel was permitted, on the contrary, to walk majestically down-stairs, as if he had been the best man in the county, with Mary Ridley's white hand upon his coat sleeve.

"I hope you have not been tired out with papa's treasures," she said. "You must forgive him, it is not often he has such a chance. We are one more ignorant that the other, my brother and I."

"That I cannot give my faith to as I should to anything else you might say," said Abel, with a little warmth which went beyond the calm of good-breeding. He had got his conversation chiefly from books, and was a little more formal in his talk than is common in this free and easy period. Miss Ridley was greatly surprised, but half amused too.

"And stupid as well as ignorant," she said. "Do you think it would be wrong to pretend to be interested? I was brought up in the way of deadly sincerity; but I sometimes think now that it is hard upon papa."

"You must have learned to pretend very skilfully, if you pretend to be—what you said," said Abel, venturing at the same time to look the compliment, which he thus dared to utter. Miss Ridley was more and more amused; but he added, "To me it is all enjoyment. This beautiful old house, and Mr Ridley's kindness, and——"

What had he been about to say? Mary decided that this young man, who was so grateful for her father's kindness, and so delighted with everything, including herself, was the Oxford recluse in person, who is to be heard of now and then—that grave young owl, whose perch among the cloisters has kept him unacquainted with ordinary mortals and affairs. And there was a certain truth in this supposition. Abel, even in places where he was at ease, never had the ease common to his generation. He was constantly conscious that there was no real affinity between him and those about him; and though he might perhaps hardly have recognised his family had he seen them, they were perpetually apparent to him when he was in "society," pursuing him with thoughts of the effect which would be produced by their sudden appearance anywhere. He had a kind of inkling all the time that, if he had the courage to acknowledge and speak of them, this painful consciousness would disappear; but he knew he had not the courage. He talked to Mary all the time of luncheon in the same exalted tone, she replying little, but by degrees finding that air of deference not disagreeable. Miss Ridley was not clever, and her betrothed husband was aware of the fact, and did not perhaps conceal it so carefully as he might have done. But there is nobody who is not pleased, in the long run, by having great qualities imputed to him. It is the finest form of flattery. Abel took it for granted that this country lady in her remote corner of the world knew everything that was moving the general mind of the country, and spoke to her of books, and pictures, and society, and politics. A member of a special society, even if he is less distinguished than Abel was, has means of glimpsing general society of a much higher order than his own. He had met all kinds of people, whose names are spread to all the winds. Miss Ridley felt as if she had made an excursion into the world, while she sat at the head of the table and ate her chicken. It pleased her to hear of statesmen and poets, and so many notable persons. She asked about their looks, and their ways of living; and she thought Mr Murray very interesting, though his manners were perhaps, a little, those of the old world.

After lunch the squire himself exhibited the chapel, which was falling somewhat out of repair and the younger people went out to see that part of the Castle that was in ruins. The ruined front included a tower, which Abel remembered well it had been one of the feats of his boyhood to climb. But the Ridleys shook their heads when he asked if they could go up.

"Not for the world," said Mary, turning pale; but though Roger agreed with her at first, he changed his mind the next moment.

"I don't see why we should not," he said. "All the little ragamuffins in the neighbourhood used to do it when I was a boy. Have you a steady head, Murray? Are you used to climbing?"

"Don't, Roger!" said his sister; "papa will not like it. Oh, don't!"

"Why shouldn't I? Charley can stay and take care of you."

"That I will," said young Landale; "while you break your necks we will run on to the village, and see that the doctor is handy. That will be the most friendly thing to do."

"Mr Murray, pray don't go," said Mary. "I am so much afraid it is dangerous; and Roger is so venturesome."

"Be sure you groan as loud as ever you can," said flippant Charley, "so that we may know where to find you when you fall."

"Come along," said Roger. As for Abel, he had no sort of nervous feeling; he knew exactly how to climb, and which were the dangerous places. When they came to one of these, Roger, who preceded him, called him to follow upon an arch of crumbling masonry, which looked sure enough from below. "When we get over this we are in safety," he said; "so take care, cross it gingerly, as I am responsible for you."

"Not that way," cried Abel. "Stop, stop, not there! That will not bear your weight. Ridley!" he shouted in growing excitement, "stop! I tell you this is the way."

"Come on!" cried Roger, gaily. Then there was a sound of sliding, and a cloud of dust and a cry. The cry was from Mary outside, looking on with fear and trembling, and seeing her brother disappear. She gave a wild shriek, such as half enervated and half inspired Abel, who had sprung with the instinct of the moment to the spot which he knew to be trustworthy, and standing there, supported by an angle of the wall, had already caught Roger before he could fall far. But the crushing impetus with which Roger fell against him, and the fright and the excitement together, were too much for Abel, already suffering from the long strain of suppressed feeling. He laughed loud and wildly,—a laugh that seemed to the terrified spectators below to have the scream of madness in it. "I told you this was the way," he cried, laughing, but panting for breath.

Mary Ridley ran screaming towards the house, then came back again as John and the other servants rushed out. She ran back to the half-ruined staircase by which the path began, wringing her hands in despair. Abel's laughter was still pealing out unrestrained, making the whole incident horrible.

"Oh, make him stop! make him stop!" she cried, putting her hands to her ears. "Roger is killed, and the other has gone mad! Oh, make him stop, make him stop!"

CHAPTER V

"What is the matter?" said calmly a smooth and even voice. Mary was almost beside herself. The servants had all gone into the ruins with Charley Landale at their head to help, and she stood outside in an anguish of despair and horror, calling out unconsciously to stop him, to stop him! It seemed almost a secondary thing to her that Roger was killed—if there could be but silence again, if they could but be free of that horrible laugh. The voice which now addressed her ought to have been the dearest voice in the world to Mary, but its calm and even tone seemed, on the contrary, an aggravation, only a little less horrible than the sound of that laughter, which she could neither bear nor tolerate. What was the matter? She clasped her hands wildly together and pointed to the ruins. She could not say anything. Could not he have seen, if he had felt for her as he ought—if he had cared about her and her surroundings—could not he have seen at once without asking what was the matter? She had no leisure to look at, or speak to, Featherstonhaugh. Presently the mangled body of her only brother would be carried out in her sight; but, oh! if that horrible laugh could but be made an end of—that was the worst to bear.

"Some one must have gone mad, surely," said Sir Richard. "Had you not better go in, Mary? This cannot be a scene for you. Go in, and I will come and tell you what has happened. Hallo! is this Roger? Then what is the matter?" he said in his surprise. Mary shut her eyes with a sinking of horror not to see the terrible sight she looked for, but at the same moment felt a sudden lull and ease steal over her—the scream of wild laughter had ceased.

"Roger, what have you been about? Are you hurt?" Sir Richard said.

Hurt! was that all? She ventured to open her eyes, and saw Roger limping towards them, covered with dust and lime, but smiling through the incrustation. She rushed forward and took hold of his arm with both her hands.

"Roger! Then nothing has happened?"

"I am not a ghost," he said, half laughing, "and I'll give you my word if you like never to try that confounded place again. You must speak to

Murray—he is more shaken than I am. Didn't you think he was mad, with that horrible laugh?"

"What were you doing?" said Sir Richard. "Surely not the incredible folly of climbing that wall! What good could it do you? I don't wonder Mary is upset. Pray go in now; pray go in. You see he is not hurt."

"But Mr Murray! Oh, Roger, how did it all happen? How did you escape? What made him laugh so?" said Miss Ridley, shuddering. "I thought you were killed, and that he had lost his senses. Oh, Roger, what a laugh!"

"Pooh! Some fellows have that fiendish way of laughing, and he got nervous. Don't you see it's all right now? You'll have to thank him, though," Roger added, hastily; "but for him I should have been carried down feet foremost, as the people say. I don't know what we can say to him—he has saved my life!"

"Oh, God bless him! God bless him!" cried Mary. She made a step forward, then turned again, with a visible tremor.

"But are you sure he is—quite—quite——Mr Murray," she added, growing very pale, and putting out her hands to him as he approached from under the old doorway, "oh, how can I thank you? You have saved Roger's life!"

Abel was paler than she was, and his face looked like that of a man absolutely worn out and exhausted. "It was nothing," he said. "I knew one way was safe, but not the other. The upper arch always crumbled at a touch—but I frightened you, I know I must have frightened you. It is a foolish weakness I have. I laugh when I am agitated."

"Oh, never mind that. You limp, too; we are a nice pair of cripples. Come along," said Roger, "let us lean upon each other. I must have come down upon you with all my weight."

"I knew that arch would go. I was prepared for it. I am only limping out of sympathy," said Murray, with again a harsh, though momentary, laugh. Mary ran in before them, still with a little shiver, and met the squire coming out, dignified, to know what was the matter? "I don't know who was laughing like that, but it was very vulgar and very objectionable," he said. A few hurried words, however, allayed Mr Ridley's displeasure. "God bless me!" he said, devoutly, and hurried out to thank the stranger who had saved his son's life. "Though Roger ought to have known better than to have run such a risk," he said, seriously, as the agitated group came back to the house. All were in commotion, the servants fluttering to and fro, the very cook, her hands covered with flour, coming out to gaze. "I'll bet that gentleman's been here before," John said, privately. "Bless you, he knows all the ways of th' ould place as well as I do that was born and bred on the Waterside;" and Sir Richard, the only spectator who was quite unmoved, recollected, and had observed as none of the rest did, what Murray said. They made much of him when they got indoors, paying a great deal more attention to his nerves than to Roger's foot, which was bruised though not seriously hurt. Roger, however, declared himself quite able to walk as far as the village with them, when at last the young men took their leave. They all set out together—Sir Richard going the same way as the others as far as the head of the lake. Roger was jealously on the watch as they passed through the village, lest by any chance they should meet Lily; but they had got past all danger, as he thought, and were once more on the open road by the waterside, when, with a sudden leap of his jealous heart, he saw her approaching. They all perceived her at the same moment. It is not necessary, in those simple regions, that a young woman should put on a hat or bonnet every time she goes out. Lily's beautiful head was uncovered. The wind playing with the locks about her forehead brought out tiny curls from the neatly braided hair, and freshened the colour in her cheeks. She was not made of roses and lilies, like Miss Ridley, but her dark hair had gleams of colour in it, and her eyes were like the dark brown mountain streams, dancing, glancing, yet profound as the depths into which they plunged. Lily was not at all unaware of the admiration with which she was regarded, and she felt before she came near them the little thrill of interest that ran through the group of young men whom she approached. She did not at first perceive that Roger was among them, but his absence did not make her indifferent to the other spectators. She came with a little stumble of embarrassment, more apparent to herself than the lookers-on, feeling their scrutiny, and feeling, as is common enough, her ankles twisting, her dress blown about. Much abashed was Lily, but yet she had no particular wish to escape from the eager lookers-on, who were watching for her as if she had been the queen. This was how the foolish girl felt it—as if she had been the queen! just as she herself would advance, her eyes as wide open as ever they could be, to watch the queen passing, and devour every look of her and every line of her dress. This was just how the silly young men would stare at herself. "Gooses!" thought Lily. She had never learnt grammar, but she understood the minds of men.

"This is the girl who is said to be the prettiest girl in the whole dale, up the water and down the water," said Featherstonhaugh, with a little conscious impropriety, feeling that the interest he felt in her was excessive. As for Murray, his heart began to beat again wildly in his ears. This time he must confront his sister face to face. Would she, could she, recognise him? The idea was enough to set all the blood astir in his veins. And Roger awaited her coming with a tumult in his, that could scarcely be kept from making itself visible: his heart began to thump against his breast, his throat grew dry, his colour went and came. She was his Lily, whatever happened. No one had any right so much as to look at her but he; and yet they were all staring, and he could say nothing. A wild fury seemed to glide like fire through his blood, kindling him as it ran along—fury that would burst out uncontrollable, like fire, if any door should be opened for it, any occasion given. Charley Landale was the only innocent person of all the four, who had no further thought than to take "a good look" at her, and make up his mind whether she were really as pretty as every one said.

Thus she came on, feeling awkward under their gaze, yet not particularly desirous of avoiding their gaze, with, indeed, a kind of pleased consciousness of it, which added to the blush that wavered upon her face. Her lips were parted with a half smile. She took them all in with her eyes, which looked steadily in front of her without dwelling on any one. As she came nearer she distinguished Sir Richard, that great potentate, who was in the front; but, notwithstanding that he was much in her thoughts, she did not distinguish Roger. It was almost like acting the spy upon her to see her advance thus in her soft vanity, with the smile on her lips, not knowing he was there. "Good evening to you," she said, as rural politeness made proper, and passed on, as it was right for a girl to do. The sound of her voice startled two of them, as if a gun had been fired by their ears. Murray could not tell what revelation might follow—and Roger grew sick and faint to see her go by him without so much as a suspicion that he was there. He would have felt her vicinity, he thought, if she had passed him in the dark.

After all, it was not much to excite them so: for they were all excited, except placid Charley; a country lass, bashful, yet with a pretty vanity, smiling and walking past a group of young men who admired her, but whom, except the one whom she did not perceive, she did not know. There was not much in this for such expenditure of feeling. And they said nothing when she had passed: even Charley, with a "By Jove!" of admiration on his lips, saw that it was more expedient to say nothing. He did not understand the paleness and quick breathing of Ridley by his side, nor the silence of the two before them. They had all made a kind of pause when Lily passed. They went on with quickened paces after, and soon they came to the point where their paths separated, and Roger turned back. All the glare of sunset was upon the lake as they parted near the waterside.

"I don't pretend to be a talker," said Ridley, grasping Abel's hand, "but I shall never forget that I owed my life to you to-day."

"It was nothing," said Abel, off his guard. "I should have stopped sooner than I did. I knew your way was insecure."

"However it was, I owe *you* my life, and I shan't forget it," said Roger. "If ever you want a good turn that I can do——"

"Good night; you must not think it was anything," Murray said returning the pressure of his hand. He, too, was agitated by all that had happened, and by the last incident as much as any. He watched Ridley making his way backward, still slightly lame, with all the benevolence a man feels for one whom he has served. "Mrs Landale said well he was friendly. It is the best name for him," he said.

"He has occasion to be friendly to you, and so has all his family," said Featherstonhaugh. "But—you knew the old tower before?"

"I!" The blood rushed to Abel's face. "What makes you think so? I—have had no opportunity of knowing it before."

"I thought you were quite familiar with the place. You said something—I beg your pardon—perhaps I misunderstood."

"I said I knew his way was unsafe; any one could have seen that at a glance."

The eyes of the two met. Murray thought there was suspicion in the looks of Featherstonhaugh, and this not only filled him with alarm, but with irritation too. Sir Richard, however, repeated his excuse. "I misunderstood you. I thought you spoke of it with previous knowledge. You will bring Mr Murray to Featherstonhaugh, Charley, to see me. I fear there is nothing to show him much worth the trouble. A few pictures—that is all."

"Only the best collection in the north country," said Landale; and with a slight complacent smile and nod, half acquiescent, half deprecating, Featherstonhaugh went on upon his separate way. "He is a prig," said Charley, when he was out of hearing; "but all the same, he has some fine pictures, and understands them too."

"Being a prig does not prevent a man from having fine pictures, nor, unfortunately, even from understanding them," said Murray, with a sigh. "There are no such compensations as one used to believe in. The poor man is not always the cleverest, nor the lord of many acres always a fool."

"I should hope not," said Charley, roused; for though his acres were limited in extent, it was his class which was thus by implication attacked. "And what did you think of the little dressmaker?" said the unsuspecting youth. "I say, both those fellows are in for it. Ridley, you know, we saw with her; and as for Featherstonhaugh, did you see how he stared at her? I admire a pretty girl, but I would not look as if I could eat her up. It's to be hoped there will be no mischief between those two."

"I thought Sir Richard was engaged to Miss Ridley?"

"And so he is; but that does not make it better, but worse," said Charley, with much discrimination. "And they are two determined fellows. If it came to a scrimmage I should like to be there."

"I don't think, in such a case," said Abel, trying to subdue his own excitement, "that Sir Richard would have much chance."

"Oh, I should not like to say that. Featherstonhaugh's very quiet, but he's deep. I've observed," said Charley, producing his innocent aphorism with much gravity, "that the more quiet men are, the deeper they are. I don't know if you've noticed that."

Murray's mind was not sufficiently at ease to remark this simple wisdom. He said with a kind of bitterness, "What she feels on the subject has not much to do with it, I suppose."

"What, the girl? Oh, yes, if she happens to be of the sort that have a will of their own. A girl like that can make herself very disagreeable, I've heard. I suppose on the whole, anyhow, it can't mean much good to her," said Charley, taking a sudden thought. "It would be better for her on the whole if she wasn't so pretty. Don't you think so? Though Roger Ridley is as obstinate as a pony, and if he once took a thing into his head—but, after all, I don't suppose he could be quite such a fool," Charley said, with a pause of consideration. Abel looked at him keenly with a suppressed glare in his eyes.

"Such a fool as to think of making the dressmaker his wife?"

"Oh, come!" cried Charley; "when you put it in words—and in cold blood—no one surely would be quite such a fool as that."

There was a singing in Abel's ears, a convulsive tremor ran through him. It was his sister of whom this innocent babbler was speaking; but who could suspect anything of the kind?

Roger strolled back by the waterside; but then he recollected that he had something to do, which made it necessary for him to pass again through the village—indeed, that he was compelled to go, though he did not wish it, by business, that infallible force which every one must obey. And when he had taken that turn he went on with more alacrity. Quite necessary! It was the blacksmith he thought he wanted to see, for servants never give your orders correctly. He went on—but not directly towards the blacksmith's. A green lane is more pleasant than a hard high-road. He would go that way for the sake of his foot, which certainly hurt him a good deal. He could not help wondering what that little flirt would say if she knew that this very afternoon he had been in danger of his life. Would she mind? Would it have made any difference to her one way or another if he had come down headlong from off that archway and broken his neck, and never spoken again? She would perhaps have met Featherstonhaugh in the lane, and heard all about it from him. Heaven and earth! Though Roger had not died, and had no intention of doing so, the idea of Featherstonhaugh reporting to Lily all the details of his dying, and making use of the incident as a means of approaching her, made him frantic.

He went very slowly through the lane. The light was beginning to wane, for it had been already late when they left the Castle. He looked up to the back window of Miss Prentice's house, and thought he saw some one there. Here was a chance at least of knowing whether she had got his letter. He made a gesture of appeal, beckoning to her, though he could not even be sure that it was Lily—a dangerous experiment. Of course, he said to himself, he had never thought of this when he came through the lane for the sake of his bad foot. Neither had Lily ever thought of it when she went by chance to the staircase window. But the result was that she did stroll out, and that he did meet her, at Miss Prentice's back-door.

"What is it?" she said. "Oh, I mustn't stay; you mustn't keep me. I only came because I was so frightened; *she* might see you making signs. I wish you wouldn't make signs like that. If any one saw you, oh, what would become of me?"

"It would not do you any harm," said Roger, "for I know what you would do, Lily. You would simply cast me off and pretend to know nothing about me. You know that is what you would do."

"Oh, but it would be quite true. What do I know about you? I know you are young Mr Ridley, a gentleman, far, oh, far above me. All the world knows that; and I don't know what I know more."

"You know I love you, Lily, which is what no one knows but you."

"Oh," she said, with a toss of her head, "I am not so sure about that. I know what you say; but what young men say and what they feel is very different."

"Who taught you that, Lily? Can you look at me, and then tell me that you think I don't feel what I say?"

"Oh, as for that—but every book you ever open says so, and all the old people say so; they ought to know. Never believe a lad, Miss Prentice says—and far more when it's a gentleman."

"Did you get my letter, Lily?"

"Oh, yes, I got your letter; I couldn't quite read it all. Did you ever learn to write, Mr Ridley? or is it taught in the grand schools? For a long time I couldn't tell who sent it," said Lily, telling her little fib with a steady look at him, and all the innocence in the world.

"Then I suppose heaps of other people write you letters like that?"

Lily laughed with malice and enjoyment of the fun. "Did you think that you were the only one that ever said he cared for me?" she said, with merry scorn. As for Roger, he was quite desperate, and did not know how to meet this levity, which broke his heart.

"You should not take it so easily," he said, "for Lily, but for— Providence—it would have been the last letter I ever wrote to you or any one. I was as nearly as possible killed to-day."

She gave a little cry, her face paled and reddened, and she clasped her hands together. This encouraged him to go on, which he did in that tearful solemn tone with which a man represents himself as an object of sympathy when he is very anxious to make a tender impression and very doubtful of his success.

"I was climbing the old tower to show a stranger the way, and put my foot by accident upon a bit of the wall that would not bear me; and there would have been an end of me, Lily, and of all my love and all our meetings. I don't think you would have minded a bit: you would have gone on with some one else, and thought nothing more of Roger Ridley. You would have——"

"Oh, never mind what I would have done!" she said, stamping her foot; "that's best known to me. What happened then? what happened then? that's what I want to know."

"You see, I was saved! What with the other man, and what with throwing myself into the corner as I fell——"

(He had thrown himself upon Murray, whose arms were out to catch him: but he did not think it needful to inform her of that.)

"Who was the other man?" she asked, drawing her breath hurriedly.

"It was—a man who is on a visit to Landale—a man that you met this afternoon walking with—never mind the man. I was behind him, but you never saw me. You were willing to let them stare at you, though you never saw I was there."

"Could I stop them from staring at me? But I mind the man. He was a handsome gentleman. I will always look at him again when I see him. He must have a good courage, and a good heart of his own, too."

"Shall you look at him for my sake or for his? You might say at least that you are glad that I was saved."

She gave another toss of her pretty head, and laughed. She was not so simple as not to know the advantage of a question in suspense like this. "Everybody is glad when somebody else is not killed," she said; "but, good-night, I must run in. Oh, yes, I must run in. Miss Prentice will be looking out as she goes down, and if she should find me here— —That is her step, I do believe!" And with extreme consistency Lily came out, quite outside the door of which she had been making a fortress, and closed it softly that she might not be seen from the house. Roger took this opportunity to seize her hand, but Lily was *farouche*, and shook herself free from the touch. She looked at him seriously as they stood there under the shadow of the wall. "Yes, I am glad that—nobody is killed," she said.

"Nobody—anybody! that it was I, don't matter much?"

"Perhaps," she said, with a laugh. This was not much comfort; but Roger, drawing as near as was permitted, looked at her tenderly, gratefully, thinking of what he should say next that would most thoroughly reveal his feelings. What could he say? She knew very well all that he meant, though she pretended to take everything so calmly. She stood with the most innocent air in the world, waiting till he should speak. Then, with some of the flippancy of her class, Lily cried, "And did you hurt your tongue, Mr Ridley, when you fell?"

"You are very cruel. You ought to pretend to be sorry at least; and you might give me an answer to my letter. Did you like what I sent you? I thought you—you might have something to say to a poor man who was nearly killed to-day— —"

This pathetic speech, given with all the tender reproach possible, would have been too much for the gravity of any looker-on. And Lily burst out laughing, with seeming disregard for his feelings.

"You are not much the worse," she said.

"I shall be a great deal the worse if you laugh at me. Lily, why are you so unkind? You know there is nothing in the world I would not do— —"

"Were you really with the other gentlemen?" she said. "I didn't see you. There was Sir Richard. Oh, I saw Sir Richard, and young Mr Landale, and a strange gentleman—but I have seen him before—I know I have seen him before; and you were there? I am glad I did not see you. I should have laughed or something. Perhaps I did not see you because I was looking at Sir Richard."

"Then you have seen *him* before?" said Roger, setting his teeth.

"*Seen* him before? Oh, hundreds and hundreds of times! I see him most days, going or coming, almost as often as I see you——"

"He is a villain, then!" cried Roger, hotly. "He is engaged to—a lady."

"I know; he is engaged to Miss Mary. What does that matter? *I'm* not keeping company with him," said Lily. "If you think I would take another girl's leavings—if she was a princess!—I would scorn it. And I don't think of the like of him. They come and they go, it don't matter to me. What have I got to do with the gentlemen? A nod or a smile out of civility, but no more."

"That is quite right, Lily," cried Roger, radiant. He came a step nearer and took her hand softly. "But you don't mean that for me?"

"Why shouldn't I mean it for you?" she cried, throwing off his hand. "But there's some one coming," she added, with a little shriek, and fled within the shelter of the door.

Roger, after lingering for a minute in hope of her return, was about to turn disconsolately away, when she suddenly appeared again, between the half-opened door and the wall, and pulling out with one finger a piece of velvet round her neck, showed him his little locket suspended to it. "There!" she cried, and suddenly shut in his face and bolted the garden door.

From which he limped home, tantalised yet happy, thinking of his possible rivals no more.

CHAPTER VI

Elizabeth Murray was very busy about her poultry all the height of the summer. She had so many broods of chickens to look after that she scarcely knew how to turn. With all her ordinary work to do, these extra cares filled up her time so that the day was not long enough for its occupations. Dick was very helpful and handy, and they laboured together without grudging, with that unfailing and unvarying industry which those exercise who know that all the fruit of their labours will be their own. No other man or woman drudges with such patience as the little landholders, who have no master over them, and nobody to share their gains; and in many cases no other class live so sordid and miserable a life. Elizabeth and her boy laboured day and night, and never found it too much. She went to the market Saturday after Saturday, and worked all the week through among the chickens and the cows. It never occurred to her even to think that she was getting near the end of that platform of middle age on which most of the more serious work of life is done, or that by-and-by rest might be a necessity; nor did she think her life so hard, as many a poor worker, not doing half so much, has done. She was busy in the poultry-yard in the evening of one of those long summer days, which her eldest son, though she did not know it, was spending so near. At that season there are always chickens in a delicate state of health to be looked after. Two were lying already in a warm basket close to the fire, which was warm enough to singe their down off—and the hospital was likely to be larger before night. The sky was all ablaze with the sunset, if she had ever thought of the sunset. Sometimes, indeed, she would raise her head, and look round her for a moment, seeing all the glories that filled the silent sky and air, but taking no special notice, except to say to herself that this splendid weather was going to last. "Good for the chickens and a' living things," Elizabeth said to herself. But she heard her boy's step coming sturdily up the hill (for Dick had been absent since the morning) long before he was in sight. This was of more interest to her than all the sunsets; and yet, when she paused and looked down for him, what a sight was spread before her! all coolness and greenness and shadow above, the light fading out, the colour departing from the green turf and tiny fields, from everything except the beck with its chain of little pools, which reflected heaven in all its glory. Overhead the rosy clouds were hanging still, brilliant with every tint that reflection can give; while spread out before her lay a wonderful panorama—the broken ground of the braes, close at hand, for a foreground, and beyond them, between the openings of the hills, whose great shoulders shut in the view on either side—far beyond them, yet claiming the attention by its blaze of radiance—the water, far away shining like a sheet of gold in the sun. To look down from this shadowy, cloudy place, already almost dark in the early failing shadows, and see that burnished shield throwing back the light, and all the canopy overhead brilliant with crimson and purple, was a wonderful sight.

"I have brought you a letter," Dick said; he did not add who was the writer, but handed it over quickly. It had been lying in the window of the toll-house for two long days, and Elizabeth gave a little cry when she saw the writing. She forgot the supper and Dick's fatigue, and everything but her eldest son, who wrote so seldom. A letter from Abel! there had not been one for—Elizabeth well knew how long. Had not she counted the months and the days? But even to herself she pretended not to know; and the sight of it thrilled her through and through; a flush of sudden colour came to her face, and the water to her eyes. When such an unusual thing as a letter came to Overbeck, it was common that he or she who received it should run it over first, thus getting the cream of novelty and sweetness—then read it aloud. Elizabeth did the first—she read it, devouring the lines: but her countenance changed as she went on, and when she had ended she put it down with some irritation upon the table, and proceeded at once to give Dick his supper. "If it's needful that he should write seldom, he might be pleasant when he writes," she said, with a spasm of disappointment and offence choking her voice.

Dick came up with a sturdy resounding step, but not quickly. Sometimes he would become inaudible, as he crossed "a boggy bit," or took a devious way, crushing the fragrant bog-myrtles beneath his feet. When he arrived at last, he found Elizabeth, with a clean apron on, waiting his arrival for supper. Everything was ready for him. The chickens in their flannel infirmary chirped feebly now and then by the fire. The cat, curious, with a growing interest in the chirpings, purred about, knowing she dared not approach. The old collie, not interested at all, but tolerant, lay, though it was hot, and he felt it so, in front of the fire, which threw a reflected tinge of redness upon his shabby black coat.

"Is it Abel, mother; and what does he say?"

Dick began his supper calmly. He was not so much excited about Abel as to neglect his meal. But Elizabeth was roused out of the common routine altogether. The first morsel she tried to swallow choked her. "I cannot eat," she said, pushing her plate away. "Oh, Dick, one thing I've asked from the Lord; it is, that my bairns should thrive and do well. Me—what do I care for me? I'm willing to work, and if I have daily bread I want no more; but my lads and my lass—my lass, my Lily, the only one I have!"

"What is wrong with Lily?" Dick said, looking up with interest. "And what has Abel to do with that?"

"Ay, you may just ask; never to have taken any notice, never asked where she was, or any single thing about her, and then, all in a moment— oh, you're not to think I'm blaming your brother," said Elizabeth, with a sudden compunction; "if he never showed an interest before, reason good he should show it now."

"Is there anything wrong with Lily? Give me the letter, and I'll see for myself."

"Ay, lad, there it is; it's gone to my heart, and I cannot read the words out loud. It would be like believing, it would be like taking all for gospel that was said again' my bairn."

Dick prepared himself for this pause in his meal by two or three large mouthfuls to begin with, and by cutting and preparing a few more, to be eaten as he went on. He was concerned, having a sturdy and honest affection for his sister; but he was hungry as well. He had to spell over the letter, not being great in "written hand," but this was what he made out at last:—

> "Dear Mother,—You will think it long since I have written, and so it is—but I will not take up your time and mine by excusing myself. I have a great deal to do, and that I know you will understand; and then my life has got to be very different from yours. I get into a kind of despair when I think of it. How could I make you understand my life? Yours is all fresh air and nature; mine is all artificial—close rooms and talk and books. Sometimes I think it would have been better if I had never left you, then we should have understood each other. God knows if we ever can now.
>
> "I am writing to you, however, not merely to give you news of me, or to ask how you are, but to put you on your guard about a danger which, perhaps, you know nothing of. A friend of mine has been in your neighbourhood, living at one of the gentlemen's houses" (Abel had smiled to himself when he used this expression, so familiar in the days of old), "and I have heard from him of a girl in the village, a very pretty girl, who is with the dressmaker, and whom a great many young men admire. I cannot doubt by

the description that it is my sister Lily. She has the young squire, Roger Ridley, going after her, and I don't know how many more. You know that this is not a safe thing for a young girl. It might come to no harm with her, and I hope would come to no harm; but it is a thing her mother ought to know, and her friends should keep an eye on her. Of course my friend did not know it was my sister, so I heard everything, and there is nothing wrong; but you know well that a girl's name should not be bandied about, and should not be talked of in connection with a gentleman's name who could not marry her, who is far above her. Do not be affronted that I speak so plainly. I am sure when you know, by all I remember of you, that you will take care of Lily and set everything right.—Your affectionate son,

"Abel Murray."

"Well," said Dick, with his mouth full, "I see nothing to vex you in this, mother; he speaks very sensible. I meant to tell you the same thing. It is what you ought to know. I was meaning to say to you, 'Bring Lily home,' this very night."

"Oh!" said Elizabeth, wringing her hands. "I knew you would be both in one story; it only wanted that. And what could I expect from two lads, that can no more see into the mind of a simple lass! That's what you do, all you men folk—put your own ill thoughts upon her that is as innocent of harm—oh, that's what you do! In the course of Providence, or maybe it's nature—the Lord deliver me from knowing which—you learn what an innocent lass need never know; and then all you've learned from ill folks, and all you've read from ill books, you think my bairn knows it as well as you!"

To this most unprovoked and undeserved attack Dick made no reply. He held his tongue, being partially compelled by circumstances to that wise reticence, and occupied himself with his supper. It was the wisest way. After a while Elizabeth, who was influenced in a way she could have hardly believed, by her clumsy Dick's support and approval of what his brother said, calmed down out of her own offence and indignation, and began to consider the question too.

"If you've heard that, and he's heard that, there may be something at the bottom of it: is that what you mean to tell me?"

"Nothing against Lily," said Dick, "and *he* says nothing against Lily; but she's young" (he was two years younger himself), "and if a gentleman says to her she's bonnier than all the rest put together, how is she to know it's not true?"

"And so she is," said Elizabeth, with a gleam of pride; "there's no one o' them, no one o' them you could name the same day!"

"Well, mother, well; that makes Abel all the more right in what he says, and me the less wrong. You wouldn't expect Mr Roger, the Squire of Waterdale, that will be member of Parliament and the Queen's counsellor, to marry Lily Murray, the cotter's daughter at Overbeck?"

"He might search far and wide o'er the world to get one like her," said the mother. "And wherefore no'? her brother is as good a gentleman, and has as much chance to be the Queen's counsellor, as himself."

"And that is all you know," said Dick, with a groan; "when her brother hears all that's said about Lily, and never has the heart to say, 'Hold your peace, lad, it's my sister.' Much good it will do her to have a brother that is like that."

"What would you have him say?" said Elizabeth, with a shrill note of pain in her voice. "When he's living among gentlemen, would you have him publish to all the lords and ladies that make much of him that he's a cotter's son?"

"That would I, mother; it would be better for himself," said Dick, with composure. "It may be grand to be a gentleman, when you have a right to it, but pretending—what good can that do? and when there's something to be found out, it's aye found out soon or late. I would rather be known for what I am, and nothing to find out all my days."

"You?" said Elizabeth, with a certain contempt; "it's no' you that anybody's thinking of"—and with this expression of impatience, which sensible Dick took for what it meant and no more, she fell into silence; and then was it not time to supper the cow?

After this there was nothing said all the rest of the evening. Both had their work to do, and they went early to bed when that work was done, for why should time be wasted and candles lighted for nothing? But when the two separated for the night Elizabeth said, "It's a good thing to-morrow is Saturday," and Dick replied, "That's true, mother." It was all that was said.

Very early on Saturday morning, as was her wont, Elizabeth Murray took her way down the long winding road with her heavy basket. Dick came with her as far as the toll, where the cart passed that carried the heavier part of her produce, and he said, "I wish ye speed," as he left her. "Speed" might mean anything—success in her sale, as much as success with more important matters. It was unnecessary for him to particularise. She nodded her head solemnly in reply. By this time Lily's danger had become the first thing in her mother's thoughts, and the kindness and goodness of her brother in sending that warning. He that had so many things to think of—he that was not like just a country lad—even he, that had lost sight of his home, and was a gentleman, and could not be expected to mind upon everything, as if he had never stirred from Overbeck. So much had his mother's mind changed that this was how it struck her now. Her heart swelled with pride and gratitude to her boy. He was out of reach of their ordinary commonplace interests, but yet he could bestir himself to save Lily, to serve herself. She was nothing but grateful to Abel now—but Lily lay heavy on her mother's heart. Elizabeth knew the ways of girls. There would be no harm in Lily's thoughts, no meaning, no understanding of harm: but at the same time nothing but harm could come from the gentleman lover. The young squire, who was so much her superior, had perhaps caught Lily's heart. Was her child to bear that burden of love impossible—love that could never know an earthly close? Elizabeth sighed; she knew what it was. Had not she been a rustic beauty, too, in days of which her children knew nothing? and it might be, was followed and wooed like her child, before good Abel came and stuck to her through thick and thin, and was married for gratitude. Even at forty-five women have not forgotten such incidents; and was it to happen over again to her child? "Oh, to have a bonnie face, it's more a curse than a blessing!" Elizabeth said to herself, as she went down the hill,—"at least for a poor lass." This thought carried her far afield, far back into the past. She had been happy enough as Abel Murray's wife, and very happy with his children. Now was it all to begin again? and Lily, her one Lily, was she to bear the burden too? But though her mind was heavy with this thought, Elizabeth had to take her place in the market all the same, and get through as usual the selling of her butter and her eggs. When that was over she went to Miss Prentice's. She took with her a little offering—a pound of her sweet fresh butter, and a pair of young chickens—and before she could see Lily, which was her chief object, she had to interview Miss Prentice, who was busy, as it was Saturday. "Good morning to you, 'Lizabeth," she said; "I hope I see you in health. I am sure I am much obliged to you for the chickens. I wish, though, it was not Saturday, when we are all so busy, for I would have liked a word with you about Lily."

"I hope she's giving satisfaction, and doing as you bid her," Elizabeth said, forcing a smile, but with a very wistful, watchful look that almost betrayed her anxiety. ("She has heard something," said Miss Prentice to herself.)

"It's not exactly to find fault. Oh, yes, she gives me satisfaction. There's not a word to say against her work. She's improving fast. I can trust her to cut out a body and put it together; and she has what you might call a real fine feeling for the trimmings," said Miss Prentice. "But just you look here, 'Lizabeth Murray. What is a young woman to do in the face o' that?"

"O' what?" said Elizabeth, growing pale. They were in Miss Prentice's own room up-stairs, and the dressmaker had taken Lily's mother by the shoulders, and pushing her towards the window, was pointing with her finger at the other side of the village street. "Look for yourself," she cried, excited. But all that Elizabeth saw when she looked out was a few ordinary passengers going by from the market: to be sure, there was also visible a gentleman riding slowly along the middle of the road. She gazed at the foot-passengers first, and saw no harm in them,—they were all very decent folk; but by-and-by Elizabeth saw that the gentleman turned his horse, and came back riding very slowly, and looking down from the elevation of his saddle to the window of Miss Prentice's workroom, which was below.

"That what's happening 'most every day," said the dressmaker with excitement; "it's no fault of hers. Whiles it's one and whiles it's another. It's enough to turn anybody's head—me myself, that am an elderly woman. They're all givin' each other the word, you would think, to see them. I was thinking of sending for you, 'Lizabeth Murray, to say, for no fault of hers, but just to keep her out of mischief, you would do well to take your Lily away."

"But—you're sure it's a' for her?" said the mother, with flaming cheeks. She was red, but not with shame—a little with pride, a little with recollection. She could not be so angry as she ought. Poor lads! was it not natural they should try their best to get a look at so bonny a face? She had just seen her daughter on her way to Miss Prentice, and Lily, all blushing and bright with the pleasure of seeing her, seemed to the mother to be so well worth looking at; and then Elizabeth, too, had been worth looking at, and knew what trouble it brought.

"There's not much doubt about that," said Miss Prentice. "You see they think they're free to stare at *her* when they would not stare at a lady. It's not a very nice way to show that you're a gentleman, *that*; but it's very common. I would not mind if it was just the strangers that passed; but there's some that come often, too often. Some would say they would never come without being encouraged; but I'm fond of Lily, and she's a good girl, and I would not say that."

"She must not encourage them. Oh, that must never be—that can never be!"

"Here she is, coming to speak for herself. Lily, you can take your mother to your room and speak to her there; but, mind, young Mrs Weston must have the children's frocks to-night; and I've given my word. Nay, dinna scold her," said Miss Prentice, whispering in Elizabeth's ear; "but give her a word of good advice. I'm aye at her, but she'll pay more attention to you."

"Oh, Lily! what is all this I hear?" said the mother, when they were up-stairs, another story farther up. Miss Prentice's was the highest house in the village. This was an attic room with a sloping roof and a skylight window, on each side of which was a bed. Here Lily had lain in the early morning, when the occupant of the other bed was fast asleep, and had looked at her locket in the dawning. She sat down upon her bed now, having placed for her mother the only chair in the room; and when she heard this question she first looked Elizabeth in the face with audacious innocence, and then she slightly tossed her saucy head.

"I've done nothing wrong," she said, and then added after a moment, "If there's anything wrong it's no' my fault."

"But there is something wrong. Oh, Lily! trust your mother. Who would you tell if you did not tell me? My lass," said Elizabeth, passionately, "you're like myself over again; and I know what it is. Oh, Lily! trust to your mother. Nobody's angry at you; nobody says a word against you, but— what's wrong?"

To this Lily for some time would answer nothing. She hung her beautiful head; she folded hems in her apron; but she would not speak. By-and-by, however, by judicious abandonment of the solemnity of her first address, Elizabeth obtained a response. "It's nothing wrong at all," Lily said, pouting; "it's—it's the lads—and the gentlemen——"

"The lads—I'm not afraid for the lads, Lily."

"I daresay no'," said Lily, with another toss of her head.

"But the gentlemen—that's another story. What have they to do with the like of you? They have ladies of their own kind to spend their time with. What business have they to come and vex and trouble a simple lass like you?"

"Oh, they do no harm," said Lily, with a conscious smile upon her face.

"They canna but do harm," said her mother. "Oh, Lily! if I could but tell you! Their ways are not like common folks' ways. You'll never bide an honest lad coming courting to you—a good lad that will work for you and give you a house of your own."

"That's what our forewoman says; as if I wanted a man and a house, and all that! I'm young yet, and why should I not have my freedom like the rest?"

In Lily's sphere it was thought quite innocent and natural that a girl should have her freedom, and see the world, as well as a young man, before she settled down. The wander-year was a sacred right to all.

"I'm saying nothing against that. Have I ever tried to stop your freedom? I know my Lily, and I dinna fear. But hear what I was going to tell you. The gentlefolk have winning ways. They take their hats off to you, and they speak soft to you, and they make you think you're a queen; but, Lily, that a' comes to an end, and how are you to bide a common man, and a rough courting, and all our country ways after that?"

"I want no man nor courting either—if you would only let me be."

"But I cannot let you be. Who have I but you, Lily. There's Dick, a good lad, more able to look after me than I'm able to look after him; and Abel," said Elizabeth, lingering on the name, "Abel—he's a grand gentleman, and wants nothing of his mother. But, Lily, a woman's glory is her daughter. *My* lass, I've none but you. It's you that's my crown and my credit. And will you no' be a honour to me, Lily? Will you let men and lads, even if they be gentlemen, make free with your bonnie name?"

"Who's done that? There's none I know that would do that," cried Lily, sharply, with a movement of anger and pain; and then she fell a-crying and betrayed the existence of something more than the mere gazing and admiration Miss Prentice was aware of. Elizabeth discovered with dismay that the young squire had gone further than vague adoration of her child's lovely looks, and that there had even been talk of marriage between them. "He said it," Lily avowed—"not me. I did not promise, and I would not promise. I thought you would say—what you've been saying, mother; and me—do I want that? I was only joking; I was never thinking. He said it; but I said nothing—neither one thing nor another. I just laughed."

"But you'll have to give an answer; you'll have to say one thing or another, Lily." Elizabeth was much alarmed, not believing in the young squire; but she was somewhat impressed and solemnised too, for it was an honour. Nobody could say but it was that.

"Not me!" said Lily, with a toss of her head.

And there was a pause, for so serious a position of affairs had not been contemplated, and Elizabeth felt the necessity of thinking it over before she could settle what to do.

"It was him then that passed the window, riding so slow, on a big black horse?"

"That passed the window? There's always some one passing the window," said Lily, in a careless tone.

"And turning back to pass again, and staring in?"

"Oh, that's their ill-bred way; they're very ill-bred. But I know who you mean, mother: that's somebody else. That's Sir Richard Featherstonhaugh, from the other side of the water."

"Lily, Lily! Is this what it's come to? And you let them both speak, and never trouble your head? Oh, Lily lass! do you see the way you're going? You must come back with me; you must come home. There's no gentlemen there to turn your head. Oh, he did well—he did well to give me warning. He is the one of us all that knows the best!"

"Who has been telling upon me?" cried Lily, growing pale. As usual, she was full of resentment against the betrayer, but thought little of those evils of her own which were thus found out.

"One that thinks of what's best for you," said her mother, slowly; "one that's far above both you and me. A gentleman, and more than a gentleman."

Lily had grown slightly pale, and her lips parted with wonder. Who could this be? She became doubly alarmed at the thought of some one watching her who was worthy of so many praises. "I don't know who you can mean," she said.

"Who should I mean but your own brother? though I fear—I fear you're no' worthy a thought of him — —"

"Abel!" said Lily, under her breath. It gave her a shock, as if Abel had been a spirit and could see her, while himself unseen. "How does Abel know? Was Abel here?"

"He sent me a letter. He has a friend that has seen you, Lily. Think how it must be when young lads, strangers, *gentlemen*, can make so free with your name."

"I know, then, who it is!" cried Lily. "I never thought much of him— and to spy upon a girl! He's the gentleman that is staying with Mr Landale, and that looks so grave and never says a word."

"Oh, I would like to know that gentleman, Lily! I would like to ask him about my boy." Elizabeth for the moment forgot one interest in another. Lily was so far safe that her mother was by her side, and had warned her at least of the danger. But Abel, where was he? And she had not seen him for so many years!

That afternoon she passed him without knowing, without one thought. She had left Miss Prentice's house full of difficulty and doubt. To take Lily away instantly seemed out of the question. The dressmaker was very busy, and frowned at the idea of losing a "hand," and Lily's fair face clouded at the very thought. What could Elizabeth do? She asked Miss Prentice to be careful, and entreated Lily, with her heart in her mouth, as she said, "Oh, to mind what she was doing, and to let nobody make free with her bonny name!" And then she went away sadly, her mind full of thought, her heart full of care, and brushed against her son Abel in the village street and never knew him. He recognised her in a moment, and very strangely the young man looked to his friends, who thought he had been taken ill. His countenance fell, and took upon it a ghastly hue; large drops of perspiration hung on his forehead. He stumbled as he crossed the street, and was like to fall. "It is a faintness," he said, with a dismal smile. But Elizabeth went on her way straight, and with her heart sore and full of thought. She was too full of care to see him, though he was in her way.

CHAPTER VII

Lily was very penitent while her mother talked to her, but after Elizabeth went away her seriousness relaxed. What harm had she done, after all? She had not encouraged any one, or beguiled any one. When she was spoken to, she replied civilly again. When a gentleman took off his hat to her what could she do but give him a smile and say "Good-day to you, sir"? Was that a sin? When they talked nonsense what did she ever do but laugh? They got nothing from her. If they fell in love with her it was at their own peril,—it was no fault of hers. Thus her compunction melted away, for what harm had she done? All that day she worked patiently and closely at the children's frocks for young Mrs Weston at the Vicarage. She never so much as put her head out of the window or thought of breathing the fresh air. Nothing could be more industrious; and prettier little frocks or neater were never manufactured. Miss Prentice had felt that it was a great compliment paid to her by Mrs Walter Weston, who lived in London, though she was now on a visit to her husband's father, to entrust her and not a London workwoman with the children's frocks; and that the work should be so satisfactory pleased her mightily. "You must mind what your mother told you," Miss Prentice said, next morning, "but I'll not keep you from your Sunday walk. Take your walk, but take some one with you, and mind who you speak to, Lily." Lily promised "faithfully," solemnly. She tripped out, looking up the street and down the street, and saw no one. Who was likely to be in the High Street in the middle of a summer Sunday? To be sure, there were the village people at their doors, and lads and lasses setting out, like Lily, for their walk. She thought she would go down to the waterside and pay a visit of benevolence and kindness to old Bess, the wife of the old boatman who looked after the boats at the Castle. That would be a nice walk, and yet it would be out of everybody's way. Quite out of the way, for it was not one of her haunts, nor was "any person" likely to look for her there. And yet such an unlikely thing might be as that "somebody" might have something to say to old Simon about the boats, even though it was Sunday. Thus both conscience and fancy were satisfied—conscience, for most likely "they" would be looking for her in an entirely different quarter; and fancy, because there was still a possibility, a far-off unlikely chance, that Providence might somehow bring "them" there, without intention. And when all was done, it was a bonnie walk,—the water softly lapping on the shore, the sunshine twinkling in all the wavelets, the green banks warm in the afternoon light, the trees softly shading over her, covering her path with scattered shadows. All this made the beginning of the walk very pleasant to Lily. She had been so good that she had a secret, half-drowsy consciousness that events would turn out to her advantage and bring her pleasant harm—that the temptation from which she had fled would be brought to her, without any fault of hers—perhaps no very unusual state of mind.

This, we must pause to say, was at a period considerably later than that treated of in the beginning of this history. Abel Murray had been for several weeks at Landale, had been on the eve of departure, and had stayed, doubling the originally proposed length of his visit before he made up his mind to write to his mother, which he had done with great precaution, sending his letter to Oxford first, that the postmark might not betray him. In the meantime he had made himself popular in the three great houses of the neighbourhood. Old Squire Ridley, in particular, had adopted him among the number of his closest friends, and because of the accident from which he had saved Roger he had been made free of the house, and had grown into the most intimate relations with the family generally, so that Mrs Landale playfully complained that though *her* guest, it was the Ridleys who had the most of him—playfully: yet the Landales, perhaps, were not quite so pleased as they still professed to be. They had remonstrated when he talked of going away, and insisted on the prolonging of his visit, but still there was a little soreness in their minds as to his constant coming and going to the Castle. If it was Roger that was the attraction, they all thought that certainly their Charley was worth as much as Roger; and if it was Mary— oh, if it was Mary, then it was most foolish, and more to be deplored than any other folly could be. For what could come of that but disappointment and trouble? Mary was engaged, and even if she had not been engaged, she never would have had anything to say to a man who, whatever he might be in the way of family, &c. (and nobody really knew what his family was, whether he belonged to the Atholes or not), was certainly not a rich man. It was madness, they all thought; but no one had a chance of saying so or warning him against it, and day by day he spent at the Castle, often, indeed, in company with some member of the Landale family (asked there much oftener on his account, which was something in his favour), but also often without. Mary was very kind to him. He had saved her brother's life, and he pleased and amused her father, and he was very much devoted, simply and reverentially, to herself. Mary was beginning to perceive that she was not likely to have very much devotion from her husband. Sir Richard was not an impassioned lover. He had taken his wooing very easily from the first;

it was more like the settlement of an alliance between two princely families than honest loving. She was the only person for him to marry, his fit mate; the one lady in the district who could add something—a bluer blood, a more distinguished lineage—to him who had so much. Therefore Sir Richard Featherstonhaugh had proposed to Miss Ridley, and, with faint reluctance, had been accepted. There was no passion in the business, and when Mary saw this new-comer, silent, reverential, and devoted, with a veiled light of passion in his eyes, she—liked it. It is a sad confession to be obliged to make. She was like Lily, though she was so much above Lily. She was flattered—and it softened and warmed her heart, a little chilled with the indifference of others and with the absence of emotion in herself, to see the light in this young man's eyes. She would not for the world have done him any harm. If she had been able to accuse herself of having done anything to cause this, she would never have forgiven herself for doing it; but the mischief was done before she found out, and she felt he was happy when he was by her side, when she spoke to him, when he had little services to do for her. Poor fellow! and she had so much cause to be grateful to him. Why should she not give him, it being so little, as much pleasure as she could?

Sir Richard, too, as in duty bound, had invited Abel to Featherstonhaugh, and there he had found among the visitors people whom he knew. Nowhere in all the neighbourhood was there so much society, and so good. The great house was full of guests, and Sir Richard was not indifferent to any one whose presence in his house was pleasant to his visitors. But though he received him and was civil to him, he did not like Murray. A certain suspicion in respect to him was always in his mind. He had seen his admiration for Miss Ridley, which was a distinct offence to the man who was going to marry her, but did not much admire her; and he had perceived that Murray, with a similarly jealous and displeased feeling, had seen his own eyes straying after Lily. These were very good reasons why he should dislike him, and be on the watch for something against him. He had made all sorts of covert inquiries into his origin—asking if he were connected with various Murrays whom he professed himself to know; and these inquiries had become very unpleasant, very disagreeable to Abel, so that he felt the existence of a *sourd* suspicion, which, had it shown itself at first, would have made him end his visit abruptly. But other reasons, now far more strong, had come in, inducing him to stay. He could not tear himself away. While he was there was he not a kind of protection to his sister? though it seemed to him that he would rather die than acknowledge the village Lily for his sister; and how could he banish himself for ever from the place which held Mary Ridley? Once gone, it must be for ever—that he knew—and thus lived on the edge of the precipice, daring the danger which seemed to him so terrible, but with which, when his feelings were excited, he could yet play. He had, indeed, it seemed to himself, surmounted for the moment all the most evident dangers. No one had recognised him, and yet he had seen many people whom he recognised; and he had never betrayed himself, though it had been sometimes difficult enough to keep on his guard. Was he not safe on the whole? and for another week or two—a few precious days or moments stolen from fate—surely there would be no risk if he should stay.

This, however, has but little to do with Lily, straying along the side of the water, with a smile on her face, and confused happiness in her heart. It was not happiness, it was expectation, a sense of all joyful things that might be coming, a confusion of hope and pleasure. She walked on with a half smile, with the shadows and sunshine flickering over her, and the wind busy about her, blowing her ribbons here and there, ruffling out the short locks that lurked under the braided hair on her forehead. Lily thought this was dreadfully untidy, and gave herself a good deal of trouble to smooth them down again, altogether unwitting of the time when "a fringe" should be counted a beauty. The cottage of Bess and Simon, to which she was going, lay in a little circle, half hidden by the woods before you reached the Castle. It was a very solitary little place, open to the lake, but shut in on three sides by the trees, which there were low down, almost to the water's edge.

Now it was not the custom in the district to go on the water on Sundays; but Roger was restless, and beyond rule: he had gone to church in the morning, as in duty bound, but he had not known what to do with himself afterwards. His mind was in a ferment and agitation about Lily, to whom he had said everything a man can say, without eliciting any response,—she had laughed, and she had eluded all his entreaties. No lady would have treated him, he said to himself indignantly, as the little village coquette had done. He was out of patience, and out of heart—exasperated, yet ever more and more bound to her, and feeling it impossible to break his chain. What was he to do? He had strolled down to the beach, and thrown himself into a skiff in the restlessness of his mind, and there he lay, swaying with the swaying of the water, floating where it liked to take him, his oars shipped, himself lying moodily in the boat, thinking—wondering what was to become of him, what she would do, whether he could tear himself away and try to forget her. That perhaps would be the best thing; but could he do it? The future was dark enough to him, even happiness being full of pain. Happiness would be to marry Lily—but if he married Lily, what should he do with her? how present her to his father? how get his marriage acknowledged and approved of? To lose her was despair; but to gain her—would that be so very much better? Poor Roger! he knew very well that Lily had not, could not have, any such love for him as filled his bosom for her. If she loved him at all, it must be in so much lighter, slighter a way, no more than liking, perhaps no more than vanity. This he knew very well by moments—and at this moment felt it to the bottom of his heart.

When all at once he saw a white dress fluttering, lingering along under the flecked shadows and sunshine. And it seemed to Roger that he knew the turn of the pretty figure, the swift yet lingering pace. He raised himself up in a moment and seized his oars; but even while he was in the act of moving, stopped suddenly, and, with those oars touching the water, stayed and gazed at what was going on before his eyes. He was not near enough to see the blue spots on the white cotton which he would have known for Lily's Sunday gown, but he had no doubt that it was Lily; but then, springing suddenly through the trees, came another figure, a man, throwing a dark shadow, by Lily's side. He could hear, or thought he could hear, her little start and scream, and saw in a moment, lighted by jealousy and a kind of hatred which he had begun to entertain for this inappropriate rival, that it was Featherstonhaugh. Roger set his teeth. If it had been any other man, any man who had a right to address her, who was free as he himself was—but Featherstonhaugh! Mary's accepted and betrothed lover! Roger's brain and his heart seemed to take fire. Lily gave a little scream, but she was not afraid, and Roger looking grimly on from his boat saw her stand listening and answering with the same half invitation, half repulsion, with which she had so often treated himself. They stood and talked, and Roger looked on. He could not hear what they were saying, but what he saw drove him frantic. It made him wild even that she should stop to parley at all. Not a look, not a gesture escaped him. He saw Featherstonhaugh put his hand on her arm, and though Lily tossed it off with a quick movement of her elbow, she was not angry. Then he seized her hand—but Roger could bear no more. He swept towards them with a few hasty strokes, and dashed his boat up upon the beach with a jar and scatter of the pebbles, springing on to the path beside the two, almost before Featherstonhaugh had dropped in amazement the hand which upon a second attempt he seemed to have been allowed to take.

"I beg your pardon," said Roger, quivering with passion. "I fear I am interrupting a *tête-à-tête*." And he glanced at the intruder who was to be his sister's husband with suppressed fury.

A man caught in such a position cannot well look anything but foolish. Featherstonhaugh was taken entirely by surprise. It is bad enough, in any case, to be found in intimate discourse with a village girl; but to be found by his rival, and his future brother-in-law, could anything be more uncomfortable? He flushed with angry impatience and discomfiture.

"I suppose, Ridley, a man may speak, without offence to you, to any one he meets?"

"Certainly," said Roger, taking off his hat. "I did not know that you enjoyed this lady's acquaintance to such an extent; but, certainly, I at least have no right to interfere."

"Oh," cried Lily, frightened, "you are angry! Why are you angry? It is not my fault."

"It is no fault at all, I presume," said Roger, "but an agreeable meeting, which I can only apologise for interrupting."

"You need not speak so fine for me," said Lily, rousing herself. "I was but going to see old Bess in the cottage. I was not thinking upon gentlemen, neither him nor another—least of all upon him," she added in a low tone, with an accent of contempt in her voice. This tone made Featherstonhaugh unreasonably angry, and in an equally unreasonable way mollified Roger. She stood between them, two dark and clouded faces, her own somewhat anxious and frightened. But Lily was no coward. "I cannot hold you from quarrelling, if you will quarrel," she said, "but it shall not be about me. I'm wanting none of you; but I'll speak when I'm spoken to, whoever it is, and answer to no person for it, but my mother," said Lily, after a pause,—"the only one in the world that has a right to find fault with me. Good-day to you. I'm going on, as was my meaning, to see old Bess."

And with this she swept away, simple Lily in her cotton gown, bearing the part and aspect of a princess to the two astonished young men. They stood as she left them staring at each other, mutually discomfited. Roger, who had confronted his rival in all the rigour of righteous wrath a minute before, feeling himself so ridiculously in the wrong that he did not know what to say. Featherstonhaugh took advantage of his sudden downfall.

"I hope you see the mistake of a too hasty judgment?" he said.

"Mistake!" cried Roger, roused. "Mistake about her, if you like, who shames us with her innocence; but none about you. Have a care, Featherstonhaugh! If you think I will stand by and see one woman duped, and another played with——"

"You do me immense credit," said the other, with a pale smile. "I never knew I was such a Lothario."

"By heaven I will teach you then," cried Roger, setting his teeth, "if you put yourself in my way."

"And what is that royal road?" Featherstonhaugh asked, controlling himself and driving the other to fury. Roger had advanced a step, his eyes glaring, his throat dry with excitement—when an unthought-of interruption came. A trim figure of an old man, bowed but precise, moving slowly along the upper path beneath the trees, came suddenly in sight. It was the old vicar, Mr Weston, who had christened both of them and all the parish beside. The sound of his steady, measured old footstep rang against their excited ears like the very steps of Time himself. They fell apart by instinct, they composed their looks and banished from their voices all sign of the enmity with which they had turned on each other. Mr Weston was not deceived. He had heard high words as he came up, and had even seen the threatening looks of the two young men, and divined that they were on the edge of a quarrel, though he did not know what kind it was. The very sight of him stopped everything. Ridley was already conscious that to quarrel with his future brother-in-law about Lily was not a thing that was possible. Passion is a fine thing, and all-prevailing, people think; but when it can bring nothing but ridicule and social ignominy, men very rarely indulge their passion. His hand, which had been raised to emphasise his words, if nothing more, fell by his side, his angry countenance cleared. "What, Roger!" said the old man, "and you, Sir Richard! then I shall have company for the rest of the way. But you must come to me, for I cannot go to you."

The vicar had not been out for weeks before. He had been ill, and had been shut up in his own room during all the course of summer. This was the first day he had been able to go out. He was walking slowly, with evident weakness, enjoying the air and the landscape, but making slow progress. "I shall be glad of an arm from one of you," he said, as the young men obeyed him and scrambled up the bank from the beach. How could they disobey such a call? He had all the authority of tradition, of natural respect, and conventional propriety in his favour. They would each have made a considerable sacrifice rather than allow him to perceive any struggle. His calm assumption of friendship between them subdued them more than any remonstrance. "You have been on the water, I see?" he said. "Think you it is a good example for you to set, the two chief men in the county?"

"You must blame me only; Featherstonhaugh is perfectly innocent," said Roger, quickly.

"Only because it did not occur to me," said Featherstonhaugh. "I cannot pretend to have been better employed."

"Ah, lads, lads," said the old man. "I will take your arm, Roger, if you please. You will be foolish, whatever we elder folks may say. We learn to give ourselves no needless trouble as we grow old. And to wear yourselves out rowing on a warm day like this, instead of creeping quietly along a sunny bank as I do—but I don't suppose you are likely to mind me."

And he went on talking quietly, leaning heavily on Roger's arm, talking meaningly, though he veiled his meaning, taking it for granted that they were two friends, two brothers, as they ought to have been. Thus he led them with him to the Castle, neither of them venturing upon a word which was in opposition to the *rôle* he assigned them. Once, indeed, it occurred to Featherstonhaugh to take advantage of the interruption and to go home; for it was not particularly agreeable to him to visit his betrothed wife, under the risk of being exposed by her brother. But unfortunately this blessed fancy, which might have been the saving of all of them, though thus suggested by some good angel, was never carried out. He went on, unconscious that he was going to his fate.

The meeting with the squire and Mary was cordial and friendly. They were both anxious to show their pleasure at the sight of the vicar, and Mary gave her brother to understand that she would be personally offended should he steal away, as he had been too much in the habit of doing. Mistaken precaution; he would have taken the first opportunity to get away, and go back to the beach and waylay Lily on her return, had it not been for this warning and for that attraction of hostility which kept him fascinated to the place in which his adversary was. But Mary's senses were too fine not to perceive that there was storm in the air, that her brother and her lover were on anything but friendly terms—that they never addressed each other, never even looked at each other, and showed every symptom of a recent quarrel. The relations between them had been sufficiently strained and difficult before, and she was anxious and watchful. To keep them together, to beguile them into talk, to interest one in the other, was her womanish way of mending matters. Even in ordinary cases of incompatibility of temper it is better to leave things alone; but an anxious woman is slow to think so. She was glad and relieved when more visitors arrived, being Charley Landale and Murray, who now haunted the house at all times and seasons. Abel had never met old Mr Weston before. The vicar had been ill, as we have said, and the meeting now was quite unexpected. Murray had become foolhardy,— he had ceased to take his usual precautions. A man who has passed his own mother unrecognised on Saturday, how is he likely to fear a stranger on Sunday? He came in quite fearlessly, giving himself up to the pleasure of Mary Ridley's presence. She welcomed him as a most happy diversion in the smouldering discord of the moment, and eagerly introduced him to the vicar. "This is Mr Murray, whom I am sure you have heard of," she said.

"Yes, I have heard of him: Mr Murray, the great Oxford scholar you have all been talking of. I'm a little blind, and a little deaf, and you must forgive an old man. There is a youth at one of your colleges I would like to ask you about. By the way, he's of your own name; I forget what his college is. Abel Murray, a young man from this parish. God bless us!" cried the vicar, with a sudden start.

"What is the matter, sir?" cried Mary; "you are over-tired; you are unwell."

"No, no, nothing of the kind. It was just a sudden fancy. Perhaps you may know the young man I am asking about, Mr Murray? It's your own name."

There was a distinct pause in Abel's mind. The others were not conscious of it; but to him it seemed as distinct a pause as that which falls upon a criminal when he has to say Guilty or Not guilty. A choice seemed to be thrust upon him—truth or falsehood, good or evil. And yet the blood had begun to hurry so wildly through his veins, the mad heart-piston to thump so loudly, that nothing but a confusion and giddy darkness was round him, through which his voice came not like his own voice, as if some one else spoke. "There are many of the name," he said; "it is not an unusual one. You don't remember his college? Had you done so all would have been easy enough."

"No, I don't remember the college," said the vicar, gravely. He sat staring at the young man with his dim eyes, studying him in every feature. "He was a handsome lad, dark and handsome like the rest of his family. I saw his mother selling her butter the last Saturday I was about before my illness, and I told her how satisfied we were. He is a credit to the parish. We have never had a prodigy before that I'm aware of. And son of a poor woman, that sells her butter (and very good butter it is) in the market at Waterside, it's a great credit to him to have done so well. Strange, now, when I think of it, in this light, there's a great resemblance——"

Mechanically Abel turned his head to the light, but there was nothing but giddy darkness in his own eyes. The room swam round him, a pale mist full of inquisitive faces. "By Jove! that will be the brother of the pretty girl in the village—the Lily of Waterside, as they call her. I had forgotten her brother. I wonder what was his college?" said Charley, carelessly. He spoke lightly, meaning little as he was in the habit of speaking—when all at once his eyes caught his friend's agitated colourless face. In a moment Charley stopped short; his countenance changed, his under lip dropped, he stared at Murray with a face of blank dismay.

They were all looking at him now, every eye fixed upon him—the vicar peering with contracted eyelids, for he was short-sighted. Abel's lips were so dry that he could scarcely speak. The harsh laugh, which he could not restrain when he was excited, broke from him in spite of himself—"The college! yes, that seems the essential point," he said.

How they all stared. God help him! unhappy wretch! He stood up unawares, feeling as if he hung suspended by some waving thread of chance over an abyss. Now he was falling in wild vertigo, misery, and shame. "My lad," said the vicar, very pitifully, yet authoritatively, in the way in which it was natural to address Elizabeth Murray's son, "I hope there's no intention to deceive in what you've done. Why should you try to conceal what all can see—that you are Abel Murray yourself?"

He gave one wild glance round him. They were all staring at him, the room turning round, the light changed to darkness, nothing but a mist of terrible, upbraiding, wondering faces. Then he became sensible of one which was an embodied insult, a sneer, a smile, a look which spoke enjoyment of his misery. That drove him out of himself: he struck a blind blow towards the insulting face, and with a cry, half moan, half yell, half laugh of despair and madness, turned and dashed through the circle. Who might be in his way he knew not, and how he got out of the room he knew not. He turned his back upon them all, and dashed wildly out of the house.

CHAPTER VIII

Abel fled from the presence of those who seemed to him his enemies and persecutors in a state of mind impossible to describe. The excitement in him had risen beyond the bounds of endurance. All power of resistance was over, along with all possibility of making a stand against evil fortune. He was not bad enough for his *rôle*. He could lie by concealment, and by inference, but not directly and in so many words; and the utter self-abandonment and unspeakable humiliation of his flight meant more than mere discovery: it meant complete moral ruin and downfall. Nothing but the entire giving in and relinquishment of every hope, the sense that he had no further step to take, no expedient, no way of escape, could have overwhelmed all his powers so dismally and so completely. For one moment only he had stood at bay, seeing as through a mist the sudden lightening and darkening of the faces round him—lightening of understanding, darkening of disapproval: he felt both to his very heart with a horrible anguish beyond all experience. He had been ashamed of his low condition, of his peasant birth, of his homely family, and this shame had made him do ignoble things; but he was not all ignoble. A strong perception, when too late, of the simple truth which might have saved him, contended in his mind with the bitterness of his shame and the rage of his despair. No possibility of anything which could be done to set him right suggested itself to his frantic soul. It was all over: there was no longer any way of repentance, any rehabilitation for him. The weakness of his nature had found him out. Farewell everything—love, friendship, honour, credit! He would live no longer among the people who had found him out; he would not look them in the face again. He darted into the woods, running at full speed, not knowing where he went; anywhere, only to escape from them, only to avoid the look of them. Oh, cruel judges! oh, terrible tribunal! could he ever flee far enough to escape from it, to forget the look in their cruel eyes?

These harsh judges from whom Abel fled had let him go in the first shock, obeying that impulse of indignation which is so natural at the moment of a discovery, but so often repented of afterwards. Mary had stood aghast in her surprise, incapable of a word, and it was only when he was gone that compunctions woke in her.

"Oh, Roger! go after him," she cried, "go after him. Do you remember that he saved your life?"

Featherstonhaugh laughed out. He, too, was excited and uncomfortable after the other event of the afternoon, and this was a way of relieving his feelings.

"His knowledge of the place stood the fellow in stead. I thought so at the time," he cried. "To think he should have taken us in for all this time!"

Mary turned upon him with a keen glance of indignation. His laugh jarred upon her nerves. "Go, Roger, go," she cried; "if you do not go I will. Don't let him fall into despair: he saved your life."

"Whoever goes it must certainly not be you," said Featherstonhaugh in a low tone, catching at her sleeve.

Mary had no thought of going. She put up her hands to her eyes, crying in spite of herself.

"I think I hear him laugh as he did then," she said. "Oh, poor wretch! will no one go after him? will no one have pity on him? Oh, Mr Weston, I hope we may not all repent this day's work."

The vicar himself was very much discomposed.

"I did it for the best," he said—"I did it for the best."

The only person who kept his composure was Featherstonhaugh, whose ill angel evidently had the upper hand for that unhappy day.

"Here is a great piece of work," he said, "for the unmasking of a wretched impostor. For my part, I suspected him from the first. As for saving Roger's life, it was not much after all—any child could have done it who knew which were the safe places. But he may have other claims upon your brother," he added—"claims you would scarcely understand."

"Do you mean to insult me before my father and sister?" cried Roger, making a stride forward, crimson with rage and indignation.

His opponent looked at him with exasperating calm.

"Is there any need for heroics?" he said. "I have no intention of insulting you; but it might be well to explain— —"

"Oh, lads, lads," cried old Mr Weston; "what is this quarrelling about?— you that ought to be brothers. Hold your hands, and hold your tongues, you foolish— —"

"I think there is some mistake," said the old squire. "Sir Richard forgets himself, and so do you, Roger. Go after that unhappy young man. Let him go to his family—that is the best place for him; but tell him that if he likes to come to me in the library at any time, I will be glad to see a man of his information. Learning is of no family," said Mr Ridley, with a wave of his hand. He was the greatest aristocrat of them all, but he had a sense of the fitness of things.

"If you have such an impostor back in the house, sir, I shall desire that Mary at least may not be exposed to the chance of meeting him," said Featherstonhaugh.

"Oh, come, after all," cried Charley Landale, "Murray's no impostor. He said nothing about his people—heaps of fellows say nothing about their people. His people don't matter to us; but he's no impostor, no more than I am, or you, Featherstonhaugh. We would both sing small enough in Oxford when Murray's there."

"And Sir Richard will excuse me," said the squire, with a stiff bow, "if I say that I can take care of my daughter. Mary, it will be best for you to retire; and, Roger, I have asked you to do something for me."

"I am going, sir," said his son, gloomily; but he went with reluctance, looking back when he reached the door. "You know where to find me, Featherstonhaugh?"

And Featherstonhaugh laughed. The whole party instinctively threw themselves between the two young men—the one red with fury, the other cool, with all the exasperation of which scorn and insult are capable.

"I will go with you, Roger," said the old vicar, hastily. "Perhaps I have sinned against my brother. But no—no, I would but hamper you. Be you the messenger of mercy, and God bless you, my boy! Go! go! before it is too late."

Thus he was pushed out of the room, Charley Landale going after him. "I'll not leave him," the good-natured fellow said quickly in Mary's ear as he passed.

Featherstonhaugh made no attempt to follow. He waited almost ostentatiously to give the other full time to be out of the way, and then he went home.

But neither Roger nor his companion could find any trace of Murray. No one had seen him or could discover where he had gone. Charley Landale went home, disconsolate and feeling half-guilty, to watch and wait for his friend's return, and to give what account of it he could to his family, such as would least prejudice them against their visitor, though even the little he said threw the house into confusion and agitation indescribable. The girls cried over poor Mr Murray; the kind mother, half-horrified at the risk her daughters had run of perhaps falling in love with a nobody, and half-sorry for the nobody himself, whose "feelings" must have been terribly "hurt," sat and talked it over, neglecting the dressing-bell, and scarcely conscious even of dinner. Dinner! ought they to wait for their guest, who had never come back? Charley went out wandering about the grounds, looking for him; and even old Mr Landale himself, though indignant with "the fellow" at first, had come to be anxious too, and stared from the only window that commanded the road. But Murray never came. They ate their dinner at last when it was cold, and everything was wretched, listening to every sound outside, and starting at every footstep as if it was one of themselves who was in deadly peril and trouble. When night came, Charley, good fellow, would not go to bed, but sat and dozed, keeping a light burning in the window which was visible from the road. But, notwithstanding all their cares for him, and all the sympathy and kindness that dictated them, Murray never appeared; His things lay about his room as he had left them when he went out, light of heart, expecting to return for dinner; but he himself entered these hospitable doors no more.

The object of all these anxieties lurked somewhere among the woods in one of the shady nooks he had known when he was a boy, and which probably no one but himself and his old rustic companions knew, in the very madness of misery, while the daylight lasted. He hid himself like the first sinners—he could not bear the calm eye of the day, the cold unpitying light, that would show him and point him out to the scrutiny of men. He lay thus panting on the earth, hidden by the bushes, his mind and all his being in so wild a turmoil that, after a while, the very cause of it got obscure in his mind, and he knew only that he was a fugitive, heart-broken, ruined, and disgraced, without knowing why. He had no sooner reached a covert in the copse than there seemed to gleam before him another, better hiding-place, a cool nook by a little stream, where nobody could ever find him, where he could have a draught of water when he pleased, and the trickle of the brook to bear him company. As soon as it was dark he made his way out of the chase, and fled along the most unfrequented paths, under hedgerows and across fields, to reach this place. The country was very still, Sunday night, no one about, no one stirring anywhere. Here and there he made a detour to escape the lighted windows of a roadside cottage, whence some one might look out and see him: sometimes shrank aside into a ditch or under a tree when he saw some solitary passenger in the distance—but met no one, saw no one, and at last came to the shelter he had thought of. It was deep down among thick brushwood, heather, and whins, and young birch-trees, by the side of a little stream which flowed from the hills to the lake. The ground was damp, but he did not care. He dipped his burning brow in the stream, and drank long draughts of it. This gave him a little relief, a little physical ease; and the walk had been long, and he was unused to so much exertion. Finally, he fell asleep, with his head, like Jacob's, on a stone. The shock he had sustained seemed to take from Abel all consciousness of any claims upon him or duties to the outside world. He remembered nothing about the Landales, thought nothing of where he was to go when the morning should come, again betraying him. He thought indeed of no morning, only of safety from some immediate danger, though he could not tell what that was.

It was a very lonely place, but abounding with wild creatures — rabbits and squirrels, every kind of grasshopper and harmless insect, water-rats, moorfowl, and myriads of existences too small for names. He was woke by them as he lay, early — very early, before any human thing was stirring. He had slept feverishly, by intervals, through the night, and he woke up to a less confused sense of his misery in the morning. Gradually it broke upon him as the light came disclosing the landscape, creeping on and on. Oh, the horror of the remembering, the misery of shame, the intolerable sense of weakness, wrong, resentment, and impotence! Why was it so? Why was he born a cotter's son? Why was it a disgrace to him? How horrible! that he should be banished from the company of men, driven out into the wilds, aching every nerve of him, body and soul, miserable, abandoned, troubled, all because he was a cotter's son! Oh, wrong at which earth and heaven should cry out! Abel was not capable of realising that nothing but his own falsehood, his own cowardice, could have made his birth a shame to him — he was far beyond such an exercise of reason. He looked down from among his ferns and bushes to where the peaceful house of the Landales, where he should have been sleeping now in safety but for this, lay among the trees, and beyond it, on the banks of the shining water, saw the old Castle, whence he had been driven out, "to eat grass with the beasts of the field." That was what the old Eastern potentate had been sentenced to: was it to be *his* fate too? Somehow it gave the poor fugitive, half-distraught, a kind of forlorn comfort to remember that old story. His thoughts went back to the old Bible lessons he remembered long ago. What had the king done to have such a fate? and what had *he* done? But it gave him a little ease to realise that this had happened to some one else before.

And where was he to go? He could not show his face in this familiar place, which had again grown so dear. He would go back — back to his lonely rooms in Oxford, where he ought to be safe, he thought. But how to get there, how to stir in that garish, lavish day, which flooded every dark corner with light, so that the water-newts and earth insects had much ado to get themselves into some covert place, and how was he to walk unseen, a man? He was faint for want of food, aching with the unusual exposure, his clothes wet and torn, his hat he did not know where, his head throbbing and buzzing and all confused. But yet he might have come round out of the painful bewilderment he was in; his thoughts began to take a little shape, his mind began to occupy itself with a practical question — how to get home unseen, how to get to the road and the railway, and go back whence he had come. All might have come again to something like nature — nature sore and bleeding and wounded to the heart, but yet able to command herself, able to be restored.

But just as he had worked to this hopeful point, a jar and rustling in the branches woke every pulse in his frame again. Who was it? He peered through his covert with his bloodshot eyes, and at first saw nothing. Then gradually he distinguished something moving among the copsewood and tall bushes of heather. Who was it? What was it? A man, coming towards his hiding-place, pushing his way through the trees, leaping across the rivulets in the bog, here sinking in the marshy places, then reappearing, coming ever nearer and nearer. Abel stretched up across his little stream to watch this advancing figure, fascinated. Was it some one in search of him? Then he sat down, pulling the heather and brushwood over him to escape detection. The sounds came on, then stopped, quite close, — so close that Abel felt his very breathing would betray him. "Are you there, Ridley?" said a voice close to his ear. "So you have kept tryst. I scarcely expected you would. Get up, wherever you are, and come out." Then, after a pause, in an angry tone he added, "Is this a time for fooling? Come out, wherever you are. I can't wait here."

Abel was like one of the branches quivering over him, one moment blown this way, another that way, as different impulses swept across him. He had covered himself with the bushes, shrinking into the very earth for safety. Now, with a sudden change of idea, he sprang out from his lair, suddenly confronting Featherstonhaugh with his wild looks and haggard face. "My God!" cried the new-comer, springing backward in consternation and alarm. He did not recognise at first the extraordinary figure. Abel was very pale, his head was uncovered, his eyelids red as blood, his clothes all wet and soiled and torn. With a sudden fierceness he pursued after the other, keeping his wild eyes fixed upon him with a glare of passion and madness in them. No wonder Featherstonhaugh was afraid. "Is it you, Murray?" he said, faltering. "I — beg your pardon. I thought it was Ridley; he was to meet me here, this morning, about the boundary line. The two estates — march.

We had—words yesterday, and I scarcely expected him. I am afraid you have not spent a—comfortable night?"

"Yes, I have," said Abel, hoarsely; "better than among men—better than with the false and cruel——"

"You take it too seriously, I am sure," said the other. "What does it matter who is a man's father! We are the child of our own actions, nowadays; only, if you will do me a favour, don't go any more to the Castle. It would do you no good, and it might—do harm."

"Are you my master?" said Abel.

"No, no. Don't be excited. I ask it as a favour. Don't go. I am not taking ground as your superior, Murray."

"Are you—my superior?"

"Well, yes," said the other, with a careless laugh, growing less afraid, and feeling that in his coolness he had the upper hand; "we need not inquire into that, need we? Go home, like a good fellow, and get some breakfast. You must be cramped, lying out all night—have you been there all night?"

"Who are you that speak to me as if I were your slave? Do you think I— will do what *you* tell me—You! Who are you that give me orders?"

"Come," said the other; "Murray, you know this will never do. You've been drinking. Go home."

"I have been—what?" shrieked the unhappy young man.

"Don't make it more evident than it is. I said drinking," said Featherstonhaugh. "Now go home."

But Abel sprang at his throat before he was aware. It was an impulse, like the other. A sudden flash and tingle of passion, and then a spring. Featherstonhaugh fell like a stone among the brushwood and broken stones of the hillside, with the grip of the madman on his neck. He was a madman now. The wavering of the mental balance, which might have been restored an hour ago, was over for ever. This second assault concluded the struggle. With no enforcement of artificial restraint, nothing but the two, in face of each other, on the lonely hillside, passion leaped into frenzy in a moment. He gripped his victim by the throat and there was a long and horrible struggle; then, when the other lay still and ceased to resist, Abel, laughing wildly, got upon his knees and struck at the helpless, prostrate figure, beating him into the bog, cruelly repeating blow on blow, blow on blow—long after all blows were needless. He kept on with a convulsive motion, rising with every stroke, like a child when it imitates the action of riding, showering down his blows, with a stick which he had picked up—with a stone, with his hands—in a fury which by-and-by degenerated into horrible, senseless play, and monotonous repetition of an act which no longer meant anything; not homicidal passion—not mad rage, but only the horrible play of a distracted brain.

But by-and-by another sound roused him—the sound of a step crashing among the branches once more. With a vague recollection in his madness that some one else was coming, he rose, all bloody and horrible, and looked about him. Some man or other stood within a few feet of him on the other side of the little stream. Some one who called to him, who hurried forward, jumping the brook. The madman knew nothing, who it was, or what he wanted; but frenzy and fear are ever akin. He turned round wildly, faced to the hills, and fled like an arrow from the bow.

CHAPTER IX

It was morning, and all the usual business was well begun; the cows were out in their pasture on the hillside; the chickens about the close vicinity of the house; nothing was audible except their busy cackle and the hum of the bees, which Elizabeth Murray kept, and which were one of her sources of income—and her own steps coming and going in her house. Before you came in sight of the house you could hear those brisk steps, stately and harmonious, giving a sign of life in the pleasant stillness. Dick was in the potato-field close by; there had been a fine crop, and he was digging them up for the market at Waterside. He was whistling as he worked, but Elizabeth, whose mind was full of many cares, did not sing snatches now of one song, now of another, as was her wont. How seldom it is that the mother of children has not occasion for anxiety about one or another! and it seemed to her that she had so much. Lily; what should she do with Lily if the girl grumbled at the loneliness, as she was likely to do, or pined for her friends, and for the admiration she had called forth? All that would be natural—quite natural. After half consenting to leave her daughter and to trust to her prudence, Elizabeth had been seized with a panic on her return home, and had sent instructions that Lily should return on Monday morning; and now again she was doubtful, as was also so natural, of the wisdom of the step she had taken. How would Lily bear the solitude? Up here among the hills, nothing except the household work and the mild vicissitudes of the chickens and the cows ever happened. Elizabeth herself did not mind, because, as she said to herself, she was old, and all that was likely to happen to her in this world had happened and was done with; and Dick did not mind, for he had not begun yet to think of anything beyond his work, and life was all before him, and he had been accustomed to the tranquillity all his days—but Lily!

And on the other hand, there was Abel to think of—the lost boy—who yet was so much greater and happier and better off than ever Elizabeth could have made him. She sighed, but took herself to task for it, declaring to herself with tears in her eyes that she did not grudge his grandeur—that it was for his happiness she cared, not for her happiness through him. "But oh, it cannot come to good that he should think shame of his own folks," she sighed in the depths of her heart. Yet it was so pleasant to think of him as "a gentleman." It seemed to Elizabeth that if she could but see him enjoying that high estate, courted and made much of by the great folks of the land, she would not want to speak to him or betray him. Oh, far from that! She would live in the house with him and never betray him.

Thus she was going on peacefully about her domestic work: the chickens cackling outside, Dick whistling in the fields, the brook trickling over the stones, the bees humming, everything full of the warmth and softness of the summer day. The air was such that unless you were ill or in trouble you gave God thanks, unenvious of other blessings, for nothing but the day; and Elizabeth was a woman subject to such influences, and, in spite of her cares, a softening of happiness stole into her mind. After all, was not everything well? However anxious she might be, there was no trouble in her family. Lily was not disobedient, and Abel, though he did not come to see his family, yet "took an interest" in them. There was no reason why she should not let the sunshine and the sweetness steal into her heart, and allow herself to acknowledge that all was well.

"Dick," she cried from the window, "lad, do you no hear a sound of somebody coming? I think I hear a step by times, and surely somebody cried to us, coming up the hill. Did you not hear?"

Dick stuck his spade into the soil, and, listening, said, "Mother, I heard nothing. But now I'm quiet, ay, that was a sound."

"It's maybe Lily," said the mother.

"Lily's foot's too light to sound so far. But we'll see soon enough when they come," said Dick, resuming his digging. He resumed his whistle too. He was not curious. Whoever it was, would not they show themselves soon enough? And in the meantime he had his work. Elizabeth, too, went in, and went to her dairy, accepting Dick's philosophy. To be sure! there was nothing so much to be expected but that when it appeared would be time enough. Time enough! And so their life went on tranquil for ten long sunny minutes more.

About that time both of them held their breath and stopped their work. Dick stuck his spade again in the half-dug row of potatoes. Elizabeth came out to the door. A hurrying, headlong step, coming on in mad haste, now ceasing for a moment as it reached the bog, coming nearer, rushing on— with other sounds, broken cries, gaspings and pantings, as of somebody hunted, came to their ears. While the mother and son listened in growing alarm, old Watch, the dog—most steady of dogs—suddenly raised his old black muzzle and gave vent to a long wailing bark of alarm, which echoed through the hills. Terror fell upon the minds of the mother and son. What was it? The light seemed to go out of the sky, the echoes to tingle all about them. These wild hurrying sounds did not come even by the usual path, but, as Dick perceived sooner than his mother, descended from the higher way, a way no one ever came. This was how it was that when the new-comer reached the place at last, Elizabeth did not see him. She knew nothing till he was close upon her. A terrible figure, bare-headed, bloody, his clothes hanging torn about him, his face ghastly and distorted, strange, harsh, broken sounds coming from his lips. She turned round only when he was within a few steps of her, when she saw him, and with a shriek of terror threw up her arms and started out of his way. Dick came rushing to her help; but the stranger heeded neither of them. He burst into the house, and threw himself, all convulsed and shivering, before the kitchen fire.

"God help us, Dick—it's a madman!" cried Elizabeth. "What will we do?"

They both stood in terror at the door. There was a moment's pause of horror and dismay. Dick was pale, but he was brave. "Go you and shut yourself in the byre, mother, and I will see— —"

"Nay, nay, my lad; your mother's life is less worth than yours. But look at Watch!" she said, with a strange thrill at her heart.

Watch had been taken by surprise, and struck with terror as well as themselves. He had run terrified out of the way with another howl when the man rushed past. But now he had followed into the kitchen, without either fear or anger apparently. "He never can bide a tramp," Elizabeth said, with a strange aching wonder in her heart. They could see the huddled mass of shivering limbs before the fire. Watch went in, cautiously snuffed all round the prostrate figure, and then began slowly to wag his tail—slowly at first, and then with an appearance of wild joy, and yelps and barks of welcome. Elizabeth Murray's heart seemed to stand still. She gave Dick a look of horrible suspicion and misery. Then she made a gesture to him to keep behind her, and went in with the silence and swiftness of a ghost.

The terrible being who had thus arrived upon them had fallen down on the floor, apparently in a fit. He was lying writhing and struggling before the fire, his face distorted, his eyes glaring, foam and blood on his mouth. She went in and bent over him, then knelt down by him. She had not seen him since he was a boy. He had been twelve years old when he had gone away. She looked at him now, knowing before she looked who it was. Heaven help her! had she ever been light of heart, peaceful, happy, though this was coming? Was it years ago since she stood at her door and heard Dick whistling and the bees humming? She knew who it was even before she looked. She knew him for all his convulsed face, his terrible struggles and contortions. Abel! her son—who was a gentleman, who was too grand for his own people. The dog, faithful brute, with a truer memory than even the mother's, was licking the terrible face. She gave a great outcry, words and sobs together. "It's Watch that knows him, and not me, first!" she said.

Then she got water and dashed in his face, and rubbed his stiffened hands. She did not even know what to do for him. She knelt by his side, her face too as pale as death, unconscious cries coming from her—"Oh my lad! Oh be still! Oh let him be, good Lord, let him be!" She did not know what she said. And Dick, with a face blanched to the colour of his linen, kept plucking at her sleeve and calling softly, "Mother?" She took no notice for a long time, then irritated by the repetition turned upon him sharply, "What is it, lad?" Dick could not get any question out of his parched lips, he only looked at her and then at the writhing figure on the floor, "Can you not see for yourself?" she cried, with a groan in which there was a kind of wild incredulous laugh. "Can you not tell without asking? It's my boy Abel, him that's a gentleman; our pride and our joy!"

How the rest of the horrible morning went they never knew. Their peaceful occupations were all abandoned. In the midst of their cares for Abel—whom after a while they managed to get transferred to a bed, when the fit going off left him half unconscious and entirely prostrate— arrived Lily, all unaware of any new event at home, but with the news that a horrible murder had been discovered—Sir Richard Featherstonhaugh lying dead on the hillside, all beaten and battered. This did not seem to Elizabeth, for the moment at least, any concern of theirs; but when Lily, very frightened and half reluctant, was taken up-stairs to see her brother in his raving sleep, a gleam of painful light, a dawning of some horror seemed to gleam among them, though they could not perceive what it revealed. Lily turned from the room where lay the stranger whom they called her brother Abel, with a suppressed shriek. "It's the gentleman!" she cried; and when she had told all her story the little awe-stricken party looked each other in the face, each paler than the other, not knowing what to think. "Was he—friends—with the lad that's killed?" Elizabeth asked, turning away her face. She could not allow her children to perceive the dawn of meaning in it. When Lily replied by a tremulous account of how and when she had seen them together, Elizabeth made no comment, but by-and-by she went up-stairs and returned with the clothes Abel had worn, made up into a bundle. Lily, whose attention was still unaroused, did not notice what her mother did. But Dick, who had watched her closely, went out after her, and found her burying her bundle deep in the potato-field where he had been digging. With tremulous energy she threw up the easily dug soil, making a deep hole in a corner. She said nothing in explanation of what she did, even to him, nor did he ask—but she took hold of his arm to help her to the higher level on which he stood, and gripped it with a convulsive strain. "God grant I'm a' wrong," she said, looking as if she had been turned to stone. "Ay, mother," said Dick. It would have been more comforting to her if he had not understood her so well.

But the events of the day were not yet over; enough, indeed, had passed already to make it terrible. All this peaceful life, which had been so quiet this morning, had disappeared from them, and in its place had come a mystery and horror such as surely never before had come upon decent folk. Who thought of the mild beasts in the field, the cows grazing, the bees keeping up that busy hum of undisturbed labour, the milk that was setting in the dairy, the eggs to be gathered, all the soft growth and production of nature that was going on for their benefit? The whole had been swept away from their thoughts by this sudden wreck, this falling among them of a ruined being, a distracted life. How many anguishes had come with him! terror, suspicion, crime! and yet it was all guess-work, and there might be nothing after all but madness in poor Abel's misery. Nothing but madness! which would have seemed the most horrible of miseries yesterday, but now would be a relief from other fears. There was only Lily in the house who did not entertain these fears. She had not seen him come flying like a hunted creature to the one place that could shelter him. She had not associated him with the murder of which, on the other hand, her mind was full. Only yesterday Featherstonhaugh had spoken to her, had tried to "court" her; had made an effort to take her hand and draw her to him; and now he was murdered — murdered! lying in his blood, scarcely recognisable! The story had been brought to the village with all its terrible details before Lily started, and she could not but go over them in her mind. So living, such power in him, such a grand gentleman! and now with the life beaten out of him, a piece of dishonoured clay! She sat down and cried, sitting by the door, while her mother watched the other gentleman, who was her brother she could not tell how. Lily sat alone in the solitude, and wept, partly for the murdered man, partly out of vague agitation and excitement, partly for herself, who had lost all pleasant things and pleasant prospects. What was there for her now but solitude and forgetfulness, all the delights of her youth over and done? She put up her hand to the little ribbon with its hidden locket round her neck. Oh how sweet it had been to receive that secret treasure! and now it was all that was left to her. In all likelihood she would never, never see the giver more.

"Lily!" said a voice near to her. She gave a great start and cry and rose to her feet. Had he come after her — and so soon? Notwithstanding the sense of trouble about her, Lily's heart rose; but there was nothing encouraging in the face of the lover whom she supposed to have come after her. He was pale and haggard, his eyes bloodshot, his frame trembling. "Where is he? Has he come here?" he cried. Of her, in the old tender winning way, he took no notice at all; if it had been Dick, Roger Ridley could not have been more indifferent. "Has he come here?" he repeated, almost with impatience. Lily was wounded in her foolish expectations. "How am I to tell who you mean?" she said. She stood in the door barring his passage. The attitude meant a great deal more than was in Lily's mind. She looked like the guardian and defender of the secret that had come into the house.

Elizabeth, who was above, heard the voices and came to the window, which she opened softly, looking out with anxious eyes. "I will not betray him," she heard Roger say. Then he looked up and saw her, and beckoned to her to come down. Elizabeth hesitated only for a moment. She must hear sooner or later all there was to say. She must find out how to defend her boy, and what he might be accused of. She locked the door upon him as he lay there moaning in a stupor which was scarcely sleep, and came down. She was but a common woman, with nothing to distinguish her from the other cotters in the dale; but as she went slowly to the door to hear her son's sentence, so to speak, she marched unconsciously as a martyr might to his death. What would death have been in comparison of this which she had to face?

"I have not come here to betray him," said Roger, "but neither need you try to hide it from me. I saw him—God help me! shall I ever get it out of my eyes? I saw him, but I was too late to save. I saw him kneeling, striking at him, striking at him! God! I think I see it now."

He leant against the wall looking as if he would faint; but Elizabeth did not faint. She stood, the colour of death, with her arms crossed upon her bosom. If there had been any possibility of denial or resistance she would have resisted and denied; but there was none, and she needed no explanation. "He is mad," she said, "mad—he's no responsible—mad! Do you hear what I say?"

"I've tracked him all the way," said Roger. "I know he must have been here hours ago; more than one met *me*, but no one had seen him. God knows what people may think of the trouble I was in. I thought after a time it might put them on the scent, and then I asked no further questions; but no one had seen him. They will not think of looking for him here, if you are prudent; but you must keep him still, and not let him move. Give me a draught of milk and I will go home and watch over everything. If it is suspected where he is I will send you word."

"Mr Ridley, I will pray for you night and day on my bended knees," said Elizabeth. "Oh, he's mad, my lad! he's no responsible. And oh, you, a stranger, to take this burden upon you! What can I say? what can I say?"

"I saw him by accident," said Roger. "God help us. I am perhaps to blame; he got insult through me, and he saved my life; and Lily," said the young man, turning for a moment to look at her—"but all that's over now," he added, with a sigh.

Lily had sat down on the step by the house door. She had hidden her face in her hands and was weeping quietly, overpowered by the despair about her. He was near enough to be within reach of her, and he put his hand on her head. "Yes, it's over," he said, "it's all over," with a sudden break of sobs in his voice. Who could think of happiness, or love, or anything sweet in life now? His heart was sick with wretchedness and horror. Roger did not know how he was ever to take up the common things of existence again, how to get that spectacle out of his eyes.

It was Elizabeth herself who brought him out and served to him, solemnly, as if it had been a sacrament, those simplest elements of food, the common oaten cake and bowl of milk which was their ordinary cottage fare. Lily sat and wept—her heart was broken—but the mother, with her heavier burden, did everything. The two young creatures thrown down there in moaning and despair—she leaning her head against the cottage wall, he lying on the turf with his face buried in his hands, were lightly weighted in comparison; but Elizabeth's heart yearned over them, sorry for the trouble they were so much less capable of bearing. "You must not stay here," she said to Roger, softly. "Oh, God bless you, my young gentleman, and put me and mine out of your head, and all that's happened this dreadful day! But you're rested now, and you mustna bide here."

Roger rose reluctantly from the grass; the moment of rest had softened his heart. He stood, looking disconsolately, wistfully, at the girl whom he had so foolishly loved. He knew how foolish it had always been, and it had fled from him like a shadow in presence of all the terrible events of the morning. But when he looked back upon her now, seated there in all the abandonment of the catastrophe, her pale face lying back against the grey wall, her pretty hair falling from the comb, her eyes shut, and two great tears stealing down her cheeks, a great pang went through Roger's heart. Love and honour and pain strove in him. Could he take her to him under this shadow of madness and ruin? Could he leave her without a word? He stood for a moment irresolute—then made a hasty step towards her, and stooping down, kissed her forehead. "Farewell, my Lily! Farewell, my Lily!" he said, then turned, and went quickly away. Lily uttered a low moaning cry—she made no other response. It was all over, all over! There was nothing more to say.

Then the silence of the hills fell around the little house, folded up with its secret in it, among the great slopes of the mountains. The first night fell upon them, half a benediction in its darkness and quiet, half an aggravation of the unseen dangers that now seemed to hem them in. Dick sat up and watched all night, while his mother sat by the bedside of the fugitive, who lay between stupor and raving, and had recognised none of them, though they thought he was soothed by his mother's presence and touch. Long were the hours of darkness, though so few in the soft summer weather, which was then exceptionally soft for the north. As for Lily, she was made to go to bed, with kind tyranny, by both mother and brother, and slept, and was ashamed of herself for sleeping. And then came the dawn again, tranquil and awful, the first morning after the calamity,—the revelation of that changed world in which no longer all was well. But the cows and the chickens had to be looked to all the more that they had been neglected the night before, and that was a consolation so far as it went. The day went on quietly enough. They were on the alert for every sound, and Watch was posted out on the hillside at a little distance to give an alarm if any one should come; but no one came. And whatever might be doing down in the low country, whatsoever course suspicion might be taking, whether Abel was thought of at all in connection with the murder, or who was thought of instead of him, here none could tell. Lily, heartsick, did her share of the work, casting wistful looks down the road, and letting her heart and her eyes roam downwards upon the water far in the distance, radiant with sunshine, or dim with shadow, where all the business of life was being enacted, though she knew not how. The others were glad (if that could be called gladness) when the day was over without any incident; but oh how long was the day to Lily, with her heart fluttering away upon the far horizon, and this killing silence round her! And it was all over, the other life, all over! Was this henceforward to be the tenor of her days: this and the madman up-stairs who was said to be her brother? Had ever any one before so hard a lot to bear? Lily repeated to herself that her mother was old, and "wrapt-up" in "the boys," and Dick "did not mind;" but she who had no boys, and was not old, and whose life was over, all over! What was there so forlorn and terrible as this fate which had fallen upon her?

It had come to be dark again; night falling, the time of terror, and great stars coming out into the sky, peering over the shoulders of the hills, and leaning out of the blue to see all that could be seen. The family had come in and shut their door; never on a summer night had that door been shut before; but it was always a bulwark the more in defence of the wretched one within. Elizabeth came and went between the room where he lay and the kitchen, where Lily sat by the smouldering fire, crying in the darkness. There was no light in the room; they wanted no light to be wretched by, and even the glimmer of the little lamp on the high mantelpiece might betray them. The fire smouldered, a red speck and no more in the darkness, and the low, square windows hung like faint pictures on the wall. Dick was outside. It was not possible for him to be confined in a room with closed doors. The night was thus darkening over them, and dreariness and stillness falling like a pall, when all the echoes were suddenly roused by the harsh, hoarse bark of Watch baying, with his head up and wide throat extended. Elizabeth, who was standing by Lily, took hold of her suddenly, grasping her trembling frame with two passionate hands. This filled the girl with additional terror; but it was her mother's silent way of strengthening herself, and bracing herself for what was to come. Then Dick appeared, the defender of the house. They could see him take his stand in front of the door, to protect the entrance. Then there came a sound of voices, and Lily sprang to her feet. "He's come back again, mother!" she said.

"There may be more with him," said Elizabeth; but she opened the door, with jealous care, showing half of herself only, to parley. Was it Roger, that dark figure against the light outside? He came pushing in with a kind of rude imperativeness. "Do you try to keep me out?" he said. "No, we are all in the same ship now. Let me in. I have nowhere else to go."

"Is there more ill news to hear?" said Elizabeth.

"More ill news? No, not for you. Listen; but first light a lamp or something, that I may see who I'm talking to. That's better. Yesterday," said Roger, with a curious laugh, "I could speak freely what I wanted to say without thinking of the dark or the light."

"What is it, tell me what it is?—I must go to my lad that is alone."

"Alone! is he worse than others?" said Roger, fiercely; and then he added, laughing again, "they say it was I—I—that did it! I have fled from my father's house not to be taken up for murder. Oh, God!" he cried, with a tone of agony. They all echoed it with one impulse. "You?" they said, and Lily broke out wildly crying, half hysterical with the misery which seemed to have its crown of anguish now.

"But no, no, it canna be! you have proofs to the contrary," cried Elizabeth, upon whom this seemed an appeal against herself.

"They can prove everything," he said, with the calm of one who knew the worst. "I had an appointment with him there for that morning. I was seen going away, looking like a man that had killed another. I had quarrelled with him (oh, poor Dick, poor Dick! I knew him all my life!) the day before. There is no one but believes it. We are all in the same box," said Roger, sitting down, miserable but defiant; "there was nowhere I could come but to you."

"Oh, sir," said Elizabeth, "no harm shall happen to you, not a hair shall fall from your head—but spare him, spare him now."

"Spare him! am I harming him? I am giving my life for his," said Roger, with a groan. "I wish he had let me break my neck from the old tower; it would have been soon over. Spare him! I'm on my way now I know not where. Whatever happens to him I am lost, Mrs Murray; my life, my good name, everything. Look here, there is but one thing you can do for me; give me Lily and let me go."

Lily had heard all from her stool by the fire, where she had sat in a dull suspension of feeling, listening vaguely, too much crushed to care for anything. At these words she rose up to her feet, and stood still, rigid, waiting for what was next to be said.

"No," said Dick. "Mother, you could not be so cruel; let him bear his just burden that did it. One should not perish for another. Mother, you would not wish a sacrifice like that?"

"Oh, Dick!" she moaned, wringing her hands, "no harm shall happen to him, not a hair shall fall from his head."

"But that's not all," said Dick, "that's but a little—honour is more than life. Would you let him give up everything because Abel caught him when he was falling? I would do that for any tramp. Mother, you will never be so cruel."

"Look here," said Roger, "I've taken all the money I could lay my hands on; that ought to keep us from starving. Tell Lily to come with me. I've nothing else left in the world. Give me Lily and I will go."

"Lad!" cried Elizabeth, turning to her son with vehement self-defence, "if I give him my Lily—my Lily, as he says——"

"That will not be to give him justice," cried Dick. "Mother, think before you do it—it will never come to good."

"They would murder my lad," said Elizabeth, shivering; "they would take no excuse, they would give no mercy. But when he's better he'll know what to say for himself. They would put the stain of blood on your father's house. We could never be clear of it to the third and fourth generations. But him there, there's no trouble in his soul; he will not suffer like the one who did it. If he was in danger of his life it would be different. I tell you, not a hair of him should be touched; but there's no danger of his life. And if I give him my Lily, as he says——"

This controversy went on swift and low-toned, while the others stood scarcely listening. Roger was full of the excitement of despair; he had been warned that the warrant was out to arrest him and the officers on their way. What could he say against it? There was every proof that he was the man. He had been traced to the fatal spot, he had been seen speeding like a ghost up the hillside afterwards; he had given no alarm; and there had been that fatal quarrel the day before. Every fact was against him, even to a blood-stain on his dress, which he had got unawares as he pushed through the brushwood to see what it was the madman had done. By no way but by giving the madman up could he clear himself. And there was no time to think; all through that day he had fancied that every one shrank from him and avoided him. When the old village constable, whom he had known all his life, ventured to hint at his danger, it seemed to Roger, impetuous and wretched as he was, that there was but one thing for him to do. And he had plunged away through the woods in the twilight as Abel Murray had done before him. He would go if Lily would go with him. To this he made up his mind with the obstinate simplicity of his nature. What was there at home to make him desire to stay? He could neither marry as he liked nor live as he liked. His sister, the only bright thing in the house, was plunged into trouble. There was no comfort wherever he looked. If he had Lily to go with him, he would go.

As for Lily, she stood in a wilder excitement, still feeling her fate in the balance. She did not think of herself as having any choice. She seemed to be suspended between a wild agony of happiness and a dreary abyss of evil. To be raised, giddy, to the height she did not realise, or dropped horribly into the pit below, was an affair of a minute or two. She stood breathless, waiting—with her eyes wavering between her mother and her lover, not knowing what was to be.

"Sir," said Elizabeth, breaking from her son's detaining hold, "you're doing a great thing for me, and I'll do a great thing for you. You'll promise me to wed my Lily? You'll vow to me afore God that she shall be your wife?"

"I promise you before God," said Roger, taking the passive girl by the hand.

"Then take her—take her—before I repent. Oh, go, my lass! go with him and be a good wife to him, and make it up to him, if woman can. Go! afore I repent. I'm buying one child with another," said Elizabeth, lifting up her hands, wild tears bursting from her eyes. "I'm giving a life for a life. Oh, Lord! forgive a poor woman driven out of her senses, for I'm doing a base action. Go, go! afore I repent!"

CHAPTER X

Roger and Lily left the cottage almost immediately on their extraordinary journey. All that they had was the money which he had got before he started, a considerable sum which happened to be in the house. Elizabeth, on her side, gave Lily everything (it was not much) which was in the cottage, and with a little bundle on her arm the girl went out into the darkness with her new companion. Not even her husband! Lily was dazed, and did not know what she was doing. She scarcely felt the hasty embrace with which her mother put her from the door. In a curious suppressed delirium of excitement and wonder she floated out into the night without any independent action of hers—or at least this was how she felt. Was it her life that she was beginning as she set out over the turf and tremulous bog under that wistful clearness of the sky over which heavy clouds were rolling? Everything was darkness before her eyes, and fear in her heart. They were both young, they had done no evil, they were strong and well and cared nothing for the long walk, and the strange excitement of the moment was indescribable. They said nothing to each other as they walked steadily over the hills, Dick going with them to show them the way. They had nothing but their money, a poor provision, and their youth, and some love for each other, which was altogether in the background now. Had they been married in the natural way, this passion, now but secondary on Roger's part, on hers vague as could be, would have been the chief thing present to their thoughts. As it was they thought nothing of it. Other subjects than this were foremost in their minds. They said nothing to each other, did not even take each other's hands, but with excitement so wild and strange that everything else was dissolved in it, went away together, fugitives, victims—yet also something more.

Dick put them on their way across the hill by a wild mountain path difficult to find for any one who did not know as he did every nook and crevice of the hills. Lily, too, had some knowledge of them, and of the tricks of the atmosphere and elements in these lofty regions. Her brother left them only when the early dawn was breaking over the mountains, and they could see how they were going. There were few words at the leave-taking. Lily let fall a few tears at the renewed farewell, and they parted and went upon their several ways without looking back. She was started now, pushed off dangerously, risking everything, into the surf of the sea of life.

And it is more than words can do to tell the state of mind in which Elizabeth Murray lived for days after; her daughter gone—perhaps for ever—perhaps, for who could trust any man? to sorrow and shame; her son lying, rolling his head from side to side, sometimes violent, and requiring restraint which it was so difficult to know how to use; sometimes lying like a log, in a stupor which nothing could break. She lived on, nevertheless, saying little even to her companion Dick, and went down to the market on Saturday as usual with a brave front, and sold her butter and bore her burden. She stood in the market as she always stood, and asked everything about the murder, and made her criticisms and observations. "It would be some tramp," she said, looking them all in the face. For the young squire, even if it had been in him to strike a sudden blow and kill his adversary, he could never have beaten and crushed him savagely as had been done. She said all this without a change of countenance, for she was a brave woman, and felt that she must not save herself a single detail. She went to Miss Prentice even, and there talked it over again, though the chief end of her visit was to say that she had sent Lily to a cousin's far south, and did not fear but what the change would put her all right. Everybody accepted her explanations with straightforward simplicity as they seemed to be given, for nothing had directed suspicion to her; and nobody supposed it possible that she could have anything to do with it. The old vicar, indeed, looking very old and very anxious, hovered about Elizabeth's place, wistfully looking at her, talking to her, trying to lead her to the subject of her son. But she had never been much disposed to talk commonly of Abel, at least for many years, and fortunately she remembered this, and would not be drawn into conversation about him now. The old vicar was very unhappy. He had repented his disclosure when he saw the unhappy young man rush out disgraced and stung to the heart, and though it never occurred to him nor to any one to connect Murray's disappearance, for which there was such good reason, with the horrible event which had occurred next morning, yet the idea that the unfortunate young fellow had felt the exposure so deeply, gave the old man a grievous pang. Even in the midst of the excitement caused by the murder, he had gone daily to Landale to inquire if any news of their visitor had reached them. What could have happened to him? It might be suicide, for anything they could tell, and in that case, Mr Weston felt he too would be a murderer. "But his mother knows nothing about it," he said to himself, with a sigh of relief. Was it possible that anything of that dreadful kind could have happened and the mother not know?

Meanwhile the Landales had mourned very sincerely over the disappearance of their guest. They packed up the things he had left, his money, his little personal possessions, in a portmanteau, mournfully, as if they had been relics of the dead. He had not been heard of at Oxford. Was it from the depths of the lake that they would have the first news of him? Mrs Landale would not see the vicar when he came. "He has killed him," she said, "as sure as ever poor Roger Ridley killed Richard Featherstonhaugh." And as the months went on and there was nowhere any news of Abel this came to be the general conclusion. What a tragic summer it had been! Old Mr Weston failed visibly Sunday by Sunday after all these events, and died of it also before the winter came.

As to the other tragedy, there were investigations without number. Roger was traced to the place where it was proved he was to have met Featherstonhaugh, and where it was supposed some sequel to the quarrel of the previous night, of which there had been various witnesses, had taken place. He was traced away from the fatal spot, having been met wildly wandering about the hills, haggard and agitated, asking the people he met if they had seen some one running that way. But no one had been seen running that way, and the hypothesis was that this was the explanation he had intended to give had not his courage failed him. But even if this defence had been true, he must have at least seen that a murder had been done: yet gave no alarm. And last of all, and most damning proof of guilt, he had fled. This convicted him with every one. His father, with a groan that rent every heart, after denying the possibility of Roger's flight as long as he could, retired to his library when there was no longer any doubt of it, and shut the door, and was seen by no one, even in his own house, for days. But there was Mary left, whose situation was more pitiful still. No one dared to intrude upon her in her first hours of grief. But she did not attempt to shut herself up. She put on her mourning-dress, as heavy as a widow's, as was due to poor Featherstonhaugh, but never forsook her brother's cause, protesting passionately that he had not done it. The vicar, who would have been a witness on the trial, and who was, indeed, called before the coroner's jury to tell of the quarrel which he had seen, did what he could to bring her, as people said, to see the truth. But Mr Weston could not shake her conviction. "You will all acknowledge it one day," she said, in her passion. "I do not know how, or when, but I am sure he will be cleared." The populace round shook their heads, but were very respectful to Mary, very tender of her in her great misfortune. And another line of Featherstonhaughs, distant cousins, came in, and dispersed Sir Richard's collections, and changed everything he had cared for. Thus one great house was entirely altered, and another made desolate, and the whole face of society changed in Waterdale. And after this great convulsion there was a long silence, and the new things grew natural and became old, as is the law of human affairs.

When years had passed, however, there arose one morning a strange rumour in Waterdale. Some time before it had crept into the knowledge of the country that some madman had escaped from an asylum, no one knew where, and was at large about the neighbourhood. People in lonely places had seen a wild figure passing by, and some had heard strange sounds, peals of horrible laughter, and inarticulate cries. On one occasion Mary Ridley even heard this sound of laughter, and had alarmed the neighbourhood, and sent out all the men in the village to beat the woods, declaring that she knew the sound, and who it was. And next morning a strange story ran like fire over the whole district. It was that a man had been found lying dead in that same tragic spot, which had become memorable far and near, where Sir Richard Featherstonhaugh got his death. The news of this came on a Saturday morning, when Elizabeth Murray was in her place in the market with all her merchandise, carefully arranged as always. She had been looking ill, everybody remarked. When the story came down from the head of the water by one envoy after another, Elizabeth left her stand unprotected and uncared for, and went away. She had lost all her fine colour, and had grown old—older than her years—but nevertheless, she marched steadily up the lakeside till she came to the place where they had carried the vagrant who was dead. Such an event had made a great commotion about, and there was much discussion among the men who clustered round the empty cottage in which the body had been placed. It filled them all with wonder to see Elizabeth come, slowly and silent, but with a death-like countenance, through the midst of them. She went into the room where the dead man lay. Those who had seen him had said that he was "a fine figure of a man," though wasted and savage with exposure, his hands and feet torn with the rough places he had been wandering through, and a long wild beard grown over half his face. She went into the room, shutting out the curious gossips about who came to peep and shrink with curiosity and horror. When she came out she locked the door. "The man who is lying there," she said, giving the key into the hands of the village constable, the same man who had (against his duty—but that was easily condoned in such a place) warned Roger Ridley to flee, "is my lad Abel, my eldest son, that has lost his reason for many a year. The Lord has delivered him at last; but he's not to be made a common show, my lad. I'll come and see to him, and that all's done for him that should be done."

"Your lad?" The wondering little crowd came closer and stared at her, whispering and pointing. "Lord bless us! Lizabeth Murray, your lad?"

"Ay. Is it such a merry sight, the face o' a woman that has lost her firstborn, and that thanks the Lord? Go away to your bairns, you silly women, and let me and him be."

"But, 'Lizabeth, there will be an inquest—there must be an inquest."

"That's true," she said. She was quite calm, and made no show of her feelings, whatever they were. "But, John Johnston, you'll keep them off that come from curiosity, to glower and girn at my lad," she said, with a sudden burst of passion. Then subduing herself in a moment, "Good morning to you all; I've much to do this day," she said.

Old Mr Landale was the nearest magistrate, and to him she went direct, without pause or delay. She was a long time with him, and came out exhausted and pale, but rejecting all the anxious offers of help he made her. "We were all attached to him—all of us," the old gentleman said, attending the peasant woman to the door with still more agitation than Elizabeth showed; and after that Mr Landale convulsed his own household with the strangest news—news that threw the whole valley into such excitement as had never swept over it in the memory of man before.

Six months after, Roger Ridley came home with his wife and children— two of them—one a boy, who was heir to all the family honours, such as they were. But though Mr Ridley forgave and acknowledged his son's family with something like joy, and relief that the honour of his name was restored, there was not much cordiality, as long as he lived, between the old squire and the young squire. The little heir pleased the old man, and recommended the pretty young mother to him; but he never forgave his son the wild generosity which plunged all his family into such grievous trouble. If it was generosity or if it was cowardice, or a false sense of honour, or mere panic in face of a horrible accusation and the network of circumstantial evidence in which he was trapped, no one could decide. But when Roger came home everybody condemned him. It was said on all sides that he would have been acquitted if he had had the strength of mind to stand his trial. "*I* never believed it for a moment," every one said; and all kinds of imputations of weakness and cowardice were made against him. From these accusations it is not our place to defend Roger. Who does not feel, looking back upon a great emergency, that he ought to have done differently, and that another time would find him in a very different mind? He had thought so himself a hundred times, after that wonderful night of excitement when he and his bride went over the hills, like Abraham, not knowing where they went. No other lord or squire in all the north country had an experience to fall back upon such as Roger Ridley had. He had lived the strangest life for these years, and he had not approved of himself any more than his father and his neighbours had approved; but to be faithful to the consequences of a false step, even when you perceive it to be false, is something. He came back a sadder if not a wiser man; no longer the gay hero of the countryside, but very serious, taking almost a gloomy view of everything. His old friends said that his wife did not understand him—could not enter into his ways of thinking—and perhaps this was true enough; but the fact was that he had gone beyond himself as much as beyond Lily. And by-and-by he got into parliament as member for the county, which was a great honour, and did his duty perhaps all the better for having been transplanted for a time out of the higher places and the sunshine into the darker shades of life.

As for Lily, she came home a beautiful woman, of so unusual a style of beauty that she reigned henceforward undisputed over the water, no pretty girl of the moment being able to stand before her matured splendour. She had developed other qualities as well—a talent for dress which no one had suspected, and for hospitality and society and lavish expenditure, which took the world by surprise. She behaved quite as she ought to her mother, everybody said, sending the children to see her, and visiting her periodically with much attention. But when Elizabeth died, a year or two after Mr Ridley's return, and Dick, left alone, emigrated, shutting up the little cottage at Overbeck, it was said that Lily showed every symptom of relief. They said she was glad to be relieved from her family in these legitimate and natural ways, and it was only then that she blossomed out into full splendour. If she was perhaps always a little rustic in manner, that was thought to be piquant when she became the leading lady of the county; and by the time her children grew up nobody recollected any longer that once upon a time she had been the village Lily, the daughter of a woman who sold butter in the market. All that is over so long ago.

And Elizabeth Murray sleeps by the side of her son Abel, in the churchyard, as quietly as if he had lived and died among the fells like herself. The anguish and the struggles are only for a time. Peace is the end of all, for all men. And what does it matter now in the silence, that a little while ago there were madness and raving, and such pangs as overpowered nature, in these two mouldering forms? Time and Death tranquillise all.

THE STRANGE ADVENTURES
OF JOHN PERCIVAL

CHAPTER I

John Percival was a nephew of a banker in Edinburgh, destined from his childhood to the service of the bank—which was considered by all the family the greatest good luck that could have happened to a boy. His uncle, who like the boy was John Percival, and who was his godfather—or namefather, as we say in Scotland—as well as his uncle and his patron, and was connected with him by every possible tie, was a childless man: childless, too, in the most secure way,—not an old bachelor who might marry at any moment, but a staid married man with a wife younger than himself, yet not so young as to be dangerous. He was, though the old man did not say so, nor do anything to raise expectations, universally considered as his uncle's heir; and did so consider himself calmly, without impatience or preoccupation with the subject, and very far from wishing to shorten his uncle's life by a single day. He was thought the most fortunate boy in the family; but I don't think he considered himself as such, and especially when he set out on a wintry day at noon in the stage-coach for Duntrum, a large provincial town in the south of Scotland. It may be divined that it was not to-day or yesterday, according to the popular phrase, when this journey took place: for nowadays one whisks off from Edinburgh to Duntrum in the morning, and whisks back again at night, having several hours in which to do one's business between, and no fatigue to speak of. It was very different in those days, when from noon to nearly midnight the coach joggled over the frost-bound country; and even in his corner in the interior, where John was forced to place himself by the anxieties of his elders, who kept up a pleasing fiction that he was delicate—it was very difficult even under a pile of plaids and topcoats to keep warm. He was going to serve for a year in the bank at Duntrum to give him a knowledge of country business and the ways of rustic depositors and clients,—a knowledge which John felt to be very unnecessary, seeing that his life was to be spent, not in Duntrum, but in Edinburgh, and at the least in the manager's office, not at the counter selling money as if it were tea or sugar. He did not like this change of scene at all, perhaps because the season was at its height in Edinburgh, and all the entertainments of the year hurrying upon each other; but chiefly because it was the sordid side of business, the lower part of the profession, as this foolish young man thought, which he was being sent to study. He did not appreciate the advantage of knowing everything connected with his trade, which the elders know so much better than the young people. Indeed, to tell the truth, he was not sure at all that he was fond of banking, or thought it every way so superior an employment as many people thought. His own opinion was that if he were left at peace to live upon his own little bit of money, and pursue his own tastes, he would be a much happier man. He had a notion, indeed, that he might possibly turn out a great painter or a great writer if he were thus left to himself to cultivate the best that was in him. It was a pity that he felt the possibilities were equal in respect to these two pursuits. It might be either which would bring him fame and fortune, but certainly one of them. If he had been sure that it was either this or that, there would have been more hope for John: but he was not sure,—he thought at one time he could have been a painter, had he time and encouragement to try, and then again another time that he could be a novelist or a poet. Perhaps on the whole it was just as well for him, that, with such excellent prospects, and the certainty of coming to a good end, if he behaved himself, he should have been what he was—a banker's clerk.

But whatever it might end in eventually, it was very hard lines, he thought, that he should have to leave Edinburgh in the middle of the season when everything was in full swing. There was not much in those days, at least not the tenth part so much as now, of football and golf. These games were played, but they were not the essence of life. Strange to say, young men found other things to talk about, other things to occupy them which were not all deleterious. For one thing, they took a great deal more interest in dances and all sorts of assemblies, in which the boys met with the girls of their own class, than the ordinary run of "manly young fellows" do now. I suspect they fell in love much more freely than they do now. They wanted to meet, to talk to, to laugh with these girls, as they like now to make themselves comfortable in a smoking-room, or rave about breaking a record on the links. I do not say which is best, not knowing; but at least one must confess that it is quite different. It is possible that John had even more than one incipient flirtation on his hands. He did not at all like to leave, for a hum-drum provincial town near the Border, with all its local questions and prejudices which he would not understand, the cheerful bustle of Edinburgh, the gay assemblies and all the private entertainments that abounded at this cheerful time of the year.

"Good-bye, my boy: we'll see you back whenever there's anything great going on," said one of the friends who were seeing him off. There was a little group of them round the coach door, bright-faced young men who had made a dart from the offices of several Writers to the Signet, or even from the Parliament House—to see the last of Percival, as they said.

"Perhaps," said John, with satirical bitterness, "if well-founded information reaches the bank that the world is coming to an end."

"In that case you may stay where you are," said the other; "we'll have enough to do thinking of ourselves. Hallo!" said this young man, feeling himself vigorously pushed aside from the coach door. This was the arrival of another passenger, by whom the group of young men were pushed aside to right and left by that free use of elbows and personal momentum which an energetic woman of the lower orders uses with so little scruple. This was a strong and vigorous maid-servant of middle age and weighty person, leading a veiled and muffled personage who followed her closely, and who bore the aspect of an old lady afflicted with toothache or "tic," or one of those affections of the face which were then treated freely with enveloping wraps to keep out the cold, and external applications, and a total indifference to personal appearance. Indeed in this case, as the face was entirely invisible, a thick veil of Spanish lace, in a large pattern of heavy and close design, covering the small amount which was not entirely obliterated by plaster and poultice applied to the right cheek, there was not perhaps any inducement even to undying vanity to attempt modification or concealment. The identity of the veiled person it was quite impossible to divine—her wrapped-up head was like a melon, a "sport" with one great bulge on the right side: a faint glimmer of an eye between the crevices of the lace pattern, a little colour, was all that was apparent; feature and form and expression were all lost in the portentous envelopments. She clung close to her protector with old and tremulous steps, and occasionally a faint waggle of the misshapen and enormous head.

"Can ye no' see it's an auld leddy with the rheumatics in her head—and jist you get out of the way, my fine callants, that kenna what trouble is. Gang round to the other side of the coach if you have any more blethers to say. Steady, mem, steady! take your time, this is the town corner, the furdest frae the winds: and I'll pull up the window-glass, and ye'll not feel a breath. You'll jist be as safe as gin ye were in your auld chair with the wings at hame."

During this speech, to which the young men listened awestruck, the old lady was carefully and with much precaution hoisted into the coach, a process which seemed more difficult than her short stature and apparently insignificant figure seemed to justify, the stout woman-servant growing redder and redder under the strain, although assisted by a porter who pushed from behind. When the process was accomplished the boys burst into a genial but suppressed laugh, with significant looks at John, who for his part could not but regard with a certain fascination the mass of nodding headgear which was to be his companion in the long drive. He could not take his gaze from her. The cold journey to Duntrum, leaving dinners and assemblies behind, was reason enough for despondency: but to travel with Medusa herself in a mail-coach! if by any chance the wrappings might come off, and her unfortunate fellow-passenger be turned to stone.

"I give you joy, Jack," whispered one of the attendant youths; "here's a bonny bride to bear you company."

"I'll tell May Laurie you were in capital fettle; a fair lady by your side and plenty of time to make your court."

"Nothing of the sort, Jack, my lad; I'll let her know you were preserved from every temptation," cried another—all this in not quite inaudible whispers, at the other door.

John was glad when the coach finally started, leaving all these laughing faces behind; for he had a tender heart, and was remorseful at the thought of perhaps wounding an old and suffering person for whom he had on the contrary the greatest compassion. True, it was dreadful to see that misshapen head nodding from the opposite corner, and to know that whatever happened he must be its companion for so many hours. A horrible doubt seized him whether it would be possible for her to go so far without occasion to change her poultice or undo her cerements. He thought of the 'Veiled Prophet,' then just published, and wondered whether he might not have some ghastly revelation to undergo like that of the horrified hero. He thought in spite of himself of ill-smelling ointments and other sickening appliances. Poor creature! it might be a question with her of ease from distracting pain, or she might go on suffering, unwilling to expose her inflamed cheek, or run the risk of disgusting her companion. Poor old body! John tried to turn his back on her, to keep his eyes diverted on the view from the opposite window: but there was a fascination in the unknown which drew him back. He stole glances at her against his will, as if she had been a young beauty. He would have given much to see what was underneath the thick silken flowers of the veil, even though he was sure it would be chiefly poultices bound up with white-and-black handkerchiefs. These modes of wrappings were visible sometimes on Edinburgh streets as they are on those of Paris to-day. It would not be a pleasant sight: still it would be better than the mystery in the corner which sat there, like an image of stone, never showing any sign of life but by the occasional nodding of the distorted head. Was it palsy too, poor soul? had she all the ills that flesh is heir to? John was very sympathetic. The sight of that wrapped-up mass of suffering in the corner affected him very much. He would fain have done something to show his pity. He began to calculate how he should manage to help her out when the coach came to its first stopping-place to change horses and to afford the passengers an opportunity for "a snack." Probably she would not be able to take a snack or exert her suffering jaws. He thought perhaps he might got her some broth, which would give her no trouble except the trouble of undoing her veil. Broth was always to be had in a Scotch village about dinner-time. It would warm and comfort her, and perhaps even she could take it without undoing anything. He had a horrible desire to see the coverings undone, and yet he had so kind a heart that he would have been glad to think she could take a little broth without any trouble in that way, poor old soul!

However, he did his best to read his book for an hour or two, turning his mind from the lady in the corner. He would be out of temptation those fellows said. Well, yes, he was out of temptation in one way: but if his fellow-traveller had only been a moderately well-looking woman, even though young and responsive, he did not know that he would have been so much in temptation as with this mystery in the opposite corner, though he felt sure it was a repulsive mystery, and probably would have a sickening, and not an enticing, effect upon him. But he said to himself he would just like to know what it was. Poor thing! perhaps it was a dreadful embarrassment to her to find a man opposite to her, to be hampered in any effort to relieve herself which she might have made if alone. He could see that she pressed herself more and more into the corner, and leaned the weight of her poor head on the cushions. By degrees it occurred to him that he might make her more comfortable if she would allow him to make a roll of one of his plaids and put it at the place where no doubt her neck came, so that she could support her head more comfortably. He pondered over this a long time, and experimented on himself how he could do it, before, with much timidity and as fine a blush as if he had been aiding a beautiful princess, he at last ventured to speak.

"The cushions," he said, "are not very soft in these coaches."

The melon with the bulging side turned round to him with a swiftness he could not have thought possible, but nothing was said.

"I've been thinking," said John, "I've seen it done in—in my own family. You see, you roll up a thing like a small bolster, and then you place it just where your neck comes——"

He exemplified what he meant by rolling up a large comforter knitted in dazzling white wool, quite new and of his Aunt John's choicest manufacture, made expressly for this journey. It was large and soft, and John rolled it close till it became as round and smooth as a bolster, according to his homely simile.

"If you will let me," he said, rising, "I think I could place this——"

There was an agitated movement inside the draperies, and a voice that made John jump, between a squeak and a scream, came as it seemed out of the top of the misshapen head, "No! no! I cannot be touched. No! no!"

It made John jump; but after all, what was a voice any more than the other appearances, to daunt him when he had so honest an intention of doing well? He came a step nearer. "I am sure you will find it more——"

"No; keep away! No; keep away!" the voice repeated with shrill decision, not at all softened but made still more bewildering by a sudden tremor at the end. He paused for a moment with his white roll in his hand, and he distinctly saw the veiled figure shake with a strange sort of broken vibration, as if in one access after another of palsy, was it? or, if not, what else? He did not know what else it could be. He stood for a moment wavering, and then he retired and threw down the comforter impatiently upon the seat. "Well," he said, with a sigh also of impatience, "if you won't have it I cannot help it: still I am sure I could have made you more comfortable," he added, recovering his good-humour. And he resumed his book: but his attention was sadly distracted, for that spasmodic movement went on at intervals; and there even broke forth certain stifled sounds—was it moaning, was it the signal of some approaching calamity? He gazed earnestly over the top of his book, with a most compassionate face, and held himself on the alert to give any aid he could. But after a while his apprehensions were quieted: there seemed no reason to suppose that anything was going to happen, and these mysterious movements died away.

The lady, however, refused the broth which he procured for her when they stopped, at the risk of having no time for his own "snack." She rejected it with the same sharp squeaking voice as before, and with something of the same strangely convulsive movements,—darting away from her corner, when he suddenly opened the door at her side, with a swiftness which it was impossible to suppose such a wrapped-up mummy could be capable of, and an evident fright which piqued him a little. "No; keep away!" she squeaked again. What a cankered, sour, shrill, old woman! What did she suppose he wanted with her? It was not for her *beaux yeux* certainly. But he had heard that some women always, however old and ugly they may be, imagine a man wants to make love to them. He laughed at this to himself as he went off to get his "snack," and as ten minutes with a powerful young appetite can do a great deal, succeeded fully in indemnifying himself. For the moment he was vexed with this second repulse; but no such feeling had long the mastery in John's honest bosom. There were some fine golden oranges on the table, and he put two or three into his pocket before he went back to the coach. Perhaps she might like one in the dark hours that were coming before they reached Duntrum, when there would be no light to see by, whatever faces she might make, if she put aside the veil. He put two of them gently on the seat beside her when he returned to the coach: but the mummy only gave a grotesque fling farther back into her corner, and took no notice. Yet once again John made an attempt to be of service to her. It was when the guard, as they passed through the small town of Dunscore, as the evening fell, opened the door hurriedly and flung in a bundle of post-bags, two or three attached to each other with a strap, their metal padlocks shining in the glow of his lantern. "Last stage afore Duntrum," said the guard. It was his habit to place the mails there at this point of his journey, in order to give them up to the Duntrum authorities without delay.

"That is scarcely very safe," said John, ingratiatingly to his silent companion; "suppose you or I were less honest than we seem." He laughed, but his laugh died out of itself in that shamefaced way in which a laugh quenches itself when made at our own joke, and falling flat without response. But presently, after a while, he suggested, which was very true, that it was getting cold, and asked if she had enough wraps, or would accept one of his. This seemed to overcome altogether the patience of the veiled lady in the corner. She told him sharply to mind his own business. "There's nothing wanted from you," she said. The voice was odd, the shrill one alternating with a softer note as if two people were speaking. It had almost become a point of honour with John to overcome this persistent defiance. He approached with one of his plaids outspread, and laid it gently about her knees. The answer was a vivacious movement kicking it away.

"Will you not take a telling?" cried the shrill voice. "Away! and snoozle yourself in your corner, and let me be quit of you!" The voice was so fierce that John fell back in spite of himself, and, somewhat mortified, took the unfriendly advice. He did withdraw into his corner, wrapping himself round and round in his many wraps, until he was almost as much muffled up as his companion. And the night was cold, and there was only a very feeble lamp in the coach. He ended by "snoozling" as the old lady advised, with his head buried in the high collar of his coat; and as the windows were closed against the penetrating chill of the night, and the atmosphere heavy, he fell fast asleep.

He woke with a start some time after, with the sensation of a gust of wind blowing upon him from the coach door. Half bewildered as he came to himself, he saw that the door was open, and caught, with astonished eyes, a momentary glimpse of the face of a young woman, a sudden apparition against the blackness of the night; and then the door was closed sharply and with a clang. The coach was at the foot of a steep ascent beginning to ascend slowly. John sat up suddenly, awake but still bewildered, and rubbing his eyes. The opposite corner was vacant. His plaid lay on the floor where the old lady had tossed it, but she herself had disappeared. He jumped up still confused, and unable to believe his eyes, and groped in the corner. But there was no one there: then he put his head out of the window, and shouted loudly into the night.

CHAPTER II

The coach was crawling softly up the hill. In daylight half of the passengers would have walked up the ascent which was within a short distance of Duntrum, but they were all benumbed with the cold and the darkness, which was so intense that John, when he looked out, could see nothing but the white speck of the lamp travelling along a black line which might be a hedge or a wall, and was only visible as the light passed over it. It was like putting out his head into some awful abyss of nothing, his eyes hurting him in this black gloom which abolished them and their use. The big vehicle groaning under its burden crept on, labouring like some huge animal, jingling, creaking, reluctant, going on through the cold and the dark.

John shouted "Stop! stop!" with a stentorian voice. "A lady has fallen out of the coach! A passenger has fallen out of the coach!" he shouted, repeating it again and again; then opening the door, got out himself, dropping upon the invisible road. But it was not till some minutes later that the coach could be brought to a standstill, and he could get possession of one of the lamps, tearing it out of its place.

"She must be lying in the road," he said; "she was an old woman unable to walk." He held the lamp to the ground, as if at any moment he might tread her under foot. By this time other dark figures were detaching themselves from amidst their heaped-up wraps from the top of the coach and jumping down, stamping their feet upon the iron and ice of the frozen ruts.

"What is it? Who is it? An old body? Bless us all, an old body. She will just get her death!" There was a chorus of voices and of warm breath going up on the still air. The guard and John, each with a lamp, walked down to the bottom of the hill, accompanied vaguely by several scarcely decipherable attendants.

"I fell asleep," he said, explaining himself to the night, scarcely conscious of any auditor, "and then she was sitting there close up in the corner, as she had been since we left Edinburgh, and would never speak: but when I woke up, the door was wide open, swinging, and there was nobody——" He added, after a moment, as if he had suddenly discovered that face: "Some woman passing on the road shut to the door with a bang—and that woke me." It seemed to him as he related this that he was telling an incident in a dream; and yet he was sure it was quite true.

"A woman on the road—did you see a woman on the road? there's few foot-passengers here at this hour of the night," said the guard.

"I saw her as clear as I see you." He held up his lamp instinctively to the face of the other, which was bent like his own on the ground.

"One of you," cried the guard, "hurry up the hill and stop her if she's gone that way. She canna have gone far on this steep road. Stop her and see what she knows."

But no wayfarer was found on the ascending road, nor could all the light of the lamps find any trace of any one who had fallen. The inhabitants of the first wayside cottage at the foot of the hill were imperiously knocked up by the guard and put upon the trace.

"We canna stop the coach whatever happens," he cried, "but we'll send out a search party from Duntrum immediate. How long were you sleepin'?" he added peremptorily to John, who looked at his watch in the light of the lamp and answered—

"Perhaps an hour."

"An hour is a long time," said the guard, knitting his brows. "As far back as the brig we would be then, and at a smart pace, for the horses, poor things, scented their stables. Take your lantern, lad, if you have one, and go as far as that.—Ou ay, ye'll be paid, you needna be feared for that. Will ye come, sir, or bide? I daurna stop the coach."

John looked into the blankness of darkness before him and shivered, but it was not this only that moved him. He felt certain that the catastrophe, whatever it was, must have happened within a much shorter time than an hour,—that it had just occurred, indeed, when he woke, and when the sudden blast of the cold wind roused him with its searching chill. He felt convinced that he and his companions had already come to the farthest limits in which the accident, if it was an accident, could have occurred. His head was confused with the effort to find an explanation. What was it? After searching so far, he became convinced that the clue was not to be found on the road. Where, then, was it to be found? He made no answer either to this question in his own mind or to the guard, but turned back, leaving the others with the sleepy and startled cottagers, father and son, who had been roused from their beds, for it was already late, and were reluctantly accepting the directions of the guard, whose red coat made a spot like a fire in the darkness, lighted up by the lantern which he had attached to his belt. John turned back and began to reclimb the hill, throwing the flash of his lamp on every roughness of the road, and making his way back to where the coach smoked into the night, the breath of the passengers and the emanations from the horses forming a mist of life which rose dim yet consolatory across the light of the lamp in the midst of that chill of winter and darkness. As he came up to it his foot caught upon something almost under the hindmost wheel, and he gave a loud cry, which brought every one on foot around him. He set down his lamp on the frozen ground, and they all clustered over it in a circle. It was the heavy bundle of the mail-bags strapped together, one end of the leather strap still entangled with the step of the coach. The guard pulled them up with an exclamation.

"Dod! she's trailed the mails with her," and then he too uttered a cry, which was fierce with instant terror and dismay. "But where's the bag from Dunscore?"

The two lamps were immediately fixed upon this new problem, and their light shone upon a circle of faces, the guard's blanched with sudden alarm, all turned towards that dark mass gleaming with its metal clasps.

"It's come loose," said one voice; "it'll be on the road."

"Bah! a wheen letters," said another; "you'll no' stop us in the cold for that."

"It's just a simple accident," said the third. But the guard held up to the light the ends of a strap cut through, clean and clear, evidently by some very sharp instrument.

"It's been nae woman, it's been some robber in disguise,—it's been a got-up thing," he cried, throwing a glance of suspicion at John, who stood aghast, holding the lamp unconsciously quite close to the bundle of the mail-bags, and gazing at them as if there was something there that could elucidate the mystery. He began to put one thing to another confusedly in his mind.

"A got-up thing! Could it be a got-up thing? It was a woman certainly," he said to himself, but aloud,—"a woman certainly, and a small woman."

"Maybe a laddie in a woman's dress," said an officious bystander.

"Were there mony letters in't?" said another, with unseasonable curiosity.

"And what," said another, authoritatively, "had the mail-bags to do in the inside of the coach?"

This question made a silence in the group, which the guard broke suddenly and loudly.

"Get back to your seats," he said; "and Jamie, push them to their stiffest, those beasts of yours: this has to be seen into. It's robbery on the Queen's highway," he said, with a vague threat which cowed them all.

John got to the lodging which had been prepared for him, with a much perplexed and disturbed brain. It annoyed him beyond reason to think he had perhaps taken a mischievous boy for a lady, and wasted his polite attentions upon a young thief; yet perhaps, because he did not wish to believe this, this became an idea quite impossible to him after a little thought. He could not quite tell how he came to the conclusion, but he felt perfectly confident that a woman it was, perhaps not an invalid, as appeared — nay, certainly not an invalid: he remembered now the swift movement of surprise she had made when he suddenly opened the door on her side with the soup he had taken such trouble to get for her. She had flung herself aside from the door, but it was a woman's movement, not that of a boy. And then the woman's face at the opened door, looking in one moment from outside, closing it with such a hasty bang. No doubt of that being a woman's face, a young face, a pretty face, in a glow of colour as he remembered it. Could that be the wrapped-up old rheumatic person with the poultice on her cheek? His heart gave a jump partly of self-derision, the dolt he had been! not to discover a bonnie lass even underneath the mountain of veils and wraps. He could have sworn that not the cleverest should have so taken him in. But why, after all, should that be *her*? Most likely it was somebody passing, a country maid on the road, good-natured, giving a push to the open door as she passed. Would a fugitive have shut it with a clang like that? Not likely!

John was very ready for his supper and for his bed afterwards, being young and healthy: but his sleep was very broken, and that woman's face kept looking in upon him, from between the curtains and behind the door, at every turn and toss. He began to see it, better than he had done in the real moment of seeing it, — a pretty face, rather redder than was consistent with his idea of beauty, with a curious flash in the eyes, and anxious lines in the forehead. He saw it perfectly clear in those visions of the night, the hair dark and ruffled, a hood half drawn over the head, the lips apart. No doubt at all that it was a pretty face. And he remembered she glanced at him with a sort of laugh about the corners of her mouth, which changed to a look of fright as she saw him wake up. He had not thought of it at first, but certainly that was her expression, and the clang with which the door closed was probably due to that surprise. Was this the old woman with the rheumatics in her head? Could it be she who had squeaked and stormed at him, and ordered him to "snoozle"? He kept going over and over it in his broken sleep, seeing her more clearly every time he woke, reading more and more meaning in the details of her face which came to him one by one. Were the eyes blue or brown? Was the ruffled hair light or dark? He could not make out those most essential details, yet he thought he should recognise her wherever he saw her. The glimpse he had got of her in reality seemed nothing to the light upon her which came from his dreams. It was like seeing her again and again, and getting familiar with her face. He thought that if he ever saw it again, it would haunt him all his life. But he should see it again—of that he was determined. Then he suddenly thought to himself with a gleam of surprised pleasure, what a good thing it was, after all, that he had come to Duntrum! This seemed all at once to him a good, a delightful, a most entertaining and charming thing, but, I fear, he would have been quite at a loss, if he had been asked for an explanation, to say why.

The incident, as was natural, made a great noise in the country, and there was an examination held before the sheriff at which John was the principal witness. He described the old body to the great amusement of all present,—the lump on her cheek, and white edge of the plaster in which it was tied up, just showing beyond the great black muffler in which her face was enveloped, the Spanish veil, with large thick silken flowers, between the interstices of which only the fact that there was a face could be discovered, the shrill strange voice which he now felt to be assumed. And, finally, the young face that had appeared at the window.

"You were awoke by it—by what?" said the questioner; "by the sharp closing of the door?"

"Yes," said John.

"Then, if the noise only woke you, how could you see the face of the person who made it?"

"No, it was not the noise," said John; "it was the blast of the cold air coming in: and then the face appeared in the open, against the night, looking up a little, catching the light of the lamp. For a moment it moved with the coach, then the door was shut."

"Moved with the coach?" said the interrogator. "Do you mean she was walking by the side?"

"I begin to think," said John, slowly, "that she must have been on the step: then dropped out of sight, and shut the door."

"Are you sure, Mr Percival," said the sheriff, "that the pretty face at the door was not a dream? We all know that pretty faces are part of young men's dreams: and you are not sure at which moment you awoke."

"I did not say," said John, "that it was a pretty face."

"Ah!" said the sheriff.

"Still it is true—it was so: and young: but it was not a dream. I saw the lady quite clearly."

"It was a lady, then? You thought at first it might be a country lass passing."

"I am not sure that it was a lady," said John, "but I certainly think so— I——" He paused, then, with a slight start of astonishment, seemed to stop an exclamation that was on his lips.

"What is the matter?" cried his questioner. "You are not so sure as you were that you saw any young woman at all?"

"I am perfectly sure—on my oath, and with complete recollection of what happened, that I saw," cried John, "exactly what I have said,—a young woman with a great deal of expression in her face, and a hood on her head, looking in at me for a moment through the open door." He did not look at the sheriff as he spoke, but strained his eyes, interrogating the faces before him between the table at which he stood and the door. His heart had not quieted yet from that start, though his mind had. He had thought he saw her again, the same face, and had been startled, and then had said to himself how unlikely it was, and looking again had found there was no such thing before him, among the score or two of people who had assembled in the room. There were very few women at all: it must have been a temporary illusion, for certainly now there was no one visible who resembled that face at all. But his heart continued to beat, though he succeeded in quieting his mind and reason as I have described.

Many curious things happened in connection with this mystery. The letters which had been posted in Dunscore on that night—as was proved by the postmarks—almost without exception reached their destination within a day or two, but with the Edinburgh postmark added to that of Dunscore. There was an exception, and that was one letter addressed to the Duntrum Bank, in which John by this time had taken his place, a favoured supernumerary, with all the prestige of his Edinburgh antecedents and connection, to learn the country work. It was curious that the incident with which his name was already associated, and which formed so remarkable a part of his scanty and young experience, should thus be brought under his notice again. He heard nothing else spoken of for the first month, at least, of his dwelling in Duntrum. The one lost letter was from a small bank in the little town of Dunscore. It had enclosed several bank bills to be collected and other papers of commercial value, and was in fact, perhaps, the only important missive in the stolen bag, judging from a commercial point of view. From the discussions in the bank where he acquired the last information on the subject, John learnt that various unfortunate persons had reason to rejoice over the loss of this letter. Two or three poor men almost bankrupt had their ruin staved off for a moment, and the dread period of protested bills and mercantile dishonour deferred at least for a time: and there were many whisperings and questions whether any of the persons concerned could have been capable of so bold a stroke. But even the inventive genius of a country town, always so bold in attributing guilt, could not come to any agreement in respect to this. It could not even be said that any one was suspected. The thing had been accomplished so mysteriously in such a complete way, without leaving a trace, that the local inquisition was completely baffled. John found with mingled annoyance and relief that his own vision of the young woman at the coach door was not relied upon. He had probably dreamt it, most people thought. Like the sheriff, the community concluded that it was nothing wonderful if a young man suddenly awakened should think he saw a girl's face; probably he had been dreaming about some particular girl. And in those days the hypothesis of a woman having done any deed of note was rarely accepted and with difficulty. The natural *rôle* of the woman in those days was to keep quiet and behind backs. She was not suspected of taking any leading part. The wrapped-up invalid in the country, whom the guard and several other persons besides John had seen, must have been a man in this disguise everybody was certain. It was not a thing that could have been done by a woman. No, no; no woman could have had the nerve to do it, the people in Duntrum said.

All these things John Percival turned over in his mind, and examined as much as he had the opportunity of doing. He listened to all the gossip about all the persons concerned, and especially of those who might be supposed to be advantaged by the loss of the mail-bag, with very keen interest, and formed within himself one hypothesis after another, several of which perished in the framing, so difficult was it to make the circumstances fit in. And in the meantime he himself became a personage of great importance, and much sought after in the gentlest society of Duntrum, which was understood to be very exclusive and difficult of access. John was the representative of Percival's Bank, one of the oldest establishments in Edinburgh, which was very much in his favour. And he was, besides, gifted with a story to tell, which was almost a greater recommendation. Over and over again during that winter he was required to give his famous description of his companion in the coach, of his own attempted attentions, the soup he procured in vain, the wraps that were kicked away. There was one circumstance which he never mentioned, but which touched his heart with the strangest thrill of kindness, which was that his tribute of the oranges had disappeared along with the old lady. It was as if she had not liked to hurt his feelings by rejecting his benevolences altogether. This curious experience inspired John with a slight inclination towards the dramatic which he had not been conscious of before, and almost made him believe before the season was over that perhaps if he had been left to follow his own devices, he might have been a great actor as well as a great artist or poet. At last, however, he got over his inclination to start at every girl's face he met and examine it critically on the score of a fancied likeness to the young woman of his vision. He said that most girls were like each other, as his final conclusion. They had all fine complexions in Duntrum.

Nevertheless, there was one evening at one of the many little dances that were given in that cheerful place, when John's composure was very much put to the test. He was taken to this entertainment by his own chief comrade and crony, young Maxwell, the son of the resident partner in the Duntrum Bank, who was in something of John's own position, more highly favoured than the other clerks and naturally one of the *élite*.

"Come, and I'll show you the flower of Wittisdale, the rose of Duntrum," said this young man. "She has been away in Edinburgh the whole winter; but mind you, none of your cantrips here. I warn you off before you see her. I'll have no interlopers cutting me out. Turn the heads of all the others, if you like, with your acting and your stories, but this one is mine."

"They are all just as like each other as apples in a basket," said the cynic John.

Nevertheless, when he went lightly into the brightly lighted room following his friend, John in a moment felt his heart leap into his throat: for there, standing a little behind the mistress of the house, with a curious little air of consciousness which seemed to him to prove that she was on her guard and ready for the startled look which he gave her, full in her face as if it had been a blow—to his extreme confusion and surprise there stood suddenly before him the woman of the coach door, the woman of his dreams.

CHAPTER III

When he reviewed afterwards, in quietness, the bewildering impressions of that night, John said to himself that it was the attitude of Miss Wamphrey which struck him before he had seen her face, and before he knew who she was, and that she was the object of young Maxwell's devotion. But probably this was only an idea developed afterwards, when he had begun to think of her in the character of a mysterious creature with a secret; for, indeed, to nobody else did she appear anything but a pretty girl in her twenties, very nicely dressed, with a little air of having descended from superior heights of fashion upon those circles of Duntrum which felt themselves so exclusive. Marion had spent most of the season in Edinburgh: she had even been in London: and various other girls in the assembly had already noted several points in her attire as things that were doubtless "to be worn," since she had just come from these fountain-heads of fashion. But what John remarked, or thought he remarked, was that she stood as one might to whom there might possibly arise an occasion to fly, which was a quite absurd exaggeration of any possibility, even if he were right in his surmises: also, which perhaps was more likely in that hypothesis, that she looked as if she expected something to happen, and glanced up behind the fan, of which she made greater use than a rustic Scotch maiden was apt to do (which was one of the things that struck the other girls as probably a new development of fashion), or over the shoulder of the chaperon, whom she followed like her shadow (which also was not a habit common among the young ladies of Duntrum), with a certain keen look of alarm, of expectance in her eyes. It happened that John saw her, after his eyes, as he thought, had been attracted to her by this peculiarity of attitude and look at a moment when she had dropped her fan to greet a friend, and before she perceived himself in the little crowd.

"Hullo!" he said to himself in the sudden surprise of recognition, and unaware he said it aloud.

"What's happened?" said Maxwell, by his side; "do you see anybody you know? By the way," he added, "it is Marion Wamphrey; of course you must have met her in Edinburgh. I wonder I never thought of that before."

"Which is Miss Wamphrey?" said John. He looked in the other direction that he might not betray himself, and then looked again to see that the girl had put up her fan, and that (as he thought) the something she was expecting had happened. She had seen him. Her eyes had taken a roundness which they had not before, the alarm of expectation had gone, and a sort of panic had come in its place. He saw her (or thought he saw her) obliterate herself behind the larger form of the lady with whom she was for a moment—then look out again over her shoulder, as if standing on tiptoe. Of course, she must have expected, John thought to himself, all that was happening or was about to happen. She must have known she would meet him. She must have been prepared to be recognised. She must be now at the height of a great crisis of mind, wound up to face it out, hoping that perhaps he might have been less quick of observation, less certain of recollection than she was.

"That's her," said Maxwell, with a wave of his hand towards the group, "playing keek-bo with somebody over Mrs Brydon's shoulder. Just like her saucy ways! You'll find Marion no country cousin, I can tell you, Percival. There's not one of your Edinburgh fine ladies more——Eh? think you have seen her before? I'll be bound you have seen her before! She's been spending the season, I tell you, in Edinburgh, and you that have your *entrées* everywhere——"

"Not so much as that," said John, with modesty; "and you must remember I have had all the fun cut off this year——"

"Never mind, I am sure you must have met her. Come along, and compare your experiences. I think I'm a man of great magnanimity not to hold you off; but it's better to run the risk of trusting you," he added with a laugh, "than to give you the attraction of the forbidden."

Somehow, however, their progress was slow through the little crowd—quite a little crowd, John felt, to one accustomed to the Assembly Rooms of Edinburgh. But somehow, everybody seemed to get in the way between himself and this lady. Had there not been a whisper sent out through the friendly ranks: "Oh, keep him off me! that man with his story about the stage-coach. I cannot abide these funny men with their stories." Young Duntrum, which had admired John quite long enough, was delighted to hear that so popular a girl as Marion Wamphrey did not want to hear the story which all the others had held their breath at. It was a victory, after all, for Duntrum over the invader in their midst. And accordingly they circled round him, and called attention to a hundred insignificant things.

"Did you hear the meet was at the Four Elms to-morrow, Percival?" "Man, do you know there's every prospect of a fine frost?" "Percival, my sister has a word to say to you about the Philharmonic." "Percival, I'm saying——" He had to stop again and again to respond to their appeals; while, on the other hand, his companion Maxwell shuffled impatiently about, waiting, and grumbled: "Come on, man, never mind,—be done with your civilities. She will have given away every dance before we get near her." Finally, John found himself standing face to face with this strange heroine of his thoughts. He said to himself that, but for her own looks, he might have been shaken in his conviction that it was she. The face that he saw before him, with hair smooth as satin, and crowned with flowers, as was then the fashion, in the midst of the ball was difficult to associate with the ruffled aspect, the flush of excitement, the strange light in the eyes of the woman at the coach door. But she stood straight up to meet him, like one who is strongly set in her own defence, as if she were standing at the bar: and there was in her eyes a watchfulness, a preparedness, as of a man who keeps his arm ready to return a blow. Perhaps all this was merely in John's eyes. Maxwell seemed to see nothing unusual in the look or air of the girl whom he admired. The gay group around fluttered and jested. Nobody within sight or hearing had the slightest suspicion of anything in Marion Wamphrey that was not always there. She did not hold out her hand to him, welcoming the stranger as the other frank and kindly maidens would have done; but that was because Miss Marion was always a little high and mighty, and now and then put on airs, as one who had been out in the world and knew the fashion.

"You mustn't think anything of that," Maxwell said afterwards; "it is just her way. I like her to have a way of her own, not like all the rest," said the young man in love. But John Percival was not satisfied that it was her way. She seemed to look at him in the eyes as if trying to cow him—as if on the faintest movement on his part she were ready to strike. And this on his part excited him, and made him anxious to strike.

"I think," he said, "that Miss Wamphrey and I have met before——"

"I told you so," said Maxwell,—"I told you both so. I was certain you must have met before."

If this ass had not broken in with his assurances about a thing he could know nothing whatever about, John felt sure she would have shown more consciousness than she did. As it was, her colour, he was sure, wavered a little; but she said, with a little burst of laughing surprise: "Oh, how condescending of you to remember! I recollect well seeing you, Mr Percival. But it was only seeing you, not meeting; for you were at the grand end of the Assembly Rooms, among all the lady patronesses, and I was only at the foot of the room, and knew nobody."

"There's one for you, Percival," said Maxwell, delightedly. Though John, it was certain, had had a great *succès* in Duntrum, they were all coming to think that it might do him good to be a little taken down.

"That is very hard upon me, especially as it was so much to my loss," said John; and then he thought he would carry the war into the enemy's country. "But I confess," he added, "I remember nothing about the Assembly Rooms. I think we have met in other circumstances."

She gave him a broad look from her fully opened eyes, with a faint elevation of the eyebrows.

"There I confess you have the advantage of me," she said steadily, holding him with that look, "as I, it appears, had of you on the former occasion." Then, with the faintest turn of her head, too dignified to be called a toss, she withdrew this embarrassing look from him, with a wave towards Maxwell of the card attached to her fan. "If you want any dances from me," she said, "it will be better not to lose any time."

"You cruel Marion," cried the young man, "it is all filled up, every line."

"You should not have been so late," she said, with a laugh; and they stood for a moment with their heads together, in the easy intimacy of having known each other all their lives. And then followed a little ball-room battle, while John stood, somewhat grim, looking on.

"I that was going to ask how many you would give me!" from him, with tender reproach; and "There will always be the extras, you know," from her.

"And it's easy to mistake about an extra—if you'll be good," said Maxwell, in a lively whisper; and they laughed together over the card, which he was manipulating. John was determined he would hold his ground. She was a very pretty girl, and she was in a state of suppressed excitement (or at least he thought so), which made her doubly interesting. And it was he who was the cause of her excitement. Whatever is the reason, it pleases a man, at least of John's age, to feel that he is the cause of a woman's emotion. He was not daunted by the *persiflage* but waited calmly till the end of the discussion; then he said—

"Is there no hope, Miss Wamphrey, for me?"

"Oh, Mr Percival," she said, turning round with an air of having forgotten him, which would have done no discredit to a great lady at a court ball: and then she shook her head. "I am afraid no more than there would have been for me at the Assembly Rooms if I had aspired to dance with one of the stewards," she said, laughing; "but you can look for yourself."

"Come, give him the last of the extras, Marion," said Maxwell, delighted to exercise a little patronage.

"If you are not at home and fast asleep before that," said Marion, raising her eyes quickly, with a dart, to John's face.

He felt it like a blow, but very carefully inscribed his name at the very bottom of her list, and retired with a bow of much dignity — at which, with secret wrath, he heard her laugh with Maxwell as he turned away. It was to be war then? She meant to turn him into ridicule before he could unmask her as the heroine of the strange adventure which everybody knew. John was very moody all the evening, and did not half fulfil the expectations of the merry country ladies, who thought it was the business of their partners to be amusing as well as to dance well. John fulfilled the latter requirement, but then they all danced well at Duntrum. They did not know the waltz in those days. They danced pretty figures of country-dances and reels, and other cheerful things. It had never occurred to them that quadrilles were dull — they were the height of the fashion, and the different figures respected as almost a revelation. Nobody "sat out," and if perhaps the assembly was simple, and some of the dances a little old-fashioned, it was very gay.

It need not be said that, in the state of mind in which he was, John stayed till the last moment, and presented himself to Miss Wamphrey just as she was following her chaperon to the door, holding together a dress which had been slightly damaged in the rapidity of a last reel. There was a glance of battle in his eyes as he came up to her, with a reminder that this was his dance, which kindled an immediate response in hers.

"I cannot stay another moment, May," said the chaperon, crossly. Marion shrugged her pretty shoulders, with a look which spoke volumes of repugnance, and reluctance, and scorn, and made John furious.

"I cannot break my word to this gentleman, if he insists upon it," she said.

"Seeing I have held on all these hours, *and not gone to sleep*," said John, with something savage in his tone, "only for this."⁻

There was a last dreary quadrille being formed, and she gave her hand and allowed herself to be led to it, to fill up a side place. They stood side by side in silence for a moment, and then Marion said —

"It is very noble on your part, Mr Percival, to hold out so long. I am so sorry to have been the means of breaking your night's rest."

"It is not the first time, Miss Wamphrey," he said.

"Not the first time! This is too much of a compliment. We are not accustomed in the country to have such pretty things said to us."

"There was nothing so far from my intention as saying a pretty thing," said John.

"This is more and more tremendous, Mr Percival! It was an ugly thing, then, you meant to say?"

"What I meant," said John, "was to let you know that I have not forgotten our meeting, which has cost me many a thought."

"Dear me," said Marion, "is this all because I said I knew nobody at *that* ball? Comfort yourself. I knew nobody grand like the lady patronesses; but I had plenty of partners, and there is no need to be remorseful, even if you have the most tender conscience, on account of me."

"You know very well it is not that I am thinking of," said John, in a low tone.

"Well, I should not have expected it to be. A young man like you, in the best society, is not likely to trouble himself about a country girl he doesn't know."

"At all events, the other occasion was a very different matter," he said.

"What other occasion? One would think there was some great mystery between us. If you will come down from these stilts, and tell me what you mean——"

"That is just what I am most anxious to do—if I could for a moment suppose you had forgotten it! It was rather a different thing from a meeting at a ball."

"You had better wait a little," she said, sharply; "it is our turn for this figure."

And then they danced. I forget now what these figures were called. It was the one in which the lady on one side is led off by the gentleman on the other side, who advances to the abandoned partner with a lady in each hand. John was the man who had to stand and look on. She had recovered all her spirit, all her freshness, it appeared, and made of this innocent performance a parade of gaiety and grace. She came up to him and retired from him, holding the hand of the other with the most coquettish defiance, and swept him such a curtsy as she might have made to the king—deeper even, with mock deference and scorn, which was considered very amusing by all the lookers-on. "You should have seen Marion dancing L'Été" (or whatever it was) "with the man from Edinburgh," they all said afterwards. John had been "too much made of" since his arrival and his adventure: it was delightful that he should thus be made to feel "put back in his place" without any one being to blame. And John, I will not deny, felt the sting: but he was stimulated by it, not depressed. In the quiet of the interval that followed, while the others were dancing, he made his attack on more decided lines.

"Where," he said—"I have always been very curious—did you hide all those dreadful things you had on?—the hoods, and the handkerchiefs, and the veil."

A spark flashed up into her eyes—was it possible there was a laugh in it that showed through both the affected wonder and the actual fear?

"What in the world do you mean?" she said; "the handkerchiefs and the hoods and—have you gone mad, Mr Percival?"

"Not a bit," said John, "nor you either. We're two very sane people. How you flashed it off in a moment might be just a woman's skill—but not to drop it on the road, not to let it be found anywhere, that's what I have always admired: it shows you have great force, and it really looked, you'll forgive me for saying, as if you had done such a thing before."

She turned round, swerving a little from his side. "If you're exposed it's your own fault," she cried, hurriedly, and in a very low tone. "I am afraid to dance with you any more."

"Oh, you need not be afraid," said John. "I am not mad: and I will not publish it, not at least at this moment; but stand still, or I'll not answer for what I may do."

She stood still, a thrill running through her; but even at that moment contrived to make her tremor invisible to the others, with glances towards him and elevations of her eyebrows, and little movements of her hands. She was no soft girl to be crushed by anything he would do, but a resolute woman meaning to fight every step, and with all the odds in her favour, well known and popular, whereas himself nobody knew.

"Perhaps this is not the best moment," said John, "but I thought I must warn you. I was very much taken in, and you must have had your laugh at me: but I was awake to all the circumstances in the end."

"It is a good thing," she said, suddenly forgetting herself, "that you are awake sometimes; for a better sleeper"—then she stopped, and a deep red flush covered her face—"dreamer of dreams," she added, quietly, "I never heard of. Did you dream all this, Mr Percival, or is it a story got up out of a book?"

And then they danced again, extraordinary interruption to such an interview. John could not help, when he took her hand, giving it a fierce grip of hostility, almost unawares. He was brought to his senses, when it was with equal fierceness and almost equal strength returned. She was not looking at him, but moving in the dance with a smile on her face. Many a close clasp of love has been given in such circumstances, but seldom one of actual defiance and ferocity. Her eyes, though they were not on him, blazed, the colour forsook her face, and its very paleness shone. She had perhaps never looked so beautiful in her life.

"Come away, Marion, come away," said Mrs Brydon; "I cannot wait a moment longer."

"This is the last figure," said Marion, over her shoulder, and she danced it to the end, but quickly disengaged herself before the concluding galop, and, seizing her friend by the arm, hurried away. John did not follow to get their cloaks and carriage, as he ought to have done. There were plenty of attendants ready. He sat down, grim, in a corner to think it over, and could not be persuaded to join the young men's rear-supper, or any of the closing festivities of the night.

CHAPTER IV

Thus John found himself involved in a duel to the death, as it seemed, with an intelligence probably quicker than his own, and with many advantages over him, as he speedily realised.

Next day he surprised a group of young men in his own very bank, the centre of his life in Duntrum, where up to this present moment he had been so easily the chief personage. He came in in the midst of a burst of laughter, through which he heard the phrase, "She made fine sport of him. He'll not craw so crouse again, I'm thinking." While the sound of the laughter filled the room John came into sight, asking quietly, "Who is it that will not craw so crouse?" and the group melted before him, every man looking more conscious than the other.

"Oh, it was only a joke of some of the girls," said young Maxwell, very crestfallen.

John went grimly to his desk, and made no sign, but he knew very well that he was the subject of the joke; and they knew very well that he knew. He had not thought that his antagonist was of such force; but, indeed, to conceive and carry out so unflinchingly such a bold plan showed that she could be of no small force, and he reflected upon her and on what might be in store for him very gravely as he sat at his desk in the midst of an unusual silence in the office for the rest of the morning, paying, if truth must be told, very little attention to the country business which he had been sent to study, and which he had at that moment unusual facilities for studying, as it was market-day.

There was another party that evening, to which he went quite prepared for the fate which was about to overtake him, and which did overtake him accordingly. None of the young ladies of Duntrum would dance with John. Some of the girls looked mischievous, some regretful, but only one out of the troop of pretty creatures with whom he had hitherto been so popular, could find a single dance for him. That one was Marion Wamphrey, who pointed with a sparkle in her eye to one line in her programme which had been left free, and danced it majestically, treating him with a lofty civility which did a little to crush his spirit, but filled him more and more with the rage of battle. After that experience, John faced the chances of Society in Duntrum no more.

He withdrew before the moment when, as in most of their little assemblies, dancing began; for in those days in Scotland most entertainments ended in a dance, the young people being quite unfastidious, and as willing to amuse themselves on a carpet as on the most beautifully waxed floors. John withdrew; and he was comforted to find that he was missed. There was no longer any fun in refusing to dance with the best partner in the room when he was not there to be vexed by the affront, and there was soon a revolt against Marion, as would no doubt have happened in any case, and those who had lent themselves to her revenge loudly complained that she had driven their finest performer away. "He told us all the new figures, and the French step that nobody here has learnt yet," moaned the culprits of that night, "led away," they could not quite tell why, by Marion, "and she gave him a dance herself!" they remembered. Did she want to keep him to herself? Was that her treacherous reason? So that before the winter was half over, John would have been received with open arms had he gone back; but he did not go back. He felt himself master of the situation, and determined to retain it, even at the cost of a little self-denial, which it certainly involved, for he was a young man of his period, not of this, and loved to find himself in the midst of pretty faces, and to show the new French steps, and the new figures, and to feel himself the king of the company as he had formerly done.

However, it was all the better for business that he should have had this check in the middle of his career. For it set him on giving his attention to the country business, and to the transactions of the bank with the little banking establishments in the little towns around, branches of the Duntrum Company or of others. Especially—and this the reader will understand, without perhaps crediting John with very great devotion to business, considered on its own merits—he was eager to inquire into the business with Dunscore, which had such a curious connection with the little drama to which he had been introduced in spite of himself. And he accepted with great alacrity, about the new year, a commission to go to that place on the affairs of the bank, and to consult with the managers there concerning some changes which it was thought expedient to make. Messrs Percival in Edinburgh were delighted to think that their nephew had been chosen for this commission. It showed, as they concluded, that the boy must be showing some real business capacity, or he would not have been chosen for such an office, and also a considerable interest on his part, or he would not have devoted himself to it. So that it made a very good impression, much to his favour, at home.

John appeared, too, at Dunscore to much advantage, with his look of gravity and interest in the suggested changes, and secured the full attention of the manager, who, knowing his connection with the Percivals, felt great interest in him as a rising young man, devoted to business, and anxious to extend his knowledge. He gave John a great deal of information as to the working of the banking system in the country, and all the difficulties which a manager had to encounter. When the business was over, the conversation went off to lighter subjects: but, indeed, it grew naturally out of it that he should inquire about the lost letter which had been in the stolen mail-bag, and whether there had been any light thrown upon that curious theft and its motives. The manager was very ready to talk on this subject, which was the most romantic incident that had been known in the country for ages past.

"Indeed," he said, "since the time when one of the Cochranes dressed herself up like a highwayman, and waylaid the mails—which took place not very far from the same spot——"

"What was that story?" said John.

"Did you never hear of it? It is just such another story. It was after Argyle's rebellion in 1685, and the warrant for her father's execution was supposed to be in the bag——"

"Her father?" said John.

"Oh, ay, it was a young lass. And did it never occur to you, Mr Percival," said the manager, "that this might well be a woman's work? You see Grizel Cochrane's story is well known, and women are grand actors when they have a purpose to serve. They say you saw a woman shut the coach door just after your queer passenger disappeared."

"It is quite true; but do you think a woman would have the nerve and the courage?"

"Oh, pooh! Nerve? they've nerve for anything when they've motive enough; and courage? there's no a deevil for daring like a young lass— they're worse than the lads; they never count the cost. I would just like to know if that is not your own point of view."

"But the motive?" said John.

"Oh, deed, there was motive enough. That big letter, Mr John, conveyed enough matter to distress, maybe to ruin, two or three families. There's times when even delay will save a man's credit: but clean destruction of bills and bonds—Lord, man, it's just salvation to some poor struggling men. There was an honest farmer that had kept up a sore struggle, my own very heart was wae for him when I put his bill in the packet. It would have been a question of roup and banishment, and an honest fellow, as honest as ever ploughed field. He came here like an honourable man, and bound himself over again for the sum, with a little delay, which we were glad to grant. Ay, and there was another, a gentleman's son, a wild fellow. I'm misdoubting he put his father's name to a bit of paper the worthy laird never saw, and a grand escape he has had. No, I don't think the bank will have very much loss, excepting just that one case."

"And who was the man, may I ask?" said John.

"I ought not to tell after what I have just said, for it would be a libel if ever it was repeated, and there's no evidence. Well, as you are, so to speak, in the business, Mr John, and in a manner concerned with the robbery, I may strain a point for you. It was just Will Wamphrey, the son of auld Wamphrey, of Craigthorn. He's away abroad now, and maybe he will never hear of it, unless, as I strongly suspect, that it was one of his gilpies that robbed the mail."

"His gilpies!" said John. He felt a flush of anger at the name.

"Just that," said the manager, nodding his head. "Plenty of them took an interest in him, if all tales are true. I have always thought it was some bold hizzy that was o'er the Border after him, and away to some seaport, while these police birkies were riding the country. Ye never can get them to turn their horses' heads the right way till the guilty person's well out of reach. Wull," he said, getting a little more familiar in his accent as the story warmed him, "was a wild deevil, and never out of mischief; but his father is a douce man, and we were all very sorry for him. I'm mostly glad, though it will be a loss to the bank, that yon bit of paper is out of the way. And they say that old Wamphrey had sworn an oath that if he played another pliskie, he should be cast off without a shilling, instead of being sent creditably to try his luck again, which is what has been done."

"This, if it came true, would make it a complete romance of the road," said John.

"That is just what it is, a woman," said the other, "and the best thing he could do would be to marry the lass, and take her with him out of the gait of justice. For my Lords Justiciary would take little heed, I fear, of the romantic circumstances if she were brought before them, which would be sure to happen sooner or later if she were to bide in this country. Somebody must have seen her—you did yourself, by the way, Mr John, as I have heard."

"I saw a country woman close the door," he said. He was glad that he had the time to prepare his answer, while the good man went on. "A person passing, I have little doubt, who saw it swinging open. And it was a momentary glimpse that I could not trust to. It would be a hard case if suspicion was thrown upon a decent woman returning from her work in the fields, and doing what she thought was a kind action as she passed."

"Bless me, that is true," said the bank manager, "but I understand you were of the opinion that it might be the very miss herself."

"I never meant to convey that impression," said John, with an immovable countenance. "It was a country lass; most likely a farm-servant going back a little late from the fields."

"Oh-h," said the manager. He added, after a pause, "I have maybe been rash in making up such a story. It might be no woman after all. But there's no telling," he continued, with a laugh; "Will Wamphrey had friends in all stations, though a country lass would scarcely have had the cleverness to carry it through."

John could scarcely help applying uncivil words to this genial person as he talked. A country lass! There were different kinds of country lasses: and the way in which this mere bank manager permitted himself to talk of one who was neither a gilpie nor a miss, nor, in short, anything that came within the range of such a critic, gave him a sensation of anger. Why should it give John, who was really the only witness against her, a sensation of anger? He could not tell. Nothing could be more absurd, and out of all agreement with the circumstances; yet he called Mr Scott several unpleasant names within himself. What did he know about it? a mere vulgar, little country-town man, a village magnate. That he should take upon himself to judge, could think himself qualified! The man was extremely charitable on the subject, and took what seemed to himself much too lenient a view; but it did not, as appeared, satisfy John, whose feelings were quite unexplainable even to himself. So far as he was aware, he wanted to find out everything about the business, but he did not choose that any one else should find out, or should prejudge or venture to form theories about it even to himself. And as he went back to Duntrum, John began to take himself to task, and to inquire into the nature of his own thoughts. Did he really, after all, believe that Marion Wamphrey was the heroine of his great adventure? Had he not seized upon the idea "for fun," as they all said, to give himself a reason for making a certain intimacy, a teasing acquaintance with the prettiest girl in the room, pretending to have this tremendous matter against her? He said to himself that this had really been all that was in his mind, when her own consciousness, her readiness to defy him, her anxious look, as of one who expected to be attacked, had turned his wavering, half-real recognition into certainty. He would not have permitted himself even to think of such a thing, to do more than to perplex her with a jest, but for that foreknowledge on her part, so clearly marking that she knew all, and more than all, he could say. This had startled and shocked him into saying many things he had not intended, and into persecuting her with hints and suggestions, as if he were quite sure of what was merely a vague suspicion. He took himself to task now as he went home. Had he really any ground for the attack he had made upon this young lady? A momentary glimpse of a face in a dark winter night, was that enough to build such an accusation upon? And he had as good as accused her, if not of the theft, at least of having been seen in circumstances of suspicion on the night when the theft was made. He had begun lightly enough: he had been himself startled by her response of eye and attitude: and now that he had hunted out this fresh information, which threw so living a light upon it all, he found himself forced to the conviction that it must be true. In the teeth of that conviction, he asked himself indignantly how he had dared to believe such a thing of an innocent girl, a girl whom he had met at a dance, blooming, gay, and full of confidence in all about her. Was that the person to accuse, even in your own mind, of robbing his Majesty's mails? It was preposterous; it was as false as anything could be. It might have been, as Scott said, a gilpie, one of the many loves of this Will Wamphrey, bent on serving him, and not too particular about the method; but Marion! with her white dress and her pearl necklace, and the flowers in her hair. It was, of course, impossible; it was impossible! Having said this to himself, he added, with a quick-drawn breath, that now the chain of evidence was complete, that the only thing wanting had been a motive, and now here was the motive abundantly supplied.

John jumped from his post-chaise at the foot of the hill where that adventure had taken place. It was now the end of February, and this had been a hazy, grey day, full of cold, yet at the same time of that indescribable thrill which shows us that the sap is moving in the veins of the old earth, and spring coming, though perhaps her footstep has but touched the heights. He was so restless with the movement of the thoughts that were rising in his own breast, that it gave him a little relief to walk. It was almost dark, and nobody was about. He stood still for a little, and looked over the hedge at the spot where the coach had stopped. It was a high and stiff hedge, hawthorn, full of strong prickles, and closely grown; there was a shallow ditch on the other side, and beyond that a large field, a little undulating, with little knowes and hollows. How did she get through the hedge, or over it? Where did she disappear to? How was it that with all their lanterns and all their eyes no one caught so much as a shadow of her? He examined the place very closely, and found that a little below there was a gap through which it was just possible an adroit person might squeeze. But it was almost impossible, if that was the mode of her escape, to imagine that so soon she could have got under cover. Not far from the hedge there was a group of half-grown rowan trees, forming a thick clump at the bottom, though very thin and wind-blown in the upper branches. They had been quite invisible in the darkness of the night, and he did not think there had been any proper search made at the moment of the wide open stretch of the field where there was so little possibility of concealment.

He was full of the recollection of that night, and of interest in the culprit whom all his investigations seemed to force him to identify almost against his will; and his inclination to follow what must have been her steps in her retreat was strong. The ground, he knew, had been gone over again and again, but no trace had been found, and it was highly unlikely now, when two months had passed, that he should find any trace of her. But he squeezed himself through the gap, with the unpleasant result of finding himself almost up to his knees in the muddy ditch at the foot of the hedge. There had been a great deal of rain in the past week, and not only was the ditch full, but the field was an expanse of soft mud, a little bound together by the grass, but slippery and soft, so that it was hard to get a footing as he scrambled out of the ditch. This was not a pleasant beginning, but he was determined to make his way to the little cluster of the rowans, and make sure for himself whether there was any possible shelter for a fugitive there. A more miserable spot there could not be. How a woman, encumbered by petticoats and cloaks as his fellow-traveller had been, could have slid and scrambled along, unheard, toward that little island in the muddy field, if that indeed had been where she went—and it was the only covert within sight—he could not divine. And very poor was the covert, a bundle of saplings, not much more: slim stems of young trees growing upon a small mound. But the farther side of this hillock, he found, fell abruptly, a little precipice of five or six feet. He had nearly fallen over it, which impressed it on his mind; and when he slid down on the treacherous and muddy slope at one side, he found that the bank above overhung a little, so as to make a shelter quite available, a sort of shallow cave. Had she come here, in the deep darkness, that daring girl, and listened to the ineffectual stir of her pursuers, the gleams of their lanterns? He tried to realise the situation. It was now only twilight, but it was difficult to distinguish anything across the damp level of the field which spread dismal round him. What could it have been in the mirk of the night, getting towards midnight, and black as winter and desolation could make it! Had she couched here, cold, encumbered with her disguise, never knowing when a light might flash round the corner upon her? John shivered with sympathy, yet felt also something of the whirl of excitement which must have been in all her being.

As he stood against the damp wall of mossy earth, held together by the roots of the rowans, he suddenly saw a speck of white in a crevice among the twisted roots. He pulled it out, or tried to do so, but it resisted his efforts. Finally, digging with his stick, and pulling with his hands, at risk of bringing the whole mound down upon him, he disinterred from the network of rough and twisted stems a handkerchief, then something black and large which he could not distinguish, and finally the skin of an orange. John's heart, already panting with the toil, gave a jump into his throat. The white handkerchief was folded into a sort of bandage, and had evidently been tied round the head; the large, black square was one of the huge neckcloths (so-called) of the period. These formed, no doubt, the wonderful headgear which his fellow-traveller had worn. But the orange skin overwhelmed John with an impulse to laugh and to cry together. It was one of his oranges which he had brought in, in kindness for the poor old lady. She had remembered them in danger and horror, and eaten it while they were looking for her. That daring creature defying heaven and earth, wet, cold, miserable, and—guilty. She had eaten his orange to comfort her, the poor little demon of a girl!

And was that Marion Wamphrey all white and dazzling, with the pearls on her throat, and the roses in her hair?

CHAPTER V

When John returned to his rooms, carrying his strange spoils with him, he found on his table an invitation. For the last week or two his invitations had been few. This one had been delivered, his landlady told him, by a man and horse from Wamphrey, which was some miles off to the south of Duntrum. This was so startling in the midst of his present thoughts, that his spoils fell from his hands in the excitement of the moment. To Wamphrey! Mr Wamphrey was an invalid, the brother was absent. There had been no festivities there since his arrival in Duntrum, and that such an invitation should come now when he was about, he thought, to disclose the family skeleton, and brand its most beloved member with guilt, startled him as if there was something preternatural in it. He threw himself down in his easy-chair and tried to think, but his head went round and round.

The objects which he had carried in his hands fell on the table and unrolled themselves as inanimate things sometimes do as if there was life in them. They had been tightly done up, and fluttered out of the roll as they fell: the white handkerchief, folded like a bandage, which had been tied together at the ends, and retained even something of the roundness of the head on which it had been bound, fell quite open, revealing its use. The larger black one had also been tied, two of the ends together. She had got rid of them on the first possible moment, trusting no doubt to the thick Spanish lace of her veil, with its large silken flowers, to disguise her sufficiently: but where did she go from that little shelter in the field? how had she escaped eventually, in the dark midnight, over the slippery, wet ground—so dark you could not see your hand held up before you, so wet and soft, your foot sinking into the clay?

John sat by his fire, and asked himself why he had been so hot in this discovery, and what he had wanted to do. Did he want to convict her, to bring her to shame, a girl who had done him no harm, who (he said to himself) had, after all, done nobody any harm,—except perhaps the bank, which was impersonal and could not suffer much. It was true that it would not do to establish a precedent, and rob his Majesty's mails, when they happened to contain something disagreeable to you. But then, there were very few people in the world who would have the nerve and the strength to do that; and indeed, when you came to think, it was as much the carelessness of the guard, putting such a temptation in the way, as the boldness of the culprit, which was to blame. If he had not left them within everybody's reach, she would not have attempted to get them. The guilt was with the guard. Then, if he himself had kept awake and not gone to sleep like a great baby, she would not have done it. Did he wish he had not gone to sleep? Did he wish the guard had not been so careless? Did he wish that the family should have been disgraced, and the prodigal ruined? John caught himself up with a start. What did it matter who was ruined? No one not with the purest motives, not with the most tender meaning, had a right to take the law in his or her hands. She had made herself amenable to the law—and not only so, but the position was untenable from any point of fact: it was a crime, it struck at the roots of every security. She was a thief! a thief! and of the most dangerous kind.

Suppose it had come into her head that somebody's diamonds would make a nice little portion for her brother, the prodigal whom his own family was sending away to the ends of the earth? Would that native have saved her from the law which has to deal with a criminal and not with the crime, certainly not with the circumstances that account for the crime? He replied to himself, indignantly, that there was no analogy in that case to this. To steal diamonds is common theft; to steal a mail-bag—well! That is a worse crime: and yet he could not endure to have it said even by himself. If Grizel Cochrane, who stopped her father's death-warrant so as to give him time to escape, was the heroine of the district, how was Marion Wamphrey to be called a thief? He went on reasoning with himself, wandering through the wilds of casuistry, examining, accusing, vanquishing himself over and over, and then beginning again.

Nevertheless, when he went to Wamphrey, ten days after, there were war and battle in John's eyes. He was given, as it happened, a very cordial welcome. Mr Wamphrey, the invalid, was down-stairs, seated in an easy-chair in his library, where he could take a quiet share in the amusement of the large party; and it turned out, as it so often turns out, especially in Scotland, that he had known John's father in their respective youths, which was a thing John himself had not done, having been an orphan as long as he could remember. And the elder son had come home from his travels, the object of which John was secretly aware of; but chiefly there was Marion, in the delightful position of daughter of the house, supreme everywhere— disposing of everybody, a princess at the head of her dominions. She was quite gracious to John, treating him with a sort of amused *empressement*, a smile of triumph on her face, as if to show him how little she feared him. Her manner drove John back into a conviction of the falsehood of all his sophistries, and that this bright creature was nothing more nor less than the robber of his Majesty's mails, and had to be brought to justice. He was not even moved as he had been before by the thought of those little white shoes stumbling over the muddy field. This had subdued him utterly when she was not there. He could not even remember that orange skin which had appealed to him as the subtlest argument. Her smile of triumph seemed to turn his head—but the wrong way.

She had kept a dance conspicuously for him. She was evidently intent on proving that she did not fear him. She herself proposed, after it was over, to lead him to the farthest corner of the conservatory, to show him a rare flower of which the gardener was proud: but it was there in this position of favour that John was so hard-hearted as to fire his first gun.

"I have something of yours, Miss Wamphrey, which I must take the first opportunity of returning to you," he said.

"Something of mine? How can that be, Mr Percival? I am sure I never gave you anything of mine."

"Or rather there are two things: a white handkerchief marked with your name, and a black handkerchief, both of which you wore round your head on a certain occasion when we first met."

"Mr Percival," she said, with a change of colour, "do you think it is good taste to assail me whenever you happen to be alone with me, with this ridiculous delusion of yours?"

"They are still precisely as they were when you must have pulled them off: you know where I found them—thrust in among the roots of the rowan-trees in that little hollow under the brae. There was another thing," said John, "the skin of an orange."

When he said there was another thing, her eyes blazed up in sudden anxiety,—then they were dimmed with as sudden a shadow of relief. She had feared something else: therefore there must be something else to find there. And then her colour came back, and she laughed out, "The skin of an orange!" Oh, she understood perfectly what he meant! That was always what led him on. She understood every allusion. "That was a very innocent thing," she said; "I would like to know how you associate me with that."

"It gave me a kind of pleasure to see it," said John; "I thought to myself I was some good to her after all."

She paused, too, for a moment, casting down her eyes, and then she said: "I cannot really stand any longer listening to your nonsense about pocket-handkerchiefs and orange-skins. I hope you yourself know what you mean.

I hope you have not—lost your head altogether. I don't want to be rude and leave you—but this is more than I shall ever give you the chance of saying to me again. Mr Percival, the next dance has begun."

"Is that all you have to say?" asked John.

"Every word—and too much!" she said.

I don't know what he had expected, or indeed what he meant at all by assailing her so bluntly, but he certainly did not make anything by it: she assumed her air of relieved triumph, but held him at arm's length all the rest of the evening; and he did not dance at all, but stood in a doorway and followed her with his eyes—always seeming to see that triumphant head flower-crowned, issuing from the bandages, and the white shoes stumbling over the muddy grass.

"What are you glowering at?" said Maxwell, taking him by the arm. "Mind, I warned you—no interference with me."

"I interfere! You had better think twice before you take any step," John said.

Then it was Maxwell's turn to glower at him.

"I hope you are not taking leave of your senses," he said.

These two drove home together, very silent, Maxwell in great wrath at such an extraordinary warning, John consumed with a desire to betray to him the secret of Marion. He could scarcely open his lips for fear it should burst forth. A dozen times at least he had framed the words. She is not what you think. There is something I could tell. I could put her in jail if I pleased. This last came most frequently of all. I could put her—in jail. He said it actually under his breath. He repeated it over a dozen times. He could not understand why his companion did not hear him. He seemed to himself to have another motive in speaking from that which anybody would imagine. It was not to expose Marion but to test Maxwell. He thought if the fellow knew as much as he knew, he would give her up at once: and with all his soul, he wanted to put this other man to the test. I don't know how it was that the secret was kept, nor did John know. He thought it was chiefly the noise of the post-chaise.

Next day John was very restless and excited, unable to keep quiet or to go on with his work. He had taken his hat two or three times to go out, but then reflected that to go during the day would be to call forth suspicion, and perhaps give some other person of a detective cast of mind a clue to the mystery. He was not at all himself of the detective mind, and, indeed, the thing was not known, and certainly not prized in those days. A thief-catcher it would have been called, and "Set a thief to catch a thief" was a suggestion which everybody thought of in that connection. But he went out in the afternoon, walking sedately over the high-standing hill, and reaching the foot just as the evening began to darken. He made his way again with the same shuffling and sliding over the muddy field, and, reaching the little declivity behind the rowan-trees, began his investigation. The roots were so tangled and twisted, so loosely filled up with earth and stones, that but for the clayey consistence of the soil, and the damp that penetrated through and through, he would have feared to bring the entire mound about his ears. It took him a long time, and the evening grew darker and darker, and he had almost ceased to hope for any further revelation, when suddenly the stick with which he was digging struck upon something which gave forth a metallic sound. With a sort of fury he rushed at it again, and struggling with a shower of falling stones, and the stem of one young tree which fell upon his arm, jamming it against the side, he at last managed to extract a large article, partly metallic, which was deeply lodged among the roots of the trees. He could scarcely make out its shape in the darkness, but, half by sight and half by feeling it with his hands, made sure, with a sensation which brought the blood rushing to his heart, that it was the mail-bag. He had scarcely quieted down after this discovery, when, looking up from his extraordinary treasure-trove, he was aware of another figure coming towards him, so near already that he could make out it was a woman, and guess what woman it was. He started back into the shadow of the outlying edge, where he was absolutely invisible, and stood there, a spectator of the eagerness with which she advanced to the spot which he had found such difficulty in discovering, where these things had been hid. She had not even a stick, but tore at the roots and earth with her hands, plunging her arm in up to the elbow into the hole which John had made. It was now almost ‑entirely dark, and probably she thought this was the reason she found nothing, for suddenly, before he knew what was being done, she had begun to work with one of the elaborate methods of the time for striking a light. John stood breathless, invisible, yet so near to her that he felt her panting breath, while holding his own, quite unprepared for what was to come next, not knowing what to do. He held the thing for which she was searching, he held her secret, her freedom, almost her life, in his hands. Her fingers trembled, it took her a long time to strike that light—it seemed incredible to him that she was not aware at least that there was some one by.

Then suddenly the little flame awoke, and to him for a moment the whole strange little scene became visible. The light leaped up upon her face, pale with anxiety and alarm, and upon the background of the rugged bank, her gloves muddy and stained with the damp earth, a quiver in her person—though even then she was not aware of him for a moment, being so deeply absorbed in her search. Then she lit a piece of candle which she had taken from her pocket and held it to the crevice; but John was no longer able to restrain himself. He touched her sleeve softly with his hand. With a great start and subdued cry, kept down at that dreadful moment by a fear still greater than her fright, she let fall the light. She had not divined who he was—or she was of sufficient power to pretend so. She said hurriedly, "I was looking for something I had lost; perhaps you'll help me—I'll—I'll pay you." Her voice went out as her light had done, dropping in the dark, but leaving an impression of trembling and quivering in the air. Her terror was very real: she thought she had disturbed a tramp or beggar taking refuge in this solitary place.

"This is it, no doubt," said John, putting the bag into her hand: this time the cry of terror was not to be repressed—and yet there was a relief in the sound. Of the two, her enemy, who was a gentleman, was safer to meet in a lonely place in the dark than a tramp. "It is you!" she cried—"you!" her teeth chattering with the fright and the cold.

"Who should it be," said John, "but I, Miss Wamphrey? I saw by your look there was something more here, and I came to find it. Did you expect anything else?"

She was not able to reply. He felt that she made a strong effort to regain her composure, but could not, being beyond speech. The entire darkness seemed to palpitate with her trembling. It seemed to him as if he, too, quivered with it, standing by her side. He had put the bag into her hands, but it fell out of them upon the damp ground at their feet. He put out his hand, and gathered both of hers, which did not seem to have any strength to resist, into his hold.

"Compose yourself," he said, "compose yourself! It was better that I should find it than another. For God's sake, be calm! I will do you no harm."

She had not the strength to draw her hands from his now: she was thankful for the supporting of his grip. "I—I know what it means," she said, gasping painfully; "I—know what it means. I am prepared—to pay the penalty. I know that I am in your hands——"

"I think you will find them safe hands," said John. He drew her arm through his. "Come," he said, "take courage. I don't think you have ever quailed before."

"Mr Percival," she said, recovering her utterance a little, "why are you my enemy? I am not your enemy—nor any one's. It did no one any harm——"

"Except the law and the bank— —" he said.

"The bank—was it for the bank?" Her tone changed: her fears came back: she drew herself away. "If that is so— —"

"No," he said, "it was not for the bank. It was for you. I think two can keep a secret better than one, Miss Marion. And you ate my orange, you know."

"It saved my life, I think," she said, with a sudden low burst of hysterical laughter; and then recovering, she put her hands imploringly upon his arm. "What are you going to do with me? Oh, have mercy upon me! What are you going to do with me?" she said.

"If you will let me, I should like to marry you, Marion," he said.

A few days after, it happened that John was entertaining young Maxwell and a few more in his rooms, as it appeared that he was returning sooner than he had intended to Edinburgh. There was some talk among them of the great adventure which had accompanied his arrival, and they fell into discussion on the subject,—what the motives of the guilty person could be, and whether it was really a woman, and what had become of her. "It would be droll if you ever recognised that woman you saw, Percival," said one of the young men. John acknowledged that it would be droll, though probably she had nothing to do with it: and he asked the advice of his assembled friends as to what, in such a singular case, a man should do, and various suggestions were made, which did not perhaps throw much light on the subject. They were by no means at one as to whether they would denounce her or not, always supposing it was a woman. "Not if she is bonnie," one said, and on the whole this was the general judgment. "If she turns out to be old and ugly, with her head bound up, and all the rest of it, give her up—like a shot" (though, by the way, they did not say like a shot—the slang of their day was different). "But if she is bonnie, nothing of the kind." John went on to suggest other difficulties. What if she should be met with in Society? What if some fellow you knew was going to marry her? This made them all ponder. "What should you do, Maxwell, if such a thing were told you of a woman you were in love with?" "I can't contemplate the possibility," said Maxwell, with a laugh. "By George! but it would be a ticklish position, though," said one of the others. "Awfully hard upon Percival, still more hard on the other fellow." "I would never mind if I were fond of her," said one. "I should mind awfully," said another. (Be it here observed that the use of the word *awful* is not slang, but the Scottish language.) "You might mind, or you might not mind," said Maxwell, oracularly, "but none of us would make a woman who had done such a thing our wife." He had not the least idea that he delivered his friend's heart from a great weight when he said these words. "So then I am no traitor even to him," John said to himself.

It was felt at Percival's bank in Edinburgh, that though to marry so young might be foolish, there was not a word to be said against Miss Wamphrey of Wamphrey, and that it was a piece of good fortune that the young ass should have fallen on his feet, and made such a good connection. Marion had the opportunity, of which she availed herself quite pleasantly, of refusing Maxwell shortly after; and in spring her marriage took place. There was some story of their having fallen in love with each other over the eating of an orange, people said: and very soon after his marriage, John Percival had the satisfaction of remitting a sum of money from his brother-in-law, Will Wamphrey, in New Zealand, to the bank manager at Dunscore.

A STORY OF A WEDDING-TOUR

CHAPTER I

They had been married exactly a week when this incident occurred.

It was not a love marriage. The man, indeed, had been universally described as "very much in love," but the girl was not by any one supposed to be in that desirable condition. She was a very lonely little girl, without parents, almost without relations. Her guardian was a man who had been engaged in business relations with her father, and who had accepted the charge of the little orphan as his duty. But neither he nor his wife had any love to expend upon her, and they did not feel that such visionary sentiments came within the line of duty. He was a very honourable man, and took charge of her small—very small—property with unimpeachable care.

If anything, he wronged himself rather than Janey, charging her nothing for the transfers which he made of her farthing's worth of stock from time to time, to get a scarcely appreciable rise of interest and income for her. The whole thing was scarcely appreciable, and to a large-handed man like Mr Midhurst, dealing with hundreds of thousands, it was almost ridiculous to give a moment's attention to what a few hundreds might produce. But he did so; and if there is any angel who has to do with trade affairs, I hope it was carefully put to his account to balance some of the occasions on which he was not perhaps so particular. Nor did Mrs Midhurst shrink from her duty in all substantial and real good offices to the girl. She, who spent hundreds at the dressmaker's every year on account of her many daughters, did not disdain to get Janey's serge frocks at a cheaper shop, and to have them made by an inexpensive workwoman, so that the girl should have the very utmost she could get for her poor little money.

Was not this real goodness, real honesty, and devotion to their duty? But to love a little thing like that with no real claim upon them, and nothing that could be called specially attractive about her, who could be expected to do it? They had plenty—almost more than enough—of children of their own. These children were big boys and girls, gradually growing, in relays, into manhood and womanhood, when this child came upon their hands. There was no room for her in the full and noisy house. When she was grown up most of the Midhurst children were married, but there was one son at home, who, in the well-known contradictiousness of young people—it being a very wrong and, indeed, impossible thing—was quite capable of falling in love with Janey—and one daughter, with whom it was also possible that Janey might come into competition.

The young Midhursts were nice-looking young people enough; but Janey was very pretty. If Providence did but fully consider all the circumstances, it cannot but be felt that Providence would not carry out, as often is done, such ridiculous arrangements. Janey was very pretty. Could anything more inconvenient, more inappropriate, be conceived?

The poor little girl had, accordingly, spent most of her life at school, where she had, let it not be doubted, made many friendships and little loves; but these were broken up by holidays, by the returning home of the other pupils, while she stayed for ever at school: and not at one school, but several—for in his extreme conscientiousness her guardian desired to do her "every justice," as he said, and prepare her fully for the life— probably that of a governess—which lay before her. Therefore, when she had become proficient in one part of her education she was carried on to another, with the highest devotion to her commercial value no doubt, but a sublime indifference to her little feelings. Thus, she had been in France for two years, and in Germany for two years, so as to be able to state that French and German acquired in these countries were among the list of her accomplishments. English, of course, was the foundation of all; and Janey had spent some time at a famous academy of music,—her guardian adding something out of his own pocket to her scanty means, that she might be fully equipped for her profession. And then she was brought, I will not say home: Janey fondly said home, but she knew very well it did not mean home. And it was while Mrs Midhurst was actually writing out the advertisement for 'The Times,' and the 'Morning Post,' and 'The Guardian,' which was to announce to all the world that a young lady desired an engagement as governess, that her husband burst in with the extraordinary news that Mr Rosendale, who had chanced to travel with Janey from Flushing, on her return, and who had afterwards, by a still greater chance, met her when asked to lunch at the Midhursts', and stared very much at her, as they all remarked—had fallen in love with, and wanted to marry, this humble little girl.

"Fallen in love with Janey!" Mrs Midhurst cried. "Fallen in love with you, Janey!" said Agnes Midhurst, with a little emphasis on the pronoun. He was not, indeed, quite good enough to have permitted himself the luxury of falling in love with Mr Midhurst's daughter, but he was an astonishing match for Janey. He was a man who was very well off: he could afford himself such a caprice as that. He was not handsome. There was a strain of Jewish blood in him. He was a thick-set little man, and did not dress or talk in perfect taste; but—in love! These two words made all the difference. Nobody had ever loved her, much less been "in love" with her. Janey consented willingly enough for the magic of these two words. She felt that she was going to be like the best of women at last—to have some one who loved her, some one who was in love with her. He might not be "joli, joli," as they say in France. She might not feel any very strong impulse on her own part towards him; but if he was in love with her—in love! Romeo was no more than that with Juliet. The thought went to Janey's head. She married him quite willingly for the sake of this.

I am afraid that Janey, being young, and shy, and strange, was a good deal frightened, horrified, and even revolted, by her first discoveries of what it meant to be in love. She had made tremendous discoveries in the course of a week. She had found out that Mr Rosendale, her husband, was in love with her beauty, but as indifferent to herself as any of the persons she had quitted to give herself to him. He did not care at all what she thought, how she felt, what she liked or disliked. He did not care even for her comfort, or that she should be pleased and happy, which, in the first moment even of such a union, and out of pure self-regard to make a woman more agreeable to himself, a man—even the most brutal—generally regards more or less. He was, perhaps, not aware that he did not regard it. He took it for granted that, being his wife, she would naturally be pleased with what pleased him, and his mind went no further than this.

Therefore, as far as Janey liked the things he liked, all went well enough. She had these, but no other. Her wishes were not consulted further, nor did he know that he failed in any way towards her. He had little to say to her, except expressions of admiration. When he was not telling her that she was a little beauty, or admiring her pretty hair, her pretty eyes, the softness of her skin, and the smallness of her waist, he had nothing to say. He read his paper, disappearing behind it in the morning; he went to sleep after his midday meal (for the weather was warm;) he played billiards in the evening in the hotels to which he took her on their wedding journey; or he overwhelmed her with caresses from which she shrank in disgust, almost in terror. That was all that being in love meant, she found; and to say that she was disappointed cruelly was to express in the very mildest way the dreadful downfall of all her expectations and hopes which happened to Janey before she had been seven days a wife. It is not disagreeable to be told that you are a little beauty, prettier than any one else. Janey would have been very well pleased to put up with that; but to be petted like a little lapdog and then left as a lapdog is—to be quiet and not to trouble in the intervals of petting—was to the poor little girl, unaccustomed to love and athirst for it, who had hoped to be loved, and to find a companion to whom she would be truly dear, a disenchantment and disappointment which was almost more than flesh and blood could bear.

She was in the full bitterness of these discoveries when the strange incident occurred which was of so much importance in her life. They were travelling through France in one of those long night journeys to which we are all accustomed nowadays; and Janey, pale and tired, had been contemplating for some time the figure of her husband thrown back in the corner opposite, snoring complacently with his mouth open, and looking the worst that a middle-aged man can look in the utter abandonment of self-indulgence and rude comfort, when the train began to slacken its speed, and to prepare to enter one of those large stations which look so ghastly in the desertion of the night.

Rosendale jumped up instinctively, only half awake, as the train stopped. The other people in the carriage were leaving it, having attained the end of their journey, but he pushed through them and their baggage to get out, with the impatience which some men show at any pause of the kind, and determination to stretch their legs, or get something to drink, which mark the breaks in the journey. He did not even say anything to Janey as he forced his way out, but she was so familiar with his ways by this time that she took no notice. She did take notice, however when, her fellow-passengers and their packages having all been cleared away, she suddenly became sensible that the train was getting slowly into motion again without any sign of her husband.

She thought she caught a glimpse of him strolling about on the opposite platform before she was quite sure of what was happening. And then there was a scurry of hurrying feet, a slamming of doors, and as she rose and ran to the window bewildered, she saw him, along with some other men, running at full speed, but quite hopelessly, to catch the train. The last she saw was his face, fully revealed by the light of the lamp, convulsed with rage and astonishment, evidently with a yell of denunciation on the lips. Janey trembled at the sight. There was that in him, too, though as yet in her submissiveness she had never called it forth, a temper as unrestrained as his love-making, and as little touched by any thought save that of his own gratification. Her first sensation was fright, a terror that she was in fault and was about to be crushed to pieces in his rage: and then Janey sank back in her corner, and a flood of feeling of quite another kind took possession of her breast.

Was it possible that she was alone? Was it possible that for the first time since that terrible moment of her marriage she was more safely by herself than any locked door or even watchful guardian could keep her, quite unapproachable in the isolation of the train? Alone!

"Safe!" Janey ventured to say to herself, clasping her hands together with a mingled sensation of excitement and terror and tremulous delight which words could not tell.

She did not know what to think at first. The sound of the train plunging along through the darkness, through the unknown country, filled her mind as if some one was talking to her. And she was fluttered by the strangeness of the incident and disturbed by alarms. There was a fearful joy in thus being alone, in having a few hours, perhaps a whole long tranquil night, to herself: whatever came of it, that was always so much gained. But then she seemed to see him in the morning coming in upon her heated and angry. She had always felt that the moment would come when he would be angry, and more terrible to confront than any governess, or even principal of a ladies' college. He would come in furious, accusing her of being the cause of the accident, of doing something to set the train in motion; or else he would come in fatigued and dusty, claiming her services as if she were his valet—a thing which had, more or less, happened already, and against which Janey's pride and her sense of what was fit had risen in arms. She thought of this for a little time with trouble, and of the difficulties she would have in arriving, and where she would go to, and what she would say. It was an absurd story to tell, not to his advantage, "I lost my husband at Montbard." How could she say it? The hotel people would think she was a deceiver. Perhaps they would not take her in. And how would he know where to find her when he arrived? He would feel that he had lost her, as much as she had lost him.

Just as this idea rose in her mind, like a new thing full of strange suggestions, the train began to shorten speed again, and presently stopped once more. She felt it to do so with a pang of horror. No doubt he had climbed up somewhere, at the end or upon the engine, and was now to be restored to his legitimate place, to fall upon her either in fondness or in rage, delighted to get back to her, or angry with her for leaving him behind: she did not know which would be the worst. Her heart began to beat with fright and anticipation. But to her great relief it was only the guard who came to the door. He wanted to know if madame was the lady whose husband had been left behind; and to offer a hundred apologies and explanations. One of those fools at Montbard had proclaimed twenty minutes' pause when there were but five. If he had but heard he would have put it right, but he was at the other end of the train. But madame must not be too much distressed; a few hours would put it all right.

"Then there is another train?" said Janey, her poor little head buzzing between excitement and relief.

"Not for some hours," said the guard. "Madame will understand that there is not more than one *rapide* in the middle of the night; but in the morning quite early there is the train omnibus. Oh, very early, at five o'clock. Before madame is ready for her dinner monsieur will be at her side."

"Not till evening, then?" said Janey, with again a sudden acceleration of the movement of her heart.

The guard was desolated. "Not before evening. But if madame will remain quietly in the carriage when the train arrives at the station, I will find the omnibus of the hotel for her—I will see to everything! Madame, no doubt, knows which hotel to go to?"

Janey, as a matter of fact, did not know. Her husband had told her none of the details of the journey; but she said with a quick breath of excitement—

"I will go to the one that is nearest, the one at the Gare. There will be no need, for any omnibus."

"And the baggage? Madame has her ticket?"

"I have nothing," cried Janey, "except my travelling-bag. You must explain that for me. But otherwise—otherwise, I think I can manage."

"Madame speaks French so well," the man said, with admiration. It was, indeed, a piece of good fortune that she had been made to acquire the language in the country: that she was not frightened to find herself in a foreign place, and surrounded by people speaking a strange tongue, as many a young English bride would have been. There was a moment of tremendous excitement and noise at the station while all was explained to a serious *chef de Gare*, and a gesticulating band of porters and attendants, whose loud voices, as they all spoke together, would have frightened an ordinary English girl out of her wits. But Janey, in the strange excitement which had taken possession of her, and in her fortunate acquaintance with the language, stood still as a little rock amid all the confusion. "I will wait at the hotel till my husband comes," she said, taking out the travelling-bag and her wraps, and maintaining a composure worthy of all admiration. Not a tear, not an outcry. How astonishing are these English, cried the little crowd, with that swift classification which the Frenchman loves.

Janey walked into the hotel with her little belongings, not knowing whether she was indeed walking upon her feet or floating upon wings. She was quite composed. But if any one could only have seen the commotion within that youthful bosom! She locked the door of the little delightful solitary room in which she was placed. It was not delightful at all; But to Janey it was a haven of peace, as sweet, as secluded from everything alarming and terrible, as any bower. Not till evening could he by any possibility arrive—the man who had caused such a revolution in her life. She had some ten hours of divine quiet before her, of blessed solitude, of thought. She did not refuse to take the little meal that was brought to her, the breakfast of which she stood in need; and she was glad to be able to bathe her face, to take off her dusty dress, and put on the soft and fresh one, which, happily, had folded into very small space, and therefore could be put into her bag. Her head still buzzed with the strangeness of the position, yet began to settle a little. When she had made all these little arrangements she sat down to consider. Perhaps you will think there was very little to consider, nothing but how to wait till the next train brought him, which, after all, was not a very great thing to do. Appalling, perhaps, to a little inexperienced bride; but not to Janey, who had travelled alone so often, and knew the language, and all that.

But whoever had been able to look into Janey's mind would have seen that something more was there,—a very, very different thing from the question of how best to await his coming back. Oh, if he had loved her, Janey would have put up with many things! She would have schooled herself out of all her private repugnances; she would have been so grateful to him, so touched by the affection which nobody had ever bestowed upon her before! But he did not love her. He cared nothing about herself, Janey; did not even know her, or want to know her, or take into consideration her ways or her wishes. He was in love with her pretty face, her fresh little beauty, her power of pleasing him. If ever that power ceased, which it was sure to do, sooner or later, she would be to him less than nothing, the dreary little wife whom everybody has seen attached to a careless man: Janey felt that this was what was in store for her. She felt the horror of him, and his kind of loving, which had been such a miserable revelation to her. She felt the relief, the happiness, ah, the bliss, of having lost him for a moment, of being alone.

She took out her purse from her pocket, which was full of the change she had got in Paris of one of the ten-pound notes which her guardian had given her when she left his house on her wedding morning. She took out the clumsy pocket-book, an old one, in which there were still nine ten-pound notes. It was all her fortune, except a very, very small investment which brought her in some seven pounds a-year. This was the remainder of another small investment which had been withdrawn in order to provide her with her simple trousseau, leaving this sum of a hundred pounds which her guardian had given her, advising her to place it at once for security in her husband's hands. Janey had not done this, she scarcely could tell why. She spread them on the table—the nine notes, the twelve napoleons of shining French money. A hundred pounds: she had still the twelve francs which made up the sum. She had spent nothing. There were even the few coppers over for the *agio*. She spread them all out, and counted them from right to left, and again from left to right. Nine ten-pound notes, twelve and a-half French napoleons—or louis, as people call them nowadays—making a hundred pounds. A hundred pounds is a large sum in the eyes of a girl. It may not be much to you and me, who know that it means only ten times ten pounds, and that ten pounds goes like the wind as soon as you begin to spend it. But to Janey! Why, she could live upon a hundred pounds for—certainly for two years: for two long delightful years, with nobody to trouble her, nobody to scold, nobody to interfere. Something mounted to her head like the fumes of wine. Everything began to buzz again, to turn round, to sweep her away as on a rapidly mounting current. She put back all the money in the pocket-book—her fortune, the great sum that made her independent; and she put back her things into the bag. A sudden energy of resolution seized her. She put on her hat again, and as she looked at herself in the glass encountered the vision of a little face which was new to her. It was not that of Janey, the little governess-pupil; it was not young Mrs Rosendale. It was full of life, and meaning, and energy, and strength. Who was it? Janey? Janey herself, the real woman, whom nobody had ever seen before.

CHAPTER II

It is astonishing how many things can be done in sudden excitement and passion which could not be possible under any other circumstances. Janey was by nature a shy girl and easily frightened, accustomed indeed to do many things for herself, and to move quietly without attracting observation through the midst of a crowd; but she had never taken any initiative, and since her marriage had been reduced to such a state of complete dependence on her husband's wishes and plans that she had not attempted the smallest step on her own impulse.

Now, however, she moved about with a quiet assurance and decision which astonished herself. She carried her few possessions back again to the railway station, leaving the small gold piece of ten francs to pay, and much overpay, her hour's shelter and entertainment at the hotel.

Nobody noticed her as she went through the bustle of the place and back to the crowded station, where a little leisurely local train was about starting—a slow train occupied by peasants and country folk, and which stopped at every station along the line. English people abound in that place at all hours, except at this particular moment, when the *rapide* going towards Italy had but newly left and the little country train was preparing in peace. Nobody seemed to notice Janey as she moved about with her bag on her arm. She took her ticket in her irreproachable French "acquired in the country," which attracted no attention. She got into a second-class carriage in which there were already various country people, and especially a young mother with a baby, and its nurse in a white round cap with long streaming ribbons. Janey's heart went out to these people. She wondered if the young woman was happy, if her husband loved her, if it was not very sweet to have a child—a child must love you; it would not mind whether your cheeks were rosy or pale, whether you were pretty or not, whether you had accomplishments or languages acquired in the country.

Looking at this baby, Janey almost forgot that she was going out upon the world alone, and did not know where. It is a tremendous thing to do this, to separate from all the world you are acquainted with, to plunge into the unknown. Men do it often enough, though seldom without some clue, some link of connection with the past and way of return. Janey was about to cut herself off as by the Fury's shears from everything. She would never join her husband again. She would never fear her guardian again. She must drop out of sight like a stone into the sea. There was no longing love to search for her, no pardon to be offered, no one who would be heart-struck at the thought of the little girl lost and unhappy. Only anger would be excited by her running away, and a desire to punish, to shake her little fragile person to pieces, to make her suffer. She knew that if she did it at all, it must be final. But this did not overwhelm her. What troubled Janey a great deal more than the act of severance which she was about to accomplish, was the inevitable fib or fibs she must tell in order to account for her appearance in the unknown. She did not like to tell a fib, even a justifiable one. It was against all her traditions, against her nature. She felt that she could never do it anything but badly, never without exciting suspicions; and she must needs have some story, some way of accounting for herself.

This occupied her mind while the slow train crawled from station to station. It was the most friendly, idle, gossiping little train. It seemed to stop at the merest signal-box to have a talk, to drink as it were a social glass administered through that black hose, with a friend; it stopped wherever there were a few houses, it carried little parcels, it took up a leisurely passenger going next door, and the little electric bell went on tingling, and the guard cried "En voiture!" and the little bugle sounded. Janey was amused by all these little sounds and sights, and the country all flooded with sunshine, and the flowers everywhere, though it was only March, and dark black weather when she had left home.

Left home! and she had no home now, anywhere, no place to take refuge in, nobody to write to, to appeal to, to tell if she was happy or unhappy. But Janey did not care! She felt a strange elation of ease and relief. All alone, but everybody smiling upon her, the young mother opposite beginning to chatter, the baby to crow to her, the nurse to smile and approve of the *bonne petite* dame who took so much notice of the child. Her head was swimming, but with pleasure, and the blessed sensation of freedom—pleasure tinctured with the exhilaration of escape, and the thrill of fright which added to the excitement. Yet at that moment she was certainly in no danger. He was toiling along, no doubt, fuming and perhaps swearing, on another slow train on the other side of Marseilles. Janey laughed to herself a little guiltily at the thought.

And she had escaped! It was not her doing primarily. She might have gone on all her life till she had died, but for that accident which was none of her doing. It was destiny that had done it, fate. The cage door had been opened and the bird had flown away. And how nice it would be to settle down, with this little mother, just about her own age, for a neighbour, and to help to bring the baby up! The kind, sweet faces they all had, mother and baby and *bonne* all smiling upon her! When Janey looked out on the other side she saw the sea flashing in the sunshine, the red porphyry rocks reflecting themselves in the brilliant blue, and village after village perched upon a promontory or in the hollow of a bay. She had never in all her life before felt that sensation of blessedness, of being able to do what she liked, of having no one to call her to account. She did not know where she was going, but that was part of the pleasure. She did not want to know where she was going.

Then suddenly this sentiment changed, and she saw in a moment a place that smiled at her like the smiling of the mother and baby. It was one of those villages in a bay: a range of blue mountains threw forth a protecting arm into the sea to shield it: the roofs were red, the houses were white, they were all blazing in the sun. Soft olives and palms fringed the deep green of the pines that rolled back in waves of verdure over the country behind, and strayed down in groups and scattered files to the shore below. Oh, what a cheerful, delightsome place! and this was where the little group with the baby were preparing to get out. "I will go too," said Janey to herself; and her heart gave a little bound of pleasure. She was delighted to reach the place where she was going to stay—just as she had been delighted to go on in the little pottering train, not knowing where she was going, and not wishing to know.

This was how Janey settled herself on the day of her flight from the world. She scarcely knew what story it was she told to the young woman whose face had so charmed her, and whom she asked whether she would be likely to find lodgings anywhere, lodgings that would not be too expensive.

"My husband is—at sea," Janey heard herself saying. She could scarcely tell what it was that put those words into her head.

"Oh, but yes," the other young woman cried with rapture. Nothing was more easy to get than a lodging in St Honorat, which was beginning to try to be a winter resort, and was eager to attract strangers. Janey had dreamed of a cottage and a garden, but she was not dissatisfied when she found herself in a sunbright room on the second floor of a tall white house facing the sea. It had a little balcony all to itself. The water rippled on the shore just over the road, the curve of the blue mountains was before her eyes.

I do not say that when she had settled down, when the thrill of movement was no longer in her brain, Janey was not without a shiver at the thought of what she had done. When the sun set, and that little chill which comes into the air of the south at the moment of its setting breathed a momentary cold about her, and when the woman of the house carefully closed the shutters and shut out the shining of the bay, and she was left alone with her candle, something sank in Janey's heart—something of the unreasonable elation, the fantastic happiness, of the day. She thought of "Mr Rosendale" (she had never got so near her husband as to call him by any other name) arriving, of the fuss there would be about her and the inquiries.

Was it rash to have come to a place so near as this—within an hour or two of where he was? Was there a danger that some one might have seen her? that it might be found out that she had taken her ticket? But then she had taken her ticket for a place much farther along the coast. She thought she could see him arrive all flaming with anger and eagerness, and the group that would gather round him, and how he would be betrayed by his bad French, and the rage he would get into! Again she laughed guiltily; but then got very grave again trying to count up all the chances—how some porter might have noticed and might betray her, how he might yet come down upon her furiously, to wreak upon her all the fury of his discomfiture. Janey knew by instinct that though it was in no way her fault, her husband would wreak his vengeance upon her even for being left behind by the train. She became desperate as she sat and thought it all over. It would be better for her to leap from the window, to throw herself into the sea, than to fall into his hands. There would be no forgiveness for her if he once laid hands upon her. Now that she had taken this desperate step, she must stand by it to the death.

CHAPTER III

Ten years had passed away since the time of that wedding tour.

Ten years! It is a very long time in a life. It makes a young man middle-aged, and a middle-aged man old. It takes away the bloom of youth, and the ignorance of the most inexperienced; and yet what a little while it is!—no more than a day when you look back upon it. The train from Marseilles to Nice, which is called the *rapide*, goes every day, and most people one time or another have travelled by it.

One day last winter one of the passengers in this train, established very comfortably in the best corner of a sleeping carriage in which he had passed the night luxuriously, and from which he was now looking out upon the shining sea, the red rocks, the many bays and headlands of the coast, suddenly received such a shock and sensation as seldom occurs to any one. He was a man of middle-age and not of engaging aspect. His face was red, and his eyes were dull yet fiery. He had the air of a man who had indulged himself much and all his inclinations, had loved good living and all the joys of the flesh, had denied himself nothing—and was now paying the penalties. Such men, to tell the truth, are not at all unusual apparitions on that beautiful coast or in the train *rapide*. No doubt appearances are deceitful, and it is not always a bad man who bears that aspect or who pays those penalties: but in this case few people would have doubted.

His eyes were bloodshot, he had a scowl upon his brow, his foot was supported upon a cushion. He had a servant with him to whom he rarely spoke but with an insult. Not an agreeable man—and the life he was now leading, whatever it had been, was not an agreeable life. He was staring out at the window upon the curves of the coast, sometimes putting up the collar of his fur coat over his ears, though it was a warm morning, and the sun had all the force of April. What he was thinking of it would be difficult to divine—perhaps of the good dinner that awaited him at Monte Carlo when he got there, perhaps of his good luck in being out of England when the east winds began to blow, perhaps of something quite different—some recollection of his past. The *rapide* does not stop at such small places as St Honorat, which indeed had not succeeded in making itself a winter resort. It was still a very small place. There were a few people on the platform when the train rushed through. It seemed to pass like a whirlwind, yet notwithstanding, in that moment two things happened. The gentleman in the corner of the carriage started in his seat, and flung himself half out of the window, with a sudden roar which lost itself in the tunnel into which the train plunged. There was an awful minute in that tunnel: for the servant thought his master had taken a fit, and there was no light to see what convulsions he might have fallen into, while at the same time he fought furiously against the man's efforts to loose his wrappings and place him in a recumbent position, exclaiming furiously all the time. He had not taken a fit, but when the train emerged into the light he was as near to it as possible—purple-red in his face, and shouting with rage and pain.

"Stop the train! stop the train!" he shouted. "Do you hear, you fool? stop the train! Ring the bell or whatever it is! break the —— thing! Stop the train!"

"Sir, sir! if you will only be quiet, I will get your medicine in a moment!"

"Medicine, indeed!" cried the master, indignantly, and every furious name that he could think of mounted to his lips—fool, idiot, ass, swine— there was no end to his epithets. "I tell you I saw her, I saw her!" he shouted. "Stop the train! Stop the train!"

On the other hand, among the few insignificant persons, peasants and others, who had been standing on the platform at St Honorat when the *rapide* dashed past, there had been a woman and a child. The woman was not a peasant: she was very simply dressed in black, with one of the small bonnets which were a few years ago so distinctively English, and with an air which corresponded to that simple coiffure. She was young, and yet had the air of responsibility and motherhood which marks a woman who is no longer in the first chapter of life. The child, a boy of nine or ten, standing close by her side, had seized her hand just as the train appeared impatiently to call her attention to something else; but, by some strange spell of attraction or coincidence, her eyes fixed upon that window out of which the gouty traveller was looking. She saw him as he saw her, and fell back dragging the boy with her as if she would have sunk into the ground. It was only a moment and the *rapide* was gone, screaming and roaring into the tunnel, making too much noise with the rush and sweep of its going to permit the shout of the passenger to be heard.

Ten years, ten long years, during which life had undergone so many changes! They all seemed to fly away in a moment, and the girl who had arrived at the little station of St Honorat alone, a fugitive, elated and intoxicated with her freedom, suddenly felt herself again the little Janey who had emancipated herself so strangely,—though she had for a long time been frightened by every train that passed and every stranger who came near.

In the course of these long years all this had changed. Her baby had been born, her forlorn state had called forth great pity, great remark and criticism, in the village where she had found refuge,—great censure also, for the fact of her marriage was not believed by everybody. But she was so lonely, so modest, and so friendly, that the poor little English stranger was soon forgiven. Perhaps her simple neighbours were glad to find that a prim Englishwoman, supposed to stand so fierce on her virtue, was in reality so fallible—or perhaps pity put all other sentiments out of court. She told her real story to the priest when the boy was baptised, and though he tried to persuade her to return to her husband, he only half believed in that husband, since the story was told not under any seal of confession. Janey never became absolutely one of his flock. She was a prim little Protestant in her heart, standing strong against the saints, but devoutly attending church, believing with simple religiousness that to go to church was better than not to go to church, whatever the rites might be, and reading her little English service steadily through all the prayers of the Mass, which she never learned to follow. But her boy was like the other children of St Honorat, and learned his catechism and said his lessons with the rest.

There were various things which she did to get a living, and got it very innocently and sufficiently, though in the humblest way. She taught English to the children of some of the richer people in the village: she taught them music. She had so much credit in this latter branch, that she often held the organ in church on a holiday and pleased everybody. Then she worked very well with her needle, and would help on an emergency at first for pure kindness, and then, as her faculties and her powers of service became known, for pay, with diligence and readiness. She found a niche in the little place which she filled perfectly, though only accident seemed to have made it for her. She had fifty pounds of her little fortune laid by for the boy. She had a share of a cottage in a garden—not an English cottage indeed, but the upper floor of a two-storeyed French house; and she and her boy did much in the garden, cultivating prettinesses which do not commend themselves much to the villagers of St Honorat. Whether she ever regretted the step she had taken nobody ever knew. She might have been a lady with a larger house than any in St Honorat, and servants at her call. Perhaps she sometimes thought of that; perhaps she felt herself happier as she was; sometimes, I think, she felt that if she had known the boy was coming she might have possessed her soul in patience, and borne even with Mr Rosendale. But then at the time the decisive step was taken she did not know.

She hurried home in a great fright, not knowing what to do; then calmed herself with the thought that even if he had recognised her, there were many chances against his following her, or at least finding her, with no clue, and after so many years. And then a dreadful panic seized her at the thought that he might take her boy from her. He had known nothing about the boy: but if he discovered that fact it would make a great difference. He could not compel Janey to return to him, but he could take the boy. When this occurred to her she started up again, having just sat down, and put on her bonnet and called the child.

"Are you going out again, mother?" he cried.

"Yes, directly, directly: come, John, come, come!" she said, putting his cap upon his head and seizing him by the hand. She led him straight to the presbytery, and asked for the *curé*, and went in to the good priest in great agitation, leaving the boy with his housekeeper.

"M. l'Abbé," she said, with what the village called her English directness, "I have just seen my husband go past in the train!"

"Not possible!" said M. l'Abbé, who only half believed there was a husband at all.

"And he saw me. He will come back, and I am afraid he will find me. I want you to do something for me."

"With pleasure," said the priest; "I will come and meet Monsieur your husband, and I will explain— —"

"That is not what I want you to do. I want you to let John stay with you, to keep him here till—till— —He will want to take him away from me!" she cried.

"He will want to take you both away, *chère petite dame*. He has a right to do so."

"No, no! but I do not ask you what is his right. I ask you to keep John safe; to keep him here—till the danger has passed away!"

The priest tried to reason, to entreat, to persuade her that a father, not to say a husband, had his rights. But Janey would hear no reason: had she heard reason either from herself or another, she would not have been at St Honorat now. And he gave at last a reluctant consent. There was perhaps no harm in it after all. If a man came to claim his rights, he would not certainly go away again without some appeal to the authorities—which was a thing it must come to sooner or later,—if there was indeed a husband at all, and the story was true.

Janey then went back to her home. She thought she could await him there and defy him. "I will not go with you," she would say. "I may be your wife, but I am not your slave. You have left me alone for ten years. I will not go with you now!" She repeated this to herself many times, but it did not subdue the commotion in her being. She went out again when it became too much for her, locking her door with a strange sense that she might never come back again. She walked along the sea shore, repeating these words to herself, and then she walked up and down the streets, and went into the church and made the round of it, passing all the altars and wondering if the saints did pay any attention to the poor women who were there, as always, telling St Joseph or the Blessed Mary all about it. She sank down in a dark corner, and said—

"Oh, my God! oh, my God!"

She could not tell Him about it in her agitation, with her heart beating so, but only call His attention, as the woman in the Bible touched the Redeemer's robe. And then she went out and walked up and down again. I cannot tell what drew her back to the station—what fascination, what dreadful spell. Before she knew what she was doing she found herself there, walking up and down, up and down.

As if she were waiting for some one! "You have come to meet a friend?" some one said to her, with an air of suspicion. And she first nodded and then shook her head; but still continued in spite of herself to walk up and down. Then she said to herself that it was best so—that to get it over would be a great thing, now John was out of the way; he would be sure to find her sooner or later—far better to get it over! When the train came in, the slow local train, coming from the side of Italy, she drew herself back a little to watch. There was a great commotion when it drew up at the platform. A man got out and called all the loungers about to help to lift out a gentleman who was ill,—who had had a bad attack in the train.

"Is there anywhere here we can take him to? Is there any decent hotel? Is there a room fit to put my master in?" he cried.

He was English with not much French at his command, and in great distress. Janey, forgetting herself and her terrors, and strong in the relief of the moment that he whom she feared had not come, went up to offer her help. She answered the man's questions; she called the right people to help him; she summoned the *chef de Gare* to make some provision for carrying the stricken man to the hotel.

"I will go with you," she said to the servant, who felt as if an angel speaking English had suddenly come to his help. She stood by full of pity, as they lifted that great inert mass out of the carriage. Then she gave a great cry and fell back against the wall.

It was a dreadful sight the men said afterwards, enough to overcome the tender heart of any lady, especially of one so kind as Madame Jeanne. A huge man, helpless, unconscious, with a purple countenance, staring eyes, breathing so that you could hear him a mile off. No wonder that she covered her eyes with her hands not to see him; and then covered her ears with her hands not to hear him: but finally she hurried away to the hotel to prepare for him, and to call the doctor, that no time should be lost. Janey felt as if she was restored for the moment to life when there was something she could do. The questions were all postponed. She did not think of flight or concealment, or even of John at the presbytery. "He is my husband," she said, with awe in her heart.

This was how the train brought back to Janey the man whom the train had separated from her ten years before. The whole tragedy was of the railway, the noisy carriages, the snorting locomotives. He was taken to the hotel, but he never came to himself again, and died there next day, without being able to say what his object was, or why he had got out of the *rapide*, though unable to walk, and insisted on returning to St Honorat. It cost him his life; but then his life was not worth a day's purchase, all the doctors said, in the condition in which he was.

Friends had to be summoned, and men of business, and it was impossible but that Janey's secret should be made known. When she found herself and her son recognised, and that there could be no doubt that the boy was his father's heir, she was struck with a great horror which she never quite got over all her life. She had not blamed herself before; but now seemed to herself no less than the murderer of her husband: and could not forgive herself, nor get out of her eyes the face she had seen, nor out of her ears the dreadful sound of that labouring breath.

JOHN

CHAPTER I

"Djohn, Djohn!" cried the boy, "come back: the mother is looking for you—something has happened. At once, at once, you must go home!"

"What has happened? Is she ill? Has she hurt herself? Has there been an accident?" demanded John, a tall lad of sixteen, dressed, like the first speaker, in country clothes of French cut, but with a certain difference which marked his different nationality.

"There has been an accident, but not to her. Make haste! It is very exciting. It is a gentleman that is hurt, and he is your father. Half the village is at the door. So go, quick, quick! I have run before them all to tell you."

"A gentleman who is my father! My father is dead years ago," said the elder boy, with a flush on his face.

"Nevertheless it is quite true what I say. Come quick, come quick! I am going back: something new may have happened even since I came away."

With that the little French villager rattled off on his noisy shoes, full of excitement, down the stony street towards the railway station, calling to some other youths, as he passed, also to come quick, for that something tremendous had happened *chez l'Anglaise*. That little group clattered after him, all agog in a moment with the precious thought of some distraction; for few things ever happened in these regions. But the person most concerned hung back. He had never been out of this village in his life—he knew no other mode of existence; yet when Jean called to John that his home was the scene of a mysterious catastrophe, John held back with a proud shame and horror which could not endure publicity. Perhaps his slowness of brain took a moment more to fathom the mere fact of a catastrophe; but in reality his heart was already beating loudly in his breast, and his head beginning to buzz and swell, while still he kept up the fiction of walking deliberately and yielding to no excitement. What was it that had happened? Nothing had happened in all John's life but what happened every day. He had been born and lived always in that little town of Cagnes. He was the son of *l'Anglaise*, and, as a matter of fact, though he had been brought up just like them, he was not the same as the other boys. There was something in him different: he was slower than they were, more deliberate, more calm. He did not quarrel as they did, noisily, with shrieks, and sometimes tears; but he was more dangerous than the rest when his composure was really disturbed. His mother was a very shrinking, quiet woman, who lived in a small house with a big garden on the lower slope of the hill. She was one who said little to anybody, even to her son whom she adored; but she was a very useful person in her quiet way, and though she was English, and silent, and a stranger, was rather popular than otherwise in Cagnes. Everybody knew *l'Anglaise*, who was a feature in the small community, not like anybody else. People who knew her well called her Madame Jeanne. She had arrived there quite by accident in the first grief of her widowhood, with a pathetic story, as was commonly told and reported. She had gone to meet her husband, a sailor, at Marseilles; but instead of finding him had received the news of his death—and being very lonely, had strayed on distracted until she saw the little town of Cagnes rising upon its hill above the prosaic line of the railway, and all the green and lovely country round. She had stopped there at hazard, in the sickness of her heart; and there her son had been born, and she had lived ever since. I am not aware that any one had heard this story from her own lips. Certainly John had never heard it; but he understood somehow, as everybody else did in Cagnes, that this was his mother's story. So many things there are in the world which have come into the common mind somehow, exist by some vitality of their own, and do not need to be re-told. John would have gone to the stake for it, and so would half the population of Cagnes, that his father was a sailor and died before he was born. What, then, did this ridiculous little Jean, Jean au Meunier, the miller's son, mean by his ridiculous story? John would not follow down the steep and stony street, where every step made such a noise on the flags, as if he were moved by that absurd tale. But presently he dived down one of the side lanes which led down the slope of the hill, almost perpendicularly between two lines of houses, until you came to the broken slopes farther down, where you could zigzag your way among the prickly aloe bushes, and the terraces of the olive gardens. His mother's cottage lay at the foot of the hill, with its large, sloping, sunny garden, in which the trees in blossom, peach and apple, stood out against the grey background of the olives, and the last of the winter oranges made a show for more than they were worth upon the darker green of the trees. John's heart beat very loud indeed as he tumbled down these steps, slipping and springing in his haste; but he was half-disappointed, half-relieved, to find no crowd, no commotion about the house. The door was locked as usual, and the key hid under the great white bank of marguerites, as it always was when his mother had gone out. There was not a sign about of anything but the ordinary calm.

Some one, however, called to him from the road, as he stood, not knowing what to do next, in front of the gate.

"Hé, le Djohn!" cried this passer-by, "thy mother is not here. You will find her at the Hôtel de la Gare, with the gentleman who is dying, or like to die."

"What gentleman?" cried John, striding over the broken ground towards the speaker.

"Do I know? Some one who came in search of her and thee. It is thought thy real father. But why ask me? Go and see for thyself!"

John paused a little till this man had passed, disappearing into the valley. He would not allow a mere peasant, a clodhopper, to see the commotion in which his mind was; but as soon as the passer-by was out of sight he took to his heels and ran all the way, which was more than a mile, through the opening of the valley to the white Route Nationale which ran along the coast, on the other side of which was the little new station and a half-built house, emblazoned with the ambitious title of Hôtel de la Gare, in the meantime not much more than a *café*, where the Cagncis went on Sundays to drink their bocks and breathe the dust they love. Here, sure enough, there was a crowd at the door, and many signs of excitement—the men standing about and describing something to each other, two railway porters surrounded by the closest group, and the women all pressing up the steps, shaking their heads and asking questions of the proprietor, who stood blocking up the doorway. John had run as only a boy can all the way until he came in sight of this little throng; then he altered his aspect, slowed down by degrees, thrust his hands into his pockets, and came the rest of the way in slow marching time, as if he were going along for his proper diversion, and had nothing on his mind. There was a great outcry, however, before he reached the spot, and he saw his mother led out into the balcony and placed there in a chair, apparently fainting, one woman sprinkling water upon her head, another fanning her, two or three hanging about wringing their hands. When John saw this he made a sudden forward movement, and forced his way through the crowd, which, as soon as it was seen who he was, gave way before him.

"It is her boy—let him go to her. Djohn, God bless thee! be good to thy poor mother. Let him go in, let him go in, Père Rondilet—it is her boy."

But, notwithstanding these encouragements and the readiness of everybody to help him, it was not so easy for John to attain to his mother. There were two rooms which opened upon that balcony, the doors of both of which were shut and guarded, one by a spare, trim, English-looking man, the other by one of the women who knew Madame Jeanne, and who now took John's head in her two hands, kissed him, leaving a tear on his cheek, and begged him to have patience a little.

"Thy mother has had a great shock," she said. "She has an attack of the nerves—how could it be otherwise after such a discovery? Wait a little till she comes to herself, my little friend." "Little friend" does not mean anything so soft and tender in English as *mon petit ami* did; but we must take the faults of our language along with its qualities.

"What does it mean?" cried John. "What lies are they all saying about my father? My father was dead before I was born."

"I beg pardon," said the English-looking man, in very slow and difficult French; "is this the English lady's son?"

John answered abruptly in English, perhaps even a little rudely. "Who are you?" He was very much irritated and troubled, poor boy. He divined a certain inferiority in the man, and the horrible question, Was this perhaps his father? crossed his mind.

"I am Mr Rothbury's servant—I may say his confidential man; and I know everything," was the strange reply.

The good woman who had just spoken to John stood open-mouthed with admiration to hear the boy whom she had known all her life thus express himself in a foreign tongue with an aplomb which was extraordinary, and which the strange gentleman *quite* a gentleman in the opinion of Mère Pointêt, understood and replied to with so much deference. Decidedly John, who had been brought up among them all, and considered just as one of the other boys, had more in him than anybody thought.

"What do you mean by everything?" said John. "And who is Mr Rothbury? I don't suppose there is anything to know."

"This is not a place to explain, if you are not acquainted with the circumstances, sir," the English valet said.

John was not at all accustomed to be spoken to in this tone; and though it was meant to be very respectful, it seemed to him something like mockery. He grew very red with the idea that he was being laughed at.

"Perhaps you mistake me for some one else," he said. "I can speak English because my mother is English—that is all; and I won't stand being made fun of, I can tell you. Though you are," he added after a moment with reluctant candour, "a great deal bigger than me."

"I am not making fun of you, sir. I am your father's valet; it wouldn't become me, especially with him, poor gentleman, lying dead on the other side of the door."

"Lying dead!"

A kind of horror seized upon John. He had never, that he knew of, been so near to any one who was dead. He drew back a step, with the timidity that is born of awe.

"Would you like to see him, sir?" the valet said.

"What does he say?" said the Mère Pointêt. "It is just: you ought to go and see him, you who belong to him. Thy mother is too much agitated—it would kill her to remain there; but thou, boy, go—it is only right, since the man is thy father, whatever he may have been in his life."

"I have no father—my father died long ago," the boy cried.

But presently, without wishing it, he found himself in the room which the valet unlocked to admit him. A man lay on the bed in his ordinary clothes—the clothes in which he had travelled. Nothing as yet had been done of those last offices which are performed for the dead. The windows which opened on the balcony were half-closed with shutters, but open enough to let the sounds without come in; the room was, if not "the worst inn's worst room," at all events the bare, newly-plastered, half-furnished room of a poor railway hotel. There were no curtains, no veil of any kind to conceal the terrible fact of that big figure lying there, in all the dreadful ordinariness of a tweed travelling suit, and boots upon which the dust of the road still lay.

"You must not think it was the shock alone," the valet said, moving on tiptoe, and speaking in a whisper. "It was a great shock, of course; but it happened yesterday. My master saw Mrs Rothbury standing on the platform at the station as the train went by. Shows how much he had thought of her, doesn't it, sir, that just a glimpse like that as we went by was enough, after all these years? To be sure, the train slowed as we went through the stations. I saw the lady too, and I believe it was you, sir, along with her; but then I had never seen my poor master's wife. And he didn't know anything about you, if you'll excuse me saying it. He would have come back here last night if he hadn't been taken so bad. He's been ill a long time, my poor master has—gout and many other things. But when he saw you, sir, there was no holding him. 'Struthers,' said he (my name is Struthers, sir)—'there's a child, she's got a child—and a boy too: what I've always wished for was a boy.' The doctor had to let him come this morning,—he wouldn't be kept back; but he said to me, the doctor did, 'It's as much as his life is worth.' Family quarrels are dreadful things. I don't want to say a word against your mother, sir. She had her reasons, no doubt of it; but my poor master might have been a better man as well as a happier if——It's not for a servant to make remarks. Come a little nearer this way."

"I don't want to see him," said John, trembling. "I don't know who he is. I don't wish to hear anything more about him."

"He is your father, sir," said the valet, reproachfully; and John stood still with a strange fascination, yet repugnance, while the man withdrew the handkerchief which covered the face. The boy trembled from head to foot at the sight. It was a face in which there was little of the dignity and solemnity that so often comes even upon the homeliest faces when death has touched them—a large heavy countenance with bloated features, and eyes half-closed, with something of a stare in them under the light-coloured, scanty eyelashes. It was impossible to believe that the man was dead. The redness natural to it had hardly departed from the coarse face; a few limp locks of hair, laid over in life to hide the baldness, straggled now about the swollen temples—not a face to be remembered as that of a boy's father. John stumbled away, covering his face with his hands. What did it mean? His father?—but he had had no father since ever he was born.

Presently he was told that his mother was better—that she wanted him to take her home; but she did not say anything to him when he went into the next room where she was. She had her little black bonnet on, which always made so great a difference between her and the village women in their white caps, and which John had been unconsciously proud of, as a sign that she was not as they were, but an English lady such as he had read of in books. Her face was covered with a thick veil, and she took hold of his boyish arm with a sort of clutch, holding it against his, and almost resting her head upon his shoulder, for she was a little woman, and he was taller already than she was. In this way he led her through the crowd at the door, feeling the importance of it, even though he felt his heart turned from his mother in the shock of this discovery. She had deceived him in some dreadful way, he scarcely as yet knew how; but, at all events, he was her protector now, her defence against all these prying people. He held her up with his arm, and he made signs to them with his disengaged hand not to press upon her, not to speak to her. He was her protector, that was certain,—even though he might be angry with her, it was his business to take care of her, and not that of any other person in the world. They went along together, she always holding fast by his arm, her head bowed, her face hidden by her veil, along the white line of the Route Nationale, where scattered groups stood about every house, though thinning as they went on, and stared at her and him—until they turned into the valley road and the slopes of broken ground, beyond which the cottage lay. It was only when they were there, and no one within sight or hearing, that she spoke.

"Oh, John, you are angry with me," she said.

"How can I be angry with you? But you have deceived me, mother," said the boy.

"I have never deceived you—nor any one. All that—that was said of me, that I suppose you have heard—was not from me, John. I said nothing at all. I meant always when you were older to tell you, but I never thought you seemed to care."

"Not care!" he said.

He could not have told her even now the pang which was hot in his heart for the loss of his sailor father, the young father of whom he had dreamed so often, who had been coming home so joyfully to his wife and child, and whom death had seized in the middle of his happiness. He had thought of him so often, imaging him forth to himself, that it almost seemed to John as if he could have painted a picture of the young man sweeping the horizon to be the first to see land—that land which he was never to see. He meant to paint a picture of it one day, which should move every heart. He had almost heard the swish of the waves along the vessel's side, the sound of the wind in the sails, and seen the wistful look in that face,— which now he was to learn had never existed, never looked out for land, never borne that disappointment which had wrung his son's heart for him so many, many times. It was with a visionary anguish that the boy realised all this. "Not care!" What was there that he had cared for more? Scarcely even this mother, bowed down with trouble, who clung to his arm. The mother, though he loved her, was still a mortal and fallible: little questions rose between them: she came to decisions which were not always just according to John's way of thinking, and said things that jarred upon him. But the father was beyond all that. He was the true ideal, without fault, full of unknown treasures of tenderness and wisdom. It would have astonished that mother beyond measure, she who thought she knew her son so well and possessed all his affection, to know how much closer still that vision was to John's heart.

"You never said a word," she cried now, with a vague pang; "you never asked a question. How was I to know? But I meant always to tell you when you should be older. Oh, John! I know now that I was very rash and imprudent; but then I did not think of that, I was so young, and life was very hard upon me. I was disposed of just as they pleased. I was more unhappy than any one can ever know. And I have never regretted it till now. I have lived a life of peace with my own child. I have been quite happy—I who was so wretched, John."

"I wish you would tell me how it all happened," he said, almost coldly.

He turned his head away from her. He gave her still the support of his arm—so much support as was in it, for it began to tremble in her close pressure and even with her slight weight. He was so young, such a child, to encounter such a sudden tempest of feeling; but he did not in any way return the mute caress with which from time to time she pressed that boyish arm. It is seldom, perhaps, that a mother is to a child as she thinks she is; but she consoled herself that he was angry, and had perhaps some right to be angry now; and she waited until they had reached the house—the little home full of all the associations of his life—before she told him her tale.

She had married—or rather had been married with very little consultation of her own wishes—an inexperienced girl, overcoming her own repugnances (of which, indeed, how could a mother speak to her boy?) in the belief that she was loved for the first time in her life; for she had no parents, no brothers or sisters, nobody to give her any affection. She had, however, found, even in the first fortnight of her married life, that the love which she longed for was as far from her as ever. An accident, the most foolish and purposeless—the husband getting out of a railway carriage and being left behind as the train went on—had left her, troubled, miserable, alone, with a whole day to think over her fate. And in that moment, in her girlish rashness, she had decided it. She had escaped, leaving no clue. Chance had brought her to Cagnes, the little smiling, ancient town on its hill, which had pleased her fancy. It was a place where no one was likely to look for the little runaway English bride; and though she had no doubt that pursuit had been made, she had never been disturbed by any inquiries— never till the day before, when, standing accidentally in the little railway-station with John, as he must remember, she had seen her husband's face look out, and knew that she was recognised. Then she had known what would happen. She had hung about the station all day to see if he came back. And he did come back, but so ill, and in such a tempest of passion, that it had been fatal to him.

She told her tale very quietly, shedding a few tears; and she said at the end, "I do not know if it was wrong: it was breaking my marriage-vow; but I did not know when I made that vow what I was binding myself to—nor how unbearable it would be. And I have never, never regretted—oh, John! never till to-day."

"And why do you regret it to-day?" asked the boy, harshly; "because you have been found out, or because he has died?"

"Oh, John! oh, John!" cried the poor woman, covering her face with her hands.

¬

CHAPTER II

Perhaps he was not so kind as he ought to have been to his mother. At sixteen how can it be expected that a boy could enter into a woman's feelings and put himself in her place? It seemed utterly wild to him—without reason, without sense, a defiance of all laws. What a thing to do! to fling off the people who belonged to you, whoever they were, because they had made a mistake about a railway train!

After her story was told, there was not very much conversation between the mother and son. He went and worked in the garden a little with great energy: which was John's chief work, for the garden formed a great part of their living,—what with the flowers, which were sent into the Nice market, and vegetables, which were the staple of their own food. And then suddenly he threw down his spade and went out, feeling that he could think it all over better if he were out of reach of any call upon him. He went up the valley, which was so green and sweet—the valley where farther up the violets are grown in furrows like corn, filling the air with sweetness, though they have no higher destination than the greasy boilers of Grasse. John clambered up one side of the hills to a favourite spot among the trees, whence he could see all the wide landscape stretching out before him—the soft sea, in all its shimmering tints of blue, and the long cape of Antibes stretching far out into the water. There were not many of his comrades who cared at all for the view; but it was inarticulately dear to John, who never said anything about it, but climbed to that mount of vision in all his perplexities, to take counsel of the boundless horizon and the long-stretching lines of the hills. But to-night it made his heart sick to look out upon that vast panorama of sea and sky, one more blue than the other, crossed by soft whitenesses of cloud and shadow, and looking like one quarter, at least, of the great globe. How often had he gazed out over it, and thought of his sailor father nearing home! Oh, the fine vision of that hope unfulfilled, that life so full of gentle wishes long subdued, of longing love and expectation, and almost certainty of happiness to come! And now he was told that it had never been. This it was which filled him with the very rage of grief and loss. Hot tears like fire filled his eyes. No father, no sailor coming out of the unknown, with light in his face to bless the memory of his child!—no father at all, except that horrible figure at the hotel, the swollen and bloated face, the dead glare under the eyelashes, the ignoble countenance. John was French enough to fling himself down on the hillside, amid the bushes of cistus, and dig his hands into the soil in a paroxysm of pain and misery, though he was also English enough to be ashamed of this frenzy, and to pick himself up and do his best to subdue it. Must he give it up for ever, that vision which had accompanied him during almost all his conscious life? She said it had never come from her—she had not deceived him; and perhaps it was true, though he was quite unconscious that he had never betrayed to her that fancy and longing of his heart; but, at least, she must have known what the neighbours said—the story that some one must have invented, but which every one held as the truth, and he most of all. John wondered whether if he had ever betrayed that ideal she would have let him know that it was an illusion, and that his real father was very different. He doubted very much if she would have done so, or if he would ever have known the truth at all, except for the catastrophe of to-day; and with this thought a chill doubt of his mother and of everything in earth and heaven came into the boy's heart. Who would ever tell him the truth if she did not? and was he sure that he knew everything now, and that it might not change again, like a dissolving view? The foundations of the world were shaken, and he was not sure that at any moment the earth might not yawn and a gulf open before his very feet.

The day was darkening when he came down again from the hill. Lights were twinkling all round the horizon: the steady light on the point of Antibes, the little revolving one on the pierhead of that little town, which he had always been so fond of watching as it went and came; and in the distance, towards the east, the light of the Cap Fêrat standing out into the sea; and the little glimmer of the household lamps of Cagnes mounting in steps upon the hillside; and below a little flame from the railway and the *cafés* that surrounded it. When he turned his eyes from the sea, it was the latter that attracted John with a sort of sinister fascination. It flared out vulgarly, coarsely, into the night, so unlike the charm of those beneficent, calm lights held up on every side to guide the travellers at sea; but it drew his feet unwillingly towards the place where that horrible event had occurred which had changed all John's life for him. His father—not the father who slept under that silent shining of the Mediterranean, a father who had never been, except in the boy's dreaming soul, but whom he could not part with, who was a portion of himself—but the other, the dreadful reality, lying in the bare white room yonder, uncovered, in the clothes which seemed to make that reality more horrible still—was he still lying there as before, like a wreck, like something cast up by a wave, lying straight out, the head lower than the feet, in that awful way? John shuddered; but he was drawn, he knew not how, to the place, and stood in the dark opposite for a moment, looking at the glaring light and the men who sat at the round tables in front of the *café*, talking loud and all together. They had discussed the event till it was exhausted, and all the new lights it threw on *l'Anglaise*, Madame Jeanne; but now they had returned to their natural topics, and were as noisy as ever, quite unmoved by any recollection of that lump of ended being which lay up-stairs. He stood and watched, with a strange throb of horror and rebellion against that thing to which it appeared he owed his life, and at the same time with a sense of grievance in the carelessness of the men who paid no respect to it. As he stood there, the half-closed shutters were softly opened in that room, and a shadowy figure came out upon the balcony. John knew by the white cap that it was a Sister.

"*Pour l'amour de Dieu taisez-vous, mes amis,*" said a soft voice, audible in the interval of the clamour below.

There were faint lights in the room into which she went silently back. Charity was watching over him, then,—watching and praying. John went away home very quietly, overawed, and saying nothing even to himself.

He was too late for supper, which was arranged on the table, though untouched; but he had no mild reproach to encounter, as he would have had in an ordinary case. His mother was seated at a little table, with a piece of paper and a pencil in her hand, writing, and then pausing to count her words and strike out now one, now another. She was saying over those words to herself aloud as he came in, and only looked up at him, not saying anything to him, continuing her task.

"Beg you to come to guard my son's interests. Beg you come, for boy's sake. Beg come— —" She went on, withdrawing or changing a word every time.

"What is it, mother?" said John. These were almost the first words he had addressed to her since he had heard her story.

"I am writing a telegram. It will cost a great deal to go to England; I am trying to put it in as few words as possible."

"May I see it, mother?"

How happy it is to have a subject, something to discuss which is not the one absorbing thing, at the time of a great crisis! The two came together once more over this paper which had to be written so carefully. There was very little money in the house. Indeed they did not live much on money, these two people, but on their garden, and by simple ways of barter, with the smallest possible dependence on any currency; and to have to pay so many francs at the post office for a telegram struck them with dismay. In this point

Madame Jeanne, who had lived for one part of her life in a country and class given to telegrams, was more at her ease than John, to whom it seemed incredible that as much as five francs, or even more, could be given for a mere message—a thing that was nothing, and benefited nobody. He asked her a great many questions on the subject.

"Who is this?" he said; "and why do you want him to come here?"

"He is my guardian, John."

"Your guardian? But he does not seem to have taken much care of you, mother."

"He did, as far as he knew. He thought that to marry me to some one who—would take care of me—was the best."

"But then he did not choose well—or else——"

"I was to blame, John. I don't want to clear myself. I was young, and I thought only of the moment and not of what was to follow. I didn't even know," she said, dropping her head abashed before her boy, "that God was going to send me a—child to comfort me. Oh!" she cried, taking his hand suddenly, "I am not sorry! I am not sorry, though I am to blame. How do I know how you would have been brought up? And we have lived very happily; and you are a good boy, a good boy, my own John——"

He let her cry upon his shoulder, but he did not know what answer to make. He could not yet forgive her the loss of his father—the sailor who had never come home. But his voice was more gentle as he said, "Mother, if it is to be sent to-night, I must run to post with it now."

The telegram was made up at last. It was not written in telegramese, and it cost more money than it ought. The reader will see how many words might have been spared. It was addressed to C. Courthill, Esq., Grosvenor Square, London.

> "You will have heard I am here and my husband dead. Have been living here all time. Beg you come take care of my boy.—Jane."

He ran with it all the way, counting the francs in his hand—eight francs, enough to have bought a great many things. He grudged the money very much, wondering why there should be so much haste, and if a letter would not have done as well, which would have cost twenty-five centimes and no more. But there are some things in which even a big boy must give in to his mother, especially when all the francs are hers. He returned more slowly, thinking this time more than he would have acknowledged of his supper.

And thus the day that had made such a change in his life, and indeed made far more changes than he had the least idea of, came at last to an end.

In the morning he said more cheerfully, "Don't be so discouraged, little mother. When the funeral is over and those people have come and gone, we shall forget everything, and things will go on just as before."

Madame Jeanne shook her head; but she was thankful for the softening in her boy's tone, and said no more.

He thought a great deal during the interval that elapsed before the arrival of the people who had been summoned from England and the formal funeral which followed immediately. It was not that there was any connection between this event, so far as he realised it, and the development of his own life. But a touch of fiery stimulation had been given to his mind, and his thoughts flew beyond this very unpleasant, but, so far as he was aware, inoperative catastrophe, to the real matter which was of importance, which was, what was going to be done with him? He was not so submissive as a French boy. Something of the English breeding his mother had given him, and the English books he had read, had given independence to his thoughts. He had made up his mind not to settle down, half-peasant, half-villager, to the lowly life of the country, to grow vegetables for his own nourishment and flowers for the market at Nice. He wanted to go away from Cagnes—to go to Paris, perhaps even to London, and study art. Since ever he had known himself, he had loved a pencil beyond any other toy. He had scribbled upon stones, upon palings, upon doors, upon every wall that came in his way, since ever he could remember. The consequence was, that he had got as far unaided as a kind of caricature—perhaps the first step, as it is the easiest. He made sketches of the country-folk, which were very amusing to their neighbours, getting a kind of flying likeness with a burlesque touch, with the end that everybody was delighted by all the portraits in his picture-gallery except their own. His ardent desire was to go to Paris to perfect himself in his art, to become a great painter, and to send home a great deal of money to his mother. Perhaps he did not think very much of the lonely life she would lead, of the change it would make to her; but he did think of acquiring a very handsome house, perhaps the chateau which was on the very top of the hill, and commanded all the views—on the one side the sea, with Antibes on its promontory, and on the other the mountains and the valley, the great Rocher of St Jeannet, which cleaves the lines of little hills asunder, and the snow of the Maritime Alps behind. What backgrounds he would get for his pictures in that beautiful country! He would come back from Paris and the studios as soon as he was rich enough, and live there in the lovely spring, and study and make sketches, and live the old life which made his mother happy. Yes, he would take up that life again, and she would be as happy as ever, if she had only the patience to wait. But after this great disturbance John did not feel as if he could settle. He had said that things should go on just as before; but when his mother shook her head John's mind too made a great and sudden start, and he saw that things could not be as they had been before. At sixteen one is almost a man: the other lads were beginning to think of the time when they must draw their numbers, when independence would begin; he, as an Englishman, would not be called upon to draw any number; but he could not live upon his mother any longer—he must get to his work and begin his life.

He had resolved to talk to her about this the day after the funeral, when everything, he thought, would be over, the Englishmen gone back again, and the ordinary conditions of existence resumed. It might be hard upon her after all the excitement; but John felt that he would be cruel only to be kind, and that it would be best to have it over. The looks of the Englishmen did not altogether please him. He was French enough to have a little hostile feeling to these two middle-aged, or rather old gentlemen (as he thought), with their looks of exaggerated gravity and trouble, who came into his mother's cottage as if they disapproved of it highly, as if it were something they had a right to interfere with. What right had they to interfere? They had, of course, to do with the funeral, at which John, in a very curious jumble of feeling, had to walk as chief mourner, not knowing whether he were more gratified by the importance of his position, or overawed by the melancholy, or anxious to have all the fuss over and everything settled back into the old lines. But he was angry when both the Englishmen accompanied him back, all being over, to his home. He did not want them there again. He wanted to be rid of them, now that their business was completed. And they talked to each other over his head, as it were, as they walked along, amusing themselves by discourse and discussions of what was to happen to a certain "he" with whom they seemed to have a great deal to do. "He must be made a ward in Chancery," one said, "and proper guardians appointed"; and "his education will have to be attended to," said the other,—"of course he can have had none hitherto." "What a chance for a lad like that!" John felt a little sorry for the boy, whoever he was, whom they discussed like this. Madame Jeanne rose to meet them as they came in, darkening the little house with their big, black shadow. Everything was in solemn order to receive them, and she herself dressed in black, looking as John had never seen her look before. She was very pale, but had a kind of dignity about her in her black dress. She bade them be seated as a princess might have done, and then she drew John close to her and took his hand in hers.

"I understand," she said, her voice rather faint but firm, "that you have come now to speak to me about my boy."

"There are a great many things to speak to you about, Janey," said Mr Courthill, the man to whom the telegram had been sent. "You could not expect that our departed friend should have shown you any consideration after the way in which you treated him."

"I expect nothing," said Madame Jeanne, hurriedly; "I am quite willing to allow that I deserve nothing from him."

"And he was not aware that you had a child."

"No; I did not," she said, drooping her head, "know myself—or else it might have made a difference."

"I am glad to hear you say that—I am very glad to hear you say that; all the same, when you did know, it was your duty to have communicated a fact which was of so much importance, and which would, as you must have known, have given him so much pleasure."

Madame Jeanne shivered a little, as John felt, but she made no reply.

"Is not this losing time?" said the other lawyer. "You will have opportunities afterwards of reading lessons to Mrs Rothbury, Courthill. She may have taken a foolish step—she certainly did—but we can't change that now. She might have had a better provision had she acted otherwise. Our part is to tell her what is the state of affairs now——"

"I am coming to that. I only want you to feel, Janey, that you have no right to expect any consideration——"

"I expect nothing," she said—"nothing!" dropping John's hand to clasp her own together. Then she turned to him again, and took it back in hers. "The only thing that vexes me," she said, sadly, "is that I have ruined the boy. I ought to have thought—Who was I, to keep the joy all to myself? I acknowledge humbly that his father ought to have known."

"I am glad," said Mr Courthill, "to see you in such a proper frame of mind."   —

"Mrs Rothbury," said the other, impatiently, "I don't see that my part is to moralise. I must tell you without any more circumlocution that your husband has died intestate. There is no will."

"There is no will?" She looked from one to another with the blank of ignorance. What this meant for her or for her child she was without the faintest suspicion. "Indeed," she repeated, earnestly, "I have no right to anything. I never expected anything. I only hoped perhaps that, being proved to have a son——"

"His next of kin," said the lawyer, "and only heir."

There was a great silence in the room—a poor little cottage room, white wooden chairs and table; nothing that could be called a carpet on the floor;

roses waving in at the windows in the luxuriance of a Provençal spring, but no other ornament. The boy's acute ears took in the words without understanding them; the mother repeated them vaguely with a kind of consternation.

"His heir! what do you mean? what do you mean?" she said.

"Janey, though you deserved no consideration, no generosity——"

She turned from this moralising voice to the stranger on the other side. "What do you mean?" she said.

"You, of course, will take your lawful portion as the widow. We are aware, Mrs Rothbury, that you have not, perhaps, fulfilled the duties of a wife—but otherwise you have done your husband no wrong. There is nothing that can be objected to in your conduct—and your son is his father's natural and only heir. I have long wished him to make a will; but he never would—guided, we may believe, by a higher instinct. It was what he wished for before everything, a son who would be his heir."

Then Madame Jeanne, who had been so calm, hid her face in her hands. The tears burst forth in a flood. "I have no right, no right to anything of his. I have kept John from him," she cried. "How was I to know it was the desire of his life?"

John caught the strange news at last with a sudden glow of illumination. He stood in his clumsy peasant youthfulness, unable to say a word, or to give any evidence of his excitement, gazing at the speaker with wide-open eyes.

"And, my boy," the lawyer continued, "you must understand your responsibility, and give your mind to the training which will make you fit for it; for you will be a very rich man."

An inarticulate sound escaped from the boy's throat. Oh, the sailor who had never come home, who had left his son nothing but love and honour! It was the anguish of the pang with which at last and for ever that tender apparition floated away, which wrung that cry out of John's heart.

"But, mind you, you deserved nothing from him," said the voice of the other man, see-sawing with uplifted hand from his chair—the guardian who had delivered John's mother to her fate.

"And I would rather have nothing," she cried. "I do not deny it. I did not do my duty by him,—how can I take anything from him? And I can make my own living, as I have done so long—if you will only think of the boy."

"Mother!" said John, tremulous, with his eyes shining, "it appears we cannot take our own way again. We are not the only people in the world. I am worse off than you, because I have lost what I believed in—my father; and even my mother in a way. But now I've seen him," he added, with a shiver, "and I don't blame you. If you had only told me from the first!"

"He was an excellent man of business—a very successful man—a father you would have been proud of," Mr Courthill said.

Another shudder of emotion shook the boy for a moment. "Anyhow," he said, "that's the truth at last." He set himself very square on his feet and faced the two Englishmen with that curious sense of hostility to them, as if it were they who had injured him; and yet an attitude which was entirely British, though he was not aware of it. "And I'll stick to it. I am not one for running away," said John.

This is not the usual way of accepting a great fortune. There was no elation in his mind over an advance which was almost miraculous. The two men stood, not knowing what to make of the boy in his curious mixed nationality. To his own consciousness he had lost far more than he gained: but how were these strangers to understand that?

This was how John Rothbury, not without a sharp pang, found out his true name and his real position in life.

THE WHIRL OF YOUTH

CHAPTER I

John Rushton's early life had been so peculiar that it was not wonderful if he found himself very much at sea when he was first plunged into the curious conventional life of an English University. He was older than most of the young men whom he found there—yet not very old, if he had not been already knocked about the world a good deal and filled with many experiences: and the first year at least passed over his head in great confusion, during which he let himself go with the stream in whatsoever eddy or current he might find himself,—which perhaps was not very profitable for his moral being, nor yet for his education properly so called. Life in the University is even more than in other places a congeries of whirls, one round or dance of wildly rushing figures, each encircling some swaying standard of its own, dance of the Mænads or of the Berserkers going on for ever in a mode that sets aside all that peacefulness of study and learning which we all, perhaps, vainly suppose is, or ought to be, found in the very atmosphere of these abodes of letters. I wonder if it ever was so. Did not the young clergy whirl too, in circles of asceticism or mutual devotion, or perhaps forbidden and secret pleasure, one trooping after another in the earliest days? Certainly the young Cavaliers must have done so, and likewise the young Puritans each treading in the other's steps, holding the other's coats, rushing round and round. It is not Fashion or Society alone that puts up those unsteady flagstaff's and leads the wild dance around them. It is nature, we must believe, since they exist everywhere. John got into the rush of the idle, and flew along in a monotonous circle among them like the merry-go-round at a fair. He did not like it much, but the whirl caught him and plucked at his feet and set him all in motion in the pathway of the others. And then he fell farther down into a wilder rush, still the whirl (so called) of pleasure and dissipation: and then recovering with an effort got back into the rush of the cultured and æsthetic and whirled through the world of pictures and furniture and poetry, finding no rest for the sole of his foot. His head was a little dazed with all these gyrations: he was a steady fellow, in fact, liking to feel firm ground under him, and to live his own way. And it was chiefly because his guardians and best friends—though in fact the sway of the guardians was virtually over—were intent upon conforming him to the recognised models, and subduing his instinct to be independent, a word into which they read other meanings, that he had come to the University at all, a place for which he felt that he was not fitted by previous training, nor likely to do much good in any way. At the beginning of his second year John returned a little ashamed of himself, feeling the strong likelihood that he would be led into one or another of his previous follies, and the almost conviction that he would find himself spinning like the rest in the contagion of youth and activity before he knew.

He was pondering upon this with a little discouragement of heart, wondering within himself with a rueful touch of humour when the first bevy of comrades would arrive and which it would be, when a summons came to him to go and see the Warden, which was rather an alarming call, considering that the work which had been given to him to occupy his vacation had not been done any more than the work of the previous year. He pulled on accordingly that shabby little pinafore (worn the wrong way about) of black stuff which in Oxford is called a gown, and took up his cap and went across the quadrangle, green with the chilly greens of October though sprinkled with yellow leaves which every breath of wind brought down. The Warden was not an ordinary or common Don (may the rash pen be pardoned which combines such words), but a man of note and of judgment, though like other men he had his weaknesses. The chief of these was that he preferred the young men of family and great position who were put into his hands, to the humbler crew of nobodies who swarmed around them. In the Warden, however, this was not a weakness, but a matter of principle. When it is a weakness it is called by the opprobrious name of snobbishness or tuft-hunting, or other still more disagreeable appellations; but when it is a principle, it is a very lofty one, and means that it is a finer thing to exert influence over those who will have a great deal of power in their hands, than over those who will have none—and that accordingly to make a great man wise and good is a greater achievement than to influence a poor one, even if the poor one might by chance be made into even a greater paragon of virtue than the great. This is a perfectly solid and defensible principle—when it is a principle, as we say; and altogether different from that love of honours and titles which has been attributed to other heads of houses in a less elevated way. The Warden received John with an austere smile, followed by a look of great gravity. He said, "I hear, Mr Rushton, and have unfortunately observed, that very little work was got from you last year,—that, in short, your first year at the University was to a great degree a year lost to you and no credit to the college."

"I am afraid, sir," said John, hanging his head, "that it is quite true."

"And now we are at the beginning of another academical year, I should like to know what you intend. Are you to join the ranks of the idlers for good—or perhaps I should say for bad—or do you mean to make an effort to do better? I always like to know how a man means to begin: then we know where we are."

"I am sure you know, sir, better than any one," said John, plucking up a heart and facing his monitor, "that a man never means it to begin with, even if he does badly. It's not the intention that is in fault."

"Sometimes. I admit, that is the case—often, perhaps; but I am not sure, Mr Rushton, that to yield weakly to a passing temptation is not as bad, or nearly so, as to begin with a plan of merely pleasing oneself. It comes to the same thing in the end."

"I did not mean it as an excuse, sir. I was merely stating a fact."

"Very well; allowing the fact—am I to understand that you are going to let yourself be blown about by every wind, and begin without any intention at all?"

"That's logical, I don't doubt, sir," said John; "but naturally that is not what I mean."

The Warden gave up the point, and resumed in a different tone. "I don't suppose," he said, "from the opportunities I have had of seeing your work, so much, or so little rather, as it has been, that you have any very high expectations of success at the University—of distinguishing yourself, in short?"

No man, however stupid, likes to be told that he has no expectations of success; and John reddened in spite of himself. But he was very sensible, and replied with a sort of laugh, "No; I never thought I was clever, sir, if that is what you mean?"

The Warden did not deny that that was what he meant. But he said, "With that conviction, and not much enthusiasm for work, will you forgive me for asking what brought you to the University at all?"

John laughed outright at this, being struck by the humour of the question. "If every man that came up was asked that, sir," he said, "a great many of us would be in the same box, I'm afraid."

The Warden was not a man who disliked a straightforward answer. He preferred a young man who stood to his guns. "That is true enough," he said; "but there are other motives in many of these cases. Parents insist on it—or future prospects demand it. Some men would find their future profession barred to them without a University education; or, at least, would find it more difficult to get on; or would be discredited more or less among the people they are naturally with. But you, I believe, don't contemplate entering any profession?"

The rapid reflection in John's mind that he was evidently not one of those who was considered to be naturally in the society of people who cared for a University degree, was inevitable; and it perhaps moved him to the unintentional impertinence of a personal reference. "You don't say that to Scarfield, sir," he said, quickly, "and he has no more intention of entering a profession than I have." He said it quickly, and repented it even more quickly than he spoke.

"Lord Scarfield," said the Warden, calmly, "is a man who will have a great deal of influence in his generation. He will be what is called a great man in his county; he may be a power for good or evil according as his mind is trained now. I make this explanation for the sake of the prejudices which are abroad on the subject, though it is one you have no right to ask, and it has no bearing on your case."

"I beg your pardon, sir," said John; "I know I had no right to say that. I'm aware," he added, "that I'm nobody; and it's of no consequence whether I take my degree or not. But perhaps, sir, that's rather a new view."

"It may be a new view. I do not bind myself to old views. I have heard that you are or will be rich, Mr Rushton; but you have no stake in the country, nothing to bind you to it, and, I hear, rather a love of wandering. You don't want to be fitted for the exercise of great influence or to fill a great place. You have no parents, I understand, to insist upon any special career, or whose place you would fill in the world."

"It is true," said John, very red and hot, "that I never saw my father; and that he left me only money, and no place to fill, as you say, sir. But I have a mother whom I am as anxious to please as if she were a duchess, and no antecedents that I know of that would deprive me of a man's usual responsibilities. But if you think, sir, that I am no credit, and had better withdraw from the college——"

The Warden interrupted with a wave of the hand, and indeed John's voice was somewhat choked in his throat. "I mean nothing of the kind, nothing of the kind, Mr Rushton! You are a young man of sense. If you think a moment you will understand my meaning—which is that, having no special incentive, either within yourself or without, to intellectual work, I see no object you can have in remaining at the University, if it is only as a method of amusing yourself,—if, in short, this year is to be a repetition of last year, I think it well for you to turn the matter over in your mind. If,—that is the problem. It is very likely," said the Warden, holding out his hand to be shaken, in token of dismissal, "that you have it in you to solve it in the right way."

John went out from this interview with a great buzzing in his head, and the sensation of having been pricked up with red-hot irons or goaded with sharp bayonet points, for the shock was physical as well as mental. His pulses went at railroad speed. The blood in his veins stung him, it flew so fiercely to the heart and back again. Such a commotion within him must have been as good for his health as the strongest dose of the best tonic ever known. A beggar like Scarfield, he said to himself, a mild dilettante puppy, to be coddled and cooked into a great man—and I, nobody! A wild young brute like So-and-so to be of importance to his country—and I, no matter, no account! If the Warden had meant to humble him, it was a bad way to do it; if he had meant to stimulate him, to stir up all his energies, to taunt and defy and bully him into well-doing—then it might be a queer way, but it was an effectual way. And no doubt that was what the Warden meant. He had been too long accustomed to the process of flaying young men to care very much whether it hurt them or not. If it hurt them, so much the better, perhaps. The hopeless kind were those whom it did not hurt.

John went back to his rooms and busied himself in arranging his books—those books especially which he had been required to work up during the vacation, and which, alas, he had scarcely looked at—which had been the immediate cause of the Warden's address. He looked at them with his head on one side as if he had been looking at a picture, and asked himself why he had not paid the proper attention to his orders, and thus put himself above the reach of such a reproof? But he knew very well why his vacation work had been neglected. He had spent these merry months in the society and the occupations which he loved best, among a varying company of painters, now in one region of beauty, now in another, in the fresh air, in the roughest quarters, drinking in sunshine and dew, light and shade, to the very depths of his being. Ah, that was life! No doubt it was a whirl too; and the young men rushed and circled round with the others in clouds of smoke, in noisy rooms where no man could hear his neighbour speak—sometimes, too, with equivocal associates enough—a noisy ring, caring for nothing in heaven or earth except "effects" and points of view and tones of colour. But probably, because that was his own way, John lingered upon it, seeing all its good things and none of its evils. A man could not be altogether idle among all these busy men. He had to make a dash at an effect, to put in a study, to fling colour on canvas somehow, or he could not keep his place among them. It was not a mere rush of foolish feet, a mere following one or another in a hackneyed round. He rushed to his own door and secured it, "sporting his oak," according to a term which has probably grown old-fashioned, against the inroad of those foolish feet which he heard afar off clattering upon the staircase. He had to think: he would not be driven away from his point by any invasion to-day.

But when the attempt upon his doors, and the shouts that accompanied it, had died away, and the staircase was for a few minutes silent again, and John sat down among his books to think over that problem, his mind, instead of grappling with it, floated away to the scenes of his holiday, to the wilds of Brittany and the trees of Fontainebleau, between which he had divided himself. He had not gone far afield. He was not an adventurous fellow. The places where everybody went were good enough for him. He followed in his mind with a smile many a riotous expedition, setting out in a tumult of shouts and fun, but gradually stilling into quietude as one man after another came to the "bit" he wanted, or stopped short arrested in a corner to record an impression, or dashed with flying touches an effect of the ever-changing light; while the old fellows, the steady, middle-aged men who had outgrown the great hopes and ideals which still flushed the horizon of the young ones, settled themselves and pegged away at pictures which were called, not according to their subjects, but by their authors' names, as a Dupin, a Merryweather, and so on—as recognisable as the painter's card among all the bands of the cognoscenti. A smile came upon his face as he wandered among these pleasing recollections—and then he came to with a sudden start, and to the sense that he was not in the least considering his problem, but only living over again the life that he loved best. What a life it was! But he must put a stop to these reminiscences; he must think of the question before him. Then a smile came over John's face as he asked himself whether if he were to send the Warden a picture or a drawing, representing the best he could do—that would please the head of the college as well as the essay which John knew he could not do half so well? He remembered having heard some one say that if a certain minor canon with a beautiful voice had sung something out of the "Messiah" when he went up into the pulpit, instead of insisting on preaching a very poor sermon, how much better it would have been,—how much more edifying for his audience and satisfactory for himself. Then John pulled himself up again. The only distinct thing before him was that he did not mean to allow himself to be beaten. They should see that he was not to be bullied out of the University.

"If the work has to be done," he said to himself, "why, I must do it. I was a fool not to do it when I had time. But I am not going to be beaten. I shan't write myself down an ass to please the Warden. And here goes!"

Did he accomplish that essay? Did he read his books, the books which he ought to have read in the Long Vacation? All I can say at this moment is that he set himself down very squarely at his table as if he meant it, placed one of them open before him, one which he had already looked into, dipped his pen into the ink — —

But just then there came another tumult of footsteps up the staircase, and kicks against the closed doors. What a noise they made, one encouraging another to "sing out" to him, "Rushton, I say! Jack, old fellow! Confound you, can't you open?" they shouted, and a great deal more; while John sat and grinned to himself within the castle gate.

CHAPTER II

The essay, I need not say, on which John laboured, inking himself body and soul, was not by any means finished at one sitting. He toiled at it during the whole of the first week which was the term of grace. It was not a good essay. The books, read in a hurry and very imperfectly, did not convey to him by any means all the sense that was in them; his remarks were very conventional, and, if truth must be told, commonplace. That was not John's line, neither is it by any means the only one in which a man even at the University can distinguish himself. He may row or he may run, which all the world knows are still more ready ways to distinction, or he may play racquets or something else for the 'Varsity, or he may at least make a good score in the college eleven—all of which things count, at least, as much as essays. John, however, did none of these. He knew more of some things, and these not inconsiderable things, than some of the Dons, and he was no more to be compared with the silly young undergraduates who carried him (sometimes) away in their whirls, than Hyperion to a Satyr. Alas! that happens often enough: it is a mystery, one of the greatest within mortal ken, but none of us can tell why. With John it was different: it was in the carelessness of strength, not the fatal lapse of weakness, that he went astray.

But he did not know how to write an essay: he did it against the grain, and knowing all the time how bad it was, even in the midst of the current which soon began again to rush around him. He was still sitting at it labouring to finish it, seeing land he thought, and panting and struggling to get to that blessed shore, when his rooms filled one afternoon with a crowd that was very much at leisure though it had a hundred things to do. There was a capital match on at the Parks, and he must come to see it, they cried. And there were two fellows going out for a spin on the river, on whose heads a great many bets were laid; and there was—but it will not be expected of me that I should know what was going on in an afternoon in October to occupy a band of boys calling themselves men, and agog after any and every amusement. A few sat on the table dangling their legs, and shutting out the light from John's laboured page, while the others stood about—one pair calling out of the window over their shoulders remarks upon the passers-by, and another pair inside lunging at each other with John's foils, and a few more turning over the yellow novels of which he had always a great stock. "I say, Rushton," they cried, "come along; you're losing all the afternoon on that rot. We shan't see half of the match if you don't look sharp."

"Who would have thought of Jack turning out a sap," cried another, who was from Eton, and used the language of that valuable seminary.

"A fellow with his pockets full of money," cried another, "and nobody to call him over the coals."

"Oh, look here," cried the men at the window; "here's old Chortles going out for a walk, and Peters after him. Oh, you fellows, shouldn't you like to be Peters, going out for an hour and a half's *viva voce, ambulando!* that's what it is to be a pet of old Chortles, oh ho! oh ho!"

Chortles, it may be here said, was an affectionate nickname, or otherwise, applied to the Warden, on account of a peculiarity in his voice.

"Jove," cried the others, "if there isn't Scarfield sailing along with the Jolly Bruiser right across old Chortles' nose. By George, what's going to happen? Chortles' got an eye like a hawk, though he pretends to wear glasses, and Scarry, poor wretch, is as blind as a bat. Oh, good Lord!" cried the spectators, in tones of awe.

Three other young men precipitated themselves on the shoulders of the foregoing to see the fun, as they said: that a dilettante young nobleman, the pink of propriety, should know the Jolly Bruiser at all, was an unthought-of delight, and all the company crowded to see, if not with their own yet with others' eyes.

"Oh, Lord!" reported the first speaker, "to see Scarry sailing on, with a deal of side, too—not a thought of what he's coming to. Bravo, Peters! he's putting up a signal, but the blind ass doesn't see. Bruiser's in a dead funk now, trying to run away—Scarry's got hold of his arm. Oh, *by* Jove!"

"What's up now?" they all cried.

"Peters' behaving like a brick," said another, over his shoulder. "Pointing over to the other side—to Shrimpton's, by all that's dreadful!— where the last thing out is Chortles himself as large as life. Out of the frying-pan into the fire for Peters, eh?"

"Did he think he'd do it, then?" said another. "I say, you fellows, don't squeeze a man flat! Chortles ain't so innocent as he looks, not by a long way. Gives a nod, as much as to say I'll come to you by-and-by; and goes for Scarry straight— —"

Here there was a chorus of laughter, suddenly subdued.

"Silence, you fellows! he's looking this way. Just one glance, Rushy, but he sees it's your windows, and you're in for it. Oh, Jove! to see the Warden touching his hat to Jim Tucker! Jim squashed, the unjolliest Bruiser you ever saw, half a foot shorter at the least, makes tracks—and, Lord! to see Chortles holding Scarry with his eye! I'd give all my lands and castles to hear what he says!"

"Ah! it's all very well for Scarry," said another—"cool as a cucumber, don't you know, with nothing against him, and a title at his back; whereas if it were you or me——"

"Explaining he is, by Jove! Don't you see old Chortles shutting him up? Come to me this evening after hall—that's what he's saying, bet you anything! Oh, I wish I could be there to see; and, Lord! there he goes across to Shrimpton's: Peters has remembered, poor old man! He's being led to execution, and he knows it. It was all to save that prig Scarry, who will never lift a finger for him."

"I say, you fellows, are we going to stay here all the afternoon?" said— this incident being over—another of the band. John had been sitting, his pen suspended in his hand, during the little episode above described. The cloud of young men at the window had shut out the light, while the cries and stamps of the fencers who had carried on through all the tumult came in now suddenly like a solo after a chorus. John's ideas were not very quick to come at any time, and that last bit of struggling towards the end of a very unwilling literary exercise is perhaps the worst of all. You are breathless with sight of the shore so near at hand, and longing to get to it. He had not been able to refuse his interest to these incidents as seen from the window, and of course he wanted to be out in the fresh air, and the contagion of restlessness in the others—who could not keep either legs or arms quiet for a moment, and now began to sprawl all about his room, some taking sides in the mock contest between the fencers, some pulling about his books, his photographs on the mantelpiece, and even his portfolios of sketches in the corner—gained on him in spite of himself: and the obstinacy of pride was not perhaps a very sustaining motive, though indeed it was this alone, and not any pleasure in work or desire to do it well, which chained him to that hopeful manuscript. "I wish you'd go," he said, with the straightforwardness which was not out of place in that society. "Brunton, there's drinks in the cupboard; you know where to find them. Help yourselves, for goodness' sake, and go! I must get this confounded thing before I stir, and how can I get on with all of you ballyragging about?"

"Rubbish!" said Brunton. "Leave it till after. You can get it done another time."

"What other time?" said John, setting his elbows square on the table.

"I never knew Jack to be a sap before," said the Eton man. "Come on, and leave him to his fate."

Then one detachment went rushing down the staircase, filling the air with the tumult of their steps and voices. But the fencers and their audience still kept the ground.

"What a deuced waste of time!" said Brunton, turning over the sheets. "By George, Jack, you'll spoil the college! Look here, Gaison, and blush if you can for your confounded swagger of a place. See what we can do here — and the first week of term, too!"

"Rushy, my boy, you're too good to live!" said the other man.

"I'll tell you what!" said John, in his impatience — but he checked himself, for the fencers had put up their foils and were preparing to move.

"Come along," they said; "let's look up the Bruiser and see how he likes to meet old Chortles full face in the High. Let's go and have a game of billiards. Let's have a stroll somewhere. Let's do something. That fellow with his pen is enough to bore a man out of his life."

Brunton alone stayed, the most intimate, but not the most desirable, of John's friends. He was intimate solely because he had made up his mind to be so, independent of John's sentiments, perhaps because he had an admiration for John — which was the most flattering way of explaining it, and even over a sensible fellow like John Rushton exercised a certain agreeable influence — perhaps for other reasons. He had sought him by night and day. He had always been at hand when the young man wanted diversion, or even merely a reason for amusing himself — and the consequence was that Brunton had grown into a necessity, a sort of accompaniment to John's life. He had helped himself to some of the drinks in the cupboard, and now sat astride on a chair with his glass in his hand staring across the back of it at John's composition which had been resumed with doubtful success. John was unspeakably burdened and angered by the presence of this spectator, but it is not so easy to dismiss a single visitor as it is to adjure a crowd to go away. At length "I say, old fellow," Brunton said.

John made a movement of impatience with his hand, and laboured on.

"I say, when are you coming down by Iffley, the Old Hatchet way? What jolly days we had there last term. By the way, there's some one there — — Beg pardon, old man, if I'm interrupting — —"

"Of course you're interrupting," cried John. "Look here. I'm going to finish this before I budge, if the devil himself were to interfere." He threw down his pen and looked his friend in the face. "If you've got anything to say that wants saying, say it and be done with it in the name of — —"

"Ah! I knew I'd fetch you so!" cried the other. "Well, I'll tell you what it is. There's a little person there that wants to see you very badly — and a very pretty little person too. She says, 'Ain't Mr Rushton up this year? — ain't Mr Rushton a-coming out to see us? Me and mother thinks a deal of Mr Rushton. He ain't a bit like the rest of you gentlemen.'"

"Well?" said John, red, but fierce.

"Well! I told her I'd tell you. It's a poor compliment for the rest of us, Jack: but you've only to go in and win."

"Stuff," said John, "and fudge and bosh, and whatever else there is that's silly. I understand what she means. I have some respect for a woman, whoever she is."

"Oh, respect!" said Brunton; "I expect she would like something a little warmer than that. And she says you promised to bring her something the very first day you were up — and you've been up a week — hence those tears."

"I promised to bring her something?" said John, with confusion: and then he became fiery red once more.

"Don't you think you'd like a stroll?" he added; "don't you think you'd like a game at billiards? there's always some one about that has nothing to do. It's a pity to lose the whole afternoon here."

"That's a broad hint, anyhow," cried the other, laughing. "Well, I'll go — but don't forget the Hatchet, old fellow, and the arbour in the garden, and the maid of the inn. Oh, I'm off. You need not spoil your books throwing them at me."

When he was alone John put down his pen again and took out his handkerchief and wiped his forehead. His countenance was crimson and the blood all a-boil in his veins. "What a fool I am, what a double-dashed fool I have been," he said to himself. And it was some time before he could resume the work at which he had so laboured and struggled. This was a greater interruption than anything made by the comrades who had thronged and troubled him. Yet after a while he surmounted this also, and betook himself to his work with such energy that he did at last struggle through. Well! it was not very much when it was done: probably no less valuable piece of work ever took so much time before. It had cost him a great deal of trouble, and now that it was completed it was of less than no use to anybody. The unfortunate tutor to whom he would have to read it would groan his head off before it was finished, and then it would be flung with relief into the fire. And yet he had spent all these days at it, cudgelled his brains, and almost cudgelled some of the idle fellows who had tried to stop him—for this wretched thing that was nothing, which was less than worthless! Few can perhaps see this so distinctly and with so powerful an apprehension as John did. He put it away in his desk with a grim smile, and then just as twilight was coming on he went out—to stretch his limbs and fill his lungs with that damp Oxford air which is perhaps just better than no air at all.

He was swinging along over Maudlin Bridge on his walk, "thinking hard," as he would have said, when there came suddenly up out of the twilight a little figure, which stopped and clasped its hands at sight of him, with a little cry. "Oh, is it really you, Mr Rushton?" which chimed in, in a very troublous and distressing manner, with John's thoughts.

"And is this you, Miss—Miss Millar," he said, perturbed, "so far from home?"

"Yes," she said, "it's a bit late. I've been in town doin' two or three little things for mother, and I see it was getting dark, and started runnin'—and then I thought that would just make folks stare—and then I saw as it was you——Oh, Mr Rushton, you've never been to see us—though you promised——"

"I have only been up a very little time. I—I have had a great deal to do."

"Ah," said the girl, "I know what you gentlemen has to do—just to find out every day something new to amuse yourselves—not like us as has to work."

"I assure you, Mary, it was work with me—real work, though you may not believe it," he said.

She came a little nearer to him at the sound of her own name, and, looking up, said in a subdued tone, "I'd believe anything you said."

Fiercely red once more became John, hot as with a furnace-blast: but nobody saw this, not even the pair of eyes that were for a moment lifted to his.

"I'm afraid I don't deserve as much as that," he said, humbly. "I say things I don't mean, just like the rest."

"I wouldn't believe anybody but yourself as said so. Perhaps you didn't mean it then, Mr Rushton, when you promised me *that*."

"What did I promise you, Mary?"

"Oh, Mr Rushton, you can't—you can't have forgotten! You promised me a nice gold locket with your picture in it."

They were walking on now side by side in the growing dimness, and John had not even daylight to protect him, or the expression of his face.

"My picture?" he said, in dismay. "Was I such a fool as all that? You shall have the gold locket and welcome, Mary; but you don't mean to say you would like my ugly mug inside?"

"Oh, ugly, indeed!" she said; "that's just what I should like best."

Poor John, not knowing what to say, overwhelmed with humiliation and shame, yet a little ruefully elated, too, that she should like his ugly mug, made a clumsy diversion by a total change of subject, and asked hurriedly whether anything had happened since he had been away.

"Oh, happened!" she cried, annoyed not to pursue the more interesting subject. "Nothing ever happens down Iffley way: at least no more than the old thing as mother is always at me to—marry: and I shouldn't wonder if I did some day, just for a change——"

"And who," said John, with that instant impulse to kick him, which is natural to his kind, "is the happy man?"

"Oh, you know, Mr Rushton. It's Jim Kington, as you've heard before. It's a bit hard," said the girl, with something like a suppressed sob, "after seeing so much of you gentlemen and your ways, to settle down for life with such a common man."

"Would you like, then, to marry—a gentleman?" John said. He did not know why he said it—unthinking, and yet not without a thought—wantonly, because it was dangerous, because he wanted to see what she would say.

"Oh, Mr Rushton!" she said, hanging her head: and suddenly, to his consternation, he felt a timid touch, her hand stealing within his arm.

"It wouldn't be for your good, Mary," he said, with energy. "You don't know what you would have to go through. How would you like to have people looking down upon you, laughing at you behind your back, perhaps mocking you before your face, and all your little faults made a fuss about, and nobody to be at ease with. I don't think you would find it a happy fate."

"If you think I have such bad manners, Mr Rushton! but not when I take pains. I know how to hold my head as high as the best, and give them back as good — —And, besides, I am very quick at picking things up, and I'd soon learn——"

"Some things are not so easily learned," said John. "I don't think you'd find it a happy fate."

"Oh, Mr Rushton," she said, again hanging with a little weight upon his arm, holding it close, "why should I mind if he loved me?—I'd be 'appy anywhere, if I never saw a single soul, only to pass my life along of— —'im!"

She said "'im," but meant "you," plainer than words could say. And John for a moment stood still, planting his feet on the soil, feeling the whirl catch them, the quickening current, the sweep of a senseless flood: yet conscious to the very core that he did not love the girl—not the very least in the world.

CHAPTER III

It was not very long after this evening walk that John found himself in a company of the very *élite* of his college. They knew themselves to be the *élite*, and that was enough for them. Sometimes their claim to this place was rudely assailed by outsiders; sometimes it was the subject of mockery: but this mattered very little to the certainty which filled their youthful bosoms. They did not sit upon tables and hang out of windows like the others. The table in the centre of the room was strewn with prints, with photographs from pictures, and curiosities of all kinds. There was a little Tanagra figure on the mantelpiece, holding a central place in its little shrine of red velvet, and other ornaments of equal refinement arranged with the greatest care on either side. On the wall above, usually occupied by an imbecile mirror, was a round picture which Lord Scarfield, the owner of the rooms, who had a lisp, sometimes talked of as "my Tondo" and sometimes as "my Bottithelli." It was but a copy, I need not say, but it came a great deal into his conversation. He himself sat in an antique chair with a high back, at one side of the fireplace, and his little colourless head, with its very light hair, stood out almost like an ivory from the dark damask. He was aware of the fact and liked it, and so were the other *habitués* of these rooms aware of it, feeling themselves called upon to be struck by this, as they came in one by one, and nodded at their host, and sat down somewhere within reach of the table if they could, if not in twos and little groups round the wall, where a number of abstruse conversations went on, chiefly about art, but likewise upon social subjects. John had been drawn into this supreme company chiefly on the score that he knew something practically of art, though they thought in a rude way, without a due sense of its fine affinities and symbolisms—but yet with a vulgar, practical acquaintance which no doubt counted for something. When he went in Scarfield was giving a description of that meeting with the Warden which John's other friends had watched from the window.

"He ith always very thivil," said the little lord, "but I had every reathon to expect a row. Peterth made me a thign to cut and run—but why should I cut and run? The Bruither is a perthonage in his way—and Thortles loves a perthonage. I was very punctual after Hall—likes you to be punctual, Thortles doth. Thaid he was very thorry to thee me in thuch company.

'Why, thir?' I thaid. Thortles taken aback by that. 'Why thir! do I need to thay why?' 'Yeth thir, pleath,' thaid I, and I waited for an answer. Never thaw a man more done in my life."

"Chortles like a nettle, soft as silk," cried another, losing the thread of his metaphor, "when you face him out."

"It wathn't that," said Scarfield; "it wath theething the kid in his mother'th milk—that's what it was. Very fond of talking to me about my influence and tho forth. 'You tell me, thir,' thaid I, 'to exercise a good influence. Can't do that without knowing men of all thorts, thir, don't you know? Bruither's a very thelect thort. Had a very improving conversation—lotth of information in it. Know his thort quite well now. Able to exercise influence. Just your own line, thir; what you've always thaid——"

"Bravo, Scarfield!" said his intimates, in chorus. "Nobody can manage Chortles like old Scar."

"Laughed and stared a bit, and then thays he, 'If it's from tho high a principle, Scarfield!'—and let me off. Poor old Peterth got it hot after me. You're bound to put it out on thome one when you are a Don."

"I say," said an eager youth, "where can one get anything like that jolly little statue there? I'd give a lot of money for one. I suppose it costs the eyes out of your head."

"It costs personal research and knowledge," said another, "which are more expensive still. There are imitations, however, which I daresay you'd find do just as well."

"Where could one get it, Rushton?" said the young man. "You're not so high and mighty as these other fellows—you'll give a man an answer. I've got rooms as bare as a post, and I must get them fit for a Christian to live in."

"Christian!" said the man at the other side. "Don't go in for that bastard incongruity called Christian art, for goodness' sake: and don't put questions of that sort in Scarfield's rooms. He's what they call an eclectic, don't you know—mixes up styles and things in a way that makes you shudder. A priceless Tanagra there and a heavy-jowelled Botticelli over it—saints and angels, what a mixture! I could show you——"

"A lot of sweepings of the excavations," said John, in the boy's ear.

"Oh, will you, please?" said the lad. He was eager to follow wherever the learned might lead.

"Influence is the great thing," said another, whose name was Sutton. "Give us only a little time and we'll move the world. But nobody half owns the power of it yet. I was speaking to some of those fellows by the river the other day. I told them they didn't see their power. Why, they've got the lever in their hands to upset everything, if they choose! Talk of a House of Lords! I told them they're all hereditary legislators by right of their knotty fists and the sweat of their brows!"

"Let 'em wath it off first," said Scarfield, solemnly, from his chair.

"Why should they wash it off? We must meet the people on their own ground. Would you let a little squeamish prejudice or nicety come between you and the masters of the world?"

"I take a little exception to that," said another. "Why shouldn't they all learn to be gentlemen in their habits? Oxford fellows scattered here and there in every workshop and trades union, and so forth—that is what would do good. I said so to Bristowe up at the People's Palace, as they call it. I said, 'Get a few Oxford men to sit in the reading-room and mix with those fellows.' You would see a transformation in no time."

"We took a lot to Florence, don't you remember, Bailey?" said a third young man; "all excited with what they were going to see: but they were rather puzzled, though, when we got there. We had to talk ourselves hoarse explaining—and I doubt if they were much the wiser."

"Don't say so, Harry! Lady Betty had them out to her villa to tea, and how they did stare and gaze at the landscape—don't you remember?—and then at her, in her shimmering silks, like a lady of King Arthur's court—her face full of expression, and that reminiscent expressiveness in particular, which is the special portion of——"

"Woman is the great mystery after all," said a thoughtful young man.

"The ladies did their best, I must say, out there," said Harry, neglecting this challenge. "But then those fellows expected, don't you know, that it was to be the same in town. We told them it couldn't be just the same, with all a woman's engagements. Nothing much to do in Florence, but a whirl in London—but some of them didn't see it. We told them to come to our rooms and welcome; but after a while they didn't seem to care so much for our rooms. They want social advancement, don't you see—and to make friends there will be of use."

"The Bruither, tho far as I could make out," said Scarfield, "wanths a public-house—thays they all come to public-houthes in the course of time. And that's his ambition—if you like to call it thocial advancement, you can."

"The Bruiser is abnormal," said Bailey. "He's a creation of false needs and false interests, so far as Oxford is concerned. Curiosity to know what such a being is like must have been your motive, Scarfield: for I ask what would the highest illumination and the purest influence do for a man like that—all physical force and brute strength—with an ambition for a public-house: a public-house!"

"I shouldn't mind starting a public-house myself," said Sutton; "fine sphere, if you approach it rightly. Why, you might get the very lives of all these fellows in your hands, and play upon them like an instrument. Get them to drop their beer, don't you know, little by little. I once offered to take the pledge myself if one of them would. And he did—or rather she did, for it was a woman, as it happened. Oh, they're very open to influence! You can get them to do almost anything—for a time."

"Now it is fully established what an Oxford Settlement can do in a poor neighbourhood, we have the game in our own hands," said another. "Give them refined pleasures—that's the thing—and you see how it answers. In Bethnal Green they respond to Brahms and Rubinstein, as none of your smart people do. You see it is virgin soil—they never knew till now what beautiful things were."

"And yet they say the People's Palace is a failure!"

"Ah, I told you! It was not in the hands of University men. I said to Bristowe, 'Don't you think a few Oxford men mixing among them would soon change the tone?' He didn't seem to see it. But there is nothing else. Diffuse culture among the masses: let them see what it has done for us: give them examples to study as well as principles. There is no other way to work—at least it is the best. Christ and the apostles did the same sort of thing. It was more rudimentary in their day. Civilisation has multiplied the wants of humanity, and scientific methods have increased our power. We have got everything in our hands. What are politics or theories? a settlement of ours in every district, leaving our own sphere to leaven theirs—that is what the people want."

"When they don't like the Bruither better, and his public-house," said Scarfield. "I had thome of those fellowth up once to thee my Tondo. They stared, and then they made their remarks. 'I don't call her pretty,' they thaid—'not a bit; and nobody could write like that. I'm sure I cou.dn't write with my hand out like that; and them shavers in wings making eyes at her: and she might a put a rag on the babby to thave it from catching cold.'"

Scarfield was something of a mimic, and the party was in his rooms, and there was a laugh, but a laugh very speedily suppressed.

"That's not my experience," said Bailey. "I find them full of respect. If you fellows would only put your shoulders to the wheel, and all of you do something, by Heaven we'd move the world."

"Don't sneer at politics," said a young man, who had just come in. "You should first feel the swing of them, and hundreds of fellows roaring at your back. I'm in with all the strikes, don't you know. I tell them they oughtn't to stand it—not a day. A man's wages should be what he can live on comfortably with his wife and children, not any cursed balance of trade. What does it matter whether the masters get their profit or not? Confound the masters!—selfish beggars, setting up their unions too, forsooth, as if they had an equal right. The right's with the masses that have the work to do. When I see them sitting down contented and taking whatever is offered them, off I go and hold a meeting or two. And as for response!—if you once heard them shouting with you, by Jove you'd never try any of your dilettante ways again."

"Thoftly, my good fellow, thoftly," said Scarfield, from his chair. "We don't like such coarth thpeaking here——"

"Brutal," said Bailey, "brutal, encouraging all their worst instincts. That is not, from my point of view, the mission of the Oxford man. I wouldn't interfere with these rude problems: if you let them alone they will settle themselves. Why must they marry and fill the world with hungry children and get into difficulties about wages? I don't want to marry. I make myself a happy life of art and refined enjoyment. Why shouldn't they? I have no sympathy with your shouting, your talk of wages, and so forth. If they did without wives and children they would get on well enough. I can't afford wives and children. Scarfield's Botticelli to look at, or one of your own if you can afford it, is enough for me."

"There's something in strikes when you can do it," said a youth in one of the groups by the wall. "Schoolmasters, now—I'm going to be a schoolmaster—if we could strike, it would be a fine thing; but there's a hundred beggars waiting to step into your shoes."

"Then you must stop them," said John, in reply, who was nearest to him. "Pull down their houses, burn their books, blow up their schoolrooms—blind them or deafen them, if you can, still better; then they would be out of your way."

"Oh, I say," said the youth, "that would be a cowardly business; that would not be fair fighting; that would be a cad's way."

"There are no cads," said John. "Everything's fair on your side, nothing on the other—that's the new doctrine. Ask Sutton: he knows."

"Everything's fair against a rat who goes against his own side," cried the revolutionary; "everything's fair against the masters. Whenever there's force against you, you've got a licence to meet it any way you can. That is strategy, it's not a cowardly way."

"I am all for the rights of man, too," cried another youth, standing up against the wall. "And Chortles is brute force, and he's going to send me down—what am I to do?"

A sudden pause came upon the assembly. It was a fate to which all of them were subject, and the boldest held his breath. Besides, what could be done? there was nothing to be suggested amid all the expedients which theoretical revolution has in store.

"I dare thay, Ripton, you deserved it," said Scarfield, in a subdued tone.

"One is powerless," said Sutton aloud, with a sigh; "it's against natural justice, but there's no help for it. You can't stand up alone."

"We could not stand up against Chortles if he were to send us all down," another voice, still more subdued and solemn, said.

"You could bully him after in all the newspapers."

"Throw stones at his windows—but they'd have you up for that: blow up the next fellow that is given your rooms."

These suggestions were made with a perilous inclination towards frivolity which had to be stopped in the bud.

"We have no combination," said Bailey. "We're an inferior lot altogether to the working men. Besides, the whole case is different. We pay the Dons, don't you see, they don't pay us, and——Well, it's not a thing to argue about. If Chortles were to send us all down——"

"Well, this is a fine thing," said the youth, who was desperate; "you're going to move the world and upset the whole country, and you daren't jaw old Chortles, not one of you. And I've got to go down to-morrow, and what shall I say to my people?" the poor young fellow cried.

They all looked at him aghast, compassionate, no doubt, but quite unwilling to share the stigma thus put upon him, or identify themselves with his disgrace. It was John who took him by the arm and led him out, and was the confidant of his trouble, which indeed was no out of the way, or original, or unusual trouble, but only a tale of idleness, of recklessness, of the usual rush and round of careless life. "I went and apologised too," the young fellow said. "I give you my word, Rushton, it wasn't all billiards and that, as Chortles thinks—I used to go to play the violin, you know, for Bailey—and carry their messages for them, and go to their meetings. I've done a little myself in the East End," he added, with forlorn pride. "But not one of them will speak up for me, or tell Chortles if I was a fool that it wasn't all in the one way. Scarry can do what he likes with Chortles, but he never would mix himself up with a fellow that's sent down."

"I am very sorry for you," said John, "and I don't want to preach: but after this, if I were you, I would stick to my own business and get that done first of all."

"Oh, don't you think, then, as they say," cried the young unfortunate, "that it's a fine thing to work for other people? That's what they all say—to do good to the lower class that haven't our advantages."

"And in what way did you think you could do good to the lower class?" said John, grimly: but he did not pursue his subject. He kept the young man in view, and soothed him, which was perhaps better, and saw him off next day in somewhat better spirits, and with a certain sense that he was a martyr to his principles stealing into his soul—which he was able to communicate to his mother, at least, consoling, nay, making that poor lady proud, even of the sending down.

John had quite enough to do, however, with his own difficulties, which he had brought on himself as he well knew. He too had gone speechifying in his time, and tried to do good to the lower classes, carried on by the whirl of the movement of the others, whose sense of the high superiority of the Oxford man, and his certain effect upon the world, he had not perhaps ever seriously, certainly never enthusiastically, shared. To do good to the lower classes, to make a transformation by his mere presence, to influence the whole fabric of life and the rolling of its wheels—John asked himself with a blush which there was no one to perceive, what there was in him to do all this? and the very direction which his feet took, almost against his will, gave him the information he sought. Where was he going? he was turning mechanically towards the road in which he knew another person—a person very easily influenced indeed, and one who had taken too much the impressions of his mind, unconsciously at first, perhaps unwillingly to himself—was likely to be found. It was not an appointment: that would have alarmed her as well as him; though he was not now so sure of that as he had been. Was it possible that perhaps little Mary, innocent little girl as she seemed and was, was playing for what were to her high stakes, and risking a good deal in the spirit of the gamester? He did not allow this, and yet it came in. But that did not in the least extenuate his guilt or explain how his footsteps sought that way and no other in those early twilights, now wan with the November chill. What game was he playing? Was it to lose—everything—his head, his feet, his self-command in some whirl of foolish feeling which was not passion or anything real at all? or was it to win—in any shameful way? Certainly not that, certainly not that. He said it over to himself raising his head, setting down his foot with a stamp upon the ground. But while he made this vow to himself, once more against the pale background of the willows and the dusk of the damp fields that little figure rose, with its air of fictitious surprise. "Oh, Mr Rushton! are you really walking this way again?" she said.

CHAPTER IV

"But, my dear little Mary, your mother, who is a kind woman, will never press you to marry him—if you don't like him," John said.

"Oh, Mr Rushton, you don't know what mother is. She says it's for my good. They always think it is for our good when they go against us. She says I'd be a deal better with a house of my own and a man to work for me, instead of slaving in the bar drawing beer, and forced to laugh and talk with all you gentlemen."

This was a new view of the matter to John. "Were you forced to laugh and talk to us?" he said, with a sort of rueful chuckle. "That was perhaps a pity on all sides."

"Oh, Mr Rushton!" cried Mary, "that's what mother says. It's not what I think—don't you believe that."

"It might have been better, however, if you had thought it," John said.

"Oh, don't say so!" cried the girl. "Then I never should have known anything better. When I think of you with your nice clean ways, and your white shirtfronts, and your soft clothes—and Jim comes in all as he has been working——"

Mary paused with a little shudder, thinking of that honourable dew of labour which Scarfield had gently suggested might be washed off. It gave John the most curious, whimsical sensation of universal misunderstanding and general topsy-turvy to hear the girl's statement of that influence which his friends had been discussing with so much more exalted ideas of its power.

"But surely you could get him to wash?" he said, with a laugh.

"It ain't so easy as you think," said Mary. "When you're only keeping company they'll do it, and keep themselves tidy; but when they are married men!—then they think only of what's comfortable," the girl said, with a sigh. Her head inclined almost upon John's shoulder as she made her plaint, which was half ludicrous to him, not wholly touching as she hoped. "Oh, Mr Rushton, how can I ever make up my mind to such a fate?" Mary said.

"But, my little girl," he said, "you know there is always one way out of it. You needn't marry at all—at least, I mean just at present," he added, hastily.

"What, and 'ave mother nagging at me from morning to night?" said Mary, hastily; and then in a softened tone, "I'd wait—ah, for twenty years!—for one as I was really fond of," she said.

And then there was a pause, and they went on together arm in arm: and the silence thrilled with meaning to poor little Mary, and perhaps to the young man, too, half carried out by the tide with which he had been so long dallying, half upon the dry ground to which he held with a sort of desperation—"One foot on sea and one on shore." John was not of the kind of those who are "to one thing constant never": yet he felt very strongly the force of this statement of his position. He could not bear to break her poor little heart, to fling her off into the arms of the unwashed Jim; but what could he do? To marry the daughters of the masses was not perhaps the way in which Oxford men could best influence those masses for good—and yet why not so if all their theories were true? He did not speak, though it was he who ought to have spoken. It was she who, after that moment of thrilling suspense which again came to nothing, took the word.

"I've been brought up too particular," she said. "We shouldn't be perhaps when it's only to end in *that*. I've been brought up so that I'm only fit for another spear."

"And what sphere is that, Mary?" He was a little amused, but he did, there was no denying, press to his side a little slender hand that clung to his arm.

"Oh, Mr Rushton, what you said yourself that time. Don't you remember, just after you came up, you said, 'Would you like to marry a gentleman?'" She began to cry softly in the dark, clinging to him. "Oh, Mr Rushton, when you said that it was like opening the gate just a little bit—to see heaven!"

"Did it look like that?" he said; his voice trembled a little. "It would be a poor heaven, Mary. I fear it wouldn't be happy for you at all. Think! You would have to give up your own people—your mother and everything."

"Well," she said, "that's only like what's in the Bible—'Forget thine own people and thy father's house.'"

"And *his* people, don't you know, would be very angry, and perhaps would not—be civil. It may be very bad, but that is what they would do."

"Oh, Mr Rushton!" she cried, clinging closer: "but if he should have no people—like—like—some gentlemen?" Mary did not venture yet to say "like you."

"Everybody has some one," he said, hastily, offended by this imputation, and feeling for the moment a strong impulse to push her away—which, however, was impossible to him. "My dear, you wouldn't like it," he said; "you wouldn't be a bit happy; you would be out of it on both sides. And then, fancy if the man was poor—as most of us are when we offend our people. You think marrying a gentleman means having plenty of money, getting everything you wish, and nice dresses and a nice house, and all that; but it would be far worse to be poor as a gentleman's wife than as—than in a different sphere."

His taste revolted from saying "as Jim's wife," which were the natural words. John was not æsthetic, but to speak of a girl, even the maid of the inn, balancing thus between two men, was more than he could do.

"Oh, Mr Rushton," she said, again, "what should I mind being poor if—if he loved me?" Her head touched his breast with a little soft sensation as of a—dreadful thought, for which he loathed himself!—a little soft cat rubbing itself against him. But yet it moved him all the same. Then Mary said, very low, raising the whiteness of her face towards him—"But, oh, Mr Rushton!—oh, *Jack!*—you're not poor!"

His heart gave a startled leap, and then subsided. He laughed aloud, which broke the spell of the darkness and the whispering tones. "No, Mary," he said; "I'm not poor. I'll give you a little *dot* to make you happy with Jim. You shall have enough to set up in a Barley Mow of your own, where Jim, will make short work with the gentlemen. Have nothing more to do with the gentlemen, Mary. Now, come, let's step out, and I'll see you home."

"Oh, Jack!" she cried; "Jack!"—still clinging to his arm.

"No more of that, my dear little girl; no more of that. It would be a great mistake for both of us. Play is very nice, but not when it goes too far. Come, you shall have a nice little fortune, which will be far better for you" (he remembered that she would not know what *dot* meant); "and marry Jim, and make him wash, and keep him up to the mark. He is a fine strong fellow; he looks very nice in his Sunday clothes. Come, little Mary, look up and don't cry. Tell your mother she's to come and see me to-morrow. We'll do it all honestly and above board. We've nothing to be ashamed of, thank God! I'll always think of you as a sweet little friend, very kind to me; and you'll think of me, Mary — —"

"Oh, Mr Rushton!—oh, Mr Rushton!" she cried, drooping from his arm, still hanging on tight: but with something different in the hold, something—John felt it almost with a pang—which meant perhaps that she had been able to keep her footing, too, in spite of the dragging of the tide, which had almost, yet more nearly, carried himself away. Then Mary had a sudden little access of pride, and let his arm drop. "If you think I'm not good enough, after—after saying such things and making me believe! But you're all the same; you are nothing but deceivers, as mother says. Or if you think I care for your money! I want none of your money!—as if it was got out of you for a breach of promise or something to buy me off! *I* go into court on a breach of promise to get money out of you! I would rather die!"

"And there's no question of promise, breached or otherwise," said John. "Here we are, Mary, in sight of your home; and you'll send your mother to me to-morrow. Good-bye, my dear, and good-bye——"

"I won't!" she murmured, but it was under her breath. And John stood and watched till she had reached the spot where the lights of the little tavern shone out upon the road. Then he turned and walked quickly home. He was not very comfortable, poor fellow. It had cost him something to drop poor Mary's clinging hands, and something more to hurt her feelings, which he sadly feared he must have done. It was brutal, he felt. If it had been a lady to whom he had spoken so, what flogging would have been too much for him? And yet, what else—what else could he have done? Suppose he had married her instead? The suggestion filled him with consternation. He said hurriedly to himself that it would not, could not have made her happy. And yet he felt that he was ashamed of himself as he marched home. He had played a poor part. It was heroic in its way, if the truth were known; but of that wretched kind of heroism which felt almost like shame. To treat a woman badly! He never thought, whatever censure he might incur, that such a thing as that would ever be said of him. And the *dot*, which had occurred to him on the spur of the moment to quiet his conscience—no doubt it would be flung back to him in his teeth, filling him with double shame.

He was still uncertain and excited about this when Mrs Brown, the landlady of the Old Hatchet, appeared in his rooms next day. His heart began to beat at the sight of her. He was no cynic. He thought it just as likely as not, and almost hoped for the sake of some foolish ideal—that she was coming to fling his promise back in his throat. But Mrs Brown was very friendly, with no warlike ideas. "My Mary said as I was to come to see you, sir," she said. "I doubt she's got some nonsense in her head, for it don't sound likely: but something about a present, as she said you was a-going to give her for her wedding—I'm sure it's most wonderful kind of you, if it's true."

"It is quite true, Mrs Brown," said John, with a curious sick sensation, something between disappointment and relief. The ground seemed somehow cut from beneath his feet, leaving him faintly struggling for standing. Neither indignation nor lamentation—neither the moan of injured love nor the resentment of virtue assailed. A wedding-present! how much more rational, how much better every way to call it that—but he made a gasp for his breath before he went on. "Yes, Mrs Brown, it is quite true. I admire your daughter very much. I am sure she is as good as gold."

"That she is, sir," cried the good woman, with energy; "and a girl had need be that, I can tell you, to see all you gentlemen so familiar and paying her such compliments and never to give way, not a step."

"It's very creditable, indeed," said John, with a smile, which was a little rueful. He would have liked to laugh, but dared not—nor did he feel at all like laughing if truth must be told. "I am going to leave Oxford," he said, "and I'd like to show my appreciation. I hope you are quite sure that the young man is worthy of her," he added, as he pulled his cheque-book out of its drawer.

"Oh, sir, he's worthy of her if ever a man was—and they've kep' company so long, ever since she was a little slip of a girl. I'm not a bit afraid of that. Lord, Mr Rushton, you don't mean to say as this is all for my Mary! A hundred pound! if it had been a matter of ten to buy her her wedding-gown——Sir, sir," cried the good woman, getting up from her chair, "there was nothing between you but good-day and good-night, for the Lord's sake tell me that!"

"Never!" said John, the blood flushing to his face—"on my honour, and as God hears me: nothing but friendship and admiration for as good a little girl as there is in the world."

Mrs Brown went away well pleased, with the cheque folded up very small in her purse. She drew her own conclusions—which were that John had endeavoured to establish other relations and had been confounded by Mary's goodness and sense of her own place. "He's been a-trying to carry on," she said to herself, nodding her head, "and has just got as good a settin' down as ever a gentleman had: or else he's asked her to marry him, private-like, and she wouldn't. Oh, trust my Mary for that! She's one as knows her place, and wouldn't consent to nothing of that sort: but he 'as behaved 'andsome for a disappointed man, and I never will hear a word against him," Mrs Brown said.

John stood at his window for some time after she had gone, with his hands in his pockets, whistling loudly. He felt as if he were digging his heels very deep into the soil to keep himself from doing something or other which it would not have been very wise to do. The tide was very strong, and if it once caught him, he did not know what he might do. Nor did he know what he wanted to do. He was in that state in which Satan finds some mischief still for every idle hand. He might have been led to concoct a strike or preach revolution had that stream caught the foot which he was digging into his carpet: or he might have done—worse. He might very easily have been plunged into unmentionable things: or he might have flung himself at the feet of the first pretty barmaid he encountered, out of spite against this one who had—behaved so very nicely. It was not a moment to stand and consider, even with the advantage of digging out two round holes in the carpet. He snatched up his rag of a gown and his college cap—(I will not pretend that he usually wore these things out of doors; he did not: and had got into the hands of proctors, and been disapproved of by Dons in consequence more times than I can reckon. But when one goes to see the Warden one is bound to academical costume.) He went there as fast as his feet could carry him,—to do something quickly and at once was the only salvation for him.

He was received by the Warden with a sort of grim kindness. "I perceive, Mr Rushton," that dignitary said, "that you have done the work the College required of you. It is done, but it is not at all well done, I am sorry to say."

"I know it isn't well done, sir," said John, with a rueful recollection of how hard it had been to do it at all.

"You have read your books flying—probably not in the vacation at all—probably since you came up. And you have not understood very well what you read. The work is done, however, and I'll say no more about how it was done. Let me ask you, however, Mr Rushton, what you think is the use of producing such an essay as that?"

"No use at all, sir," cried John. "I thought so all the time: more than no use. It has only driven me half mad and disgusted you. It is fit for nothing but to put in the fire. It should never have been written at all."

"Do you suppose, then, that you come to the University to amuse yourself, and that no work should be asked from you?"

"I don't amuse myself a bit," cried John. "And if you call that rot (I beg your pardon, sir) work— —Well, yes, I suppose it was work, it was such a horrible task to me."

"Take care what you are saying, Mr Rushton: it's as easy for me to send you down, remember, as to throw your essay into the fire."

"I wish you would, sir," cried John; "it would give me an excuse for going away. It would give me satisfaction to see that rot burning, and myself too almost, in one way or other. I thought once I'd paint a little picture and bring you that instead."

"Oh, you can paint pictures?"

"I try," said John. He smiled a little to think that while the Warden probably expected him to produce a daub like a schoolboy's or schoolgirl's, there were people quite as good as the Warden in their way who would have needed no further information than his name as to what he could do. He who could produce nothing better than that very bad essay; he— —Well, he had heard a picture of his recognised as a "little Rushton" once, by a man who knew. He laughed in a way which the Warden did not understand and thought silly, and then he grew grave. "I think, sir, on the whole," he said, suddenly, "I will take the advice you were good enough to give me when I first came up."

"And what was that?" said the Warden, with a faint smile. "I believe I have given you a great deal of good advice."

"It was—to go down," said John; and he felt a little attack of the wounded vanity which that advice had roused in him as he repeated the words, notwithstanding that he was making them his own.

"Oh," said the Warden, with a little surprise, "was that my advice?— and why was it my advice?"

"It was chiefly, I think, because this miserable essay, which you think disgraceful, and so do I, had not been written—the writing of it has convinced me of the justice of what you said."

"But not me," said the Warden; "the essay is not very good, certainly" (he had tacitly allowed it to be "rot," in its author's forcible language, two minutes before); "still it is a piece of work creditably gone through with, though against the grain. That does not count in literature, perhaps, but it does in morals."

"I don't think so," said the audacious John: few were the men who had dared to say so to the Warden before. "Bad work is bad work, sir, if it were done with the best motive in the world."

The great man's face wavered a little between wrath and approval. There was a spark of humour in him. "Thank you," he said, "for the lesson"—while John's countenance blazed like fire.

"Oh, sir, I hope you don't think— —"

"You need not apologise. I thought a week or two ago you had better go down. I don't think so now. I need not stand upon my consistency. You had better work out the problem for yourself."

John stood before him doubtfully, shaking his head. "The tides outside are very strong," he said; "they catch a man's feet— —"

"And do you know, my young Daniel," said the Warden, "any place where the tides outside are not strong?"

All I know is that John Rushton did take his degree—a mere pass, of course—and I don't know that it was of the least use to him. But he was very strong in his sense that it was best not to be beaten, whatever the battle might be.

THE HEIRS OF KELLIE

AN EPISODE OF FAMILY HISTORY

CHAPTER I

Sir Walter Oliphant of Kellie in Fife was a man who had grown old amid many perturbations of the State and of the house. In Mary's stormy and troubled day he had been, as many were, not so certain in his beliefs, either political or religious, as a person of so much consequence in his county ought to have been. He had been the Queen's man, and he had been the King's man, without, however, being either a time-server or a turncoat. He was one of those who would have given his life to prove his Queen's innocence, but who all the time could not but feel that this would be a poor argument, and no evidence at all, against the cold chill of doubt that lingered all the time even in his own heart. And his reason was convinced of the advantages of the English alliance, and that everything must be risked rather than King James's heirship, notwithstanding the strong revolt in his heart against that which was so likely to follow, the abandonment of Scotland, and ebbing away of her dearly-bought glory and the pride of her independence, second to none. But all the active struggles of life had died away from him when he sate in his old hall, in the dreary years after the Court had gone away to London, drawing so many with it; and the change had stricken to the heart of Scotland, as wise men had known it would, although all the country had cheered and shouted when their king assumed the English crown, as if it had been by his prowess and for their greatness that he had won that other kingdom. The land was subdued and troubled in these days, yet did not venture to complain; for had not they desired that which had come to pass? And the Kirk was troubled and uncertain too, alarmed by threatenings of interference, though no great thing had yet been attempted, and the ministers still had dominion more or less, and, though many things were tolerated that had been condemned, still guided most things their own way.

But all the affairs of the world had grown dim to Sir Walter Oliphant, sitting in his little warm chamber—the room of panelled and carved oak, which opened from the hall of Kellie Castle, as all the chief rooms did and do to this day, without any chill of corridors or passages, but one room out of another, after the ancient fashion. He sat by his fire, and his mind was full of thoughts. He was an old man, but not so old in years as in condition. His life, which had been a stirring one, was far off from him, as if it had been a dream. There were times when it came up into his mind like a tale that had been told, with which he had little to do—the time when he was stout and strong, and rode out to feast and to fight, and came back to hear the shouts and the sports of his boys making the rafters ring. He thought of all these things sometimes vaguely, as of things that had been; but at present his occupation was chiefly to keep himself warm, and to think who should be the heir of his Castle and his lands when he should be carried for the last time down the winding stair. He was not much concerned about that, any more than he was concerned for all that had happened to him in the past: but the thought of who should have Kellie after him was still real in his mind. That the natural heirs were gone had caused him bitter sorrow in his day; but even that had grown far away and dim to him, and all his life had shrunk into the routine of getting up from his bed and going back to it— both tiresome processes—and swallowing the food that had no taste, and sitting by the fire that had so little warmth. Only this one thing held him, the great care of making up his mind who was to be the heir of Kellie in the days when he should be there no more.

It was not that he was without kin or heirs-at-law. There was one even at his own hearthstone who might well have ended all difficulties, being its natural inheritress. Though Sir Walter was an old man, he had a sister who was little more than a girl, though that is a strange thing to think of. His father had lived long, and had made a foolish marriage in his old age, and left behind him a child much younger than his grandsons, and who was like a grandchild to her brother. She had grown up in the house, the plaything of everybody, her right to her home never doubted, yet without any position in it. When the others disappeared Jean remained, and it might be that the father bereaved felt in the bottom of his heart some grudge that she of whom no account was made should continue when the loftier heads were laid low. But if this was in his heart he did not betray it. She grew and blossomed out, and came to her full height, which was not small, and was now of an age to be considered the lady of the house. And no doubt, the old knight might easily have given her to a fitting wooer, and thus found himself an heir among the best blood of Fife; but of this he never thought, nor of Jean his little sister as in any sense his successor. It angered him greatly when Master Melville of Carnbee kirk and parish took it upon him to speak a word to this effect. "Her, the heiress!" cried the old knight, with a roar in his throat like a wounded lion. And he would not speak to Master Melville again for many a day.

"And wha but her should be the heir?" said Mistress Marjory, the old nurse, who had long been the housekeeper at Kellie, and to whom Jean was as the light of her eyes. "Waes me for all the bonnie lads that are away! and no an Oliphant left to keep up the honour of the old house. But though she's but a lass she has the blood as well as any one, knight or lord, that ever owned the name. And wherefore should she not get a good man and raise up the race?"

"If she had a good man the morn the race she would raise up would be for his house and no hers," said Neil Morison, who was the head of the other section of the household, and in most things opposed to Mistress Marjory. He gave forth a dry laugh, as was his wont, and added, "For all so grand as ye are, the name never comes from the side of the distaff. That's aye something to our side."

"There's times," said the housekeeper, "when nae less a thing than a crown comes from that side—as is well kent in poor auld Scotland this day."

"Ye may say that," said Neil, forced into sudden sympathy, "and if we had vanquished thae English loons by our swords and our spears, as it is written in Scripture, it would hae been the better way."

"Oh, hold your tongue with your spears and your swords! It would set ye better, Maister Morison, to do what you can with our auld knight and keep sore injustice out of his head—for who should have the lands after him but his ain flesh and blood?"

"It would never do, it would never do," cried Neil. "A lass! that couldna keep her ain heid, and muckle less the old Oliphant lands—that are not what they used to be, lack-a-day, whoever was the heir."

"What are they colloguing about, the two great rulers of the house," said a young voice, bursting in as its owner did, with a sudden gush of fresh air and the fragrance of the outdoor world, "putting each other in mind of the greatness of the Oliphants, now that it's like the Flowers of the Forest, and a' wede away."

"Mistress Jean! and a' in a confusion, your hair about your haffits, and the lace torn off your riding-coat! What has happened to you? Will ye never mind what a' the house tells you, that it sets you not, a lady like you, to ride a powney about the roads like a farmer's lass."

"Or maybe worse things than that," said Neil, who had risen hurriedly to his feet on the young lady's entrance, and shot this Parthian arrow at her as he went away.

"I will shoot that auld carle some day if he looks at me so," she cried, with a sudden gleam of anger, then laughed and clapped her hands, "with my bow and arrows," she added, merrily. "We'll put him against the castle wall, and pin him to't like that bonny saint in the old picture. What's happened, said she? A great deal has happened. I have had a grand adventure, Marjory, simple as I sit here."

"Oh, bairn, bairn!" cried the housekeeper, "you'll just break my heart."

"It's been broken so often, and aye mended again," said the girl. "Wait till I tell you. I was rattling along on the Pittenweem road, my pony and me, very well pleased with the fine day, and just singing to ourselves, for it was too sunny to keep silence; when lo! I was aware of a horse's hoofs coming pelting after me. I thought what you said, never to mind, but just keep the road quietly and pay no attention. I would not even give a look over my shoulder to see if it was one of the Anstruthers or Roland Dishington, till I came to a corner and gave a glint. And it was a muckle trooper on a muckle grey horse, not canny to see, and no another soul within sight."

"Lord bless my soul! ane of the disbanded Greys!" cried Marjory, lifting up her hands and eyes. "Oh, lassie, lassie! will ye never learn?"

"My heart was in my mouth," said Jean, whose eyes were dancing, however, with excitement and triumph, "but I had to keep up my courage. I gave the pony just a touch to speed her on—and you know she cannot thole even a touch, she has such a spirit. And then there came a muckle voice, as muckle as the man, calling to me, Hey, my bonnie lass! and hey, my bonnie bird! The cannaillye! to use such words to me!"

Jean's eyes shone with a momentary gleam of rage and shame. "It is maybe my fault," she said, "as ye are always telling me, to ride alone; but who would I get to come behind? No Maister Morison, the major-domo, nor Jamie Webster, that is everybody's man, nor Jaicque the groom. No, no; there's nobody to follow Jean: so I must either bide in the house or ride my lane."

"My darlin'! and what did he do?"

"Oh, no harm," cried the girl, laughing, "since here I am, and none the worse but for the lace on my cape, that he gave a snatch at as he came up thundering, till I thought it was a real charge of cavalry, and I would be ridden down."

"Lassie! and how did ye escape? For gude sake dinna keep me in my trouble."

"There is no need for trouble," said Jean, "since here you see me: though I allow," she added, with a pleasure in working upon the old lady's fears, "that a minute longer and I cannot tell what I would have done; for he had gripped my cape in his hand, though the pony was just flying, and the muckle grey horse thundering, and my heart bursting out of my throat with fright and fury." She paused, half from the keenness of the recollection and half maliciously, to pile up the agony.

"And then? and then?"

"Then?" said Jean, looking innocently into her old nurse's face. "Why, then! there was just nothing more."

"Oh, bairn! you are enough to drive ten women out of their senses."

"Well," said Jean, "I will admit there were causes for it. But just at that moment there came another galloping, just as muckle a horse and as muckle a man, on the other side. And my man he dropped hold of my cape, and tore the lace off it with his glove, as you see. And the pony, she just set her feet to the ground as if she were riding a race, and the new man and my man they faced each other. I'm thinking nothing happened. I saw with that eye I have in the back of my head that they rode up to each other awfu' civil, like two towers; and then the trooper he took the turn to St Monance, and me I flew up the Carnbee road, and the grand adventure was done. You can see I'm not a prin the worse, except my riding-cape, and Kirsten must just sew on the lace again."

"And that was a'!" cried Mistress Marjory, relieved, but at the same time a little disappointed to hear no more.

"All! was it not enough?" said Jean; "would you have had me assaulted on the king's highway, and put in peril of my purse, that has nothing in it, or maybe of my life, which has not very much— —" Jean made a pause, and then, looking up demurely, she said in very quiet tones, "No; it was not all."

"Oh, my hinny,—you just play upon me as if I were a fiddle."

"You are much more like a harpsichord," said Jean, contemplating the housekeeper's ample person reflectively. "Yon man after he had dispersed the trooper never came rushing up as Roland Dishington or one of the Ansters would have done, but just rode steady behind as if he had been my servant." The word has or had two meanings, and probably the second of these flashed over her memory, for she made an almost imperceptible pause and reddened. "I was still a little feared: and what did I do but head the pony for yon house you know, of Over-Kellie, where you never would let me go— —"

"And then?" cried Mistress Marjory again, breathless.

"Well, they came fleeing out, and he, he came riding in. And it was who would be the most concerned, and was I hurt and was I frightened, and would I bide and rest? The Leddy—or is she the Gudewife?—for I could not tell— —"

"Some calls her the one and some the other," said Marjory, shortly. "Never you mind. You'll be telling me now the man that came up and— saved ye was— —"

"That is just it," said Jean, "and if you'll tell nobody, Marjory, I'll just whisper in your ear—he's a bonnie lad."

"Mistress Jean!" cried the housekeeper in consternation.

"Well! say he's just a country fellow, and no grand cock to his hat, nor lace on his coat: I am not saying he's a grand gentleman. But I have a pair of sharp eyes in my head,—you are always saying that,—and I cannot but see what's set before them. He is a bonnie lad; and that is just as true as all the rest."

"What do you call a' the rest?"

"You know as well as I do; or maybe you know better," said Jean, with a little indignation; "because he is Peter Oliphant, and because he is the next of kin, that's not to say that he is not a bonnie lad!"

"It might be a good reason, Mistress Jean, for you kenning naething about him, and no going out of your way to make acquaintance with him——"

"Me go out of my way to make acquaintance with him! Neither him nor any man, if it were a prince or a king! It was he that came out of his way to protect a lass he knew nothing of when he saw she was in need. Maybe you would have thought it better had he left me to the trooper?" said the girl, with much indignation.

"Oh, no that, no that," said the old woman; "but it would have been better you had not put yourself in the way of wanting protection, my bonnie leddy—no from him nor from any man!" she said.

"You forget who you are speaking to," cried Mistress Jean, with quick anger, flinging away. But she came back next minute to fling her arms round her old nurse's neck. "And that's true," she said; "I was just thinking so mysel'."

CHAPTER II

While this was going on, Sir Walter was sitting in his warm panelled chamber, pondering by the side of the fire. His old Castle, which was not one of the famous strongholds of the time, but yet an ancient house dating far back into the mist of ages, and standing four-square to all the winds that blew, a house that time could scarcely wear more than the rocks, would soon be a desolate and masterless house. Since the days of Bruce the Oliphants had been there, and the first lord of Kellie had good King Robert's blood in his veins. But now there was no one to come after him in the old home of his race. The gloom of that consciousness had settled down upon his mind, and filled him with an immense and indescribable darkness in which he went tottering, seeking for something to replace what was lost, though by moments he was not very clear as to what it was that was lost, which made it necessary for him to grope in the dark and seek that substitute. And his thoughts were very slow, wandering, and confused, though they always came back with unbroken persistency to the one point. Who should have Kellie after him? Who would replace the heirs who were no more? This had been the preoccupation of many years; it almost seemed as if all his life he had been thinking of it. His own active days had vanished away, and all the adventures and troubles that had filled his house with rejoicing and with wailing. Sometimes while he sat musing on that one sole question he would be surprised by a recollection of himself, as in the days when he rode in Queen Mary's train, or those in which he hung about the ante-chambers at St James's, half proud to feel himself one of the new masters there, half furious to see the dark looks which the Southern lords threw upon King James's train. Was that himself? or one of the former Oliphants who held a larger train at Kellie? or perhaps one of the young ones—the lads, the——, those who ought to have been here to receive Kellie from his hands. Their faces would sometimes flash out from his memory too. Who were they, old heirs of Kellie slain in the wars, or lost in the wildering world, never coming back to claim their heritage? And who was to have it now? Who would keep it safe, and guard all its rights and keep up the auld name? On this subject his thoughts would clear, his mind retained its force. It was the one clear point in the misty universe of dreams that surrounded the old man.

Almost his only visitors were the clergymen of the two neighbouring parishes, each of which claimed Kellie Castle as part of its own. He retained enough of his natural keenness to perceive that each of them took a different side in this great question, and sometimes to play upon their contradictions with something of the pleasure which the quarrels of priests and women between themselves so often afford to a man of the world. The difference between them gave him a vague amusement, or something at least as like amusement as he was capable of. Master Melville of Carnbee was a Reformation minister who had known John Knox, and who, though of a much milder temper, was yet very strong as to his duty of speaking in season and out of season, and letting no man avoid or mistake his duty without full warning of it; but Sir John Low at Pittenweem was no better than a mass priest the country folk said, and loved the great, and to speak smooth things, flattering the old laird and supporting him in taking his own way. Sir Walter listened to what they said on both sides, but he was little moved by their arguments. What he was really doing while he seemed to be listening was slowly settling upon his own plans, and deciding for himself while they talked, which neither of them was at all unwilling to do. It was Mr Melville who was his visitor the day after the incident in the last chapter, a grave man of gentle manners, with a black velvet cap upon a bald head.

"What are ye saying?" said Sir Walter. "Reason gude—ay, I've reason gude for all I say to you. It's no fit that an auld race should die out of the land."

"And yet," said the other, in the heat of argument, "if it's so ordained, it's ill striving with the Will aboon. But ye have heirs in plenty at your hand, and little danger of your name. How often must I be telling ye, Sir Walter Oliphant, there is your ain father's daughter, your ain flesh and blood, the one that has the best right? Where would ye go furder than your ain ingleside? Who could be so near to you? and young and likely and one to raise up heirs—always if it be the Almichty's will——"

"Who's that," said the old knight. "Jean! a bit lassie! how often have I tellt you, minister? just as often as you have tellt me. What would I do with a lassie in my seat, that could neither keep the house nor keep her head, a thing with neither might nor right? Na! that will not do for me."

"She would get a man," said Mr Melville.

"Ay, she would get a man! little doubt of that: and my auld lands would be sweepit up into lands that march with mine, and there would be an Anster of Kellie, or a Dishington, or a Lindsay, or the Lord knows what. No! if I have said it once I have said it a hundred times, nae lass shall reign and rule in my auld house."

"Well-a-well, well-a-well! if ye say so," said the minister. "I have no certain teaching about the heirship of a woman, though the daughters of Zelophehad had a portion with their brethren, as we read in the Book of Numbers; but I would not force the word of the Lord, and that might be a special case. But ye know well, Sir Walter, as well as I do, that failing her, there's one of your blood no far from your door that is as weel capable of keeping his ain house and his ain head as Arthur and a' his knights. And that is Peter Oliphant of Over-Kellie— —"

"Pah!" the old man spat vehemently into the smouldering fire. "I will have none of him—a country clown—a callant from the plough. And what was his father but a clown before him, with no more spirit of a gentleman than Neil, my man?"

"Neil," said the minister, "is a decent man now, whatever he may have been; but would pocket a crown-piece and hold his tongue if any grand gallant had need of him: whereas your cousin of Over-Kellie, Sir Walter— —"

"Cousin! a hundred times removed!"

"Is it you I hear shaming your own blood?" said the other. "Me, I am maybe a hundred times, as you say, or more, removed from the head of my name; but I have yet to learn," the minister added, raising his head, "that the strain of the younger is less pure than the strain of the elder when it flows in an unbroken and lawful line."

"I ken, and we all ken," said Sir Walter, subdued, "minister, that there's no better name in Fife— —"

"I am standing upon no such vanities," said Melville. "Your cousin has neither been at the College nor at the Court, Sir Walter, and maybe as well for him in these evil days; but he's a handy man at his weapons, and a lad that kens his own mind. There's no man in the parish better kent or better liked, or more a man of his word. I ken but little of my Lord Oliphant, or of his house; but well I wot there is not a better in it than Pate, or one that can master him, or daunton him, among the best of his name."

"Ye mean the lad to wed one of your lasses, that you are so hot upon him," Sir Walter said.

"I ken well," said Melville, "what lass I want him to wed; but she is none of mine. Will you see the young man, Sir Walter, and judge for yourself? I will bring him to you in my hand, for he has always been a good lad to his minister; though he would not set foot over your door-stane for other motives."

"And wherefore," cried Sir Walter, "would this farmer-lad no set foot over my door-stane?"

"For an evil reason," said the minister; "for pride, and a high head that would not stoop before any man but the king."

"Ha! ha!" cried the old knight; "bring me this clown with his high head that would not stoop under the door of Kellie Castle. Bigger men than him have entered at that door—ay, and stooped too, and even bitten the dust before them that owned it. He's then a deevil of pride and conceit, this yeoman lad of yours."

"Ye are right, and again right, Sir Walter," said the minister, gravely, "when you say that pride, the pride that you, and even myself, that should ken better, take in the vanity of a name—is a devilish thing."

"If that were all!" Sir Walter said, with a snap of his thumb and finger, which failed and gave no sound. He paused, and his countenance grew grave as he observed this, looking with a half piteous surprise at his own large feeble hand. "I canna even snap my thoom," he said under his breath. Then with a feeble wave of that hand to his companion, he added, "If it's to be done, lose no time."

This was the warrant upon which the minister brought Peter Oliphant to Kellie Castle. He had as much trouble with the young man as he had with the old. The house of Over-Kellie was still excited by the flying visit of Mistress Jean when the minister reached it; and the Leddy, or the Gudewife—for Marjory said truly that she was called sometimes one and sometimes the other, according to the courtesy or indifference of her rare visitors—could not be persuaded that the extraordinary mission of the minister had not something to do with that exciting incident. The Mistress felt that her Peter was called to the Castle to receive the hand of the Princess, who must have found time enough in the ten minutes of her stay to fall in love with him; and that this event at once and for ever established his claims as heir-at-law, and made Kellie Castle his. The young man naturally was more hard to be convinced; but he too was excited, and not in perfect command of his faculties. If Jean had discovered that he was a bonnie lad, he had still better means of discovering that she was fair enough to dream of; and though this encounter had made her first aware of him, it was by no means the first time that her humble cousin had seen the young lady of Kellie. And, in the glow of pride with which he remembered, though no such claim had ever been acknowledged, that he was the undoubted next of kin, there was, perhaps, something of a more generous fervour, a warm and noble sentiment towards the friendless girl to whom the head of the house, as all the countryside knew, was little more gentle than towards himself. When Sir Walter died, it was he who would be the nearest in blood to her to defend her rights or herself. The Lord Oliphant might be the head of the name: but he was a man who loved gear, and was secretly operating, as all the countryside believed, to draw the lands of Kellie and the old Castle to himself.

It was therefore with no small exaltation of mind that Peter Oliphant flung his bonnet upon his head, notwithstanding his mother's prayers that he would put on his better suit and the hat in which he appeared at kirk and market, to show his better breeding. "I will not stand covered in Sir Walter's presence," he said; "and, as for my clothes, they're well enough. He knows me for a country loon, whatever fine suit I might wear."

"Loon, did the laddie say? and what next? I would like to see either knight or yeoman, in all Fife, that would dare to call Peter Oliphant loon," his mother said.

"And so would I," he said, with a laugh. He was strong and straight and tall, with the brown hair and the laughing eyes that belonged to his race. But they were eyes that could look fierce enough when occasion required.

"By my troth, I would like that better," he continued, as they set out; "a bout at single-stick, or a good frank blade, I am not that ill at: but what am I to say to the old laird? a man wants lear for a presence-chamber, even if it's but an old knight's."

"You have lear enough for that," said the minister, "if you would but mind half that I have put into you, at the point of the sword, as a man may say."

"A little Latin, and a shelf of old books," said Peter; "but you would not advise me, Maister Melville, to tirl off a verb to Sir Walter, even if I could mind it, the first time he has bethought himself that I'm alive and within reach."

"My lad, I would not lippen to his bethinking himself," said the minister; "just you mind it's mostly my doing, and my credit's concerned. Na, I will not tell you, not a word, what to say; nature will tell you, and that fine spirit of your ain that never let you be overly modest before me. And I hope, so far as learning goes, I am of more account than Sir Walter, if that was of any consequence."

"Little doubt of that," said Peter; but he was wise enough to know that this was indeed of very little consequence, and that it was an extremely different thing standing before the minister in Carnbee manse, though he was a man of learning, and thus stepping suddenly into the presence of old Sir Walter, though he had no letters at all.

CHAPTER III

Peter Oliphant went into the great hall of Kellie Castle with very mingled feelings. Though he had lived all his life almost within sight of the home of his race, he had never crossed the threshold before; and a kind of awe, a kind of defiance, the inalienable attraction of an ancient family house, mingled with the indignant sentiment of a scion of the family upon whom its door has been always closed, made his cheek glow and his heart beat. This, then, was Kellie, which had been the home of his fathers, which might be his home if justice prevailed and the law of heirship and lineage. It was not a splendid place to overawe him. The house of Kellie was not rich. Whatever superfluity the family had ever possessed, Sir Walter and his sons had managed to get rid of in the days when they went to England with King James—perhaps, like so many Scotch gentlemen, in hope of advancement, but, like so many more, only wasting their small substance in a brief attempt to hold head among the great English lords ten times as rich as they were. There were few signs of grandeur in the hall: a little show of silver on the buffet; heavy old velvet curtain with tarnished embroideries; some carved furniture of noble workmanship, marked with the three crescents of the family arms. Those arms were dimly blazoned, too, on the high, carved mantelpiece, with that proud motto which poverty turns into a brag or a jest, according to the humour of the wearer—*À tout pourvoir*. Peter knew that much at least, if no other word, of the French tongue, and had said it over to himself many a day. It was but a sad word in the old house that had little to provide and few to provide for—none but the old man and the helpless girl. But if ever this house should come to the strong hands, that if strength and labour and daring could do it would, so help him heaven! carry it out to the letter! Peter's head, all throbbing and resounding with excitement, was in a state of exaltation to which he had never felt the parallel. And as it happened, the first thing that met his eye was Mistress Jean, the heroine of the other day's half-adventure. She was seated on a stool in the recess of the great window, with a great book clasped in her arms, too heavy to hold, and over which she was stooping, bent almost double. Jean's kirtle was not so well preserved nor her snood so fresh as those of his own little sister at Over-Kellie: and to his yeoman's eyes she was doing nothing useful, nor perhaps able to do anything useful—a creature not made for common occupations, but to be kept in sweet leisure and pleasure like one of the lilies of the field. *À tout pourvoir!* Here was one of the things for which it would be his duty to provide. The thought brought a sudden glow over him—the heat of resolution and enthusiasm. It was the climax of all those mingled and tumultuous thoughts that had been surging in his breast.

Jean looked up at the sound of the heavy steps ringing upon the floor, and, throwing down her heavy book, darted forward; but, seized with a sudden access of shyness, stopped and drew back before she had come up to the visitors, and stood looking at them—herself a very pleasant image, impetuous yet timid, her figure suddenly arrested in all its swiftness of motion, her lips in their meaning of speech. The sight of Peter Oliphant, so unexpected an apparition, made her dumb.

"We have come, Mistress Jean," said Mr Melville, "to speak a word with Sir Walter, so please you, and by your brother's ain desire."

"By his—ain desire!" Jean looked at the pair before her. The well-known figure of the minister, and the other, so much more interesting, still in all the novelty of recent discovery, a personage not precisely like the young Ansters of her acquaintance, wanting something, possessing something, a different kind of being. Indeed the rustic young gentlemen were but little superior even in breeding to this handsome yeoman, with his greater maturity and higher consciousness of life and its struggles. They were good to laugh with, to mock at, to dance with on the very few occasions when such an opportunity occurred. But she had met with a reality of life in the person of this modest yet ardent young man, who reddened when he looked at her, which Jean had never encountered before. At Sir Walter's own desire! was it on account of herself, for some reason connected with that meeting, which some one must have betrayed and reported? This idea had no time to grow, but it flashed upon her suddenly, almost choking her with the sudden rise and hurried pulsation of her heart.

"We will but bide a moment with your permission till Maister Neil comes forth to bid us to the knight's presence," said the minister. "And it will not be long, seeing the hour was fixed by himsel'."

"There is somebody with him," said Jean: and then her awe of the situation yielding a little as she grew familiar with it, she laughed and added, "It is one you do not love."

"And who may that be?" said Melville. His question was answered in a way much more significant than any reply of hers. The curtain over the door of Sir Walter's sitting-room was audibly thrust back, without, however, revealing immediately the person coming forth: and a voice said, speaking to the old knight within, "My lord shall hear every word of your good intentions, every word! it is the thought of a true kinsman, whatever comes. Be sure my lord shall hear: and farewell, sir, and the blessing of God."

The new-comer paused to draw the curtain back to its usual folds, covering the door, and then he turned round, and with a hasty exclamation of surprise became aware of the group in the hall. He was more conspicuous in his dress as a clergyman than was the minister of Carnbee, with something on his dark head that suggested a tonsure, though no such mark of the beast was permitted in Scotland, and wearing the cassock of a priest. He came forward, however, with much appearance of cordiality, "Ah, Brother Melville, it's long since we met! If we've both come on the same ghostly errand, I wot our penitent will get something confused in his Belief."

"I come on no ghostly errand," said Mr Melville, "but concerning the affairs of this fleeting world: which have their importance too, as you will agree with me."

"That do I—and whiles more bewildering still," said the Curate of Pittenweem, rubbing his hands. "We have no doubt the luck, my kind neighbour, to take different views on that subject too."

"It may be so," Melville replied gravely, but he added no more. He had no inclination to disclose his hand, as his opponent had done involuntarily by those last words behind the curtain. Low of Pittenweem looked at him fiercely, but without any visible change of tone.

"And how's all with you, Pate?" he said with a smile. "I heard a bonnie story the other day of one of these wild soldier fellows that are just a pest on the roads, and how he was scared away and took the road west, meddling with no person: for fear of a certain muckle rider, bigger than himself, from the Over-Kellie gait."

"Oh, and it was me, Sir John!" cried Jean; "and the loon was after me on my pony, till there came in sight——" Jean stopped suddenly, crimson all over, half with annoyance at herself for having spoken, half because of the smiling glance which Low directed from her to Peter Oliphant, and back again—a smile which developed into a low laugh of malice, and which filled her with unaccountable shame.

"There came in sight—the palladin, the grand knight"—he said these words to the accompaniment of his laugh, till every line of Peter's rustic dress, the blue bonnet in his hand, the heavy shoes on his feet, seemed to come out under the sarcastic look, as if the curate had been holding up a candle to show their roughness. And then he turned away, still laughing softly to himself, and rubbing his hands. "I will not interrupt such braw company," he said. "Good day to you, Mistress Jean: and I wish ye, madam, a good fulfilment to all your virtuous wishes; and one of those days ye can tell your mother, Pate, I'll come in for a crack, and to hear the country news. Brother Melville, we'll probably not be so long, you and me, this time of meeting again."

"Maybe not, Maister Low," said Melville.

"Wherever the — — is, there will the eagles be gathered together," said the other, going lightly towards the door, with a wave of his hand and a nod of his head. Mr Melville drew a long breath.

"That is no canny forerunner," he said, "Peter, my good lad, for you and me; but I will haste and see if the auld knight is weariet, or if he'll see you still. Bide here for me."

When Peter was left alone with the young lady, there was a pause of much embarrassment between these two young people, so suddenly brought together by malicious suggestion, and by the involuntary flash of thought that went from one to another, in the unlikely and unexpected combination, in which all suddenly, in a moment, they had been placed. Jean, who was full of saucy words at other times and in other company, at this moment, when she would have given all her small possessions for the power to throw one jibe at him, could not find a word to say. It was Peter, whose grave mood had more solidity and could better resist the excitement of the situation, who was the first to speak. "I have a charge from my mother, Mistress Jean, with her duty—which is maybe more than is due from her to you; but my mother, Lady Jean, though she is the best woman in the world, was but a farmer's daughter, and cannot get out of her head that the Laird's daughter is a Princess in the land."

"I have no quarrel with her for that," said Jean, restored to herself; "but if I am a Princess you will maybe live to be the King. Here we are, us two, and it's between us, Maister Peter. You are the just heir; but I am the more just if it were not that I am a lassie, and whose fault is that? I am sure it is by no will of mine."

"My Lady Jean," said Peter, "you say well it is my just right, as the next man of the blood; but if by Sir Walter's will it should fall to you, as may be— mind you this, whatever happens, I'll stand for you through fire and water, and be your man, and a true kinsman, as long as I live."

"No me!" cried Jean, giving a spring in her excitement. "If it falls to you, I'll fight you every step, and go to the law with you, and never yield while I've breath!"

Peter looked at her with a tender admiration—but that ineffable way of taking the girl's hot words as if they meant nothing, which not even love itself can make palatable to a girl. "Well-a-well," he said gently, "the one thing and the other they mean just about the same."

"But nothing of the kind," she cried, almost with a soft shout of passion, "nothing of the kind! they mean——" here it suddenly struck Jean quite irrelevantly, as he stood before her with a deprecating smile, by every turn of his figure and change of his face recommending himself to her, seeking to please her, asking nothing better than to serve and help her,—suddenly and supremely that he was a bonnie lad, that nobody had ever looked at her like that, nor spoken to her like that before. She stopped and gasped and put out her hand to him, which was as unexpected as any other of her movements. "Cousin Peter," she cried, "there's my hand upon it; we'll be grand enemies! We'll be true as auld Sir William's sword, that he keepit the Castle of Stirling with, that hangs there upon the wall. We'll fight fair, and never say an ill word one of the other. And there's my hand."

She expected nothing but a comrade's grasp; but young Pate of Over-Kellie had the gracious manners of the old chivalry, without knowing whence they came. He stooped low almost to his knee, and kissed the hand held out to him—an unlooked-for homage which altogether overwhelmed the rustic maiden, who was scarcely by her own nature a lady of romance. And at that moment the heavy curtain was drawn, and Mr Melville's head put out calling Peter. The sudden light of a delightful smile shone over the minister's face. "Ah!" he said, with a soft laugh, which was not of ridicule but content. It was enough, however, to send Jean back to her window-seat, all one blush, and to make Peter draw himself up almost to more than his stature, as very red and portentously serious he followed, transported out of all his nervousness about Sir Walter—into the presence of the old knight.

Sir Walter sat by the fire, which smouldered sullenly, as if it felt the inappropriateness of its presence on a warm spring day, as the centre of the scene. But the old Master of Kellie was cold, the blood ran slow in his veins, and all the fires of living were as low in him as the dull glow in the coals. The gown in which he was enveloped was lined with fur, and wrapped closely round him; and his head was so sunk into its soft collar that the effect of his upward look was as if a pair of eyes alone looked over his raised shoulder at the young man who came in. But there was life in the look, which contradicted every other sign of diminished vitality. It seemed almost to strike at Peter like the flash of a blade into the air. The steel-like light quivered, and then suddenly the old man turned his head away. There was a pause, and both of his visitors thought for a moment that the old knight had fallen asleep or lost consciousness—till at last the minister spoke, half alarmed. He touched with a finger the wide sleeve of Sir Walter's coat. "Here is the young lad, Sir Walter. Come in bye, Pate—show yourself—and be not blate. What, man! ye are here in what may be your own house."

Peter took a step forward into the room, opposite to the light which fell full upon him, his somewhat rustic air lost in the temporary exaltation of his look; but Sir Walter had returned to his fire, and looked at him no more. His voice came out of the fur collar of his gown, as out of a cave. "Ay! the young lad, say you? And what is his will, and his errand here?"

"Speak to him, man; speak to him!" said the minster, in an undertone.

"I have no purpose, Sir Walter," said Peter; "but that ye were thought to send for me; and me—I was very willing to come, as your kinsman, and to ask how you did."

"Ay!" said Sir Walter again, "as my kinsman! Blate! I see little sign that he is blate. Let him speak for himself. There are plenty of loons in Fife that will swear themselves my kinsmen, however they came by the name."

Peter was stung by this disdainful speech. "I am no loon," he said, "minister, as you well know; and as for how I got the name, Sir Walter he kens weel, seeing I am but his second cousin, when all is done, twice removed."

"Ah, so! are you all that?" said the old knight: he raised his head, and once more Peter felt himself struck as by a flame. But again the light quivered, and Sir Walter swerved, and his head sank among his furs. Then he added, averting his look, "What is your will of me, young man?"

"Nothing," said Peter. His heart swelled, a sudden sense of pity moved him for the desolate old age before him—so lonely, so void of all the charities and tenderness which ought to encircle the old. "And yet," he said, a remorseful sense of all his own advantages over this solitary, chilled, and suffering old man melting his spirit, "Sir Walter, if there was any pleasure I could do you, for the sake of the drop's blood between us, and because you have none of your own——"

"Eh! eh! what is that he says? — what is that he says?"

"Sir, I would fain, fain do you a pleasure, if that were possible," Peter said.

It was some time before the old knight spoke. "Gramercy for your kindness, lad," he said; "I have plenty to do for me all I want. I seek no service from the like of you."

"Yet it would be given out of a good heart," Peter said.

These words of manly kindness to the weak, given with an insistence of which Peter, blate of nature as the minister had said — that is, proudly shy of expressing emotion, as it is the drawback of his countrymen to be — would not have believed himself capable, made a curious commotion in the still air of that chamber, where all was stagnant, and life and charity were seldom heard. Sir Walter put out a blanched hand with a gesture to the minister, calling him forward, "Ye have tutored the lad what to say."

"I would think shame," said Melville, "to try to tutor what's native to a gentle spirit. And, Sir Walter, you are more understanding than to believe what you say."

The old knight dropped his head again, and was silent once more. Then he said, without raising his face, with his eyes fixed on the low red of the fire, and a voice half buried in his fur collar, "Did I hear ye say Pate?"

"His name is Peter — —"

"Pate," repeated the old man, vaguely. "There was once another — but keen, keen as a hawk, and gallant, and fine in every limb. Not like that yeoman from the fields. Take him hence, take him hence! There is that in the turn of his head that goes, that goes" — he made a pause, and gave forth a long slow breath "to my hert!"

And again there was silence. Peter would have stolen away by natural instinct, but did not dare to break the deep stillness by a movement, and the minister stood doubtful, hesitating, afraid to shorten an interview that might have important results, yet afraid at the same time to injure the impression that had been made.

"Ay, Pate," Sir Walter said almost to himself, "Pate — like day to night, like a prince to a churl — but just a turn of the head, a trick of the voice. Eh! ye are still here? is it a service do ye think, young man, to spy on the privacy of one that, kinsman or no kinsman, is the head of your name?" he raised himself, putting his hand upon the table — "in Fife," he added with a faint laugh, "in Fife—saving the rights of my lord. Ay, my lord, that's the question. Well, sir! I thank ye for your coming, and dismiss ye from further attendance. Master Melville, at your leisure I will see you again."

The hall was vacant when Peter, with strange visions through his brain, confused with his own good impulses and the less kind ones that came hurrying after, stepped into it again. He did not know what he had expected or hoped for, but there was disappointment and a little offence in his mind. He was not sure if he had acquitted himself as a man in this unusual trial or if he had failed. He was new to all these strange and conflicting feelings. The old man in his chamber, the death in life which Pate's animated youth had never seen before, and the young lady in the hall, had given to him equally a great thrill and sensation of the novel and unknown. Life seemed to have begun for him to-day.

CHAPTER IV

In Sir Walter's chamber, after that interview, there were many comings and goings. Sir John Low, as it was still the habit to call the curate, came every day, for the knight, in the many fluctuations of his mind, had at the last swayed towards the ritual and formulas to which he had been accustomed in his youth, and there were consolations boldly administered, though with precaution, by the curate which the minister, although no further removed than the next parish, would have esteemed sinful mummeries and offences to the truth. Mr Melville gave no absolution, which the curate dispensed with confidence, soothing the aged gentleman with rites by which his wavering mind was supported, though he could not give above half his attention to them, but sat turning over and over in his mind the one question that occupied him even when the viaticum was put to his lips. Sir John came and went, and a silent man from St Andrews, with a soberly clad attendant bearing a bag full of papers and an inkhorn, also came and went, spending hours in the Castle, and called in ever for a new discussion by the major-domo, Neil Morison, who shared all the consultations, to which indeed his master gave but the same distracted half attention which he gave to the rites of the Church. The time had come to him when he could not fix his mind to anything—whether it was those matters which were pressed upon him as for his soul's weal, or those others which were in reality the permanent subjects of his thoughts. Sir Walter, indeed, amid his dreams and distractions, which broke everything with which he was occupied as an image reflected in water is broken by every blowing breeze, was conscious of many people coming and going, who were not seen of men. While he pondered over the disposal of his property, his sons, to whom it should have gone by course of nature, came and went fitfully, more clearly realised at those moments when, in his *malaise* of mind and body, he became impotent of all other thoughts, and turned towards them as of old. Something had brought them back into the still air of that death-chamber—something which no one knew of, which the old man himself did not understand. It was the look of young Pate Oliphant, the turn of his head, something in his voice, those subtle tokens of kin which come and go, broken always, like that same reflection in water, not to be traced, but thrilling for a moment now and then through every nerve. That fugitive likeness had not inclined him towards Peter of Over-Kellie. It had struck out rather a tone of wrath, of harsh contrariety and opposition in his mind—with the impulse to push that interloper out of his way who dared to remind him of Pate, his own Pate of the other times. In his confusion of mind he did not remember how that suggestion came—had he dared to speak of Pate, this stranger who had no right? He forgot how it came. But Pate and the others had come back: they were vaguely about him, always eluding him when he would have appealed to them—present there he felt, by some secret understanding, known only to himself and them, which if he betrayed it would harm them all. And Sir John, quieting all the vague terrors in the old man's mind in respect to death—terrors only half real, too, for nothing was very real with Sir Walter—mingled other counsels, suggestions of another name in which there perhaps was an escape from the confusion of his soul.

The silent man from St Andrews disappeared one dim morning when the world was all white, stifled in an easterly haar, after a sitting of an hour with Sir Walter in his chamber—and that afternoon when the minister of Carnbee appeared he was informed that all was nearly over, and that the old knight, who had hung so long between life and death, was in the very act of ending. The curtain was held back that Mr Melville might enter; but as this was at the very moment when Sir John was bending over the couch of the sufferer administering those rites which were sacrilege to the preacher, Melville solemnly and indignantly withdrew, and stood outside till all should be over. He stood against the curtain with a stern expression on his face, his eyes half closed, his lips sometimes moving. I fear he was angry that this mummery should be permitted in a "Christian land," and thought many a harsh word of his brother, even while he prayed fervently for the passing soul which these rites were dismissing in peace. A little time after Sir John emerged, solemn too, yet with something of triumph in his look. "He hath gone forth well provided on his last journey," he said; "his end has been peace." "If you call that peace," Melville could not keep from saying; "I hope his end was also justice." "It was judgment," said the other priest, walking back as if in a procession with his little vials: and the old hall, so large, so empty, its great windows full of the whitened mist, the shroud of the haar that covered all things, looked more desolate, cold bare, and empty of life than words could say.

Before Sir Walter was carried to his rest in the family vault in Carnbee kirkyard it was known all over Fife that Kellie Castle and estates had been left by his will neither to his sister nor to the next of kin, but to the head of the family, my Lord Oliphant, then in London with King James, and not likely to put himself to much trouble in doing honour to the funeral. It is true that he was the head of the family, and also that there existed an additional link in the fact that Sir Walter had married his sister. But the fief of Kellie was one which came not from the parent house, but was acquired for his own hand by the original holder, the founder of this branch, so that its bequest to the chief was no reversion, but a free gift. Lord Oliphant was not rich; and poor as had been the state kept by the old knight in the lingering end of his days, his inheritance was not one to be despised. The knowledge made a great sensation in the neighbourhood, where there had been many speculations on the subject, the claims of Mistress Jean and of Pate Oliphant having been largely discussed. By some of the neighbours it had been believed that Sir Walter had no right to exclude the heir-at-law; but this had been warmly disputed by others, who held that the death of all the immediate members of his own family left the old knight a free hand, and that, in the absence of any legal settlement, he had a right to do what he liked with his own. His funeral brought together all the gentry from that side of Fife, both gentle and simple indeed, of the East Neuk, neighbours and tenants, a numerous company. And at this ceremony the positions of the two clergymen were reversed. Sir John of Pittenweem was not looked upon with very favourable eyes in the Kingdom, and his return to the ancient ways, though it had to be winked at by those who were aware that authority was no longer entirely on the side of the Reformed Kirk, and that protection was now extended even to something very like the odious Mass—was much against him in the opinion of the multitude. That he had "played his cantrips" about the dying man was whispered from one to another, and that he was a rank prelatist was universally known. Maister Melville, that excellent and sound divine, had now all the say.

There were other strange features in this funeral which were long remembered. For one thing, there was nobody to conduct the mourning with authority. Peter Oliphant stepped forward to follow the coffin, and no one gainsaid his right to take the place of chief mourner; but he was modest and a little backward in marshalling the others, notwithstanding the support he received from several of the chief gentlemen present, who acknowledged the title of the next of kin, even though it was known that he was not the heir. But was he not the heir? would not natural right prevail, though in opposition to an old man's testament, a doited old man! These words were freely spoken even as the long procession set out upon the heavy country road, winding dark and silent between the hedgerows. Was he not a doited old man? Had not he taken, as somebody had related, Pate Oliphant for his own son Pate, who, poor lad, had been but a rover, and broken, folk said, his father's heart? And there were some even who whispered that it was with the idea that Pate of Over-Kellie was his own Pate, and to punish that ne'er-do-weel, that Sir Walter in his dotage had left his lands away from the natural heir. This discussion, however, was not all or even the most remarkable part of what occurred. For at the cross-roads, where the way to Carnbee turned off from the highway, a young gentleman, followed by three or four retainers, came up almost at a gallop, with every sign of hard riding, and in his travelling-dress, and made an effort to disturb the decorum of the funeral by forcing his horse into the line and taking the place next to the coffin where Pate walked leading the procession. This incident caused a pause, and such an interruption of the solemnity as threw the line of the mourners into confusion, and turned the conventional stillness and whispered conversations of the funeral party into something like a brawl. The new-comer proclaimed himself the representative of Lord Oliphant, his son, sent to render the last honours to his kinsman, and could only be prevented with the greatest difficulty from taking his place forcibly at the head. This noisy interruption, and the bad manners of the young gallant, who, when prevented from taking the place of Pate, rode on himself and his followers at either side of the coffin, breaking the quiet not only by the excitement of their appearance but by the clangour of their ride, and the breach of all those Scotch decorums which have always been so rigid in respect to burial. Brawling at such a moment was not indeed unheard of, any more than at any other moment, in the temper of the times. But the depths of the peaceful country, where no such thing had been thought of, and where my Lord Oliphant had neither friend nor enemy, was displeasing to all. Nevertheless, perhaps, had it not been for the steady backing of the minister and one or two of the elder men, the position of Pate would have been a disagreeable one; for the sympathies of the gentry were more with the Master of Oliphant than with the humbler youth, whose blood they acknowledged, but whose breeding had been that of a yeoman rather than of a landed gentleman. Pate himself, however, proved his gentility by a bearing much more noble than that of the intruder. He held his place with determination and without flinching, yielding no step. And thus they carried old Sir Walter to his grave.

On the return, however, Pate was less certain of his right and less supported. It was the intruder then who had the upper hand. The elder men might look coldly upon so irreverent an assertion of the position; but the younger ones, who knew, or desired to know, the Master of Oliphant, were glad to push forward, to claim his acquaintance, and to accompany him back to Kellie Castle, where at least he had now the first right to be. Pate felt himself left behind to the company of the tenants and the smaller lairds, who, like himself, were rather patronised than on an equal footing with the great proprietors. Mr Melville made an effort to draw him into the quiet of the manse, which would have been safer; but it was more natural that, indignant and injured as he felt himself, he should prefer the sympathy of the others, who were full of angry suggestion and advice. The young man had been profoundly disappointed and cast down by Sir Walter's will. It was the destruction of his brightest hopes: but it had not occurred to him that the question was not closed, or that there might still be a chance of having justice done him. Now the utterances of companions were no longer in whispers. The doited auld man? Was he indeed a doited auld man? Pate thought of the heavy look, the dreamy eye, the sudden kindling like a flame of Sir Walter's brief words and moments of animation. He shook his head at first, but afterwards his own mind took fire. It was galling to hear the voices, already gay, of the others who clustered round young Oliphant, and streamed after him, full of pleasure in the excitement of the stranger's arrival, and also in their release from the gloomy ceremony: he and his friends came behind, and different were their tones and their looks.

"It is e'en like the impudence of thae minions of the Court," said one of the neighbours, "that follow the English fashion, and despise their native ways."

"English fashion or no," said another, "right is right. Body and banes! if it were me, I would have my lord before the Feifteen before I drew breath."

"And let them prove that the old knight was fit to mak' a disposition——"

"I'll tell ye just this, Over-Kellie," said one of the tenants, raising an expository hand. "I had a word with Andrew Morison, that is the cousin of Neil at the Castle, and the hired man of Maister Playfair of St Andrews, the writer—him ye ken of. He had a look within yon closed cha'mer, at his maister's call, to bring in the papers. And Andrew, he says the auld man was like an auld ghaist—the colour o' the pairchment spread out on the table, and his een dead in his heid."

"Which was nowise natural," said another. "I hae seen him mysel', when there was question o' a feu or siclike, that took his pairt, and a free-spoken man that would hae his argument and tak' his jest like another. You'll no tell me it's the time to test, when a man's like yon."

"If it had been a reasonable testament——"

"Or like a leal kinsman: now Sir Walter was aye considered a very honourable person when he was in his own command."

"Pate Oliphant," said one of his own comrades, "I would fecht till my last drop o' blood, before I wad yield Kellie Castle and your auld name to a popinjay of an Englished lord."

"My auld name," said Pate, holding his head high, "is in no danger, Beatoun, from any man."

"Oh, ay, ay," cried Beatoun, impatiently, "we all ken your pride. But Oliphant of Over-Kellie is one thing and Oliphant of Kellie Castle is another: and Lord! if it were but for this day's work— —"

"Cause enough, and reason gude for feud or fray; but it's law and not blood that's in the question," said another. "A bit of yellow pairchment and a muckle false seal, and the name of a doited auld man!"

All these speeches and many more of the same kind rang in Pate's ear and echoed through and through him as he rode home.

CHAPTER V

The house of Over-Kellie had not the dignity of the Castle; yet the living-room into which Peter strayed with absent eyes, flinging himself down on an oak bench beside the long table, was not entirely without pretension. The windows were high in the walls; the fire was a wide-spreading ingle, with some seats under its ruddy arch. A large oaken table occupied the centre of the room; but it was kept with greater care than was common, cleanly swept, with a pair of large silver candlesticks on the high mantel-shelf, and some carving on the panels. On one side of the fireplace a casement had been put in with a broad sill, so that the women might have light for their work, and weapons hung upon the walls by way of ornament—an old Andrea Ferrara, and some pieces of plain armour such as were worn by squires and yeomen. The only thing that made any stronger call upon the attention was the carving of the mantelpiece, on which there was what seemed a rough copy of the shield which occupied a similar position at Kellie Castle, with the motto sprawling in rather ungainly letters, out of proportion with the armorial bearings, *À tout pourvoir*, in a lengthened scroll by itself.

The Leddy, or, to compromise the matter, the Mistress of Over-Kellie, which was a title equally befitting, whether she was by right Gudewife or Leddy, came hurriedly out of the house to greet Pate, eager to hear all that had happened, and what had specially befallen himself in this crisis of his affairs. The Mistress had still hoped, or persuaded herself she hoped, that the previous news about Sir Walter's will might be untrue; and, as she followed her son up the few steps which led to the great room, had overflowed in a string of questions, echoed by her daughter Margaret, who followed close upon her steps. "Oh, Pate! what did they say till ye? was the writer there? was there any person that had authority? Pate, my man, did you lay his head in the grave?—for sure, it was your right."

"Ay," said Peter, "I laid his head in the grave—muckle good as that did me; for sure, as you say, it was my right."

"And is it true about the testament?" asked his sister.

"It canna be true—I will not believe it: it is but the ill-will of Maister Playfair," said the Mistress; "they were ever against our house."

"Mother, mother, what has the writer to do with it? he cannot alter what Sir Walter says. But maybe it is not so ill as we thought," said Margaret, with devouring eyes on her brother's face.

"Let me be! let me be! I would like a stoup of your ale, mother. The roads are very heavy both for man and beast."

"You are tired, my bonnie lad! Na, I'll not say another word," said the Mistress, while Margaret flew down-stairs to get him the refreshment he asked. "We might have thought if we had not been so taken up concerning the news. Na, na, I will not hurry you, my Patie. Just take your time, my bonnie lad!"

And she seated herself on the settle near the fire, and took up, not without a little ostentation and with a sigh of excitement, her habitual work. Margaret stood gazing on the other side of the table while he drank, and their united force of curiosity and suspense moved him more by repression than it had done by utterance.

"Well, then," said Pate, "hear this: my Lord Oliphant—that is the head of our name—if I were ten times over the first of it in Fife, no mortal man can contradict that."

A sob of opposition and protest came from the overcharged bosom of the Mistress. Mortal man she was not, but woman; and therefore resistant to every statement which diminished the importance of those she loved.

"The head of our name," repeated Pate, with a wave of his hand, in fine acknowledgment of an allegiance which was not agreeable to him. "There is therefore excuse, if excuse were wanted. It is no alienation; but might, in the language of some persons, be conceived a giving back."

Pate was not without his share of schooling; he could be sententious, which has always been a possibility to a Scotsman, when he chose.

"Given back!" said the quick Margaret, "but it never came from thence. Look at the Buik, and look at the tree. It was no fief of Aberdalghie, but won by our awin spear and our awin bow."

The women were wild with this outrageous pretence; but Pate, whose heart, he thought, was broken, bent his head down on his hands and spoke no word.

Afterwards he began to tell them what had happened, which they listened to with cries of indignation and wrath. If it had been the Prince of Scotland (or of Wales, as it was heard with indignation that the heir of the crown was now to be called) who had tried to push forth Pate from his lawful place, his mother and sister would have risked their loyalty to resist it. But a young popinjay of a Master of Oliphant, as Robbie Beatoun had justly said! And then by degrees they elicited from Pate all he had heard about Sir Walter's incompetence, and how Sir John and the Writer between them had swayed his mind, in spite of all that Maister Melville, good friend and true, had been able to do.

"I am no for fechting," said the Mistress. "I've seen more of it in my time than I would desire to see again; but to sustain a mortal wrong, and not to say a word—I would raise the country afore I would abide that."

"I would rather sell my shoon off my feet, and my gown off my back!" said Margaret, ever the first to see what was the real question.

"Whisht, mother, whisht! If it was to raise the country and haud the Castle against whoever should oppose! Ah!" cried Pate, with a sigh, "that was the way in the former days, when there was a king in Scotland."

"And what for no?" cried the Mistress, with a gleam of war in her eyes; but then she threw her apron over her head and began to cry "The Lord forgive me," she said; "to bid the lads to fecht, that are aye o'er ready; and me that have seen the son brought in stiff and stark to his ain mother's hearthstane! Oh no, my Patie, no! I am an ill woman to think such thoughts."

"If that were the way of it!" cried Pate. "But the strong hand will not serve us, mother; and he is the chief of our name. How could I rouse the fisher-lads at St Monance, that are most Oliphants, against the head of our own name?"

"There's not one of them but would follow you, Pate. It is you that are the head of the name!"

"Whisht, Peggy!—to their death and the ruin of their sma' houses, and starvation to their bairns—me that should rather feed and fend them!" Peter half turned with a wave of his hand towards the motto rudely carved upon the mantelpiece, "À tout pourvoir." He pronounced it as his equal might do to-day, Aw toutt pourvoïre. "If ye ken nothing else, you ken the meaning of that."

The women turned their eyes to it sadly, both answering, yet with reluctance, to the spell. "Indeed it was an ill day it was pitten there," said the Mistress, shaking her head. "Your father, honest man—and blessed be his rest!—was just wud of these auld words. Never was there a crown-piece to ware upon unthankful folk but yon was what he said. Yon fishers in St Monance! He would point it to me that would have held him back, and says he, 'Ye dinna understand, Marg'ret, but I understand. The haill tot provided for: that's what it means—and the honour of my name.' 'Laird, laird,' I aye said, 'you are far o'er muckle taken up with the honour of your name.'"

"Not so," said Pate.

"Never so!" cried young Margaret, kindled and shining forth, her eyes "keen with honour" in a glow of youth and brightness against the old dull panelled wall.

"And that is just what cuts deepest," said the young man—"the law, and the siller: it is either to abide the wrong, or to risk the pickle land and the old rooftree, and your living, mother. Say that Peggy is safe in Rob Beatoun's hands. But there is you and me, and them that hang upon us. Me, I could go away to the wars in Germany, where there's ever place for a Scot, like many a kinsman before me; but that would be no pleasant issue for my mother."

"O Pate! Pate!" she cried, otherwise speechless, holding up her hands in an agony.

"And the plea at law," he went on. "The plea at law! there's something that is as devouring as the grave. And it's that is the only way. Look, mother! shall I take your living and mine and fling it to thae dogues? I might get righted of my wrong; but if not we would be beggars, with a wallet on our back and a staff in our hand. And what would come of the name then, or the old o'erword of the name? My heart is just broken," cried Pate, with a wild movement of his arms. "Run the risk of everything we yet possess—or else brook the wrong. How is a man to decide? Whiles I think I would sooner perish than brook the wrong——"

"You must not do it, you must not do it!" cried the mother and daughter in one breath.

"Or be counted among the dyvors at the horn," cried Pate. "The broken men that have neither land nor dwelling to their name. The Lord preserve me! but I am in a sore strait. Dishonour one way and ruin the t'other. To be stripped of all, or to sit still like a coward and brook the wrong and the shame."

At this moment the attention of the agitated group was suddenly diverted. The sound of a horse's hoofs, urged in a headlong gallop along the road, had been audible for a minute or two: and now there rang into the air the sudden clash of the swinging gate, the bringing up of a horse upon the paved yard, and the sound of some one flinging from the saddle. "Where are they? in the big room?" some one cried: and the door swinging open admitted Mistress Jean from the Castle, breathless with haste, excitement, and agitation, her fair face glowing, her bright hair waving, her riding-skirt splashed with the heavy mud of the road. "Oh take me in!" she cried. "Oh save me, Leddy; I have no place to hide my head, and Kellie has come into a stranger's hands."

"My bonnie bairn!" cried the Mistress, rising from her seat, "who has dared to frichten you like this?"

"Oh, I'm safe, I'm safe," cried Mistress Jean, "now I'm here. But I thought I would never win here——" She flung herself into the great chair from which the Mistress had risen. "The hall is full of men," she said, pushing back her hair from her forehead, "drinking wine and holding muckle loud talk—and my brother, Sir Walter, that was lying there yestreen, only laid in his grave this very day."

"If there was any man that dared," cried Peter, flaming up in response, with a kindled eye and flashing face, "to lay a little finger upon you——"

"On me!" cried Mistress Jean, in high disdain. "He would have brooked a buffet in reply, and that I can answer for; but yonder young lord—if he's the Maister of Oliphant, as they say, he does muckle harm to a good name—he cried to me as a bonnie lass, the coward loon! and held wine to me to drink the health of the new lord—me! that am Leddy by all rules in my ain right."

"And so you are," cried Margaret; "I have ever said so—if nature and law were the same."

The Mistress shook her head. "Not for a lass, not for a lass!" she said; but her kind hand rested with a caressing touch upon the girl's shoulder. "Think no more o't," she said, "my bonnie doo! you are safe here."

"But I must think more of it," cried Mistress Jean. "I am no doo, but of a fighting race. He is riding off the morn, that painted pyet of a Maister— maybe to-night. And by St Margaret!—which is a good oath, for we bear her blood—I'll hold the auld house against him and all his! I will do it! Cousin Pate, you're my chief vassal, for you're the next of the name: you're my captain; up with you, when you hear what I say! Raise every Oliphant in Fife. They are no maidens spinning at their wheels, but buirdly men!"

Pate had started with a reddening cheek at the word vassal; but with another glance at her, a smile of wonderful tenderness and brightness came over his face, and he bowed his head with a look of mingled reverence and protection beautiful to see. "That am I," he said, "and at my Lady's bidding I'll——" He paused again. The old cloud, dissipated for a moment, came over him. "But, Mistress Jean," he said, "bethink you first what it will be. Clean rebellion against King and law."

"I have ever been a Queen's woman," cried Jean; "and that for your law!" she cried, snapping her fingers, "that takes your native heritage out of your hands, because, at God's will, not your own, you are a lass born instead of a man!"

"Eh! and from the man also—the true heir—at the will of a doited auld laird," cried the Mistress, forgetting the foremost grace of hospitality in her indignation for her son.

"How dare you call my brother, Sir Walter, a doited——" cried Jean, with flashing eyes. And then suddenly she calmed down. "It's maybe true, since both him and me we are cheated of our rights. And are ye then so slack, Peter Oliphant, that for the sake of King and law ye will not stand to defend your own?"

"Lady Jean," said Pate, "I and mine are at your orders, and our right is the same; but for the lads that would follow me, and rise at your name—the fishers at St Monance, the small farmers intill Carnbee—every man with his little gear that he has gathered out of the heavy ploughland or the stormy sea—do ye mind that every one would be putten to the horn, their sma' tenements levelled with the earth, and their bairns scattered to the winds? For this house we are ready, though it means want for my mother and banishment (at the best) for me. We were not even without a thought of it, as they will tell you,—though I allow for our own hand,—till that glowered at me in the face."

"What?" cried Jean, staring wildly, as if he had pointed to a ghost.

He pointed again in silence to the fireplace, where Jean's lighter eyes caught the rough carving with a flutter of volatile observation. "Eh!" she cried, "but it's ill done! But all this mocking, and I want a true man. What are these auld words—if I kent what they meant—to you, Peter Oliphant, and me?"

"They are just the o'erword of the race," he said, "that our fathers have left to us—the best they could, and the most meaning in the least buik.[1] To provide for all, that's what it means—no to devote them to death and ruin for our service. Mistress Jean, when you think well of it, that will suffice, I trow, for you and me."

"I trow no such thing!" cried the girl; "for what should a man die for if not for his laird's rights, or his leddy's, as the case may be? Is there aucht more honourable, Pate?—a good cause and a good weapon, and stout auld walls to hold against the world! Me, that am only a lass, the more's the pity, it would put pith into the very arm of me!"

She held it out, pushing up her sleeve—a well-knit, vigorous, brown arm, but so slim and soft that 'the tension of the general feeling was relieved by the sudden laugh into which she herself was the first to break. "But a pistol covers all that," she added afterwards. "I could load and I could fire with any man."

"But no to shoot a neighbour dead," said Margaret, with a shiver, holding the soft arm with two caressing hands, smoothing down the sleeve over it with a tender touch. The thrill ran through the other, too, though she tossed her fair head.

"I did not say a neighbour; but if it was yon fause gallant, with his air like a lady's love, and his coarse cry to what he thought was a lass of no account——Yon was no gentleman, Cousin Pate," she said, turning to him with a glance which made Pate's face glow crimson, and filled his heart with a sudden flood of pride and exhilaration. The appeal in itself carried a sanction higher than that of any court of honour. Jean's implied acknowledgment of her rustic cousin's highest claim could not have animated him more had it come from the king upon his throne.

But the lamp burned late that night in the windows of Over-Kellie, and many were the anxious consultations held under its roof. As the evening went on, it was Pate and his mother whose voices were the most heard. Jean fell, like Margaret, into the position of an eager listener, submitting for the first time to the supremacy of strength and age, leaving the decision to them, flashing only now and then, as Margaret did, an eager light of suggestion upon every new discussion as it rose.

CHAPTER VI

News were brought to Over-Kellie only in the afternoon of the next day that the new heir, who had made so ungracious an entrance, was gone. It was brought by Neil Morison, in the faded velvet doublet which was his habit of state, attended by the varlet called Jaicque (*Anglicè*, Jack), who was man enough to groom all the horses left in the Kellie stables—to wit, a sober steed of all work, now ridden by Maister Neil, and the skittish pony of Mistress Jean, who held in these old unused stalls something like the same position which her mistress held in the Castle. It was Jaicque who opened the gate, and "tirled at the pin" of the house door, and held the stirrup while the major-domo got down from his horse, which he did slowly and with difficulty. He had been Sir Walter's faithful attendant, and long confinement to his master's chamber had given to his scarcely more than middle age the aspect of an old man. He gave the Mistress a bow which almost alarmed her, it was so grand, a much finer bow than that with which he signified his sense of the presence of his own young lady, whom it appeared he had come to seek.

"I was weel aware," he said, "and it was the conviction of our Mistress Marjory, who is my Lady Jean's auld caretaker, and kens her ways, that our young damsel, Leddy Over-Kellie, would have taken shelter here."

"It was the natural place for her to come to,—my son Pate," said the Mistress, "being her own blood relation and next of kin."

"Madam," said Neil, "we've mair confidence in yoursel' as a guardian than in any man whatsomever. But we judge it quite safe for the young leddy to come her ways hame."

"I will never cross the door," cried Jean, "as long as yon painted pyet, yon fause lord, is there."

"The popinjay," said Margaret, in the background, proud of the name her lover had given.

"He is nae lord," said Neil; "his father is the Lord Oliphant, and he is but the Master, and may never be a lord at all for ought that we can tell,—

nor would it be, I'm thinking, ony great loss to the name, for a wilder or a wantoner I have never seen. Anyway, Mistress Jean, he is gane. And, so far as I hear, none of them will meddle us more till the summer, and for the present you are better at hame than ony other where."

"Till the summer," Jean said, with sparkling eyes. She gave a glance at Pate, who had just entered the room, and stood a little perplexed and doubtful on the threshold in his farmer's dress, as he had hastened from the fields on hearing of this emissary from the Castle. For aught he knew, it might have been some scornful message from the interloper which Neil brought; and he stood, his ruddy face clouded with unusual sternness, expectant and somewhat defiant. "Cousin Pate," cried Jean, over the head of the old servant, "yon popinjay is gone, and they are not coming back till the summer: the summer, and there's three months to that. Oh, if ye were my real captain, and like our forebears of the past! Neil, did you ever hear tell that Kellie Castle had held out against a mortal foe?"

"And where is the mortal foe, my young leddy? Sir Walter, my honoured master, had neither feud nor fray with any man—that is," said Neil, with caution, "not for many a year."

"Eh! may the green turf lie soft upon him," said the Mistress; "he was an auld, auld man."

"No so old as ye think—if it were not for care and sorrow. I have seen a stour about the Castle, and swords drawn, if that is what you mean, my Lady Jean. There are few castles in Scotland, nor even ha'-houses," said Neil, "that could say less."

"Eh, and that is true!" said the Mistress; "but the present times are more quiet, the Lord be thanked!"

"The most of the fiery blood is away," said the old man. "Your own son now, young Over-Kellie, there, where he stands, he has his farms and his fields to think of, and never fashes his thoom about feats of arms."

Pate, still lingering at the door, grew darkly red, and came forward with a gloomy brow. "I have my father's sword, Maister Neil," he said, "ready for any man that doubts my spirit."

"Ay, ay, I ken that," said the major-domo. "The father's sword, maist likely rusted to its scabbard, and as heavy as a plough pettle. But the young gallants have blades that flash out at a moment's notice, as free as breath, though it's the stoppage of breath they're bent upon." The old servitor laughed, a low laugh, like the creaking of a door, at his own wit. But it was at Pate's expense, and the young man felt it to the bottom of his heart.

"Yesterday was no day for a brawl," he said; "but let him cross my gait again, and he will learn if there is rust or not on a man's sword."

"I lovena the lad," said Neil. "He has nae respect either for a young lass nor an auld man. But he's no sweart with his blade, and he'll stand up to you were you Wallace wight."

It is hard upon a young man to be driven to protestations of what he would do if the occasion came, and Neil's tone was bitter to Pate, in the uneasy pride of his position, thus waved aside more or less offensively not only by the others, but by the very servants of the others, conscious of all the external differences between the place he claimed and that to which, notwithstanding his claims of blood, he had been barn. Might ill be the fate of that Oliphant who was first led away by love of a fair face, and married a farmer's daughter, and settled down on a yeoman's land! And yet that Oliphant was the source of all his claims, the honour of his house, and a far better man than if, like any swashbuckler, the laird's younger son of Kellie had died in a foolish fray, and left behind him neither heir nor land.

"Cousin Pate," cried Jean, "mind that it is you I look to. I will not say another word; but the walls, they are old and they are strong, and if the men are not stout, the knaves belie their name: and as for your auld motto, I just cast it in your teeth. Provide, then, an' ye are so fond of it! and let it be for your lady, as is your bounden duty, and you the next kinsman." She took up the edge of her riding-cape, which Margaret with affectionate devotion had been arranging on her shoulders—at the spot where the gold lace with which it was trimmed was frayed and broken—and held it up to him. "Next kinsman, and only friend," she said, putting her hand into his with a gleam of moisture in her eyes that made them twice as bright as usual: and they were bright enough at all times, as bright as stars to Pate's thought. They were not the Oliphant eyes, which in their kind were not to be despised, brown, glowing, and liquid, full of laughter and light: but blue, with such a sparkle in them as the sapphire has, and shooting out rays like arrows— that kind of blue fire which has something in it more keen than the brown, piercing and cutting like a dart. It softened with the last words, and the water swam in the darkness of the blue.

Pate said little for the rest of the day to the inquisitive and anxious women of his house; but he pondered long as he strode about the fields in the afternoon, and later in the night, when the labourers had gone to their houses, to the scattered clump of lowly cottages that sheltered beyond the farm-buildings, and all the members of the family within the house, bound to be early astir in the morning, had gone to rest. There had been talk enough and consultation. But though the Mistress and Margaret had not been able to refrain from carrying on the arguments of last night between themselves, there was a consciousness even in their minds that it was he alone who had to decide. And they had withdrawn to their beds, a little reluctant, yet constrained by necessity and a sense of duty, to leave him to himself. It was a relief to him when they were gone, and yet it troubled him to feel himself left under the flickering light of the cruse in the stillness of the house to face this problem which was his, and not another's. He had been more or less of an easy mind during all his youth, disturbed from time to time by his gentle blood and his possibilities, which from shadows, that they had been at first, had grown into present and real things, as old Sir Walter's family had failed one by one, and it had become more and more apparent that it was he, and only he, who was the heir. The lass who was the last of the house of Kellie had not seemed of much importance to Pate's eyes,—not more than she had been to old Sir Walter, who was her brother, though he might almost have been her grandfather, and to whom she was an accident, troublesome, and sometimes exasperating to think of, and therefore pushed aside and not considered at all. Neither did Pate think of her. He had been troubled at times by the consciousness that he had not been bred so well as he was born—that he had about him that something of the fields and the plough which made him different from the young gallants, the flash of whose ready rapiers from the scabbard was, as Neil had said, with wise and wounding justice, unlike the deliberate drawing of the sword which perhaps had rusted a little in its sheath. And the thought of this, and such incidents as had occurred yesterday, when the train of gentlemen who, though they resented his intrusion, and supported Pate in his rights, still crowded about the Master of Oliphant, and left his kinsman to such consolation as the humbler yeomen could bestow,—had irritated and vexed him. It seemed to Pate a humiliation, not only that they should withdraw, but that he himself should care.

But all these thoughts had gone like last year's snow, in a new dilemma very differently felt. That he should not after all be the next in succession, the just heir; that there should be some one between him and Kellie,—to have discovered this, had he ever anticipated or dreamt of such a possibility, would have been in all his previous thoughts a sort of deathblow. But somehow that dread discovery did not hurt him at all. No; nor that he should be recognised as the first vassal, the loyal servant of this intruder, who shut him out of his lawful inheritance. He had tried for a moment to be angry, even to be wounded, but he had not succeeded. It had given him a shock; but the shock had been such as the discovery of a new inheritance, a something better even than Kellie, might have given. Who was it, this true heir, for whom he was called upon to give up the claim which had been dear as his life? who commanded him imperiously as the first vassal, the nearest kinsman, servant, and officer. It would have been incredible to him that he should have accepted such a position; that he should have met the call, not with defiance, rage, denial, but with a consent and acquiescence which astonished himself; which filled him with generous emotion, with a kind of pleasure, with a soft humorous sense of something beyond reason in it, foolish, noble, more exquisite than any emotion he had ever felt before. To secure the home of his fathers, the hope of his life, the right most dear to him—for Jean! not for himself. It brought the moisture into his eyes, a dew of pain, yet warm with every sweetness. He turned round on the heavy wooden stool, beside the big table, on which he sat, and fixed his eyes on the words scrabbled in stone upon the chimney, and still more misshapen and irregular in that medium through which he looked at them. "À tovt povrvoir." What meaning had been in these words! He had seen himself the master of his father's house, the head of his name, the providence of his race. Not an Oliphant in St Monance, not a fisher on the coast, that would not be the better for him, that would not rejoice to think that the auld blood had been revived in the new master, and every ancient tradition of kindness from lord to vassal made true. It was no ignoble hope that had been in the young man's heart. No one had ever called old Sir Walter an ill laird; but he had grown old, indifferent, rapt in the shadows of his old age, no longer capable of thought or care for those around him. Whereas Pate was young, full of sympathy, full of vigour, knowing every man and caring for every house. To cry "an Oliphant!" in a street brawl, or take the crown of the causeway from any passer-by, had not been in his thoughts; but to be the defence of his own folk, the champion of Fife, one of the supporters of the common weal!

Pate rose up with a start, pricked by his thoughts, and went to the fireplace—leaning his head upon the rude carving, and gazing down at the smouldering red on the hearth. Would she be that? A bit of a lass, not much more than a child, without knowledge; also a creature of caprice, moved not, like himself, by long-held, long-pondered resolution, but by every wind that blew, by sudden impulses, perhaps unwise, by the council of the moment, born to-day and gone to-morrow. He pressed his brow upon the stone till the carving was printed upon it, as it had been before on his heart. Who could tell what mood would sway her, what strength she would have, what instruction would commend itself to her—what (and perhaps this was the great question of all)—what husband she would marry? But that question, which suddenly roused the blood in every vein, so that Pate felt a sudden flush go over him from head to foot,—that question had to be crushed at once, having nothing to do with the matter. That was not his affair. No such solutions from fairyland were to be brought into the consideration of a man's duty. The women might dwell upon them. They might so, if they would, set injustice right, and contradict the laws of nature at their pleasure; but such considerations were not for him. The question was not one of fancy or of chance, but of what he, a strong man and a steadfast, taking gravely into consideration every side of the subject, was to do: and this was what he had to settle now.

CHAPTER VII

"My friend Pate," said Sir John Low, "I cannot think that you have so little sense—a young man of havins, as I have ever kent you—as to oppose my Lord Oliphant in his lawfu' rights. The estate has been gifted to him fully and fairly by him that had the power. And you have but the drap's blood. We are not denying your blood-right. You are the next of kin; but if Sir Walter thought it the best thing to put back the auld lands under the hand of the undoubted head of the house——"

"It is just *that* that will have to be tried," said Pate.

"Man," cried Sir John, "what are you but a distant kinsman after all? And my lord also is a kinsman—maybe farder off in degree, but assured in line as the fountainhead to the stream."

"Mess John," said Pate, "we will leave counting the degrees. There is one that needs no counting, being the child of the same father, and more near in kin than I am, as I frankly allow." Here Pate lifted his bonnet from his head with a certain solemnity. "That she is a maid and not a man is naught; for the maid has succeeded to the father as long as there has been law in Scotland. And I have even heard say——"

"Mistress Jean!" cried the curate, elevating his eyebrows; and he smote Pate on the back a jovial blow, all unlike his lean form and the gleam in his eyes. "Ha, my bonnie lad! you are none so simple for a country clown. You would strengthen one ill claim with another, and win the knight's spurs by the help of the distaff! Whiles it is not a bad plan."

That Pate's cheek should have flamed at this filled him with a sense of humiliation; but it was anger and not shame that brought the red, which flushed fiercely over his brow and lent a red light to his hazel eyes.

"The lady's claim is firm as Carnbee Law," he said. "I yield to it, with no liking, nor even surety of well-doing. She may carry the auld castle that is the home of my fathers into a stranger name—the whilk would be the grief of my life. I yield to her, because I cannot in justice withstand. She claims me as her defender, which doubtless I am, being the first man—in Fife—of my name."

Sir John, who had been staring at him open-mouthed, here burst into a laugh. "And you tell me that's your reason!" he cried, in a derisive tone.

"You, or any man," said Pate, calmly. "And I would do the same," he added with a smile, turning upon the half-priest, who followed stealthily, as far as he dared, the habits of the old faith, sure of indulgence in the unsettled state of affairs—"I would do the same if I were one of your lambs, that tell you all in your ear ahint the kirk-door."

"It would be well for you, my lad, if you did the same," said the curate, reddening in his turn; "and ye should hear from me that when you lippen to a young lass you are a fool for your pains."

"What!" said Pate, "is that the counsel you give, Sir John? To leave the orphan lass undefended, and bow the head to the silken lord? That is not the lear that has been learned to me."

"Silence, yeoman!" cried the angry curate. "Are you one to teach your betters, let alone your priest?"

"Ay," said Pate, "or any honest man; and I acknowledge no priest but only him that teaches the Word—which never yet bade to pass over the weak, even when it is to your own hurt, as this is to mine."

"Here's one coming that will give you grand reason for every fule-deed you like to do," cried Sir John—"ay, and tie you up safe and fast to the lass that ye think has such a grand tocher. But bide awhile, bide awhile, Pate the pious. Succouring orphans is a fine thing when your own rights are not so clear as ye thought; but when you find a useless wife on your hands, and all the cows to milk, and the byres to clean——"

"You have an ill tongue, if you were ten times a priest!" cried Pate, with a clouded brow.

But the controversy was stopped by Master Melville, who came up hastily, quickening his usually sober steps at the sound of Pate's voice raised above its usual tone, and the laughing, scornful attitude of Sir John.

"Your look is not peaceful, Peter," he said, "nor your eye content."

"Did you expect to find me content, Maister Melville," said Pate, "with my rights taken up by others, and myself scorned before my neighbours? I would then be a man not like other men."

"The Lord of Over-Kellie," said Sir John, "was, by my faith, near upon charging me with a cartel of war to that other nobleman the Lord Oliphant; but that I am a man of peace and carry no gage."

"You might moderate your jesting, Brother Low," said Melville, "and so show yourself a man of peace. This is not the time, Peter, to bandy words, with whosoever it may be. You have your duty to do for your kindred and your name."

"It is what I am ready to do at all times," cried Pate, hastily, eager to find in the minister's face the counsel already established in his own.

"We will say good morrow, first," said Melville, "to this reverend brother. It is an evil thing to be overly much concerned with the affairs of this world, Maister Low. Here are you and me, both led away by these heathenish disputes, that should have been in our quiet studies pondering our sermons, and the Lord's Day coming on——"

"I am no man for long sermons," said Sir John, "nor am I liked the less on that account, so far as I can see."

"Well, sermons are my trade," said Melville, passing his brother-clergyman with a bow. He put his arm in Pate's, and led the young man with him, gently forcing his steps. "All he means," said the minister, holding Pate's arm tight and leading him on, "is to make you talk and give forth your foam and nonsense, the whilk he will turn into solid mischief. I hope I am no uncharitable," he added, devoutly; "but come you, Patie, my man, and talk out your soul: you are safer with me than with him."

"No, minister," said Pate, "I have no need for blethering, as you seem to think: my mind is steady and made up. The young lady is more wronged than I am. She is her father's just heir. She claims me as her first servant, and I allow the claim. I am the man nearest to her. I am fechting, and I will fecht, to the death, for her right and not mine."

"Pate! lad!" said the minister; his voice faltered, and even his step for the moment. Then he cried, "No wonder he did not understand!"

But Pate neither comprehended nor desired to comprehend the meaning of this reply. He was entirely preoccupied with his own thoughts. "That is my solemn determination," he said. "I have had my fancies; but then I kent nothing of her, nor of her just rights. I will get them for her if I can, minister: it is my first duty, as the next of the name."

"She is but a lassie," said the minister, "and a wild one; no training, no mother, grown up just like a blade o' grass on the lee. There is no telling what the like of her may do. She will take your very heart out of your life, and never ken what a gift it is. She may not even thank you. She may think it's only her right and your duty."

"And what is it else?" said Pate. "You are all the professor I ever had: if my lear is poor it is your blame. I think I have heard from your very mouth that if a man does not stand for his ain, specially for them of his own house— —"

"Oh, laddie, do not tackle me out of my own mouth!" cried the minister, peevishly; "many a foolish thing I've said. Meantime, you must mind that when the Apostle said yon, he was thinking nought of a man's house, according to your meaning of the word. Little recked that holy man of the Oliphants or any Scots name, with their pride and their clanships. What he meant was the man's wife and his bairns—and no a distant cousin twenty times removed."

"No more than three times, minister," said Pate; "make me not out more loon than laird. And as she's her father's daughter, and he so old a man, she is of the elder generation, my father's second cousin, and no more than second cousin once removed to me. And what could be nearer my own house than that? Nay, the holy man, as you say—I wot not how to call him—would e'en have been of my mind."

"Paul he was, and not always favourable to Peter," said Melville, shaking his head, yet with a tremulous smile on his face. "Pate, I will ask you but one thing. Is it for the hope of this maiden's love that you take up her forlorn cause?"

"Maister Melville," said Pate, "I ken not if I love her; but reason none have I to think that she has ever wared a thought on me. There is clear in my mind the danger, and mostly the certainty, that she will mate with some stranger and carry the auld house into another name,—the whilk would be bitter to me—more bitter than words can say."

"If it is so," said the minister, "then the Lord bless you, my lad, Pate. Laird or no laird, you are a true man, and that's better than rank or high degree."

"You mind, minister," said Pate, with a smile, "*Aw toutt pourvoïre*—you were the first to learn me what its meaning was."

"I was ever a fool," said Melville, "and ever will be! It is not that kind of lesson that makes a man win lairdship and land."

"But it is maybe the best consolation when he has to bide without them," Peter said.

They had come in their walk within sight of Kellie Castle, which stood square and strong, rising with its turrets to the sky from amid the peaceful fields, as it still stands undismayed by all the progress of the centuries. It is a little grim and grey in the darkness of its stone walls nowadays, all Scotland having been seized since then with that false reserve which discredits colour; but in these days, no doubt, much of the rough mass, especially in its out-buildings, must have shone in white or yellow, the old tints, weather-stained and glorious, which the country then loved. Pate looked towards that home of his fathers, lifting once more the bonnet from his brow. It had been a kind of idol to him throughout his youth, his every hope had centred in it; it had been his ambition, the desire of his heart—not an ignoble one. He looked upon it now with a smile full of sorrow and disappointment, and a thought, had he known it, higher than any other hope that had ever before centred upon Kellie. If it were won for her, then would it be well lost.

"Fare thee weel, auld Kellie," he said with a half laugh to hide that tremor; "thou wilt never be to me or mine; and I have glowered at thee, and longed for thee all my life long: which maybe you will say, minister, is just a judgment on me for a covetous thought."

"You will never hear such a word from me, Pate, my man," said the minister. "I have more opinion, if I dare to say it, of your good Lord and mine."

He, too, lifted his hat in reverence as he spoke, and after a moment both turned away.

"After all," said Master Melville, "this is not the subject on which I sought you in haste, my lad, Pate. I hear that yonder wild lassie, hot with her race and her youth, is for defending the auld Castle by force of arms. She will call out every Oliphant in the Kingdom of Fife, you the captain: she will fill the stores with provender, and furbish up the auld armour, and hold the place against lord and loon. It's over the whole countryside already, and the lads at St Monance all alow. There needs but a spark to fall, and there will be a blaze to light up Fife. Pate, do you think what that would be? Two whole parishes put to the horn. The men, that are the breadwinners, in prison or hounded out of the land. The women helpless with their bairns; the boats all useless on the shore, the plough in the furrow. Ever have I learned you, Pate Oliphant, that a man's first thought should be for them about him that are in want of good guiding and help to do well. You cannot stand against the law. You cannot stand against the chief of your name, that has riches and troopers at his command (though well I wot he is a wastrel, and his son after him). Mistress Jean, she is but a bairn. The right and the wrong have gone to her head, and of the consequences she takes no thought. Vain to, speak till her of ruined houses and men slain or banished. She just thinks of victory and the three silver crescents waving over Kellie, and the tyrant driven away. As if she was a queen fighting for her crown—and, waes me! we have well known in this generation what comes of that."

Pate had walked on by the minister's side, silent, his head bowed, listening. He looked up hastily, interrupting—

"A princess; but with more right than the law, and more innocence than that gowan-flower. There is no similitude."

"Nor am I making any comparisons, Pate Oliphant," said the minister with a smile; "but what is all that," he cried, as a sound as of shouting and tumult came to them over the cliffs on the breeze which is always fresh (or salt as the case may be) blowing off the Firth over the Fife braes.

They had walked far in their talk, and were now near the old village of St Monance, with its old kirk dating from the days of King David, that "sore sanct for the crown." The sound evidently came from that quarter, and both the men quickened their steps accordingly. The village consisted then, as now, of a straggling line of red and moss-grown cottages, parallel—if any parallel could be to a coast cut up in zigzags by the line of rocks—with the margin of the sea. It was entirely a fisher village, the boats drawn up high in the rocky openings of the beach, almost on a level with the houses, and nets spread everywhere, drying, or mending, or being baited at every point. But in the centre of the "toun," where the space between the houses and the sea was a little wider, was a little crowd of fishermen, their dark figures lighted up by a touch of brighter colour in a kirtle or petticoat, and the white specks of the mutches which every decent woman wore. They were all circling round a gayer figure in their midst, Mistress Jean to wit, uplifted on her pony, with her hair flowing under her riding-cap, the highest light in the picture, as her delicate face was, among all the ruddy, weather-beaten, glowing countenances round. Jean had, it was evident, been making something like an oration to her assembled vassals, and her eyes shining, her hair waving, her arm in the air, had kindled the fishers to enthusiasm. "We are Oliphants all," she was saying as the minister and Pate came up, "every one kin, far off or near, and hey for the silver crescents and bonnie Kellie Castle, that never owned master since the days of Bruce but——" she stopped with the pause of natural eloquence as her kinsman pushed into the crowd: then waving her whip, cried with all the force of her young voice, and a daring which brought the blood to her cheek, "Pate Oliphant's line, and mine."

Never was a touch more effective. As he pushed forward, scarcely hearing what she said, there rose a general shout, "Pate Oliphant and the bonny Leddy; Leddy Jean and the kind house o' Kellie! We're for them and nae land-loupers. The Bruce's blood and the auld name!"

"Mistress Jean," said Pate, "what do you here? This is no court of law, to judge between you and him that, right or wrong, is no land-louper, but the head of our name."

"Land-louper yourself, Pate Oliphant!" cried Jean, in high indignation. "Let go my bridle! If you will not tell the lads, what is left to me but to do it? and you, if you will not speak, be silent, sir! for though I do you all honour, and name you with myself, you are but my vassal like the rest. And that you ken!"

Pate's bonnet was in his hand, and he bowed low; but he held her bridle without flinching, though pony and rider both rebelled. "It is not safe for a spirity creature like this," he said, "the roaring of those loons so near her lug. Silence, lads! The lady understands, without more of your rowting, that you're all leal, and her friends."

The men had slunk a step backward in dismay at what seemed to them a family quarrel. They brightened again, and answered, "Ay, that are we!" "To our last drap o' blood!" "And yours too, Maister Pate!"—with a subdued clamour, daunted by his look, for he was not a man to trifle with, as they knew.

"My bonny bairn," Mr Melville was saying at the other side, "if you will curb your pony to an auld man's pace, I would fain go with you. There's danger baith for man and beast here."

"And what do I care for danger?" cried Jean; "it's just half the pleasure. Bid Pate Oliphant let go my bridle. Do you think, me that am 'most in arms for my rights, I will be guided by him?" She touched the excited pony with her whip, which made a bound, scattering the fisher-folk. But not Pate, who, setting his teeth, and digging his heels into the earth, held her with a grasp of iron. Jean had the whip raised again, with the intention, it seemed, this time, of striking him, when the minister called out to her—

"Slip down, lassie! the little beast is wild wud; she'll dash you against the rocks; she'll have your brains out: slip down, slip down, and you'll take little harm."

"Leddy, ye canna haud her a minute longer," cried a fisher—one rushing on each side to pluck her from her saddle. But the girl blazed over them, her hair waving in their faces, her blue eyes darting fire.

"Away!" she cried. "Away! Hold off! She may master you and me, but she'll not master Pate!"

CHAPTER VIII

There ensued after this a very dark time in the life of Peter Oliphant of Over-Kellie. When Jean found that not she, any more than the pony, could master Pate, she withdrew altogether her favour and friendship from him. Shut up within the old house, which Lord Oliphant after that one demonstration of taking possession left unvisited, she passed the lingering spring and summer, often seen about the country roads on her pony, but keeping up a seclusion within, quite uncongenial to her temper, and which even Margaret from Over-Kellie was not allowed to break. The suit at law, brought before the courts by her kinsman and next friend on her behalf as a minor, — that Sir Walter's will might be set aside as barred by her right of succession, and also as procured by undue influence, when in his age and weakness he was no longer able fully to exercise his faculties, — excited for a moment her hottest wrath. She burst forth upon Maister Melville, who gave her the information, with blazing artillery of looks and words, of which he avowed that could the first have slain him he would now have been a lost man. But the mild divine, being full of experience and observation, believed he saw behind all this fury a certain exultation. "How daured he, after denying me, and contradicting me, and leaving me here to eat my heart, while he went off to his plough, the dastard, no to answer his lady's call! And I doubt not he's laying his furrows and sowing his grain as if there was no such person as Jean Oliphant shut up in Kellie," the girl cried, glowing with rage and curiosity and eagerness. "You can tell him that it's he that is the land-louper, and no credit to his gentle blood, to turn his back on the auld house and upon me."

"No back of his has been turned on any lawful risk," said the minister; "on certain destruction no brave man will run if he is other than a fool. Ken you what your kinsman is doing, Mistress Jean? He is risking his whole living, with the chance of loss that will banish him the country — and that not for himself, as once he thought, but for you."

"Banish him the country!" said Jean, with blanched lips.

"Ay, my little maiden, you ken not either the risk or the pain. You think it is but to out with the flag, and load the arquebus, and the right will prevail; whereas it would be death to many a bonny lad, and destruction to many an honest house, and no hope to do more."

"All that," she cried, with an impatient wave of her hand, "is over and gone, since he refused and would not stand by me, nor be my captain as I bade him; but to gang to the law is one thing and be banished the country is another. And who would banish him the country for standing by his—next friend? if that is what you call it," she added, in a subdued voice.

The minister smiled within himself to see how swiftly she had accepted the position, notwithstanding her first revolt; but he proceeded to explain to her that the law cost much siller, and Peter had little but his land and his old house; and if the plea lingered long—as it might well do—till all his money was spent, there would be nothing for him when he had secured a living for his mother but to quit Scotland, either for the foreign wars, like so many of the Scots, or to sail away to one of the New-found-lands over the seas, where folk said there were estates for the asking, a fine caller climate, none of your tropiques, a new Scotland cold but fair. And then Jean wept, and declared that she would not have it, that no man should risk life or land for her cause: and afterwards dried her eyes and waved her golden locks, and declared that it was even like him, just like what was to be looked for from Pate, and showed that he was the maist fulish lad in all the land, as she had always said. But even after this she would not come forth nor make friends, though Margaret, when next she came to the Castle gate, was brought up to the hall, and many kisses passed between the girls, and still more kind words.

The cause was heard, by good fortune, with less delay than was feared, and it was thought at first with much prospect of success. Pate himself, being anxious, made more than one visit to Edinburgh, which indeed was a journey in those days.

But, alas! there was no longer any occasion for hope, when one day in July when the sun was at its hottest, and the genial earth warm through and through, and the corn turning red against the blue of the sea, as I saw it but the other year, glowing as if it would take light and flame—Pate Oliphant, just come back, and weary with the journey, stood hard by his own hall-door, leaning upon the wall, his bonnet low on his brow, and his heart full of trouble. He had flung out of the big room from his mother's questions and his sister's outcries of sympathy and distress, feeling that he could not bear even the sympathy, much less the questions: how was this, and how was that? when all he could tell or think of was just that the cause was lost. Oh, easy enough to see how it was, if they would but think, instead of asking questions! My Lord Oliphant had friends enow; he was a Lord of King James's Court; he was sib to all the nobles, and even to one of those carles on the judges' bench, with their muckle wigs and their weariful tongues. A losing litigant is prone to be doubtful of the impartiality of the law. Pate Oliphant could not but feel that, had he been Oliphant of Kellie (as he ought to have been), any suit of his would have been more safe to end as he wished.

He was standing there, idly lashing the air with the riding-switch that was still in his hand, his bonnet low on his brow, and his heart in his bosom, when there came suddenly into the silence of the afternoon a sound of horse's hoofs at the gallop on the rough road that led to the house. Margaret, who had come out after her brother, cried out with a start, "Hear till her! It is Jean's powney, the little wild beast—wild like her mistress. It's our Leddy Jean."

"Leddy, puir lassie!" cried the Mistress; "no more Leddy, if a' be true, Margaret, than you or me."

"And even so worthy of the more respect," cried Pate, rousing from his despair. There was no mistaking the breakneck gallop, which seemed to join the two, pony and girl, in one personality. Jean's one idea now, clearly told by every flying beat of the hoofs upon the road, was a fiery desire to get there, to fling herself upon the protection or sympathy of her friends. Pate flung his bonnet on the ground, and hastened to throw open the gate, receiving her with uncovered head and reverential gesture, as if she had been a queen. But Mistress Jean, in hot haste, too impetuous to pause, flashed past him like a gleam of sudden light—her golden locks flying, her complexion bright with haste and excitement. She drew up before the door, and flung herself from the pony's back without waiting for any aid. "They have come, they have come!" she cried, with only breath enough to say the words. She was so keen, however, to tell her story, that the immediate painful meaning of it was lost in eagerness. "Here am I, flung upon you like a stone, fired out upon you like a bullet out of a gun," she cried, with a laugh of excitement. "O Pate Oliphant! if ye would but have done it, you and me would have been in harness this day, and the silver crescents flying out-owre the grey wall! for they are come—they are come!"

"The silver crescents," said Pate, "are their cognisance as well as yours and mine: and they have won the day."

"Listen to me," cried Jean, shaking her half-curled locks about her ears, her eyes blazing, her countenance, in her excitement, undismayed. "I was sitting quiet in the great window, thinking no harm, when in a moment there arose sic a tumult as if a haill army had broken in; and before I could say more than a word to old Marjory, there they were, bursting up ilka stair, some from the west tower, some from the south, with a clatter of rapiers by their side, and spurs on their heels—the villain sound," she cried, "and them no better than reivers upon a poor maiden—but notwithstanding," she added, pausing with a sigh, "a bonnie noise!" She cast a sudden glance at Pate, standing there in the dust of his journey, the sun shining on his bared head. He had no swingeing rapier, but a whinger in his belt and a spur on his heel, for use and not for show, a subdued figure, not like the gallants in their bravery. He felt this glance to the bottom of his heart, divining something of it, but not Jean's instant second thought, that not one of them, fine as they might be, was such a bonnie lad!

"I am telling ye," cried Jean, renewing her tale with a flush upon her cheeks which came from her own consciousness of that thought, "that they all burst in in a moment, men's voices, and the jingling and the clattering of them, that filled the hall. It is well for me that I never stop to think, as the Mistress says; for if I had stoppit, or thought, or lingered a moment, I would have been in their hands, the popinjays! and no time for parley. I just flashed up 'most before I saw them, divining in my heart, and slippit behind the curtain that is over yonder sma' door, Margaret, you will mind? I just lingered to see that it was safe, and heard their outcry, 'Where is she?' and 'Call forth the leddy,' which proved they had not seen me—though one cried there was some person gone forth, and another that he had heard a step—which was a muckle lee, whoever told it," cried Jean, pausing in her childish sense of triumph yet injury; "you ken whether I have a foot like a trooper, to be heard among armed men."

"Thus I got to the stable," she went on, "like an arrow from a bow: and Jaicque, who is faithful, and me, that have saddled her many a day, we got on her gear before you could turn round, and away by the back of the outhouses, and the bridle-path by Kellie Mill, and never a soul to hear us or see us, all the gaping fools about being out to see the gallants' train. And here I am," she cried, suddenly pausing and looking round. Up to this moment her tone had been almost joyous, her bearing almost gay, in the heat of excitement and novelty, which were life to this young creature. She stopped, and her countenance changed. She looked round upon them — the Mistress at the stair-head wringing her hands, the young master of Over-Kellie standing at the pony's head, with a sobered wistful look of discouragement and downfall, nobody, as it seemed, sympathetic but Margaret, who, excited like herself, half crying, half laughing, had clasped the hands which still held the bridle, caressing them in the absence of other means of showing her pity and her love. "Now I am here," repeated Jean, slowly, a sudden cloud of surprise and dismay sweeping over her, "but you are not glad to see me. O Pate Oliphant, Pate Oliphant, take your hand from my bridle! Next of kin you may be, but no next of heart!"

"You silly lassie!" cried the Mistress, taking, though she was a little timid and cautious in her elder days, but two steps down the four stairs.

If I had space I would tell how Jean came to understand the saddened looks of her next of kin, and how Pate discovered that no popinjay of them all was in her eyes half the man that he was, though he had refused to take up arms or spend men's lives in a hopeless cause. They had to subdue their pride to the acceptance of their fate, which was much harder upon Peter Oliphant — born, you would have said, to no better — than on Mistress Jean, though her proud cousins called her no more than the Gudewife of Over-Kellie, scorning her blood and her rights. But the family kept their homely life there unbroken for many generations, keeping up the old name and kindly tradition long after the Lords Oliphant, though this is no brag of a child of Over-Kellie, but a sad saying, were, like the Flowers of the Forest, a' wede away. There was another lawsuit, of which no better came; but Peter Oliphant of Over-Kellie, though no more than a bonnet-laird, no doubt, "with his bairns and his oyes all around him, oh," came to be more or less a contented man. He knew French to a certain degree, as has been said, thanks to Maister Melville, whose breeding and education had been much in foreign countries; and though he pronounced it like good broad Scots, and was no professor for the grammar, here is this little composition of his in that language, beaten out as he went about his fields through many a quiet day, and pondered his life and the life of man in the long silence of the years. À tout pourvoir had been the proud device of his youth, when everything seemed within his power; but this was what he put into that old tongue of gallant device as the burden of his age, with the accent of Scotland and of long life —

"Ayant pourvu
Autant qu'a pu,
quoth Pate."

And may we all say as much, however humbly, his descendant prayeth, at the end of the dim valley from whence begins to glow over the dark braes the rising of a better sun.

[The Lord Oliphant, perhaps harshly treated above, was a man of many troubles and difficulties, much like those of Sir Walter of Kellie, whom he succeeded. He, too, died with no son to follow, and would have passed over his daughter; and a romance of mingled lawsuits and royal interference might well be made out of his history and that of his successors—but this must be for another hand. As dates are the useful things that are most apt to fail in family tradition, I do not attempt to say which of his successors sold Kellie Castle—to them a useless and unnecessary burden, though so dear to those who lost it—to the family of Erskine, who took from it in later days a title, and made it their home.]

[1] Smallest space.